Cat Tales

J. CARVER PUSEY
Inventor
of
"Cat Tales"

Cat Tales

J. Carver Pusey

COACHWHIP PUBLICATIONS
Greenville, Ohio

Cat Tales, by J. Carver Pusey
© 2023 Coachwhip Publications

J. Carver Pusey, 1901-1953
CoachwhipBooks.com

ISBN 1-61646-546-8
ISBN-13 978-1-61646-546-9

About the Author

James Carver Pusey, Jr., born in Avondale, Pennsylvania, was a newspaper cartoonist best known for his 1930s pantomime strip, *Benny*. His first strip was *Cat Tales,* which was also mostly pantomime (wordless), though a few feature vaudeville-style gags. *Cat Tales* ran in the mid- to late 1920s (and a brief resurgence in the 1930s), with the same strips showing up in different newspapers in different years. Pusey's talent with pantomime briefly took him to Hollywood, where he was one of several writers working with the Marx Brothers on the movie *Monkey Business.*

The comic strip blog, *Stripper's Guide,* includes additional material on Pusey at: http://strippersguide.blogspot.com/2014/07/ink-slinger-profiles-by-alex-jay-j.html

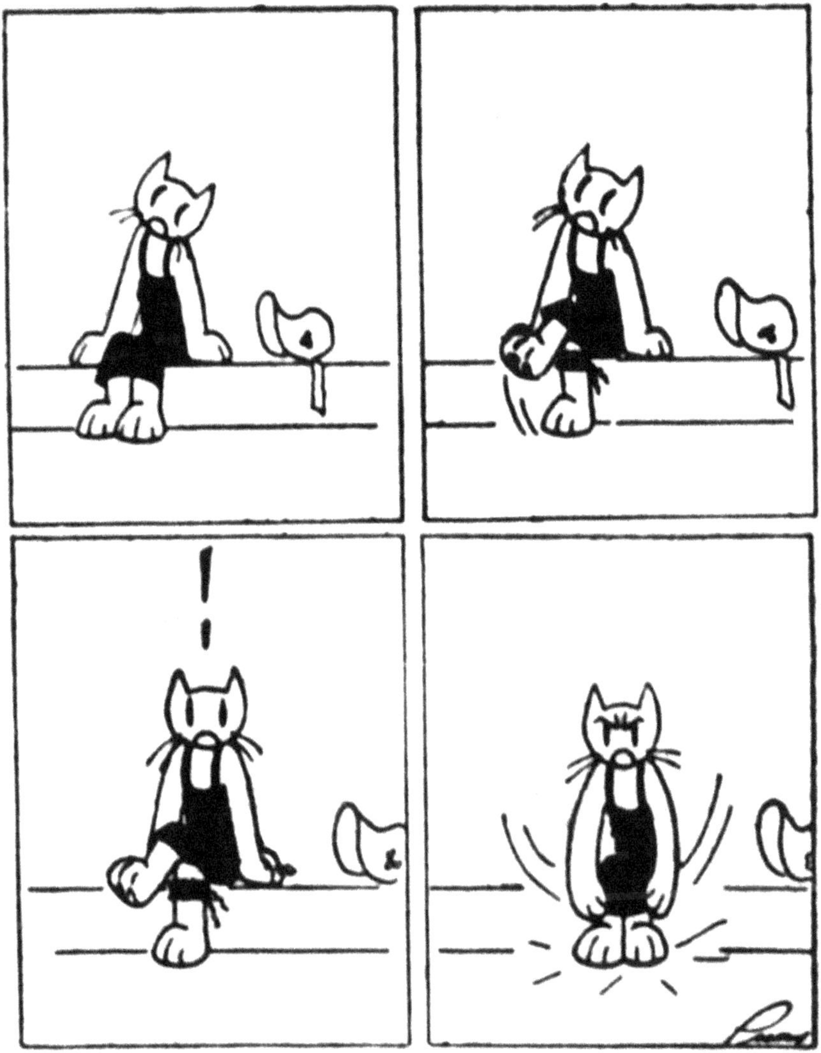
!

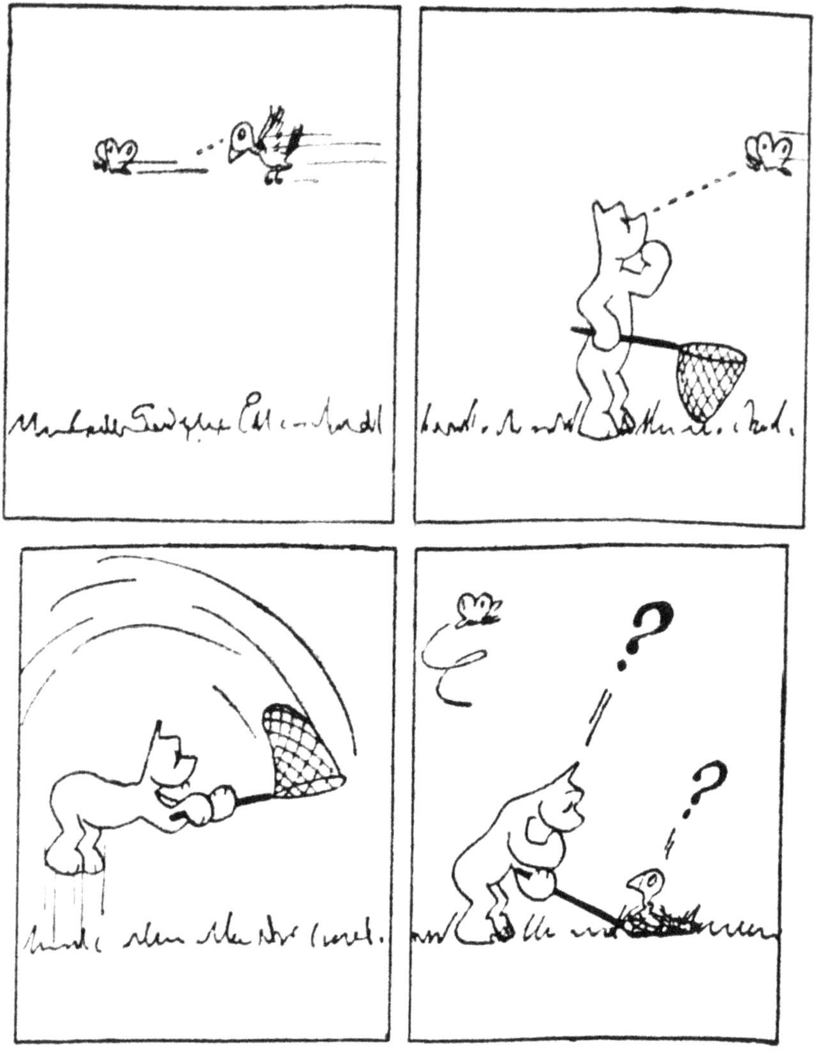

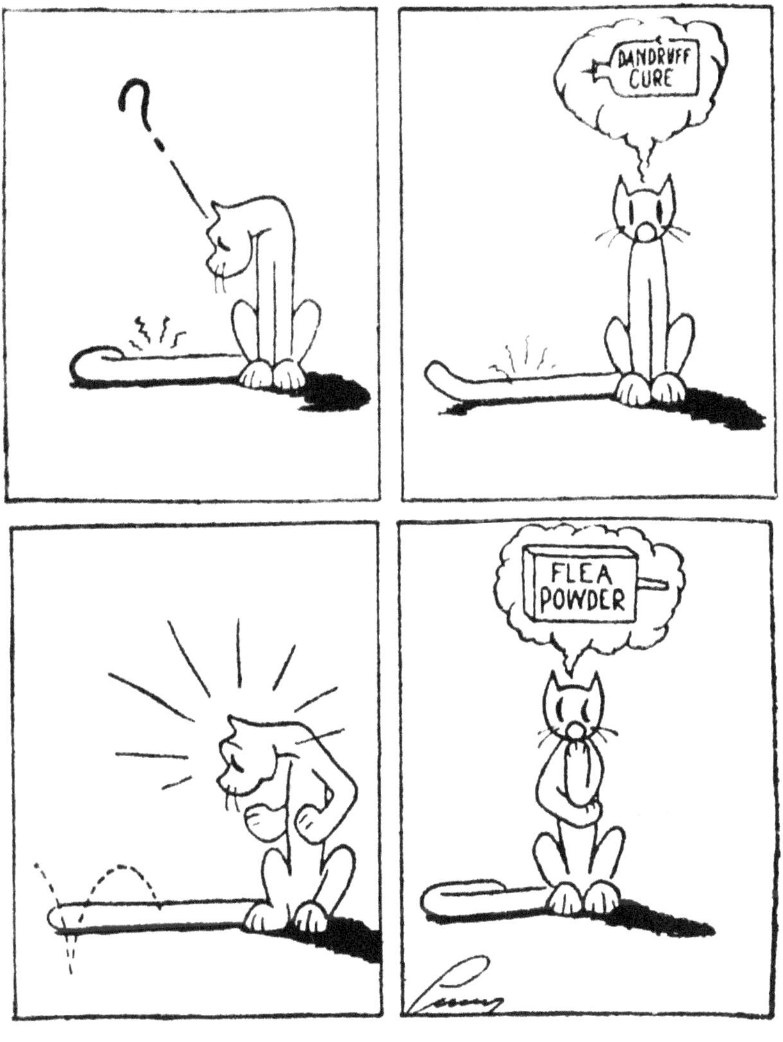
?
DANDRUFF CURE
FLEA POWDER

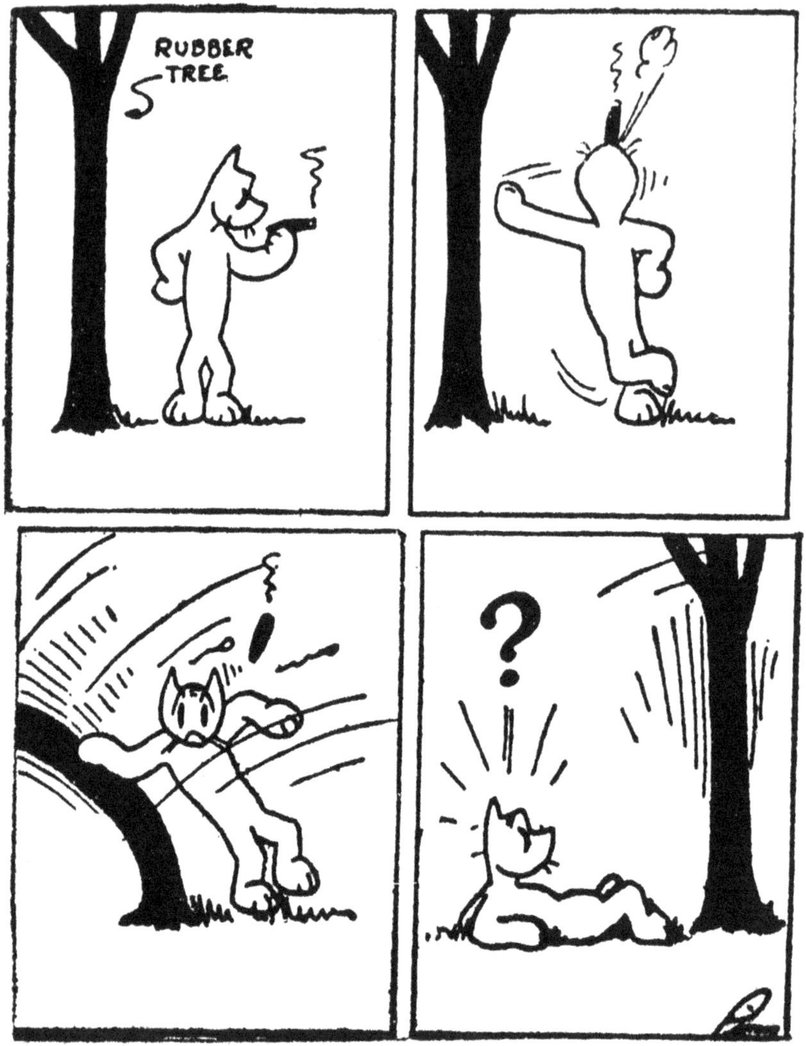
RUBBER TREE
?

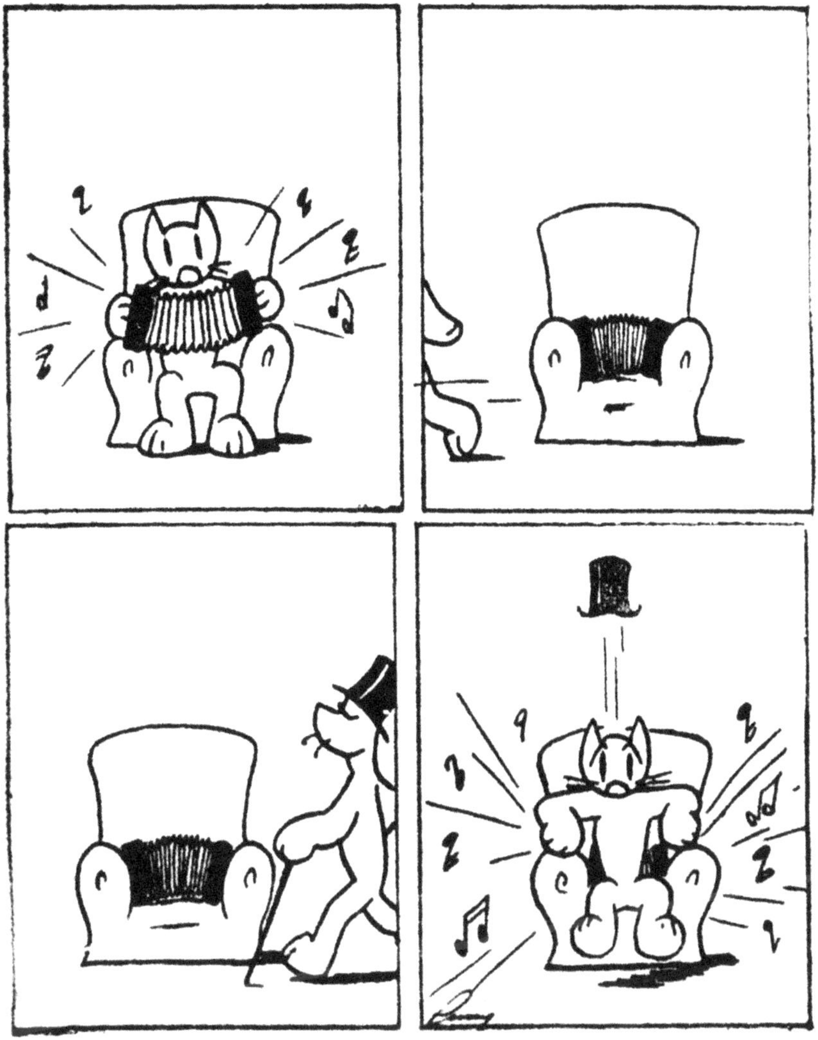

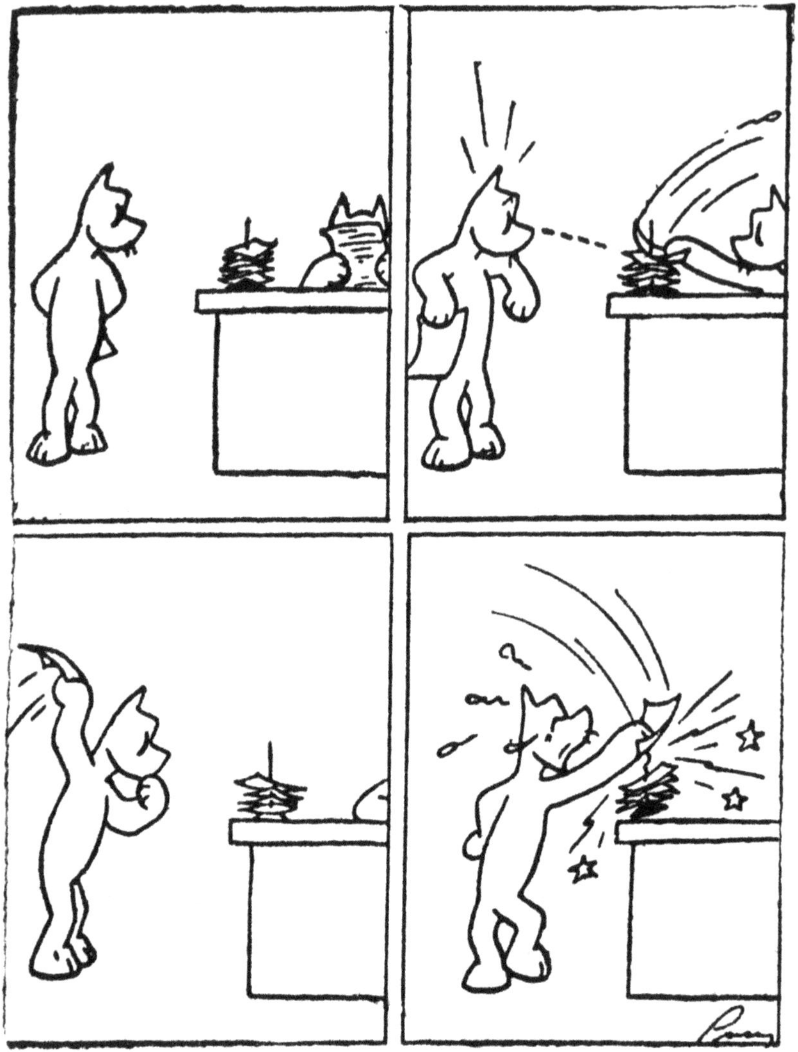

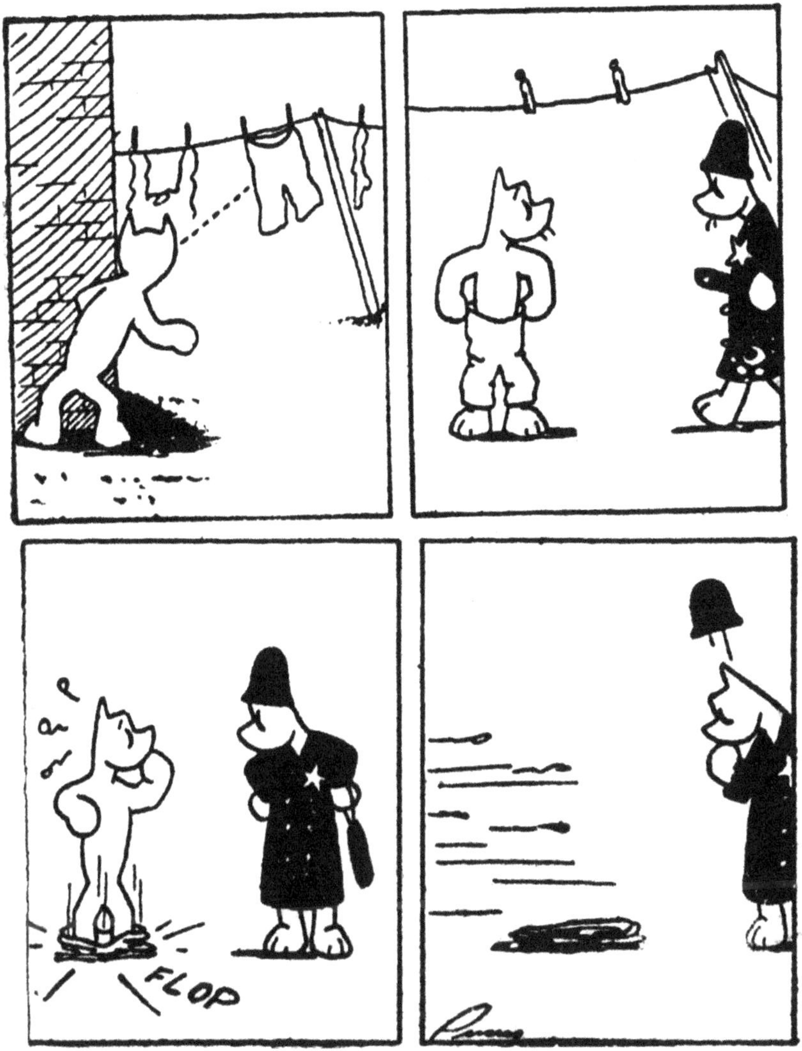
FLOP

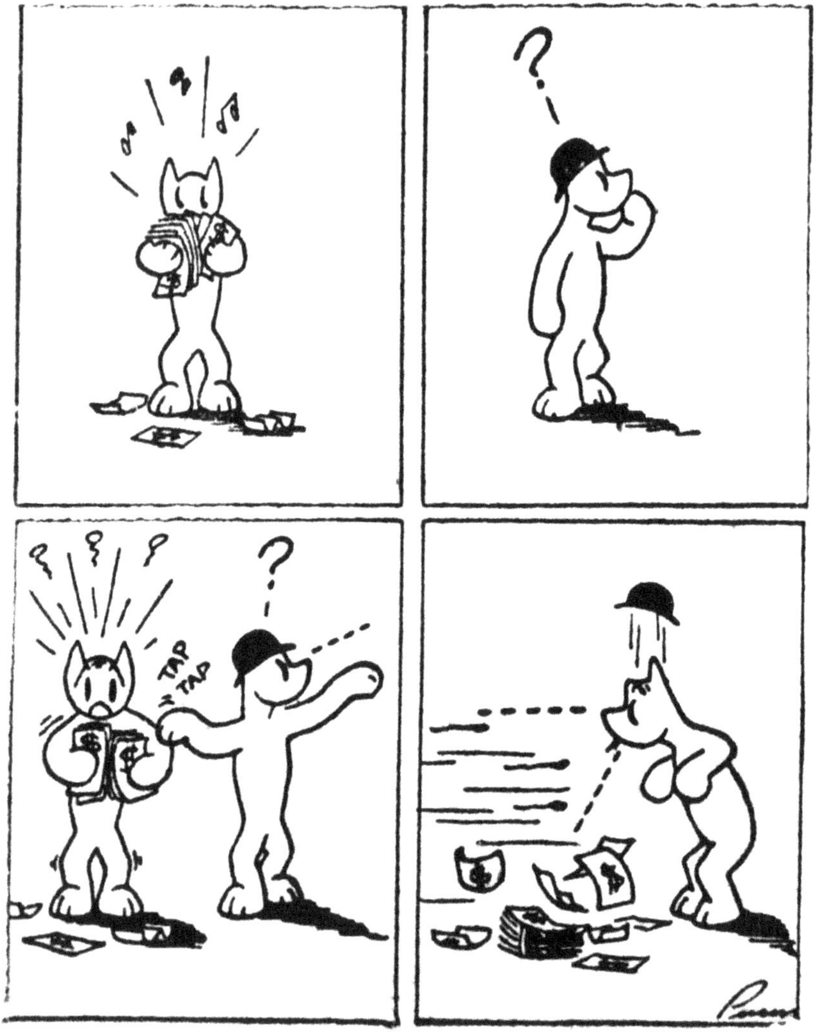
TAP
TAP

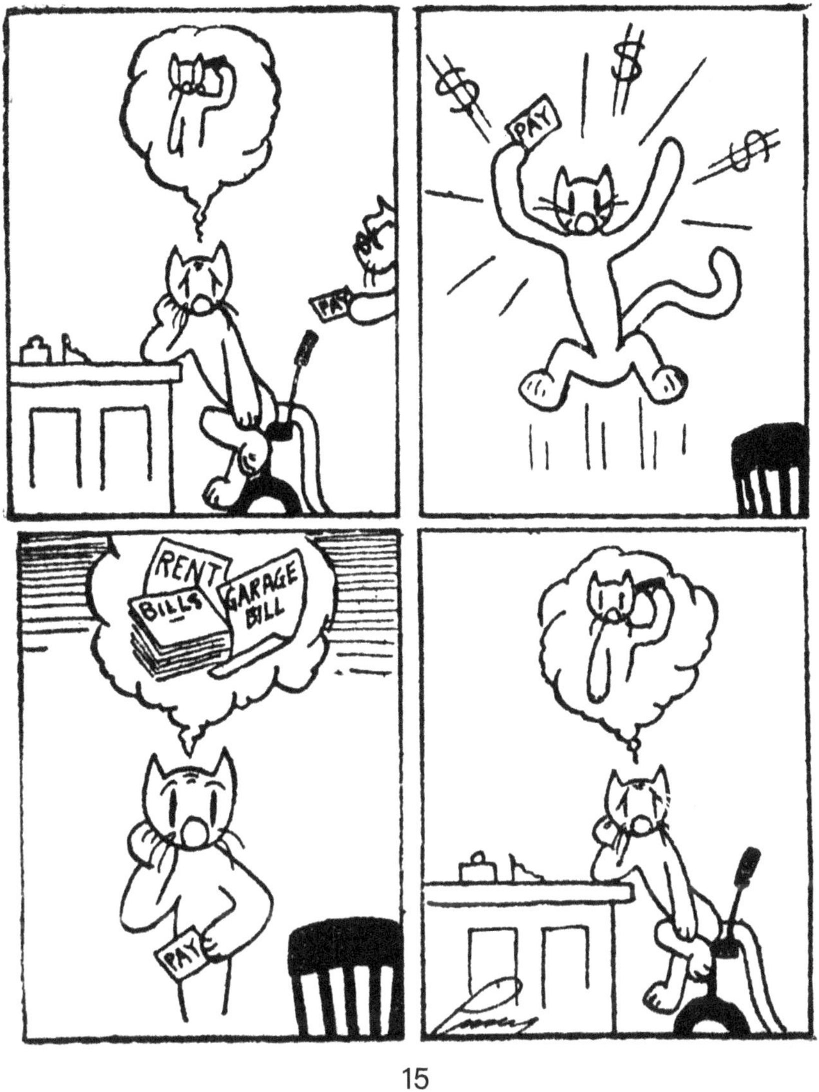
PAY
PAY
RENT
BILLS
GARAGE BILL
PAY

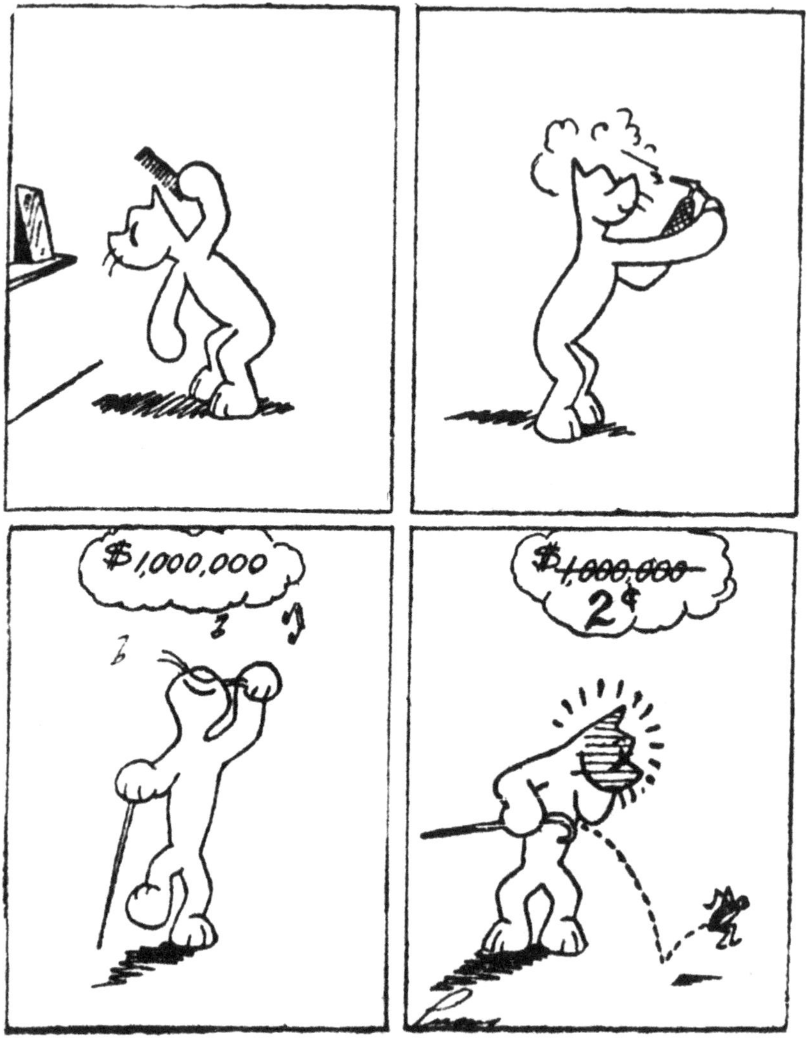
$1,000,000
~~$1,000,000~~
2¢

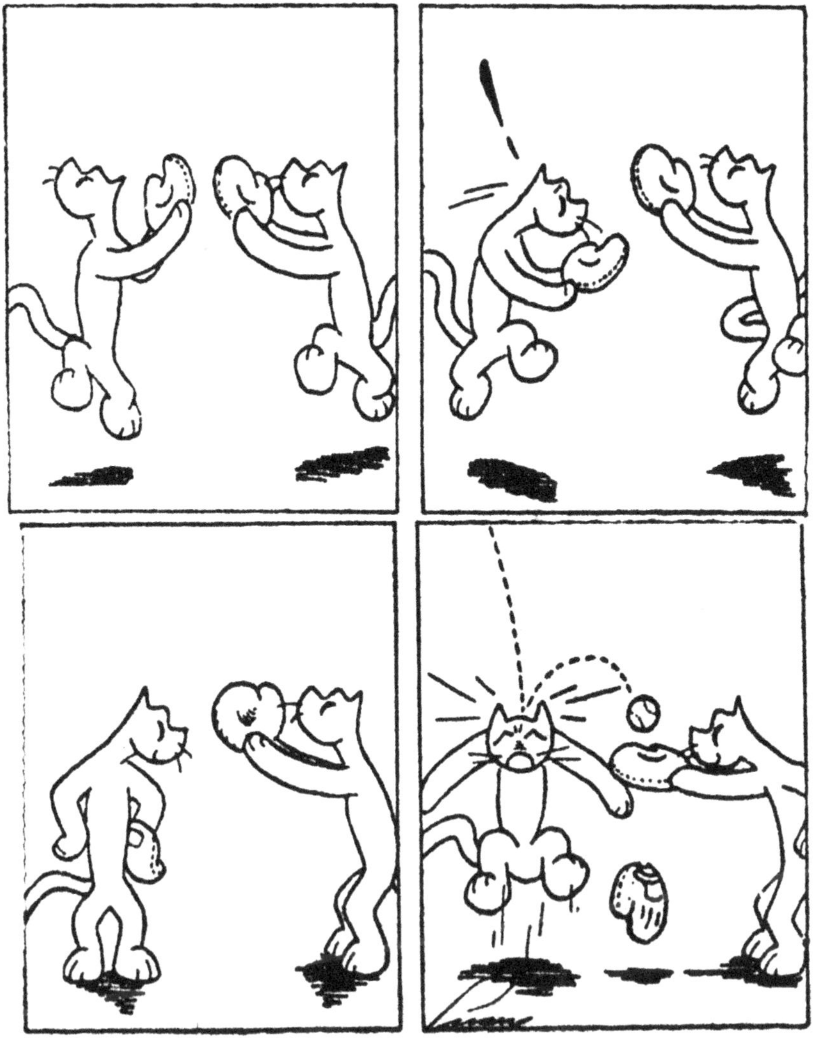

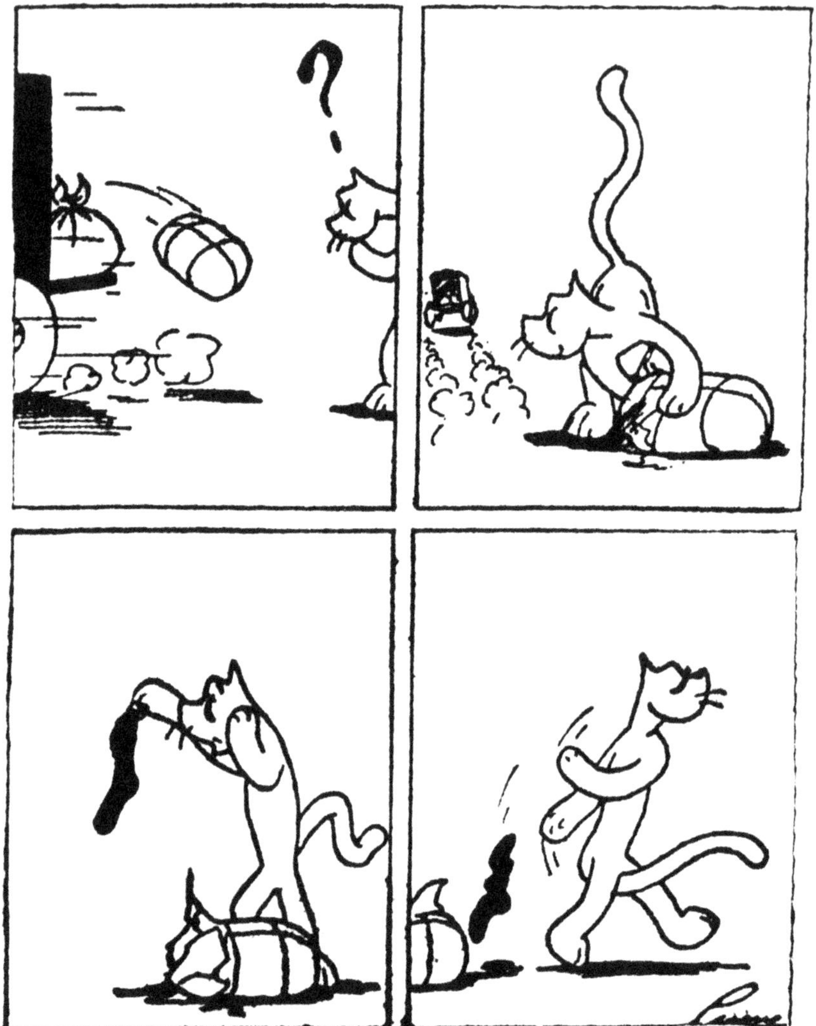
?

TO DAY
CLAREN
CAKE
THE
LOVELY LOVER
IN
LOVE
MUSH
LOVE
IN
LOVE
TO THE GREAT
OPEN SPACES
WHERE MEN
- ETC.

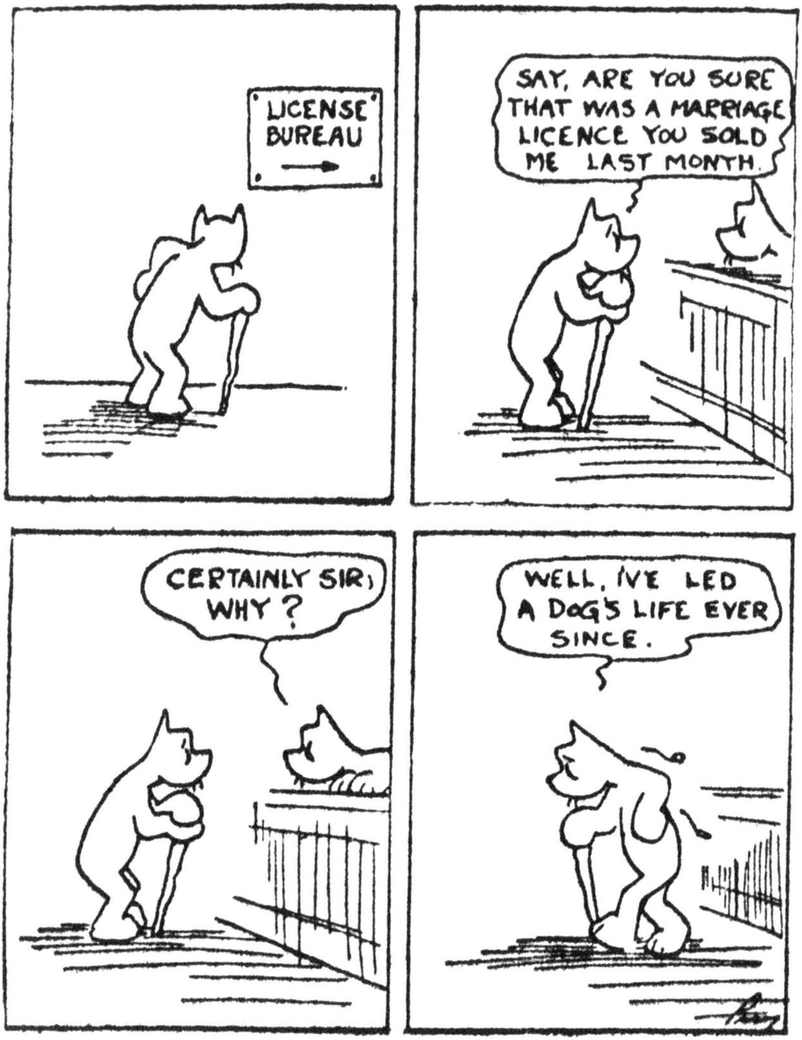
LICENSE BUREAU
SAY, ARE YOU SURE THAT WAS A MARRIAGE LICENCE YOU SOLD ME LAST MONTH.
CERTAINLY SIR; WHY?
WELL, I'VE LED A DOG'S LIFE EVER SINCE.

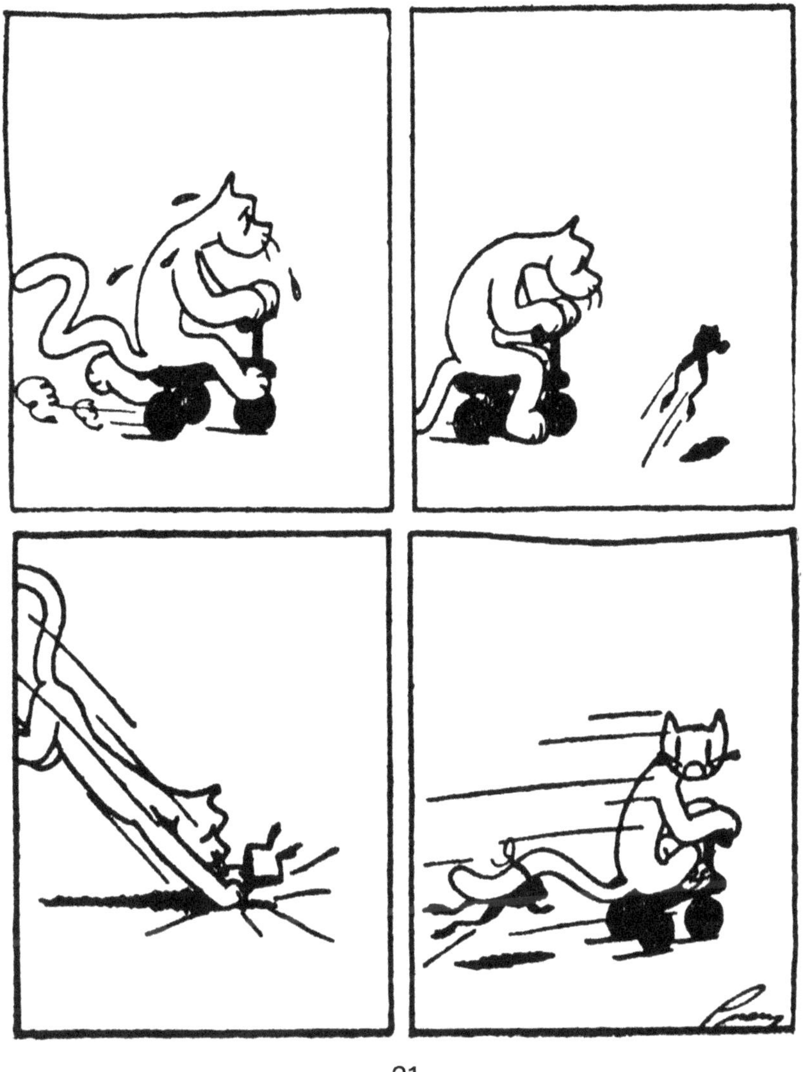

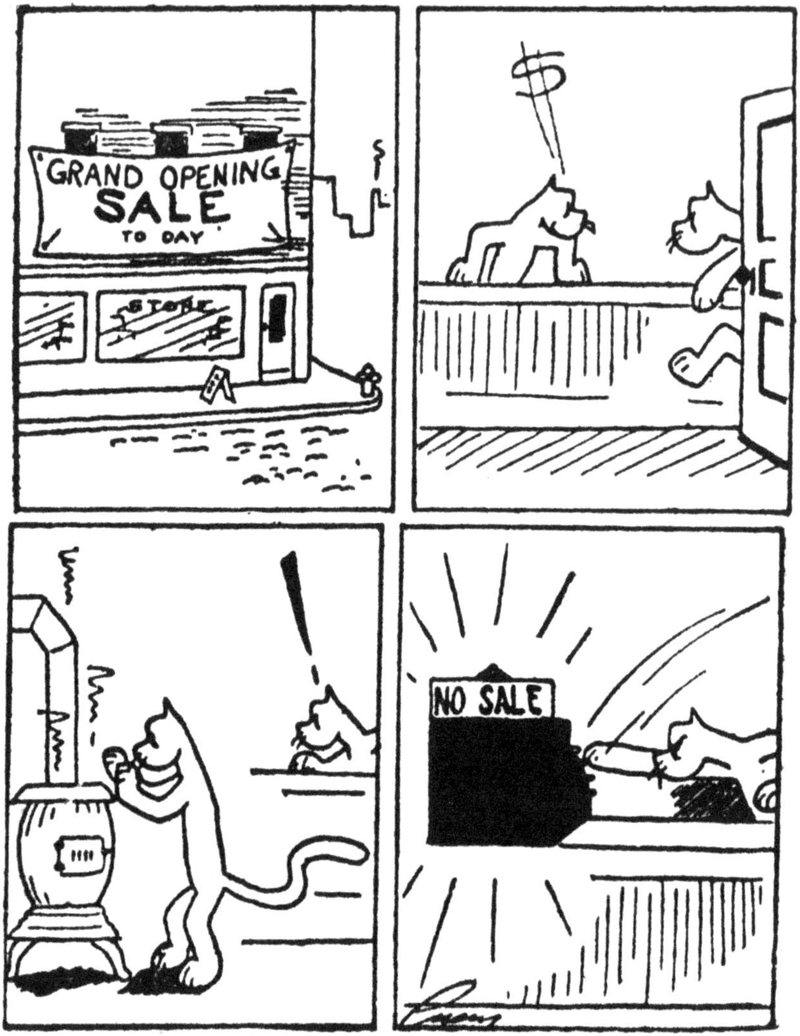
GRAND OPENING
SALE
TO DAY
STORE
$
NO SALE

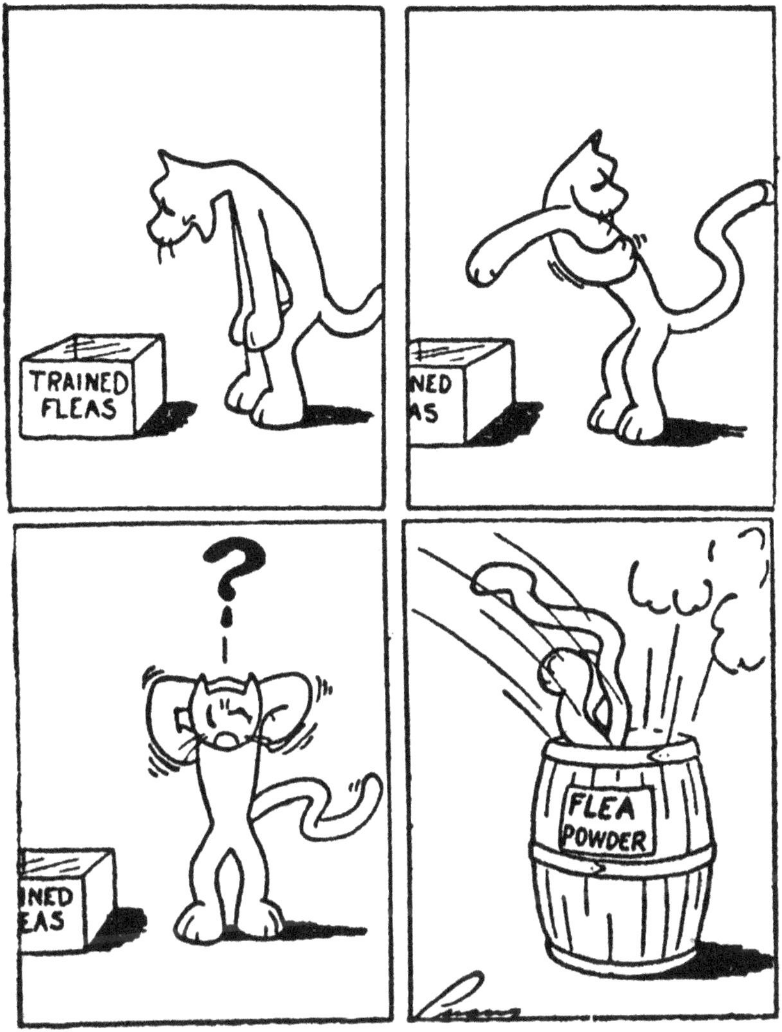
TRAINED
FLEAS
NED
AS
?
NED
EAS
FLEA
POWDER

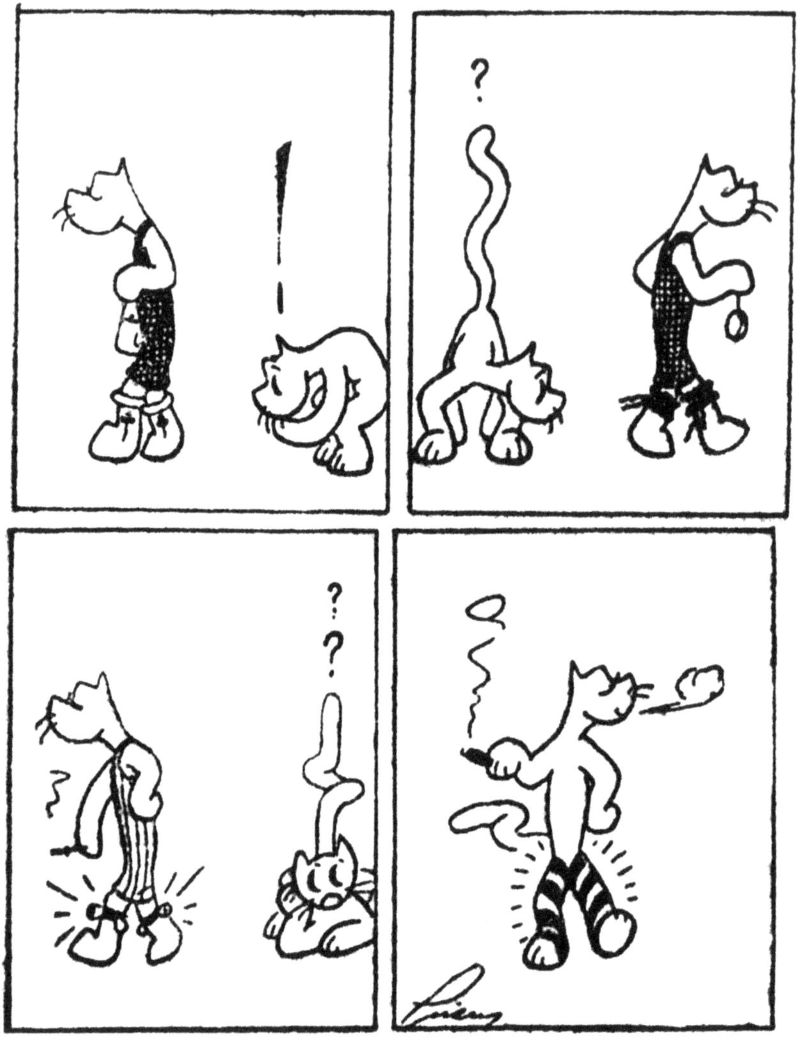

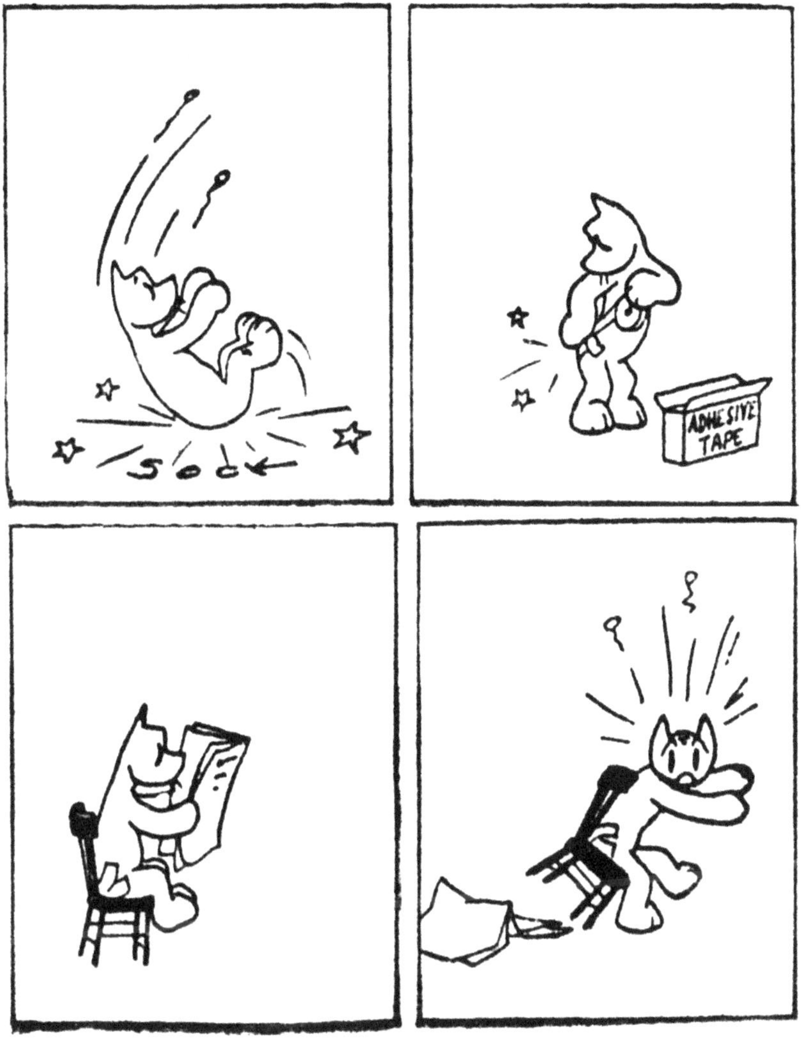
SOCK
ADHESIVE TAPE

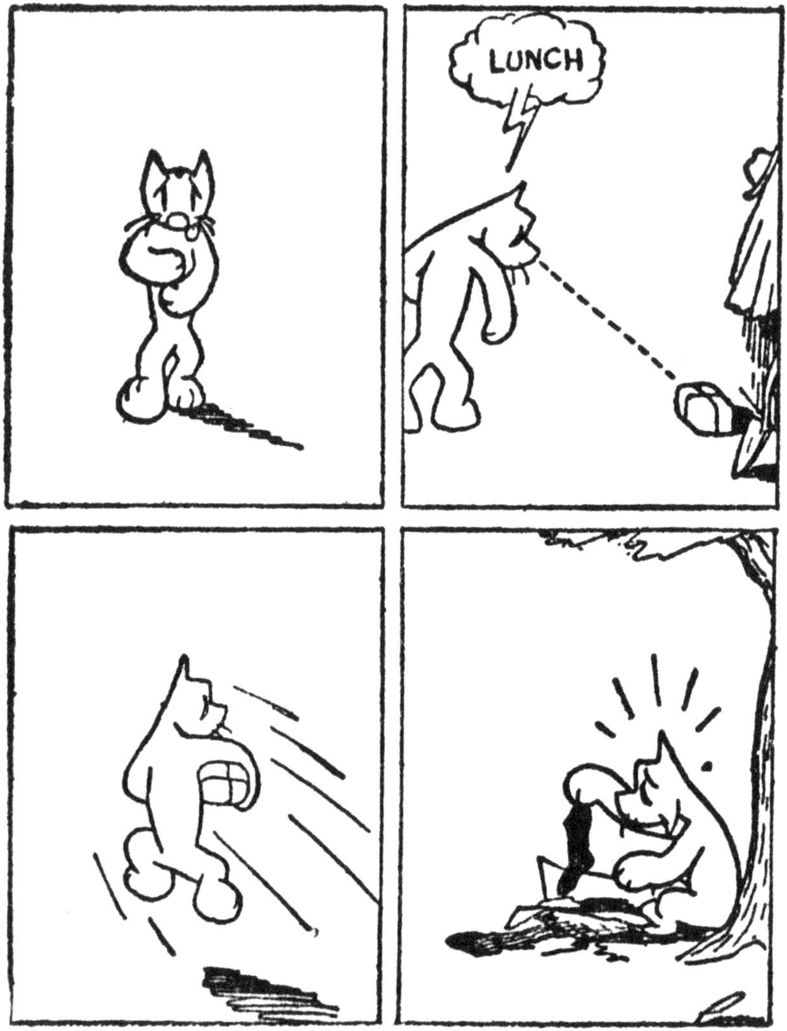
LUNCH

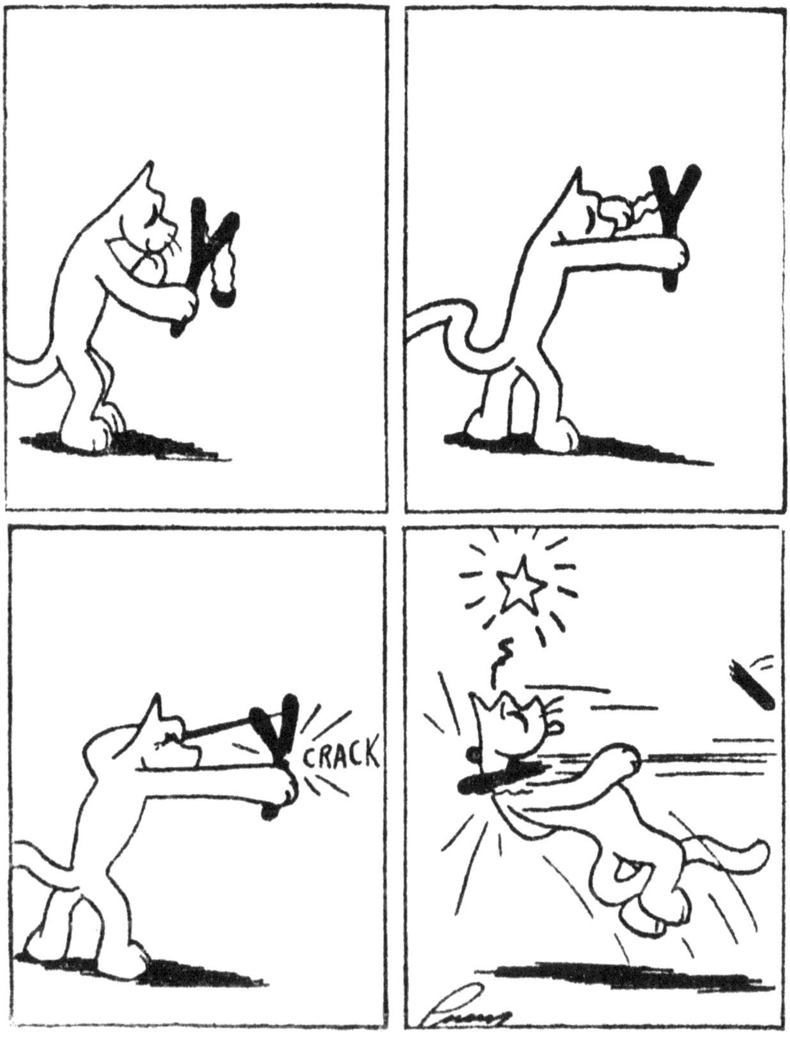
CRACK

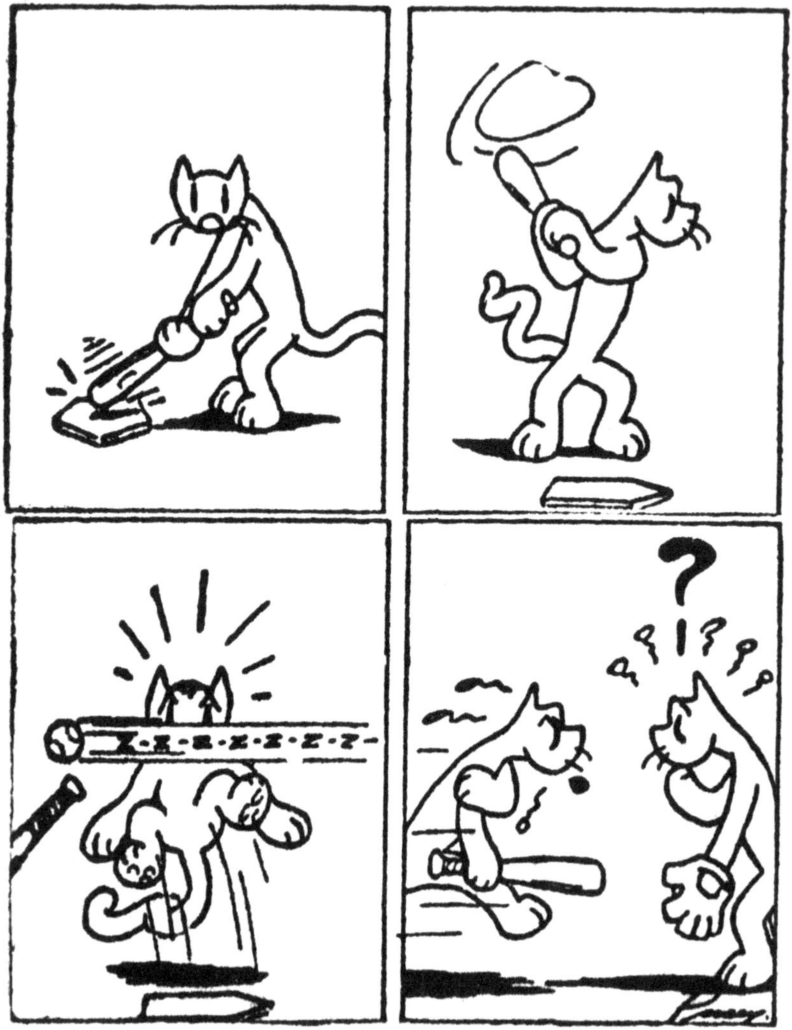

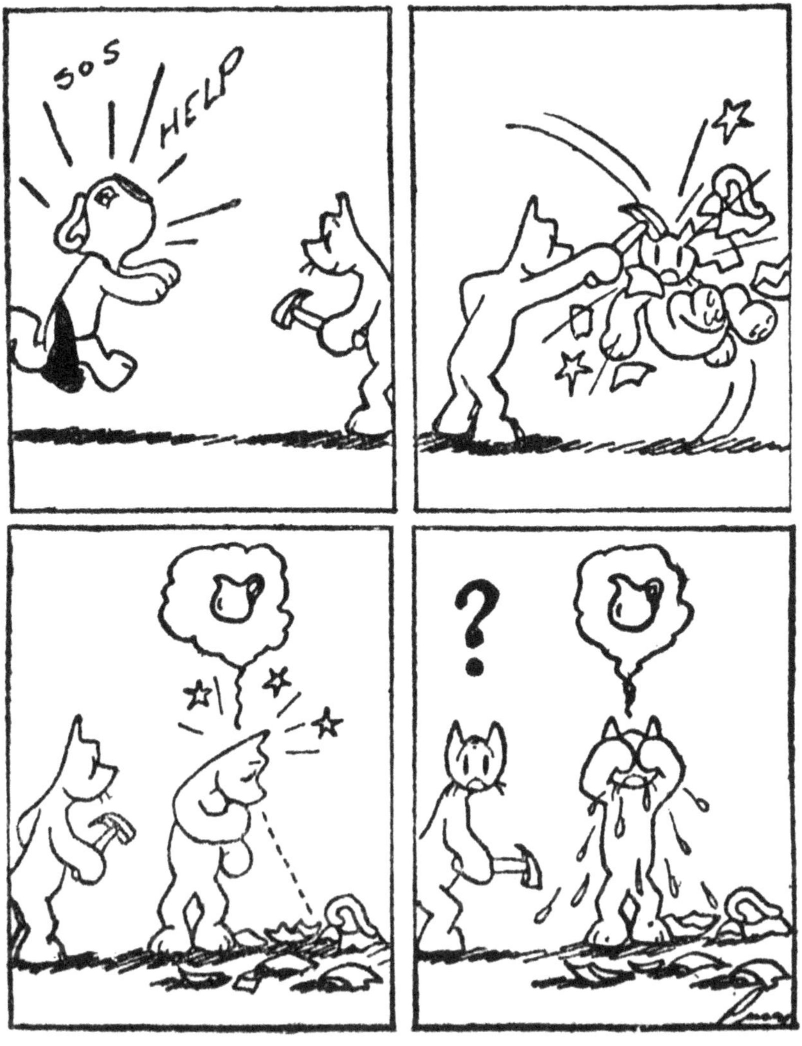
SOS
HELP
?

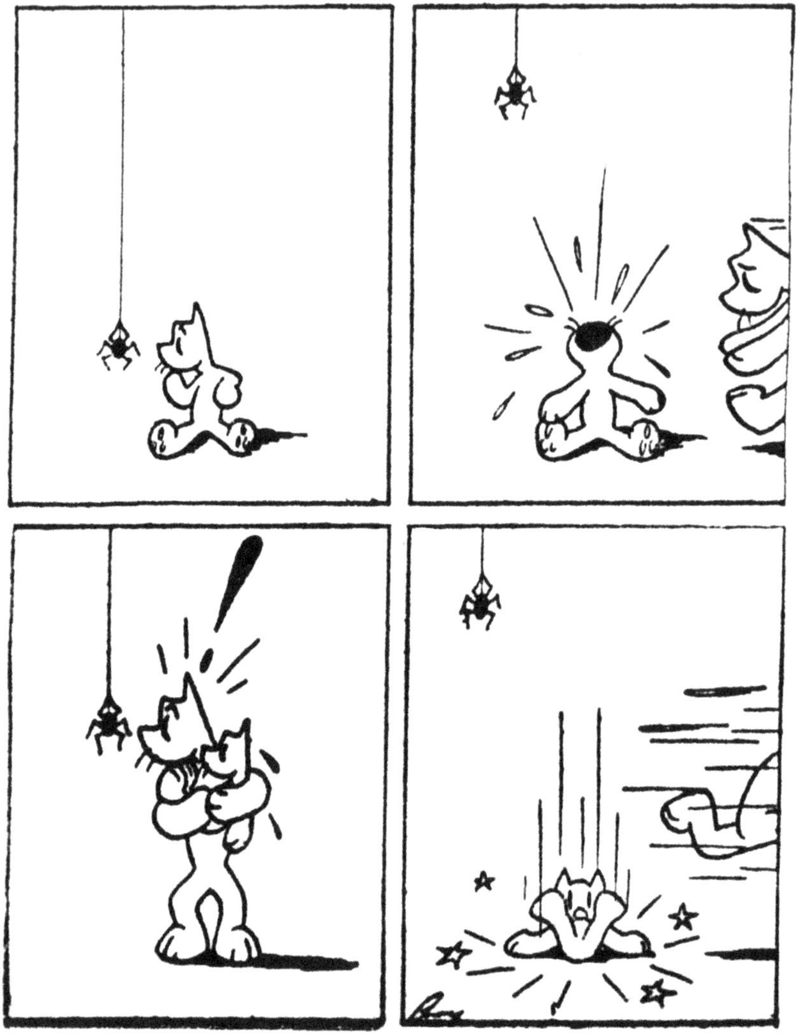

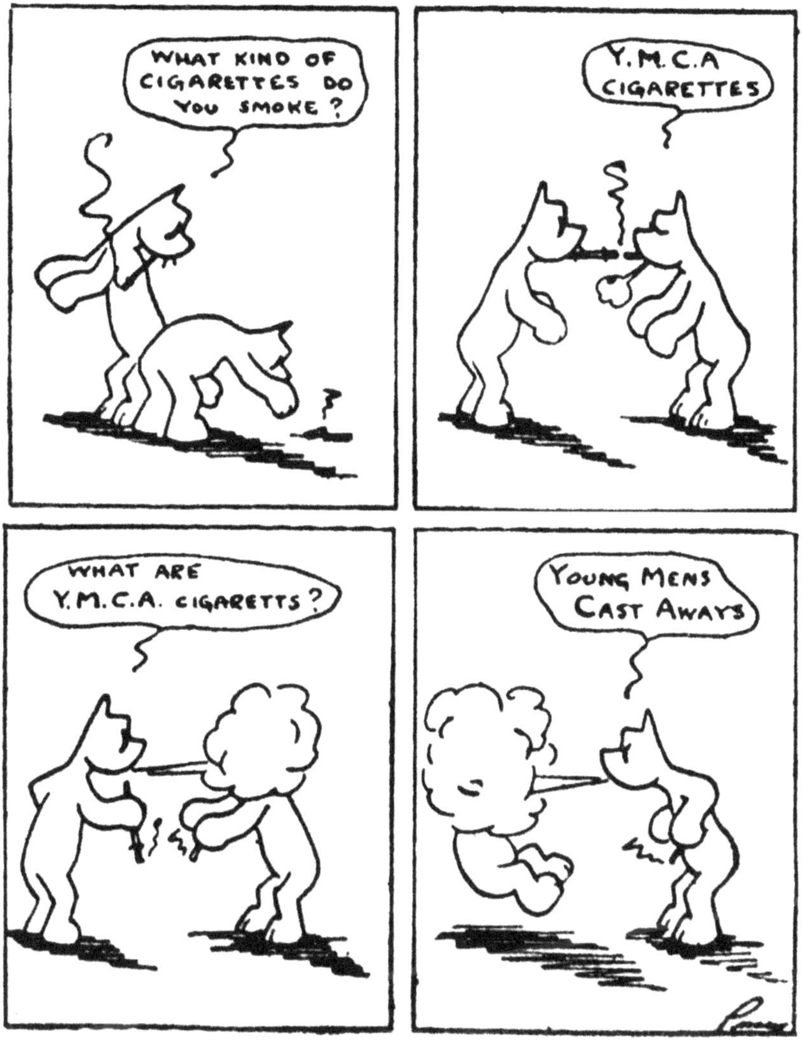
WHAT KIND OF CIGARETTES DO YOU SMOKE?
Y.M.C.A CIGARETTES
WHAT ARE Y.M.C.A. CIGARETTS?
YOUNG MENS CAST AWAYS

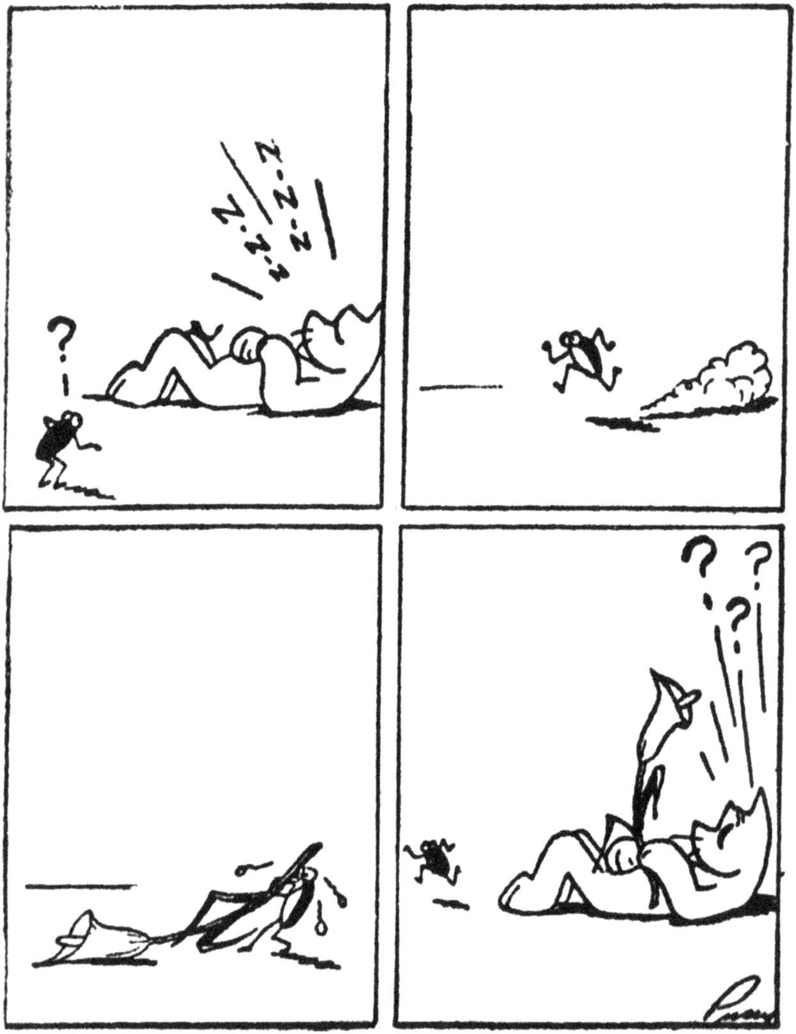
Z-Z-Z
Z-Z-Z

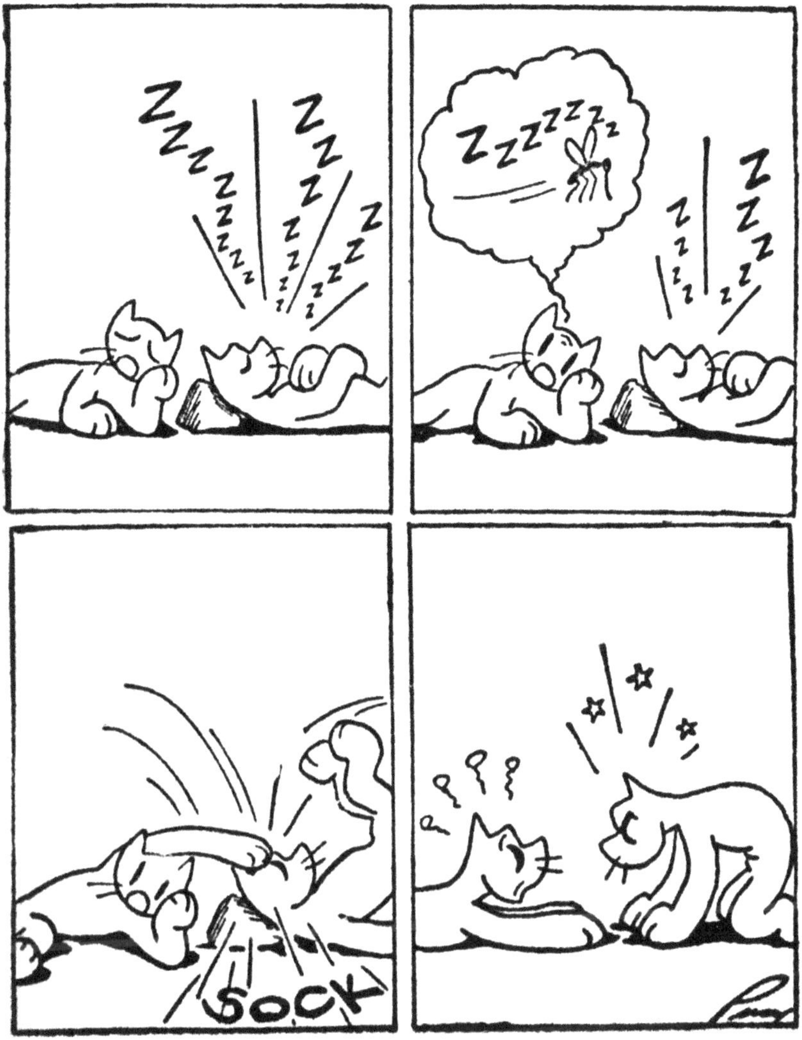
SOCK

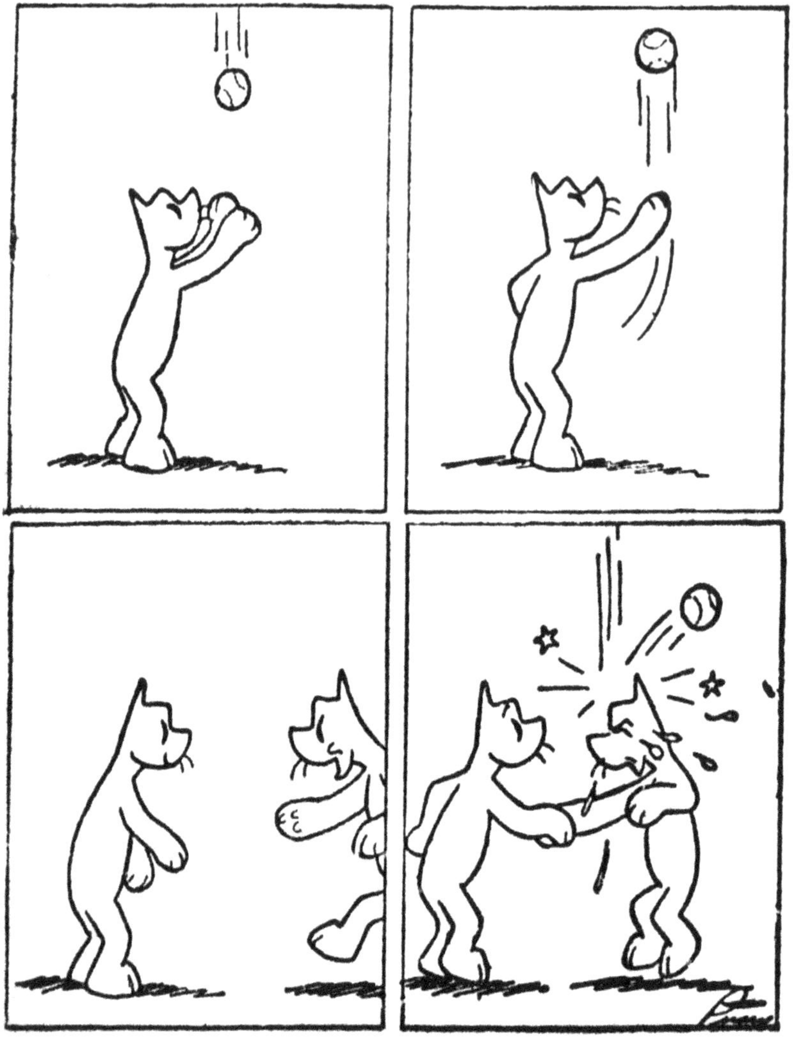

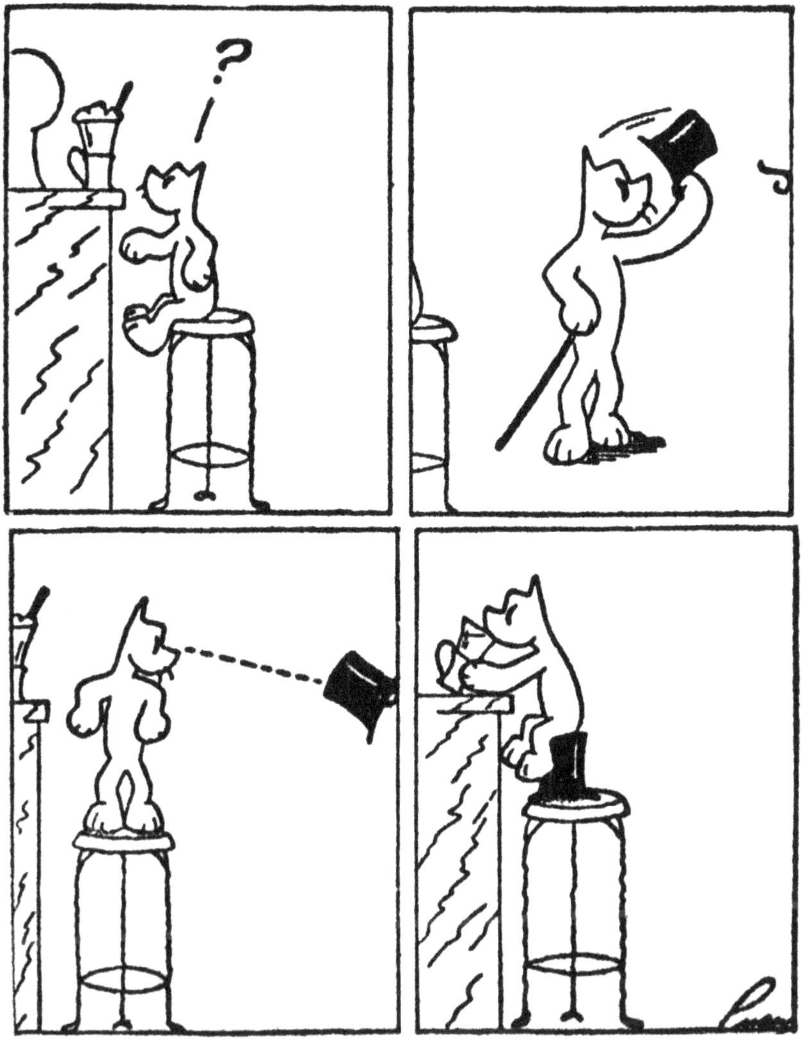
?

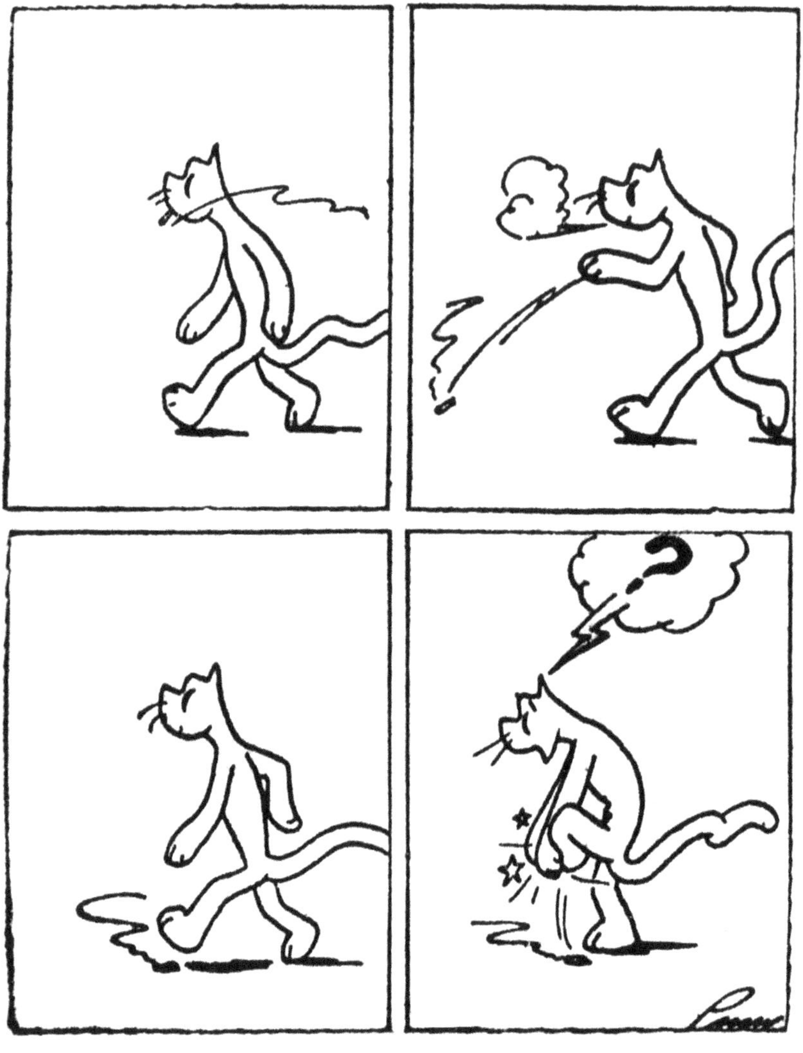
?

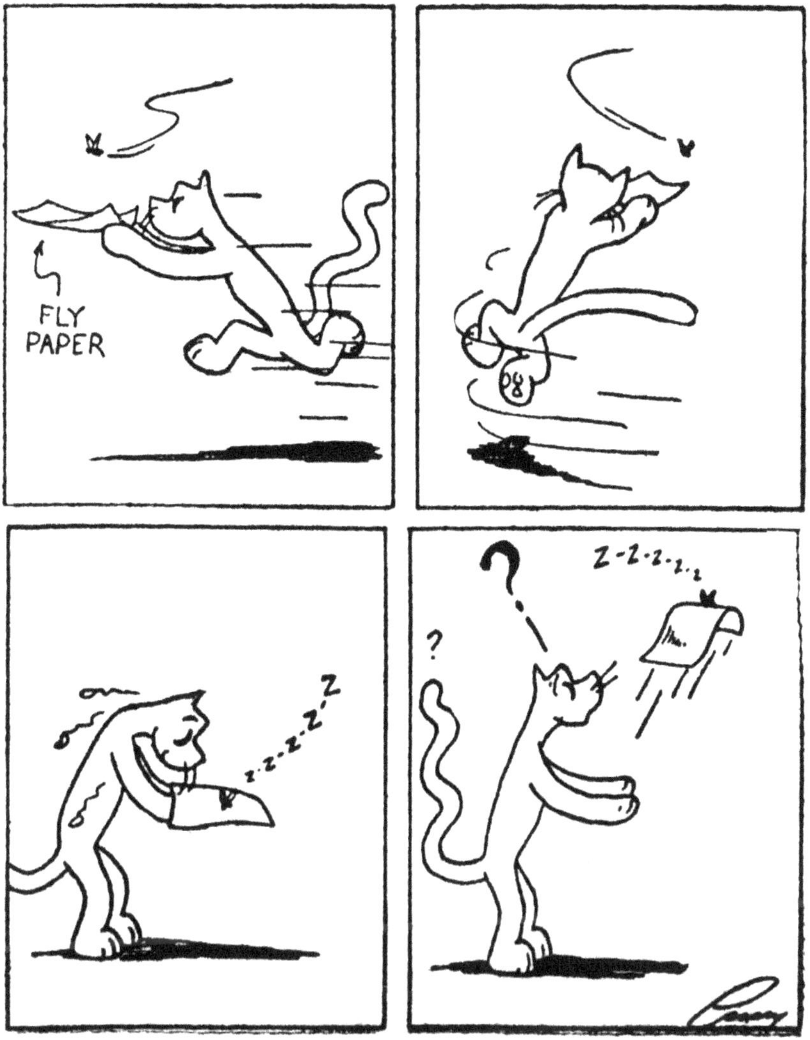
FLY PAPER
Z-Z-Z-Z-Z-Z
Z-Z-Z-Z-Z
?
?

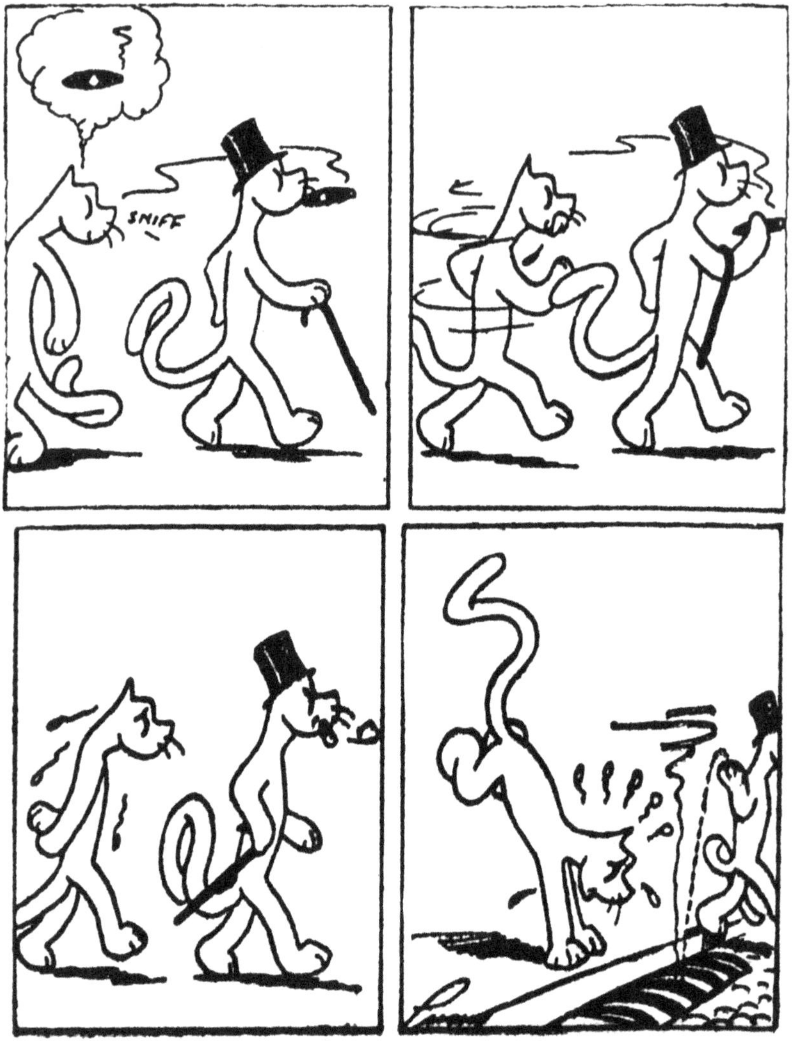
SNIFF

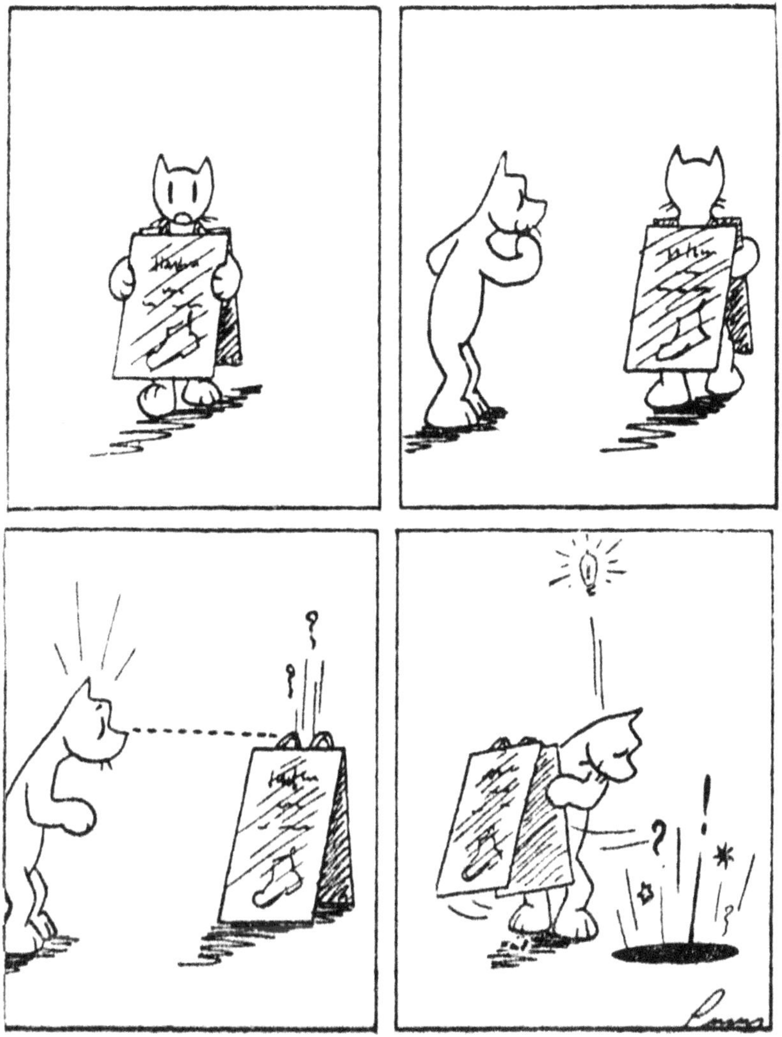

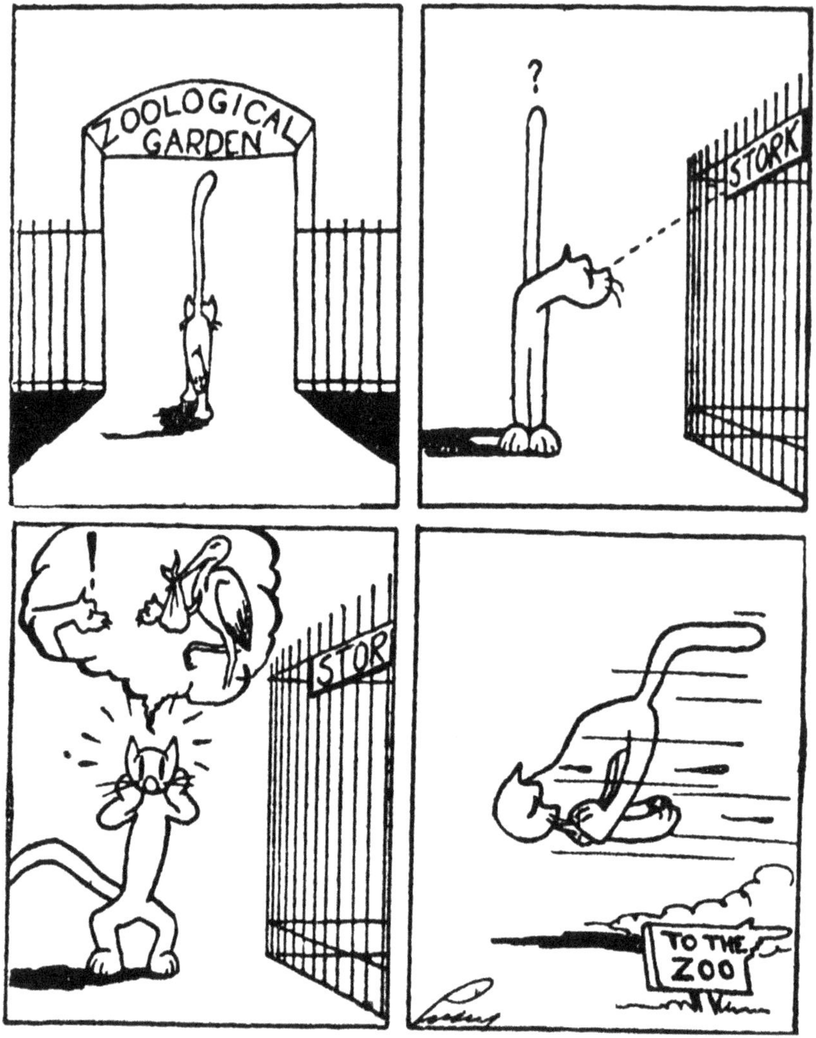
ZOOLOGICAL GARDEN
?
STORK
!
STOR
TO THE ZOO

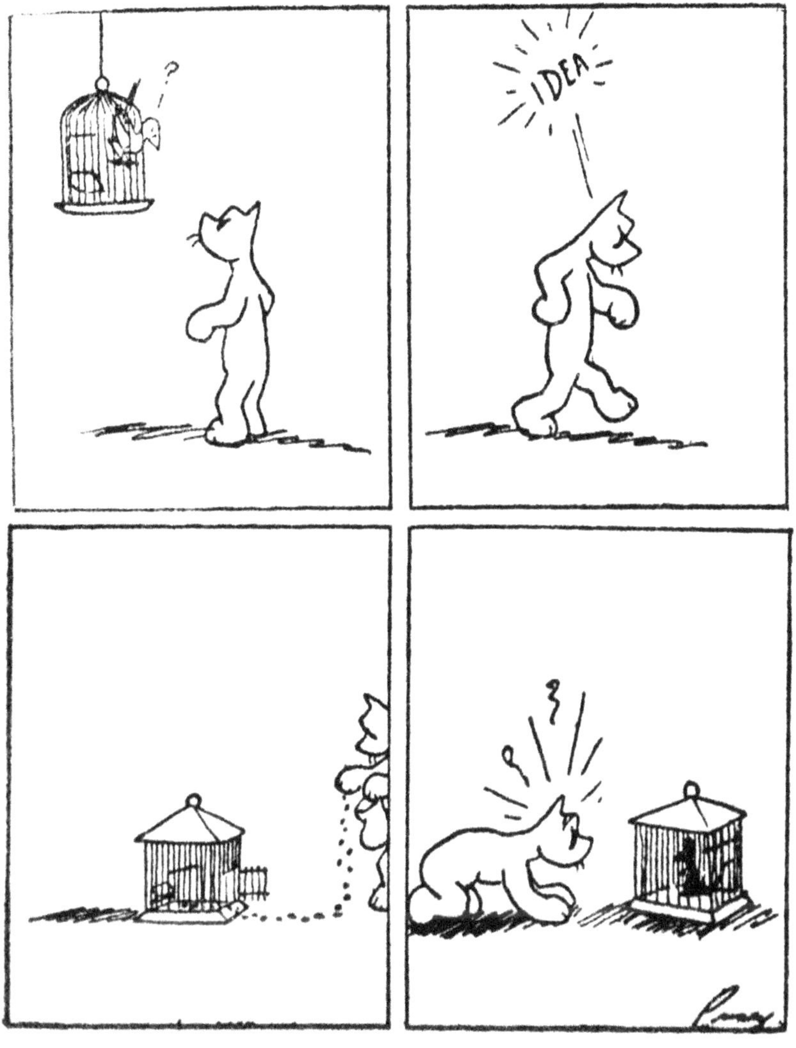
IDEA

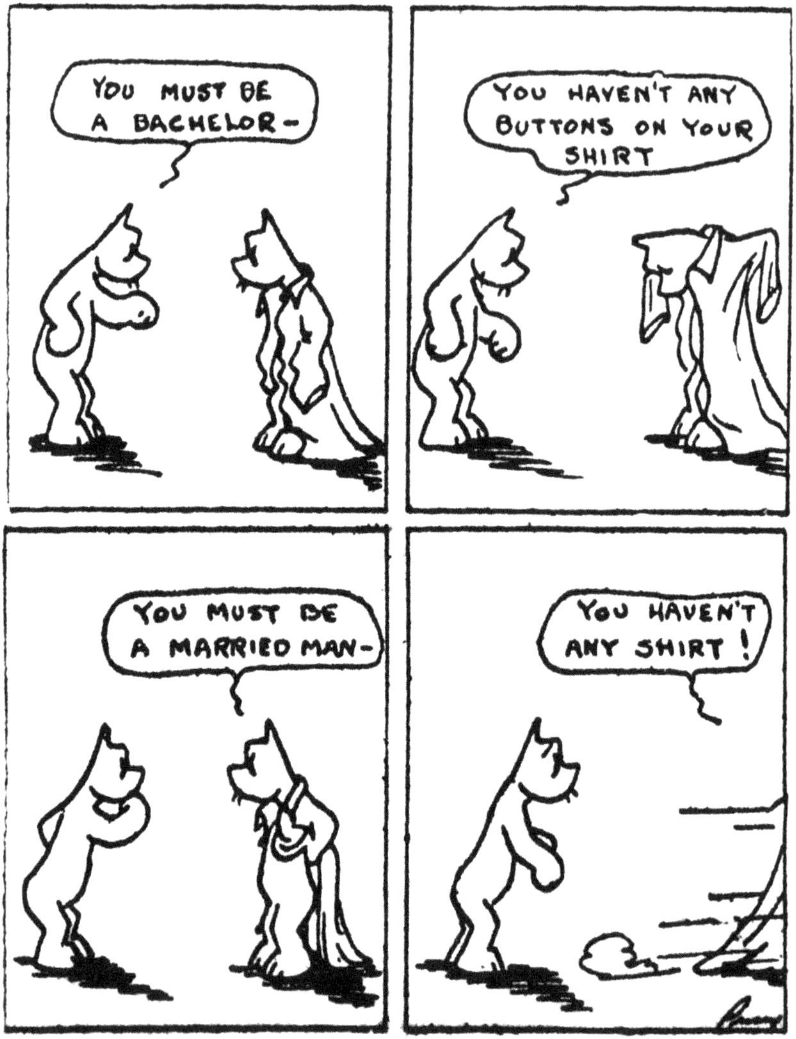
YOU MUST BE A BACHELOR-
YOU HAVEN'T ANY BUTTONS ON YOUR SHIRT
YOU MUST BE A MARRIED MAN-
YOU HAVEN'T ANY SHIRT!

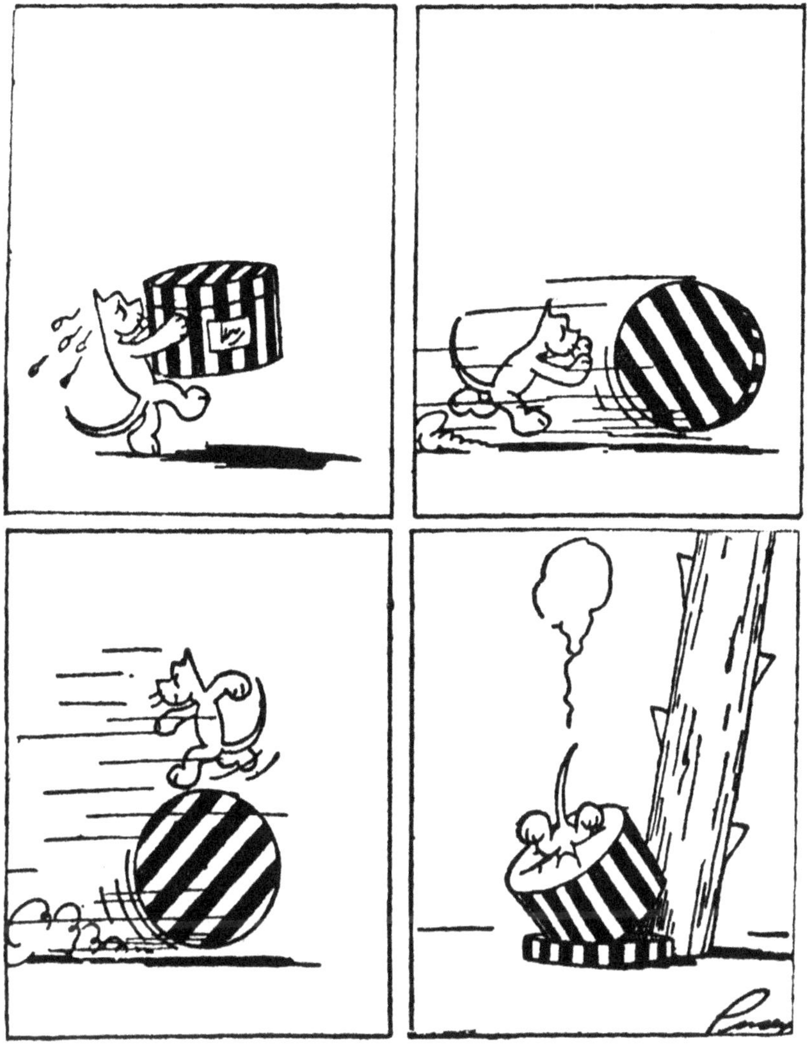

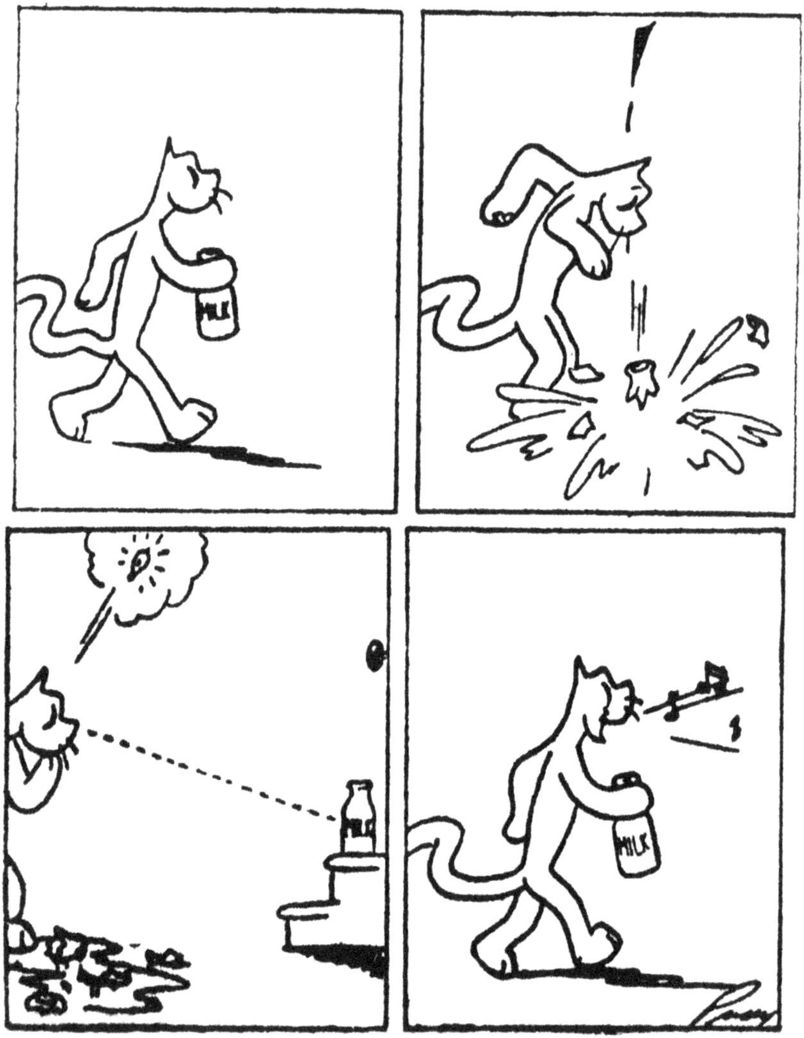
MILK
MILK

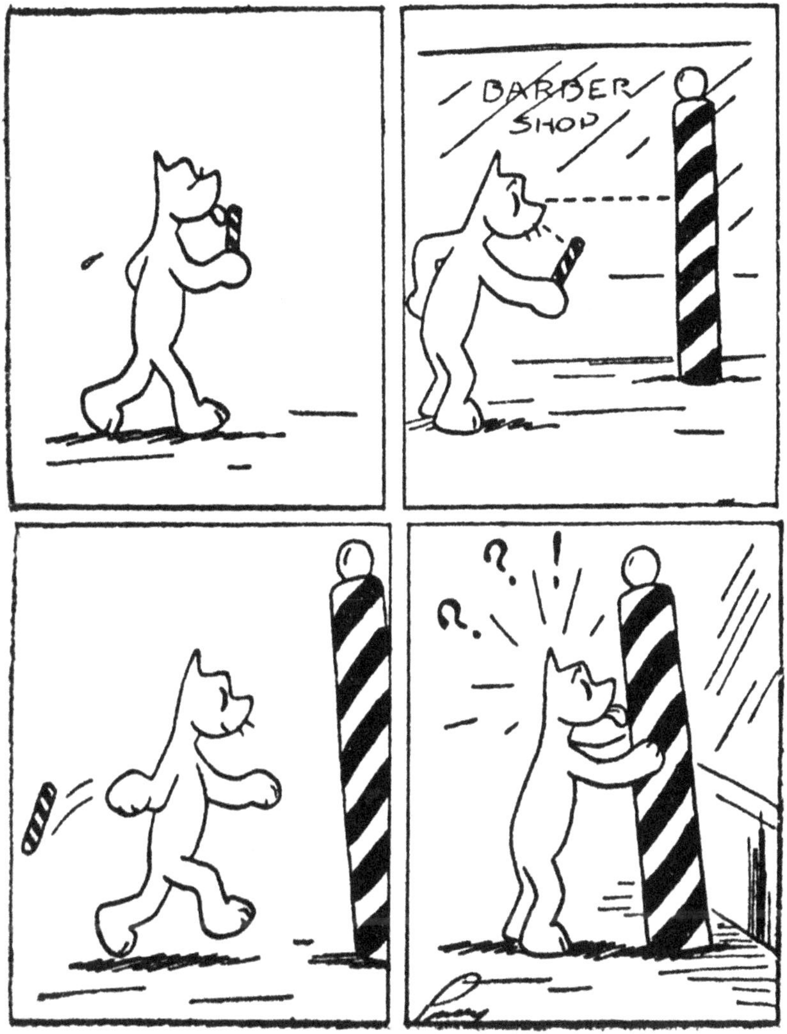
BARBER SHOP
? ? !

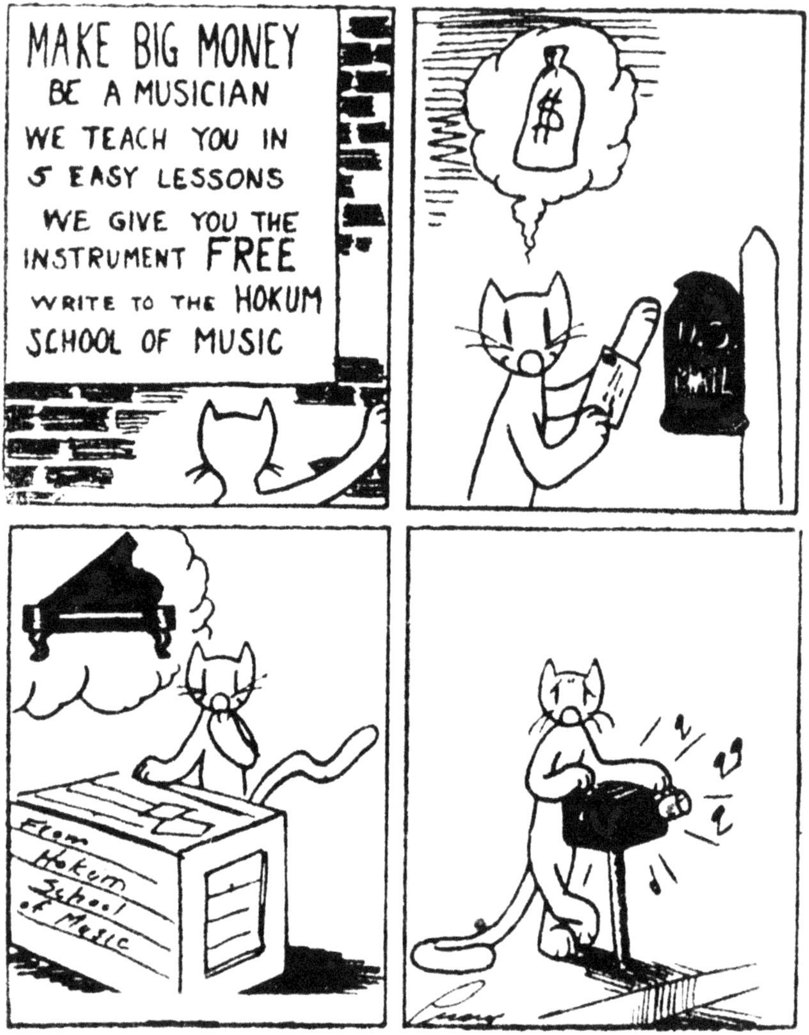
MAKE BIG MONEY
BE A MUSICIAN
WE TEACH YOU IN
5 EASY LESSONS
WE GIVE YOU THE
INSTRUMENT FREE
WRITE TO THE HOKUM
SCHOOL OF MUSIC
U.S. MAIL
From Hokum School of Music

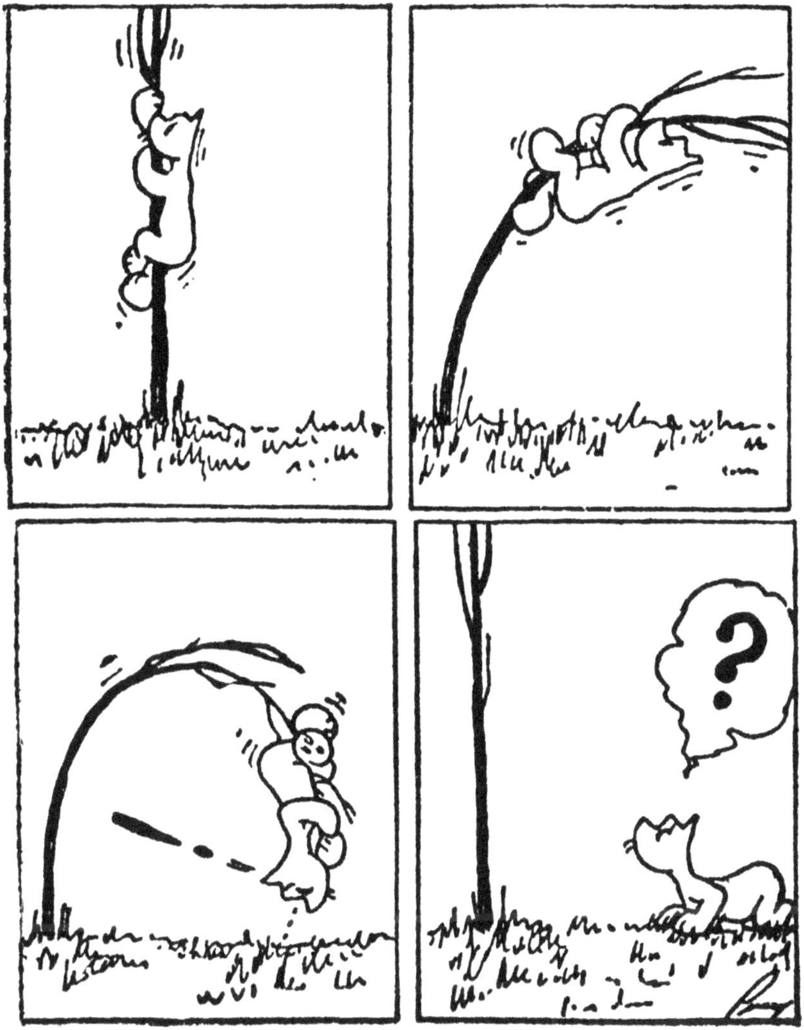
?

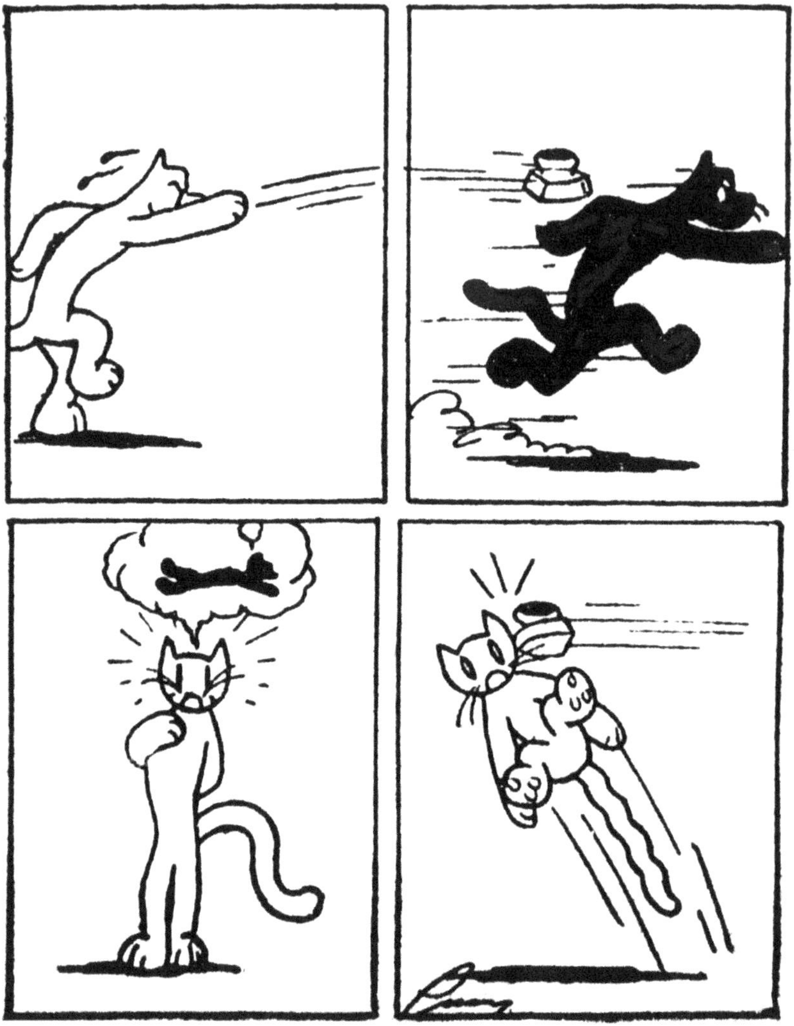

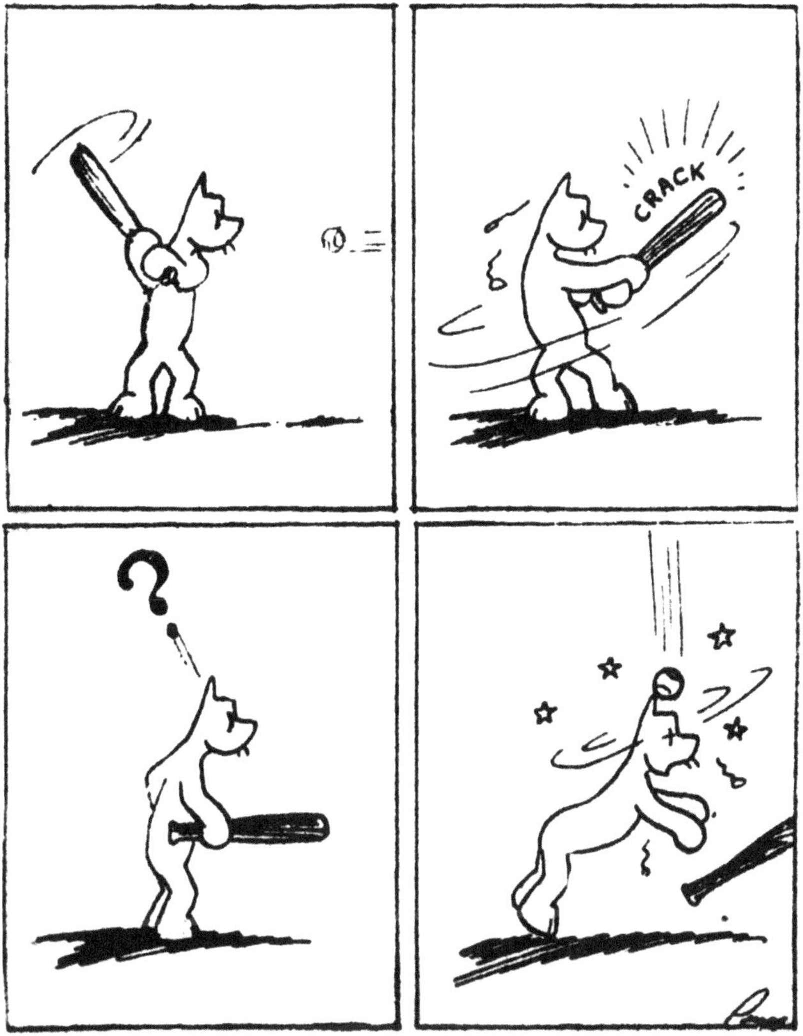
CRACK

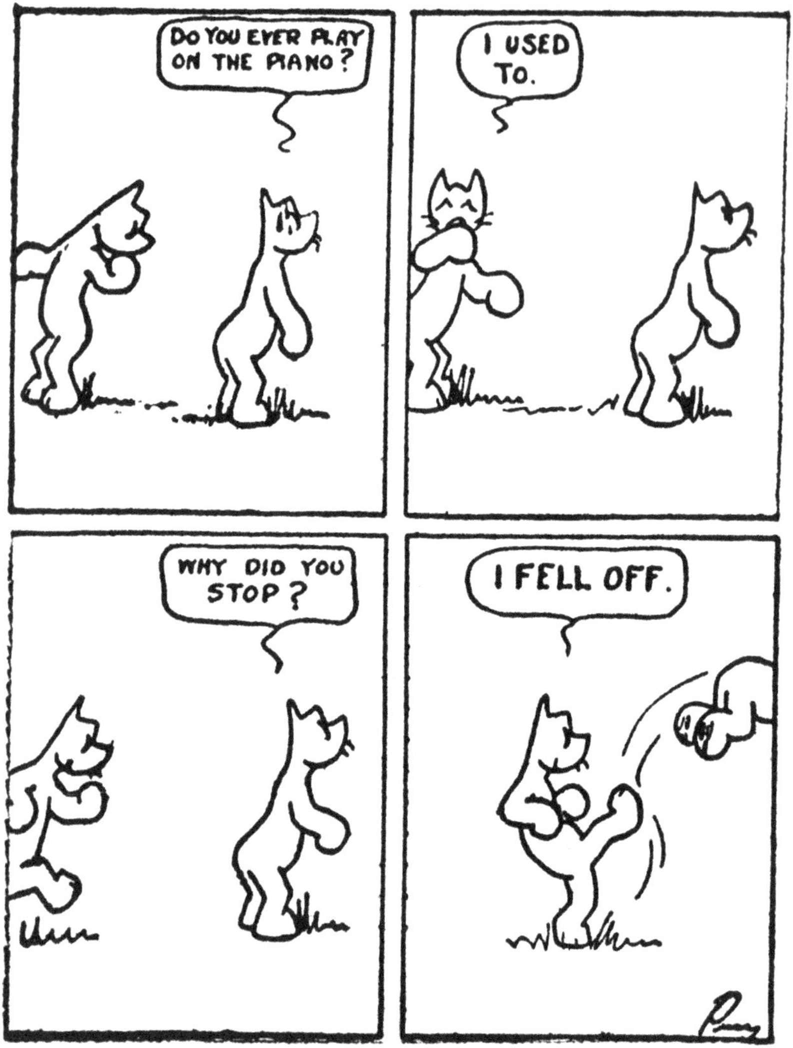
DO YOU EVER PLAY ON THE PIANO?
I USED TO.
WHY DID YOU STOP?
I FELL OFF.

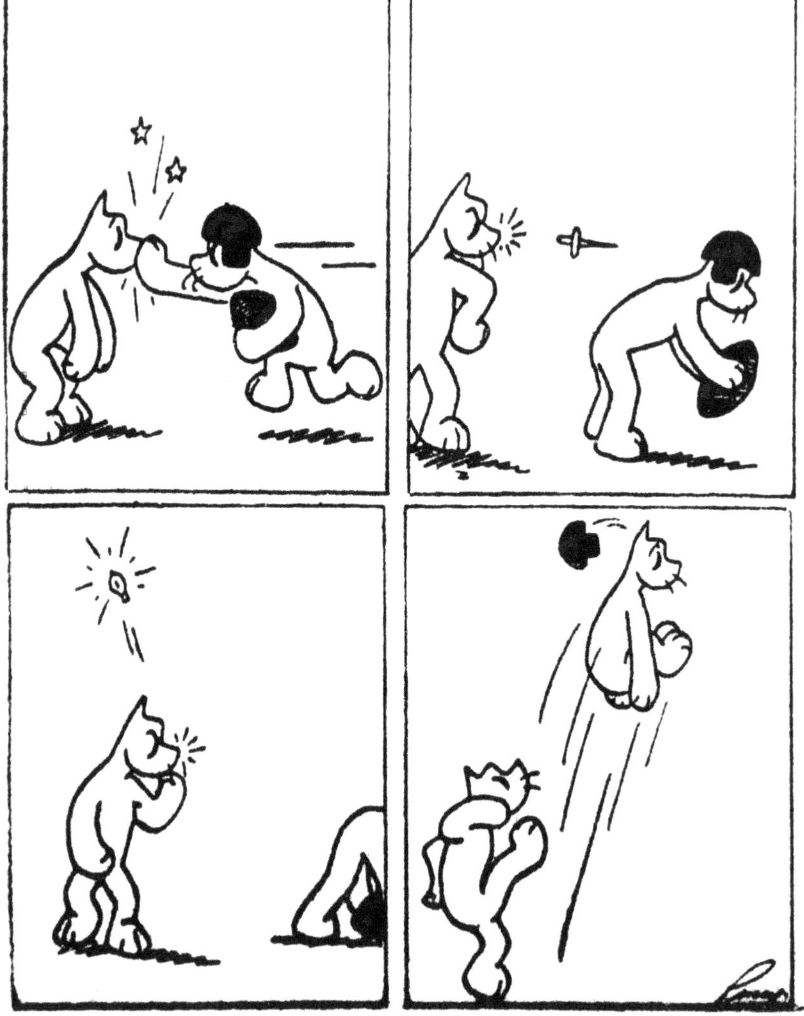

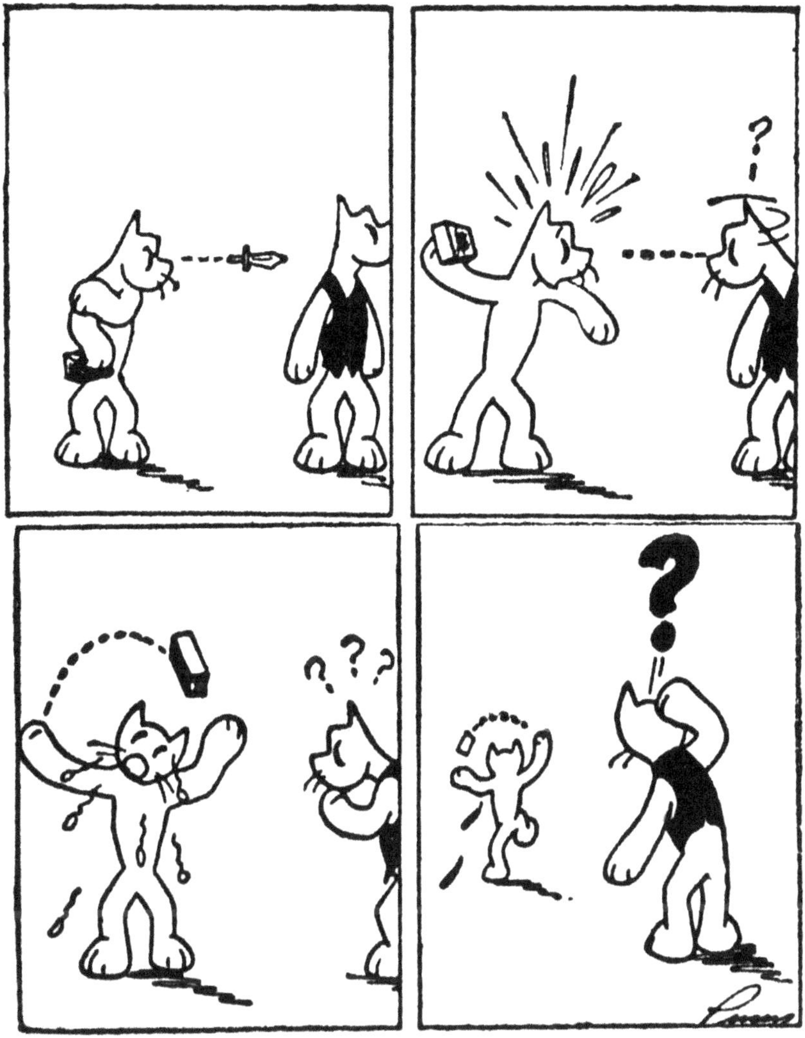

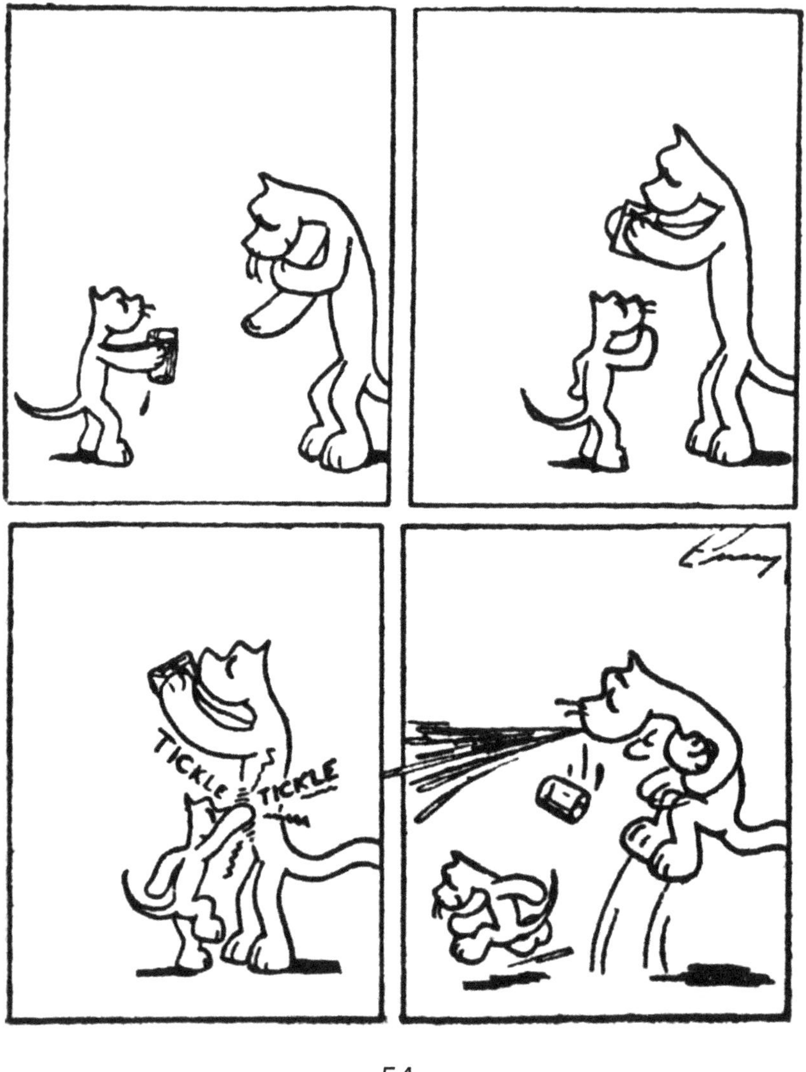
TICKLE
TICKLE

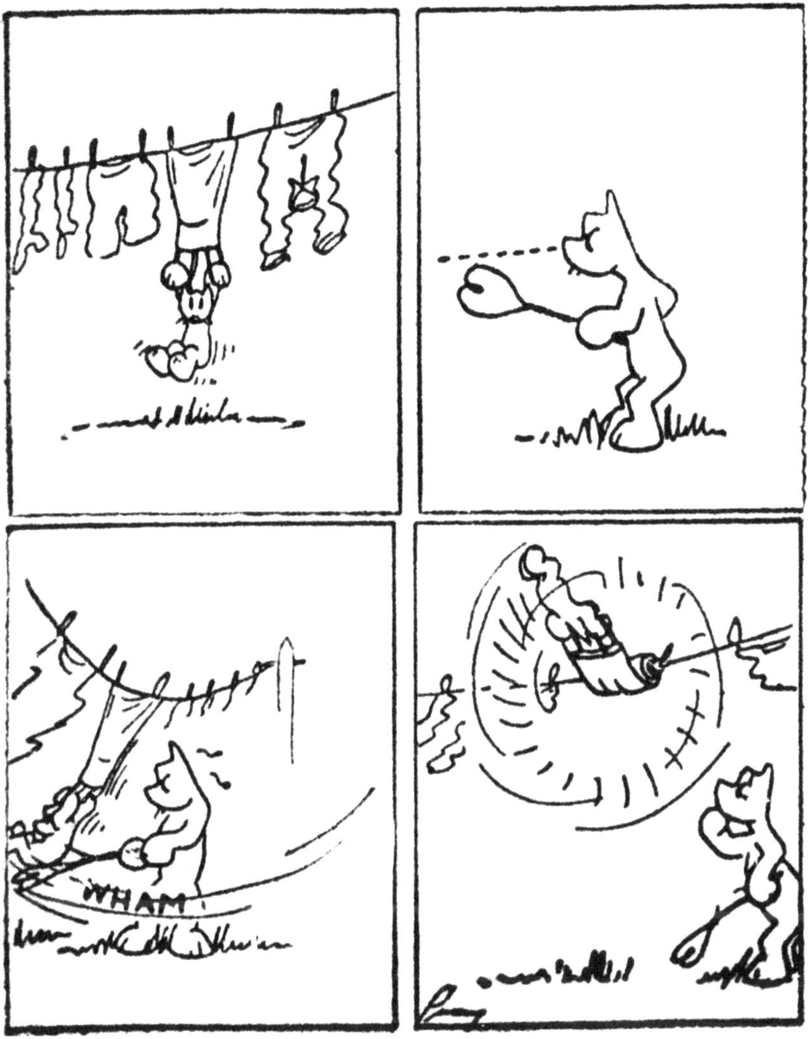
WHAM

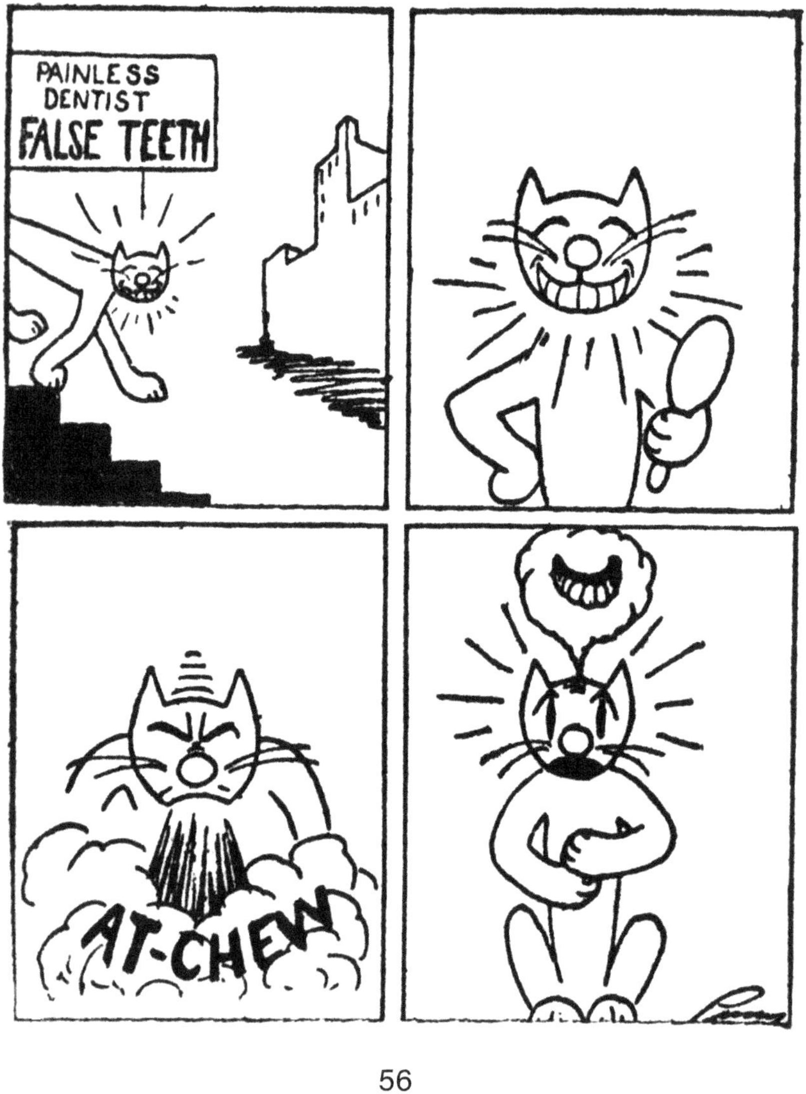
PAINLESS
DENTIST
FALSE TEETH
AT-CHEW

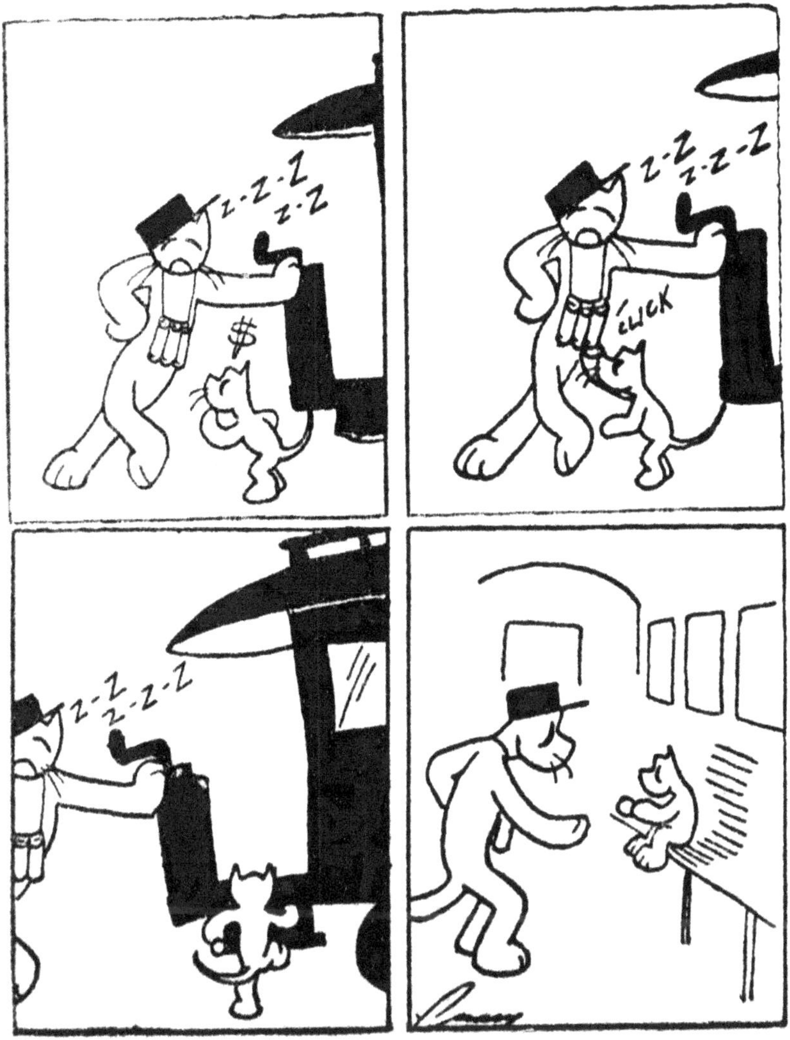
Z-Z-Z
Z-Z
$
Z-Z
Z-Z-Z
CLICK
Z-Z
Z-Z-Z

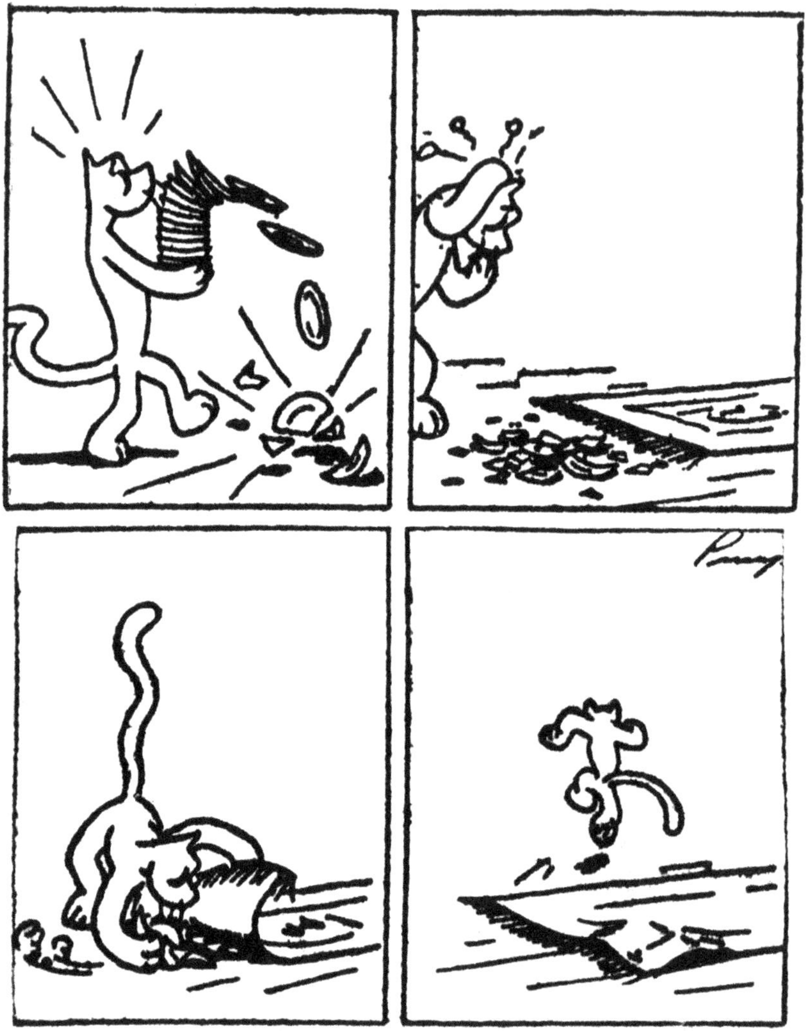

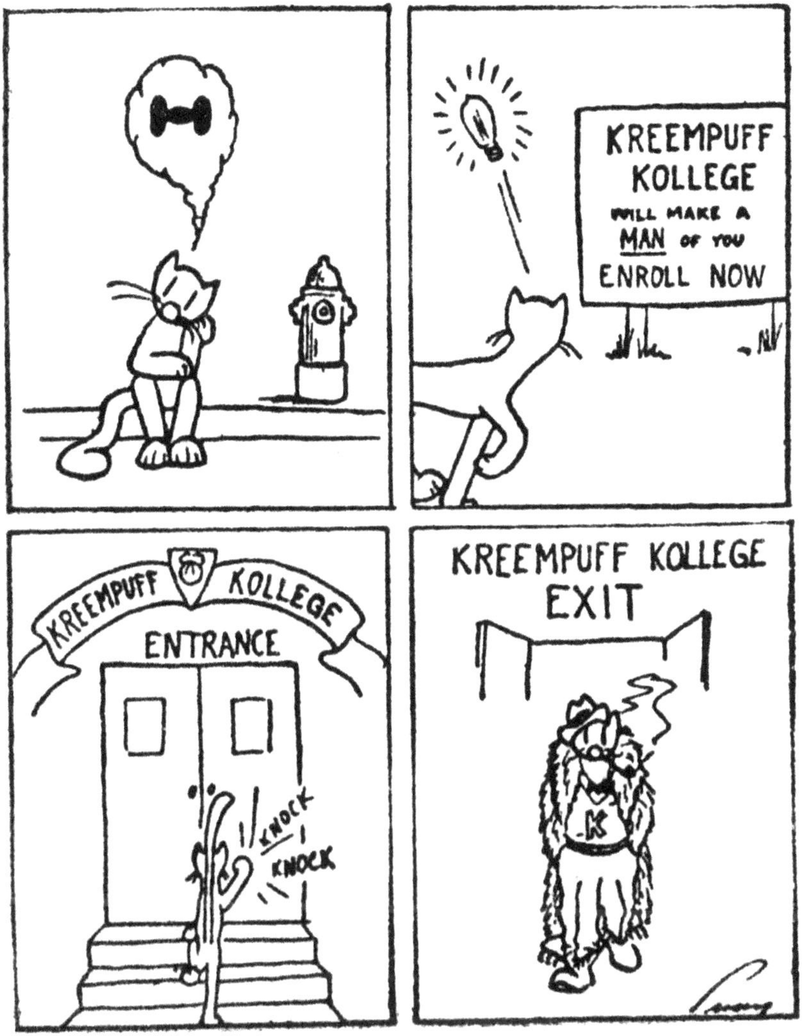
KREEMPUFF
KOLLEGE
WILL MAKE A
MAN OF YOU
ENROLL NOW
KREEMPUFF KOLLEGE
ENTRANCE
KNOCK
KNOCK
KREEMPUFF KOLLEGE
EXIT
K

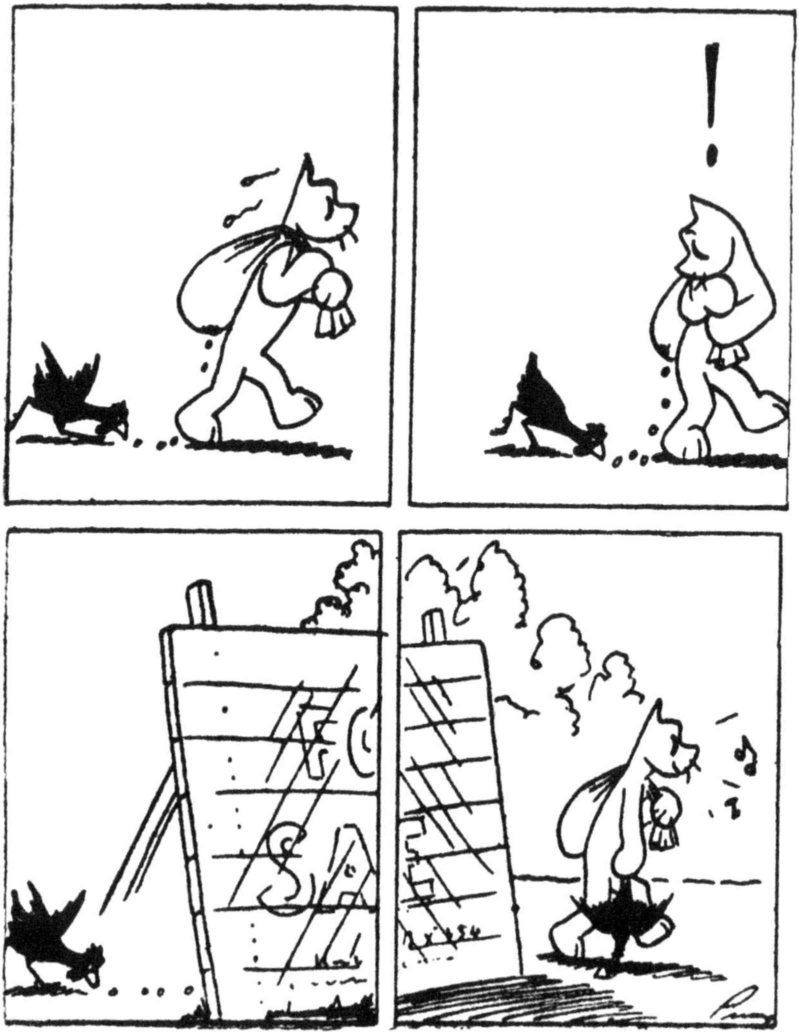
!

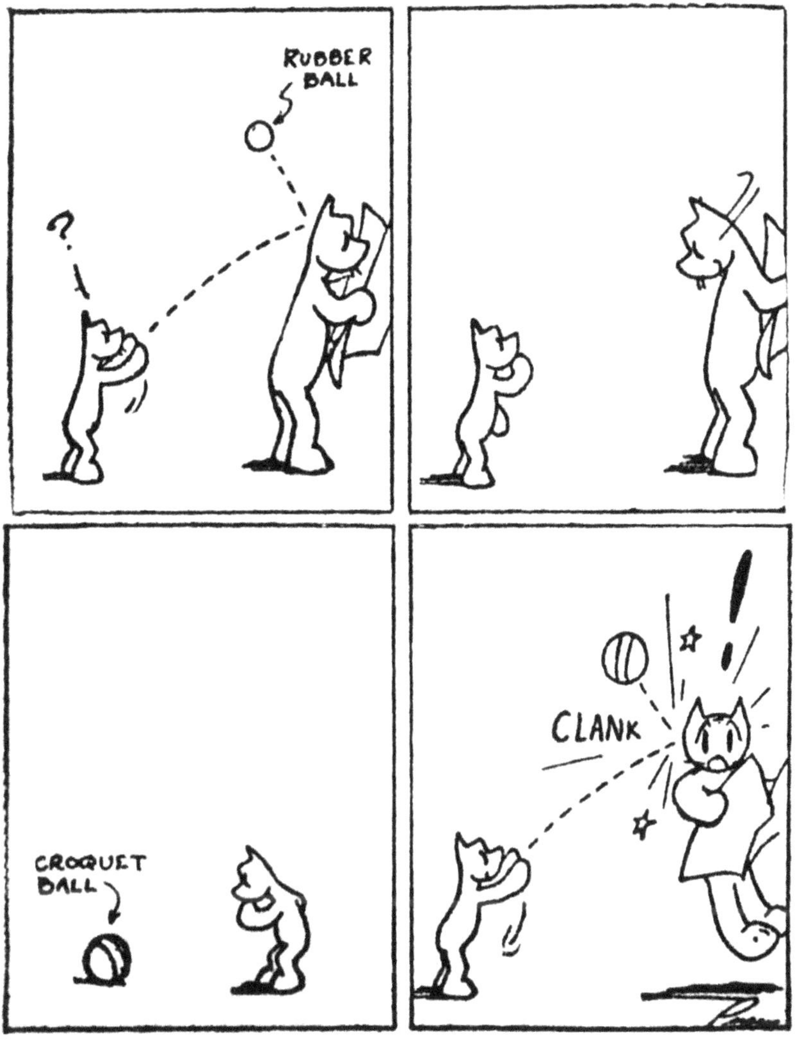
RUBBER BALL
?
CROQUET BALL
CLANK

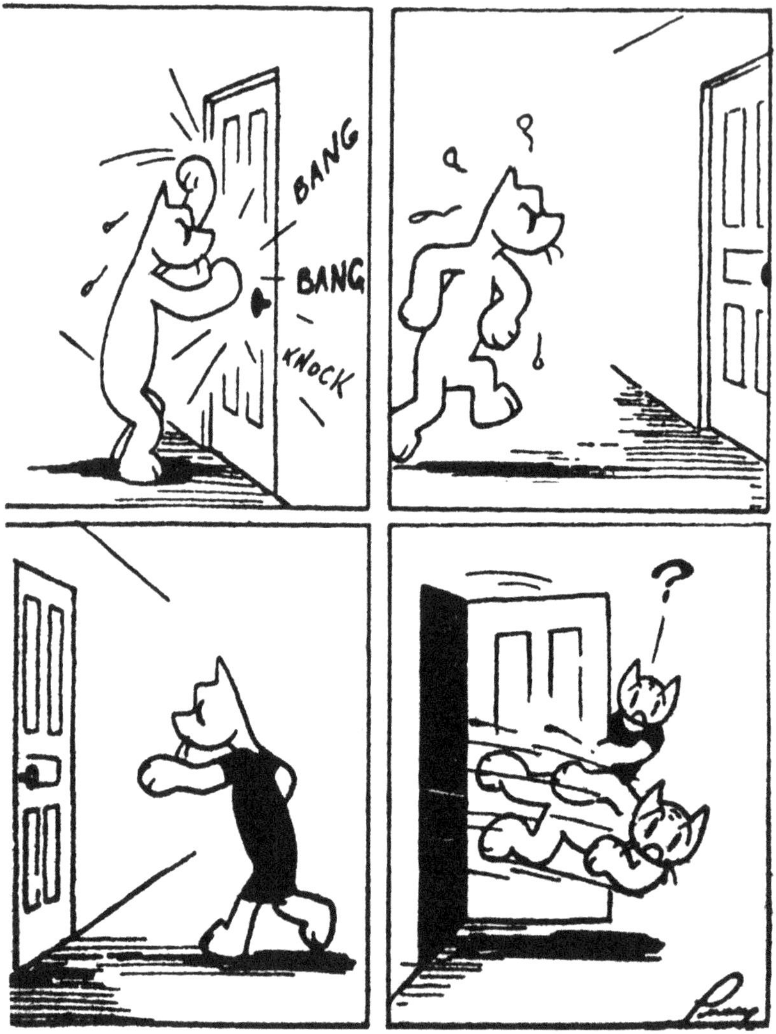
BANG
BANG
KNOCK

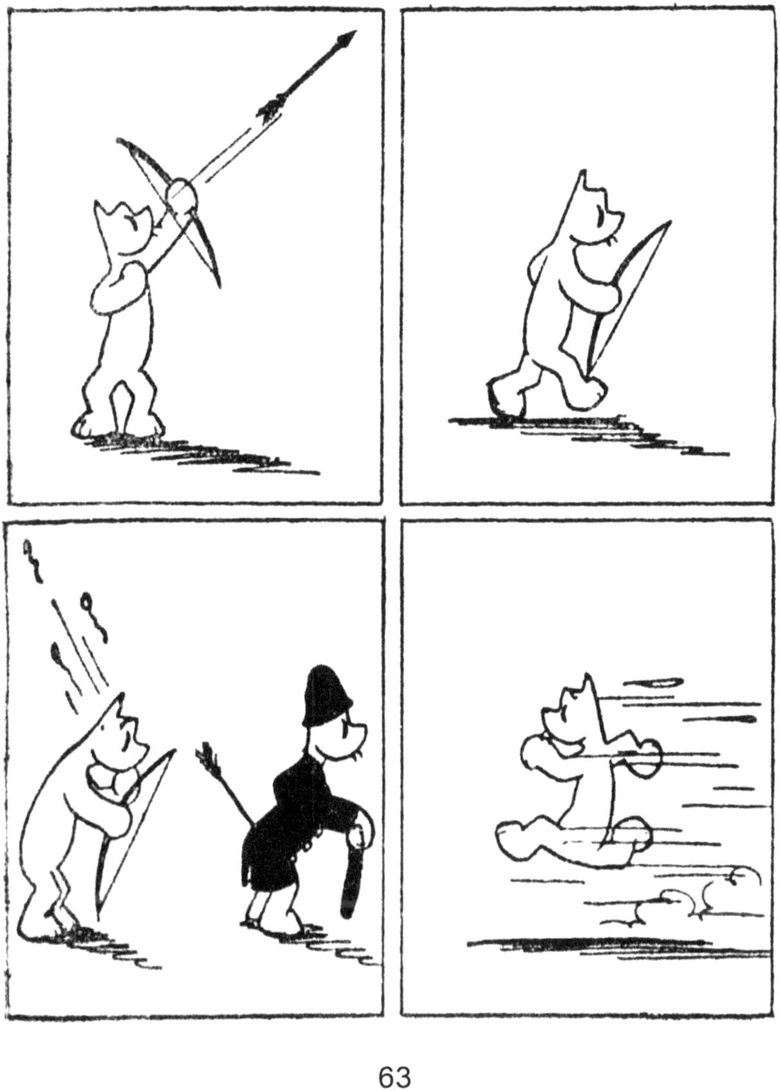

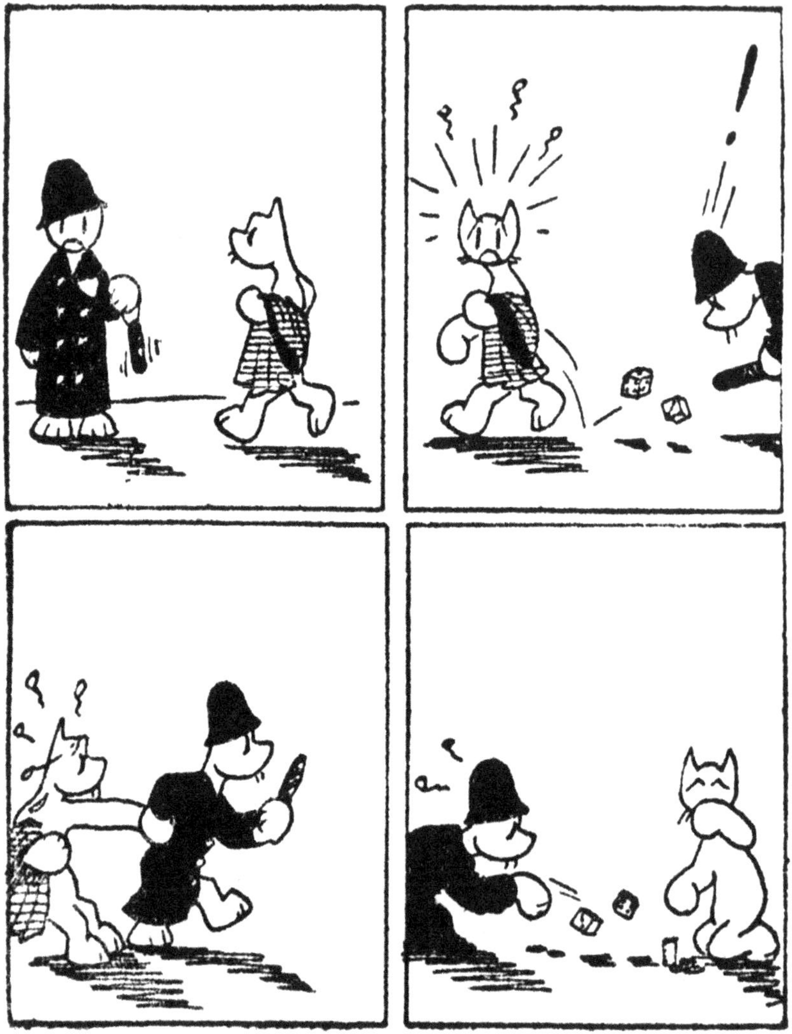

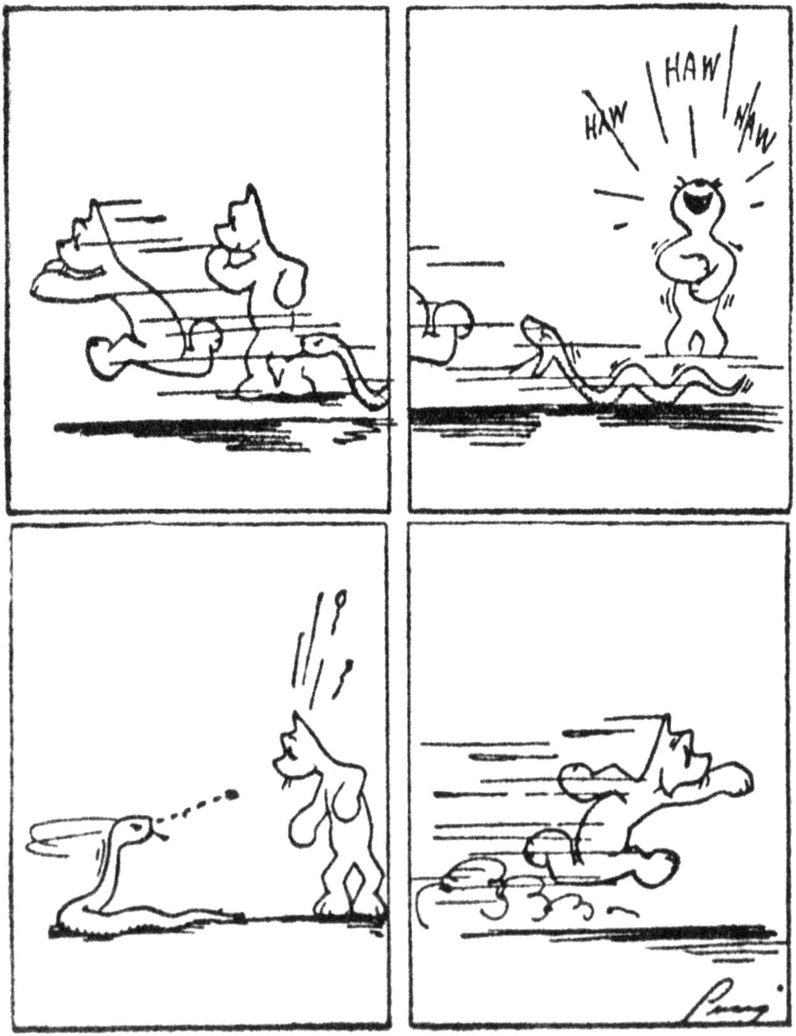
HAW
HAW
HAW

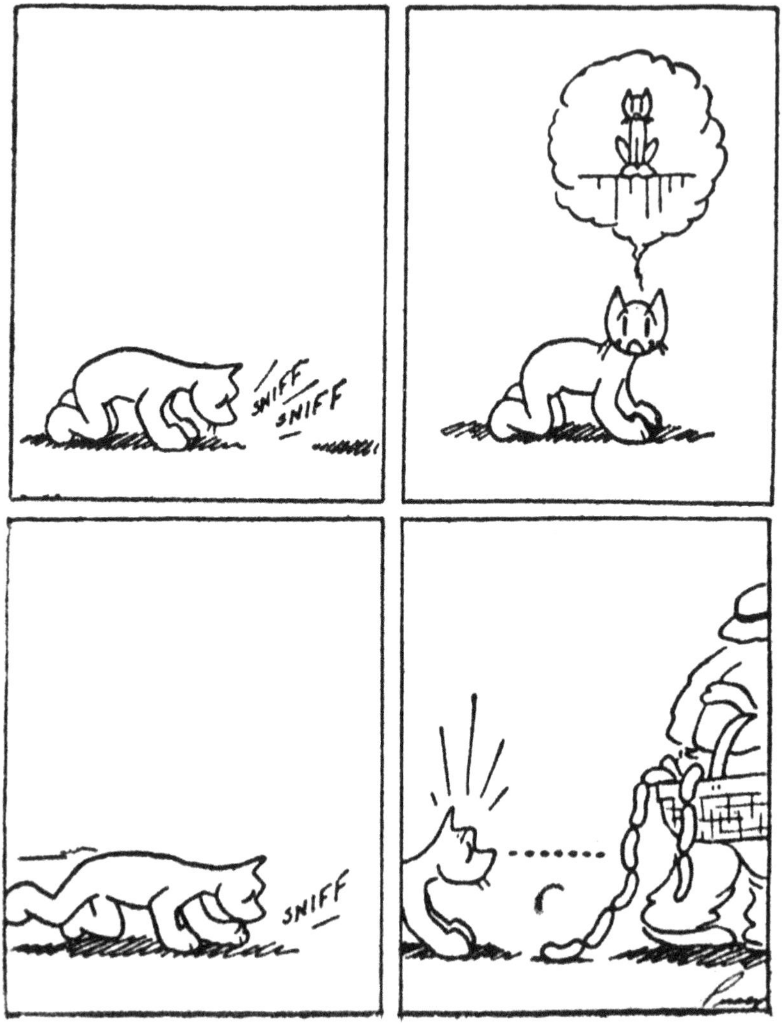
SNIFF
SNIFF
SNIFF

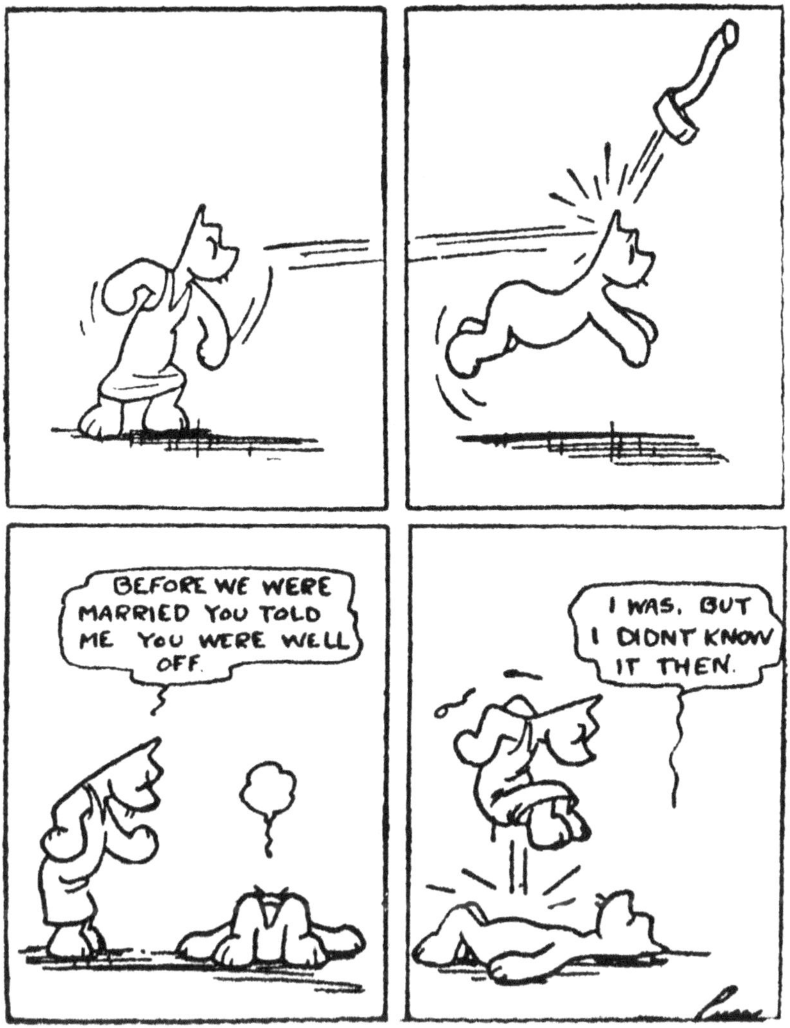
BEFORE WE WERE MARRIED YOU TOLD ME YOU WERE WELL OFF.
I WAS, BUT I DIDNT KNOW IT THEN.

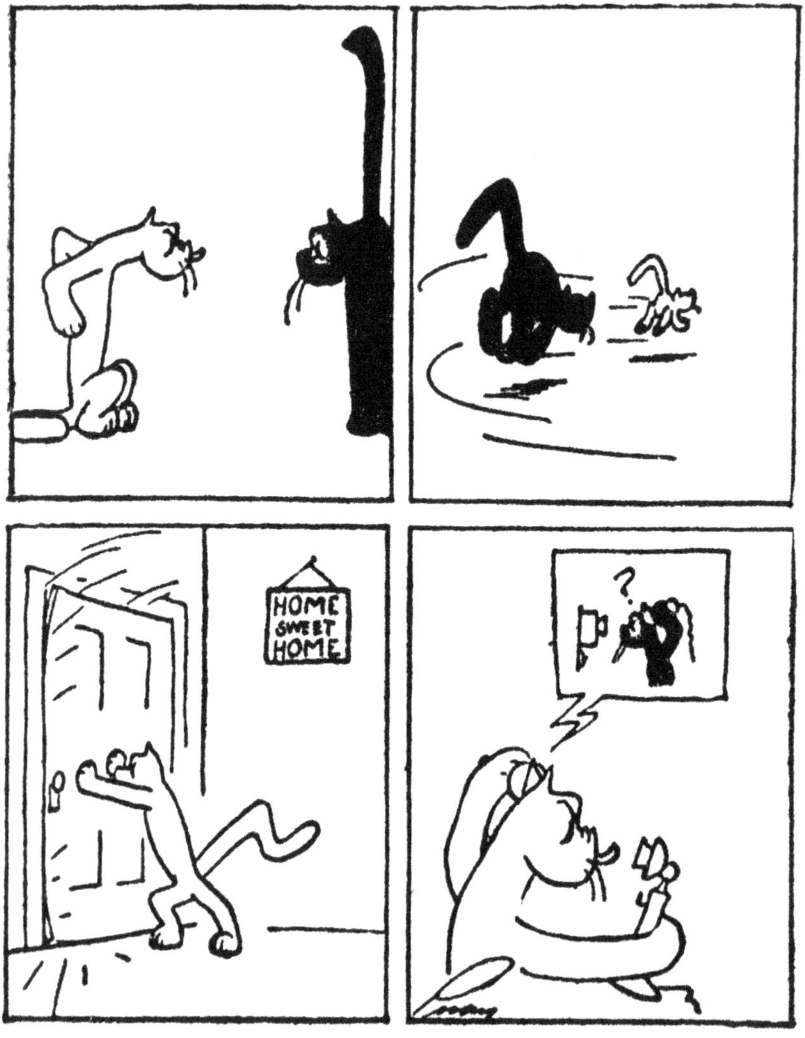
HOME
SWEET
HOME
?

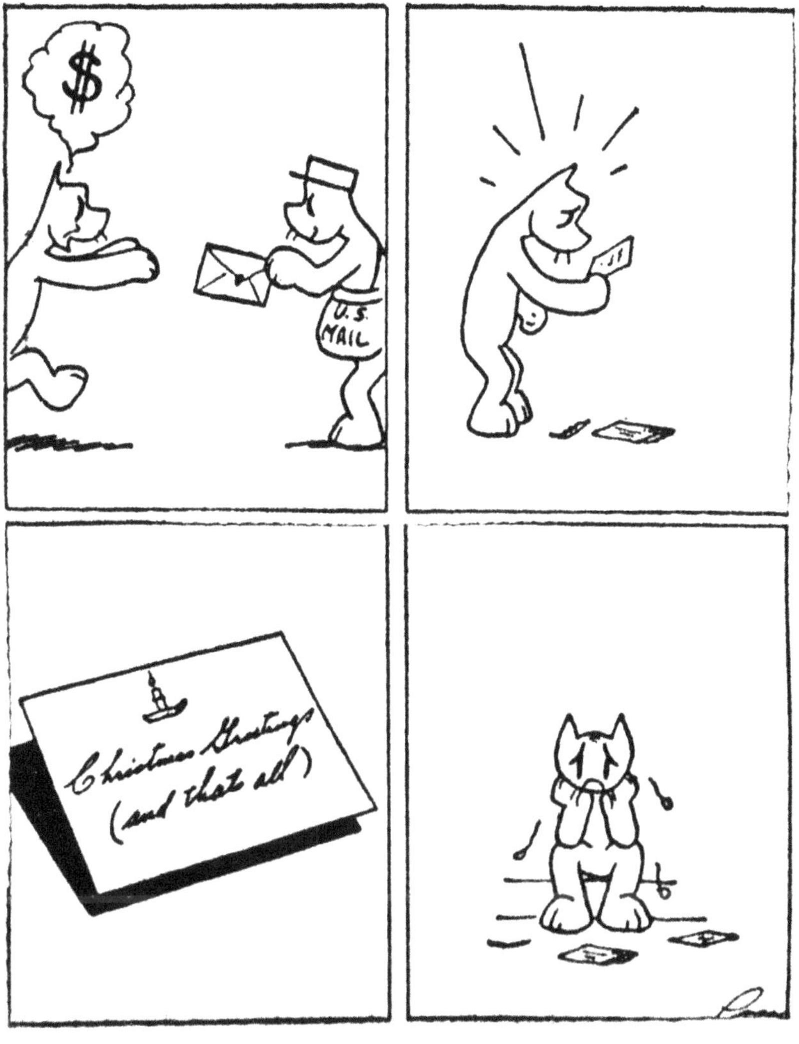
$
U.S. MAIL
Christmas Greetings
(and that all)

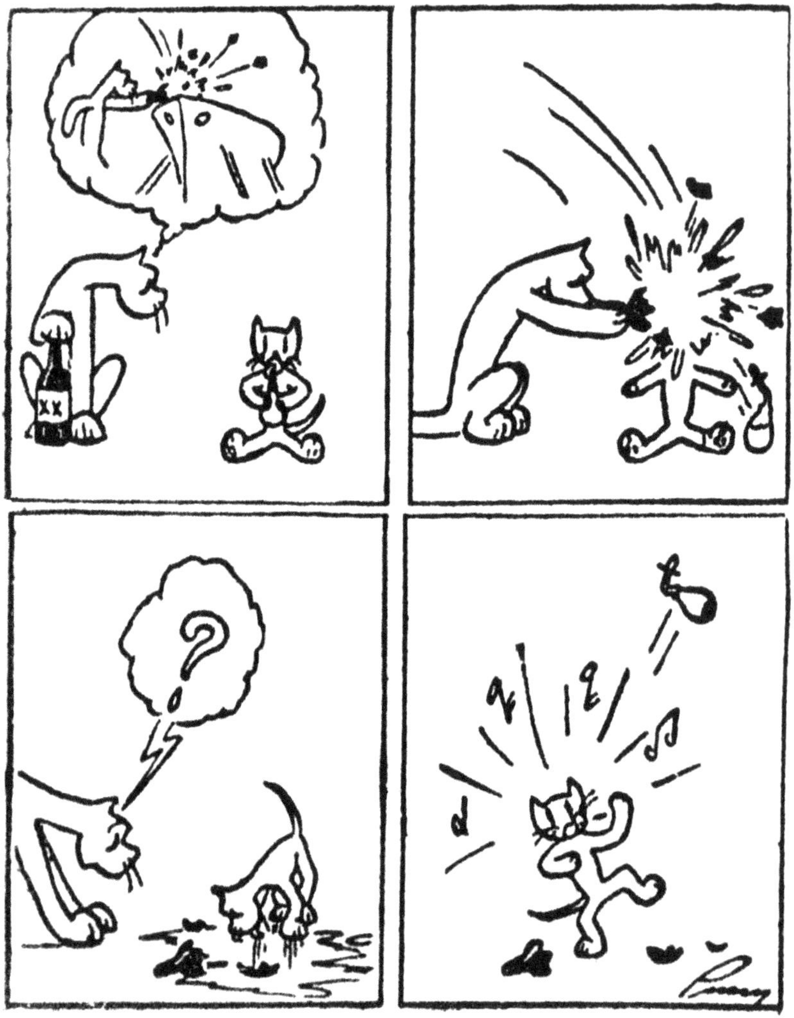

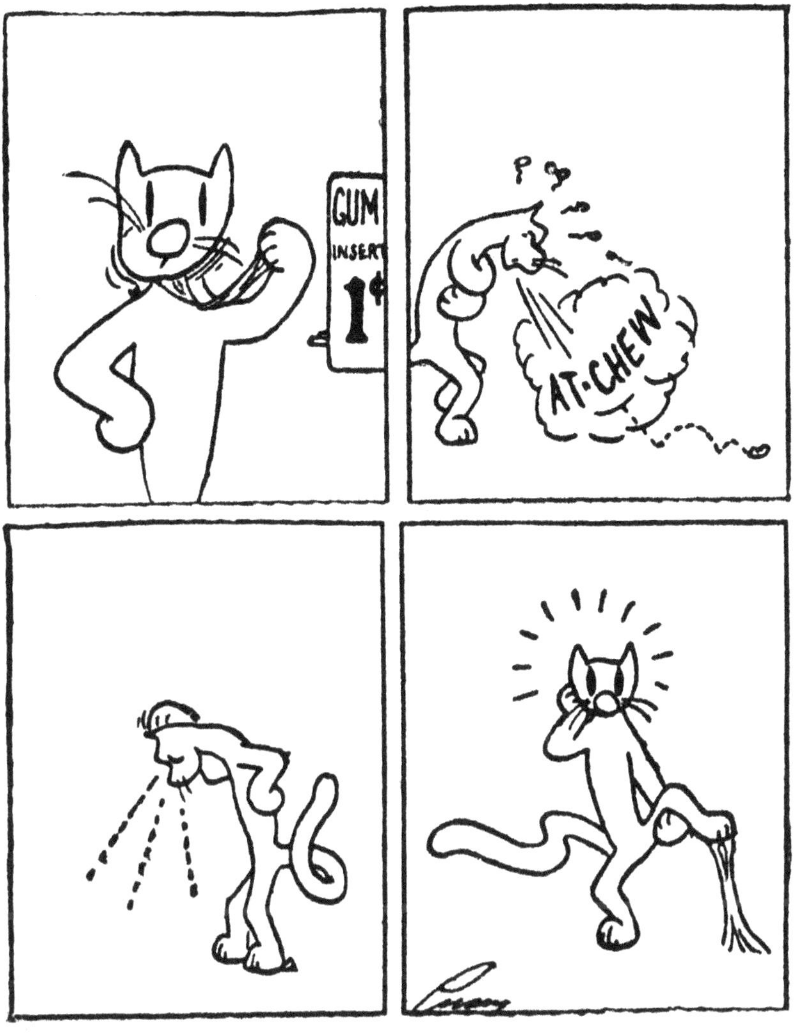
GUM
INSERT
1¢
AT-CHEW

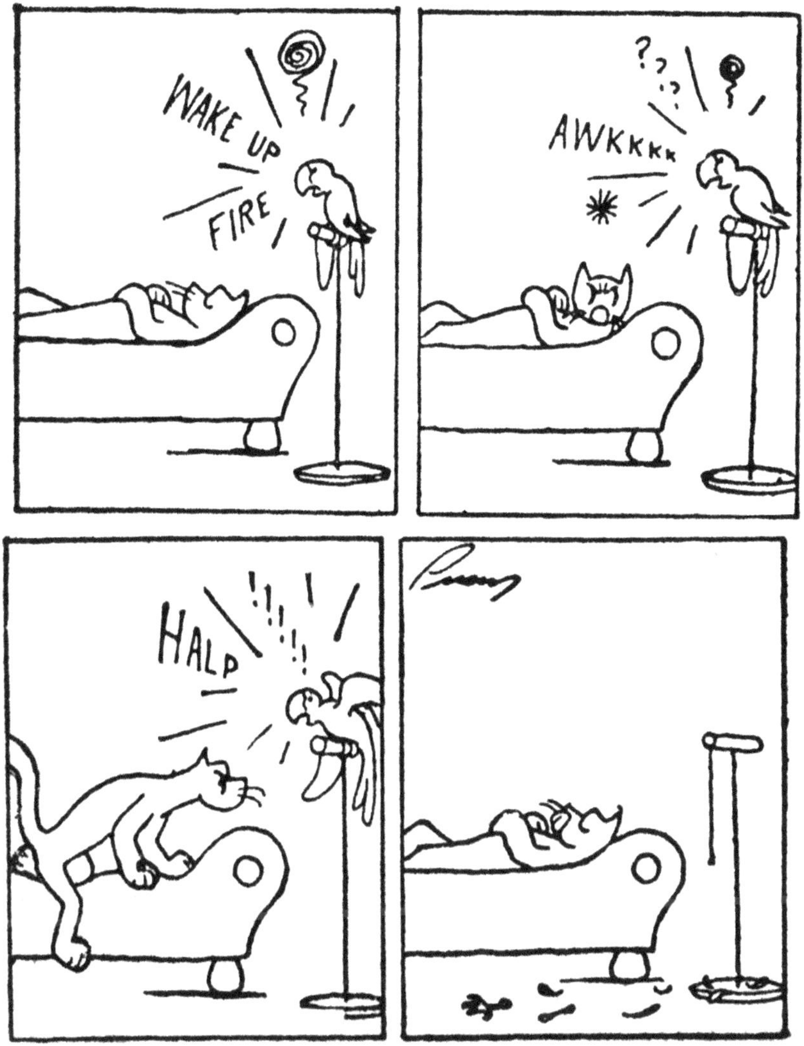
WAKE UP
FIRE
AWKKKK
HALP

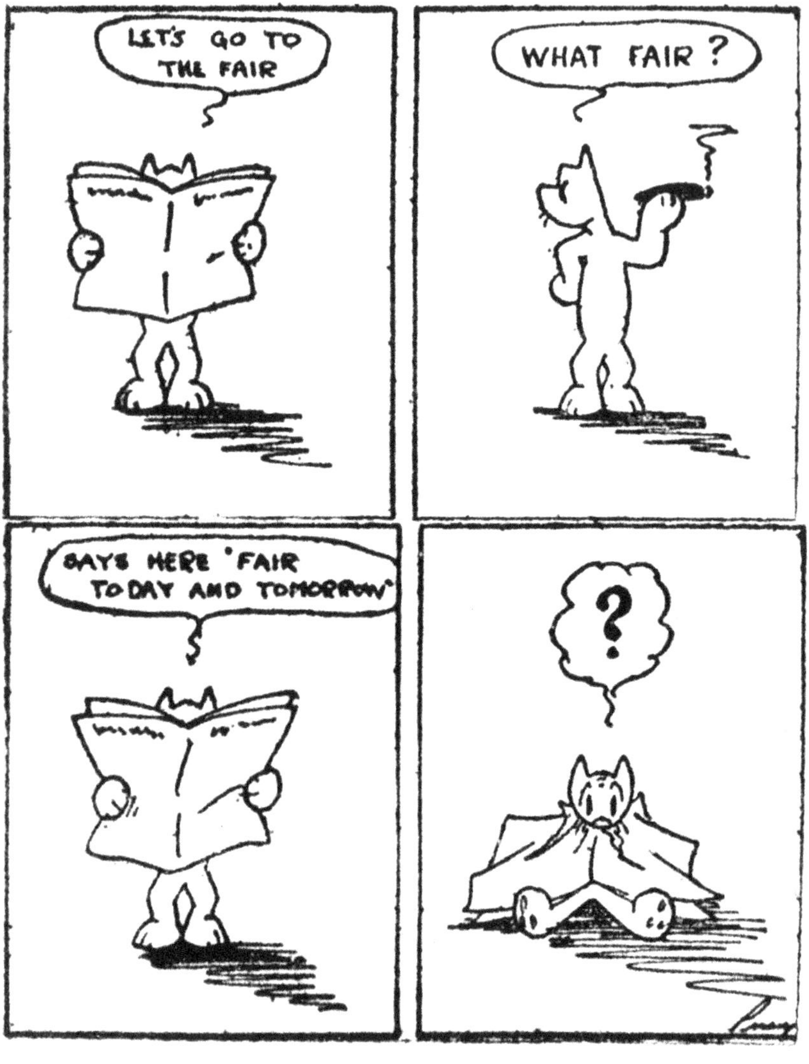
LET'S GO TO THE FAIR
WHAT FAIR?
SAYS HERE 'FAIR TODAY AND TOMORROW'
?

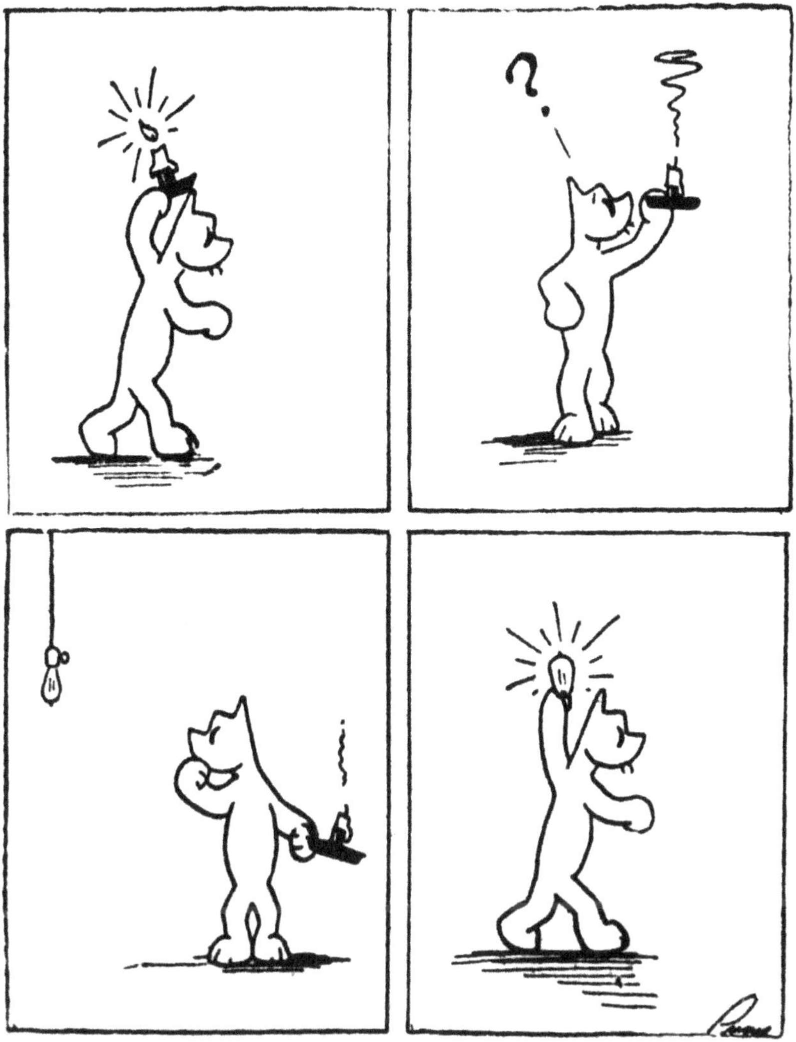
?

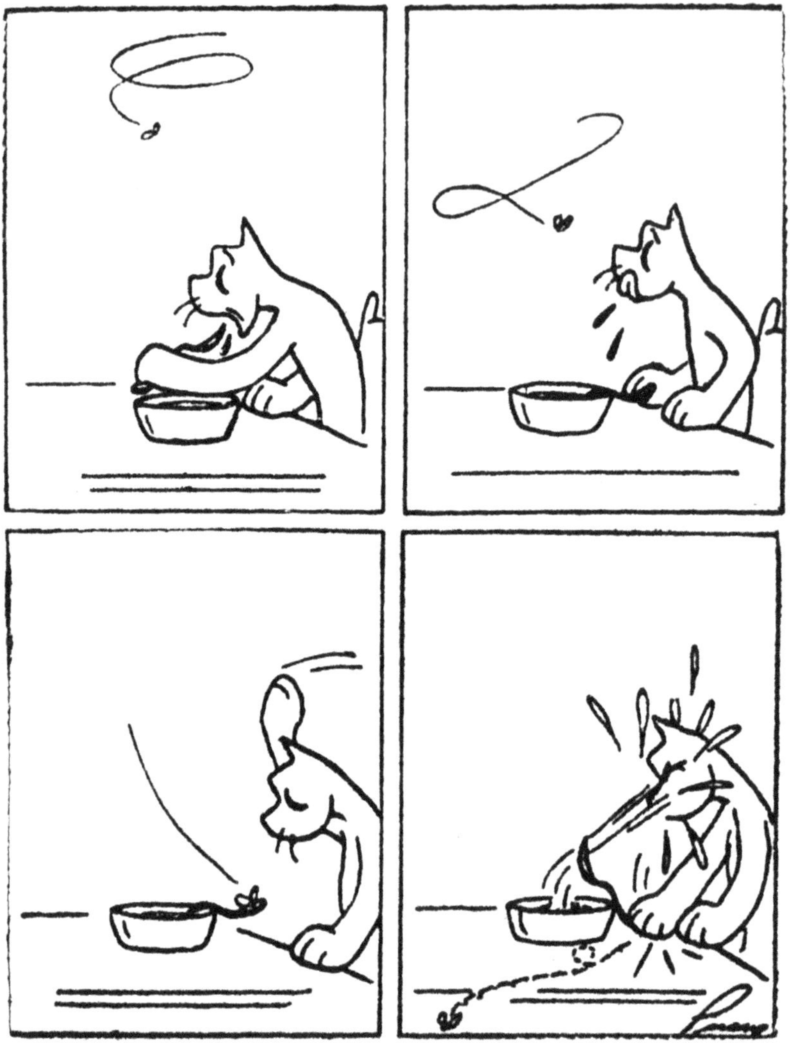

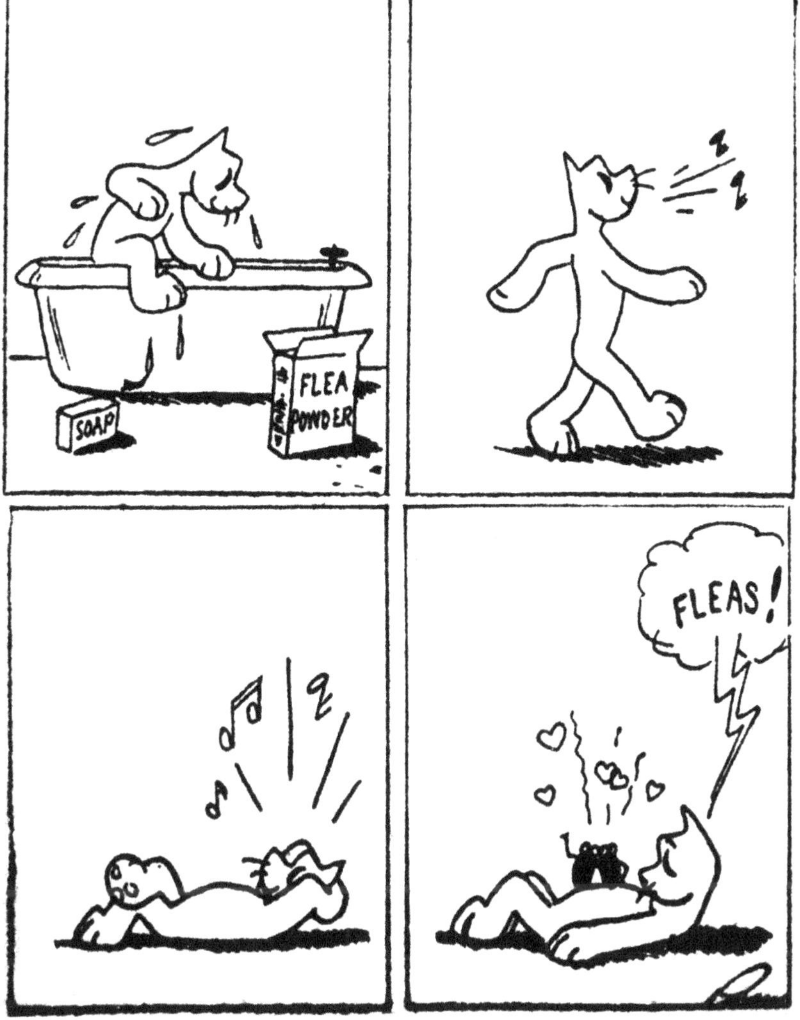
SOAP
FLEA
POWDER
FLEAS!

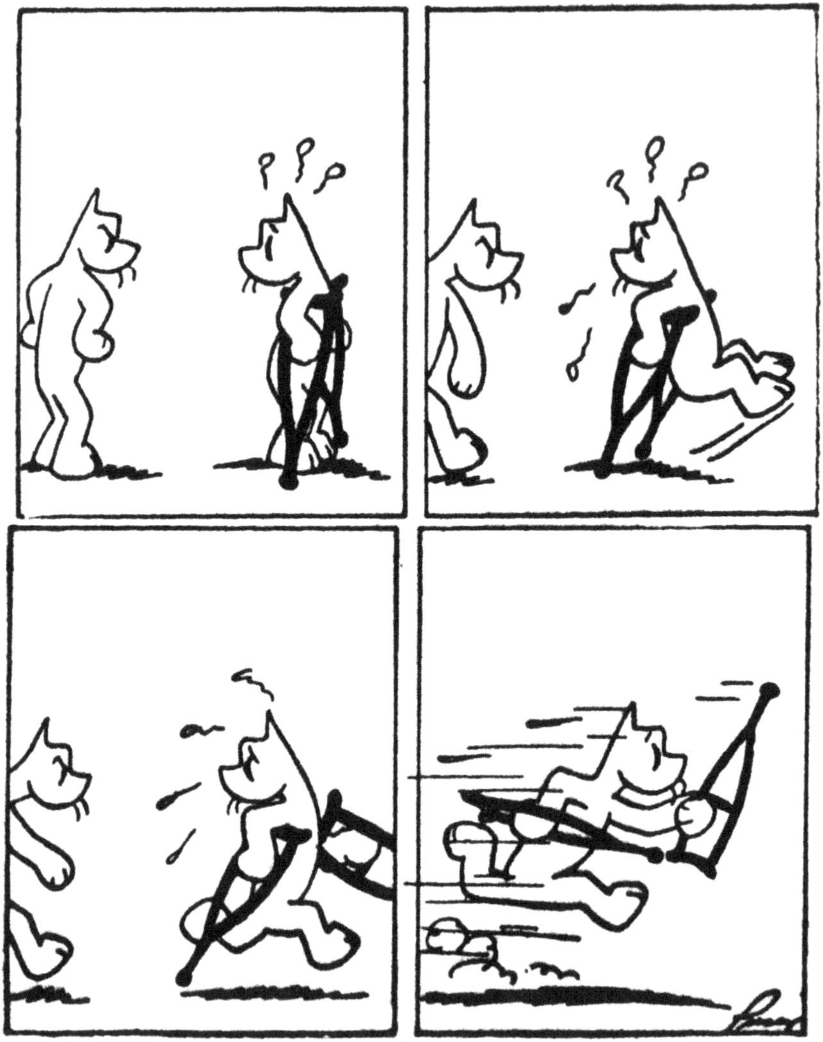

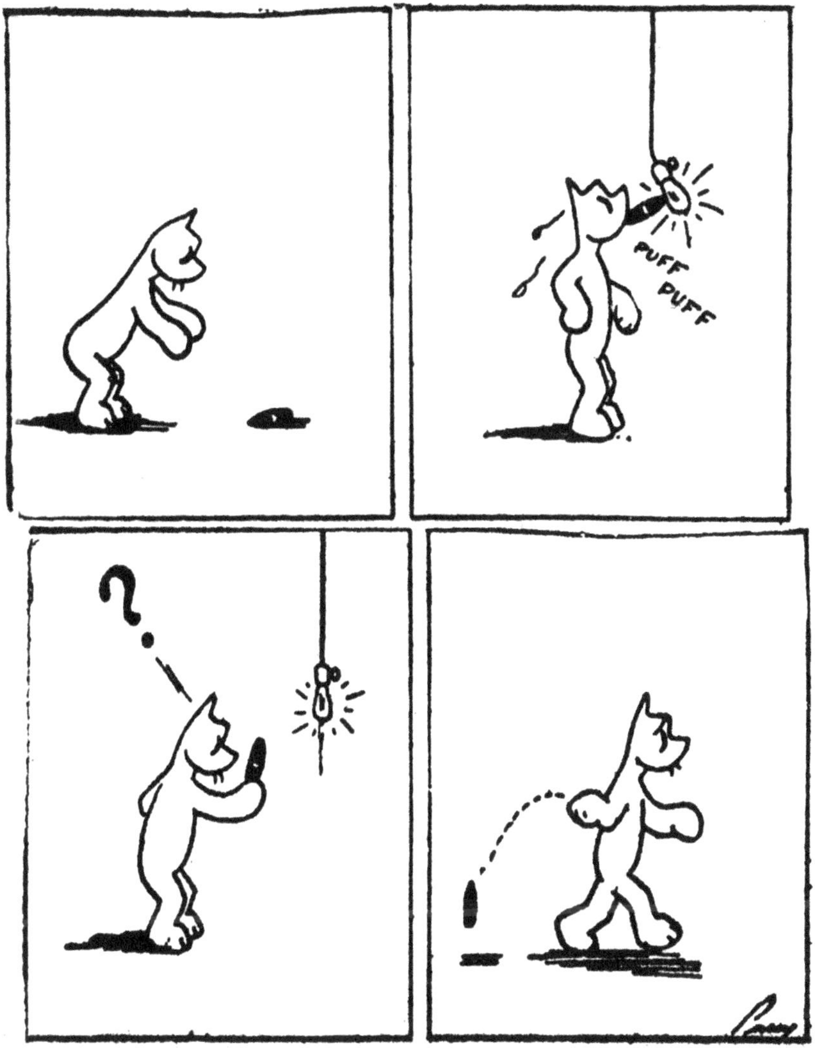
PUFF
PUFF

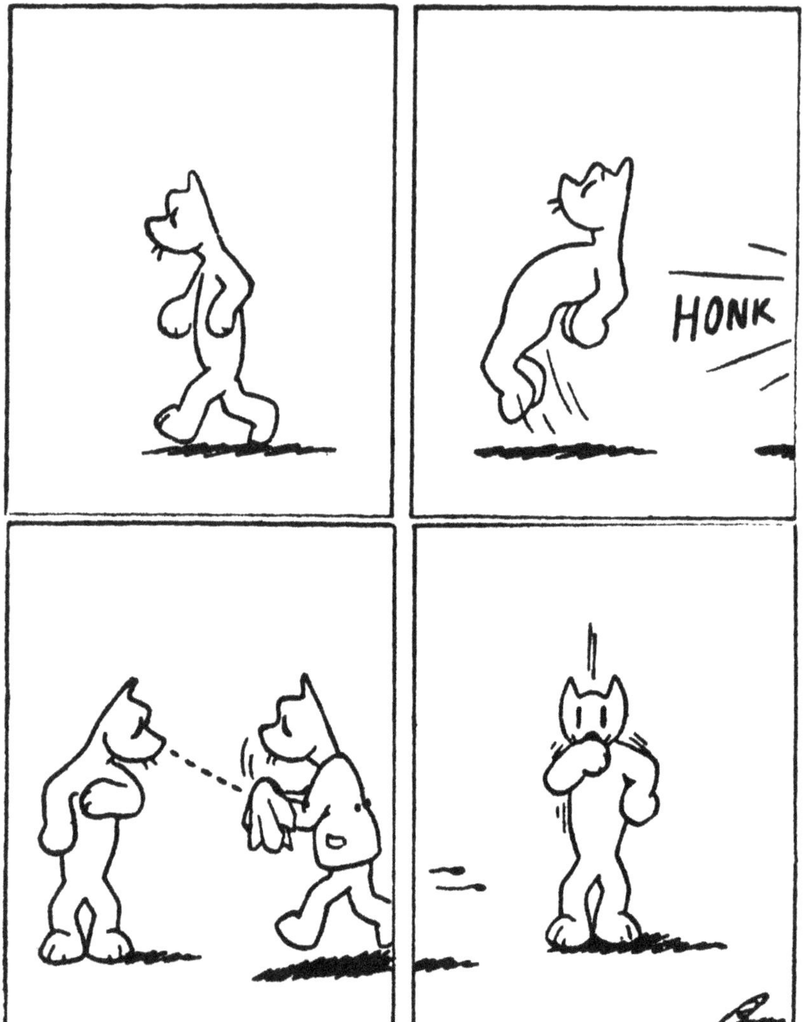
HONK

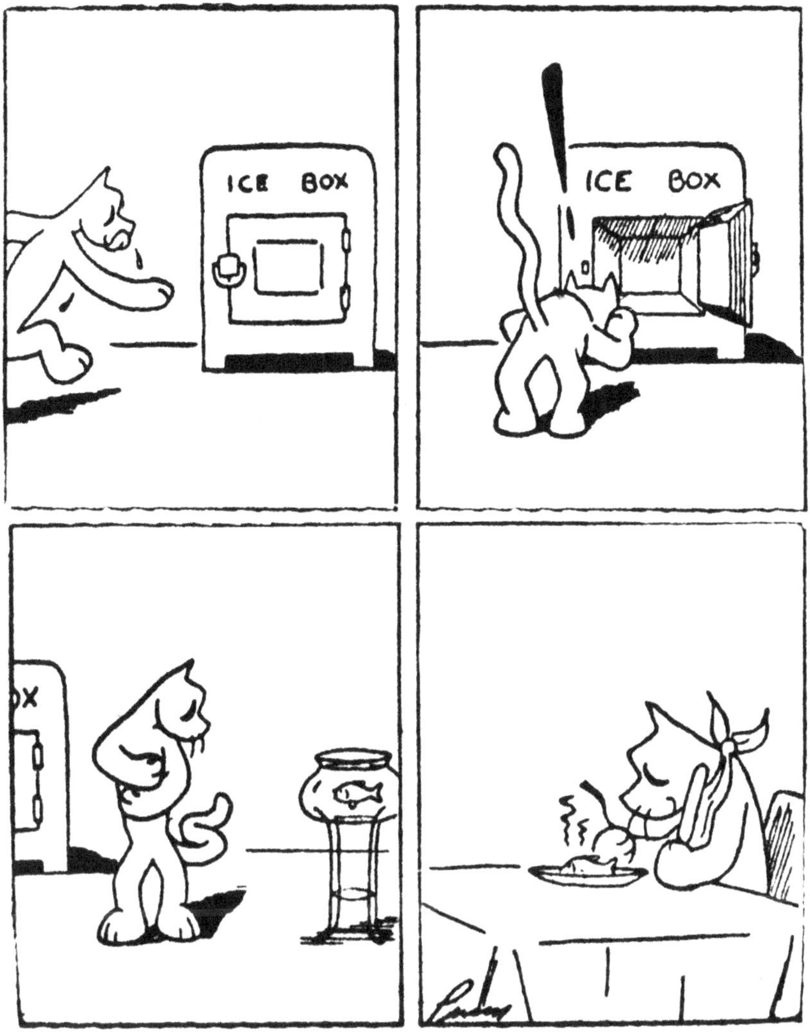
ICE BOX
ICE BOX

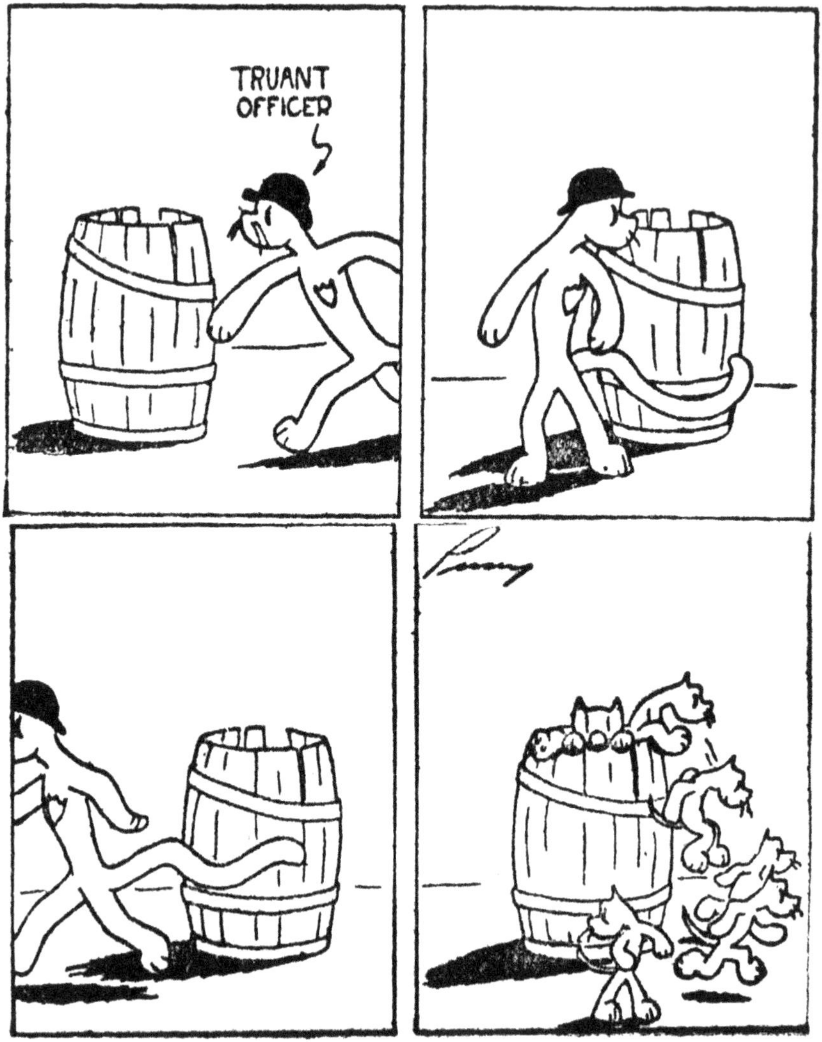
TRUANT
OFFICER

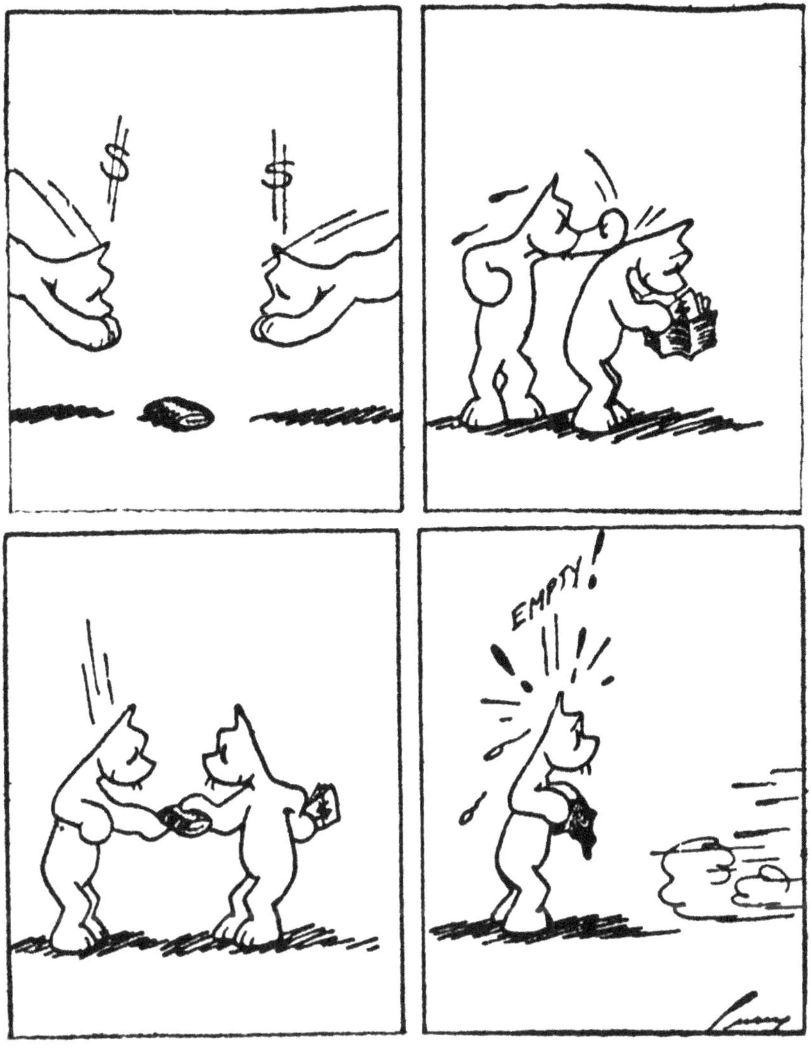
EMPTY!

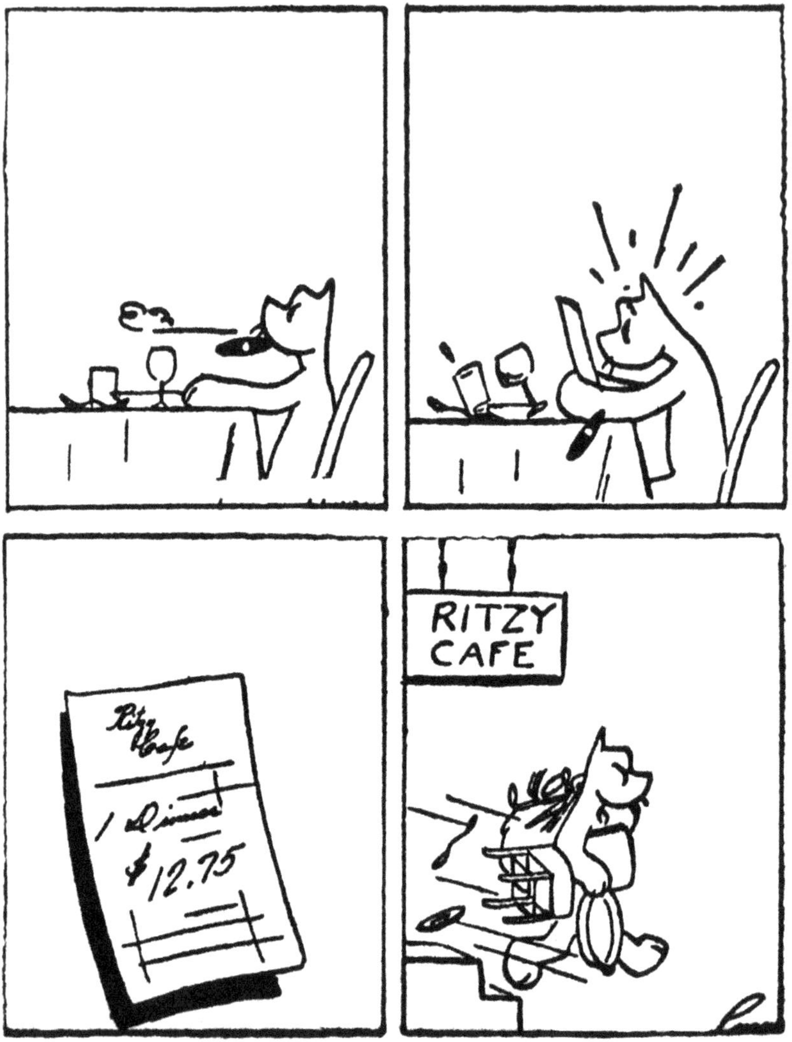
$12.75
RITZY CAFE

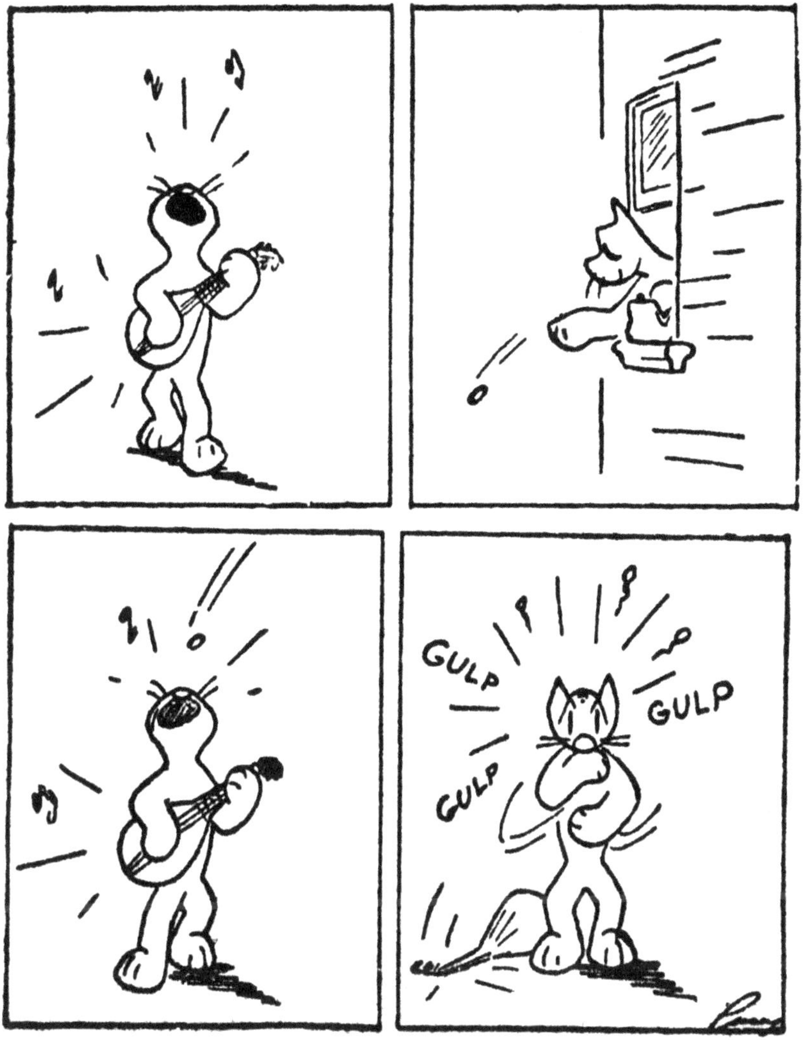
GULP
GULP
GULP

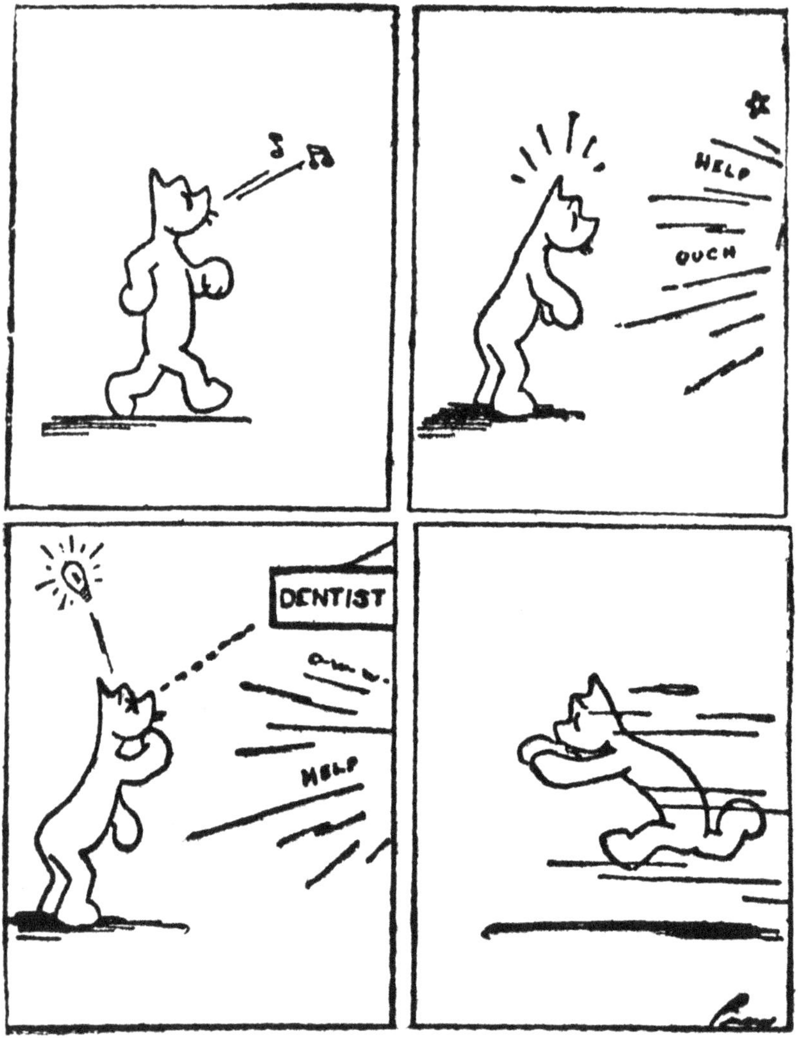
HELP
OUCH
DENTIST
HELP

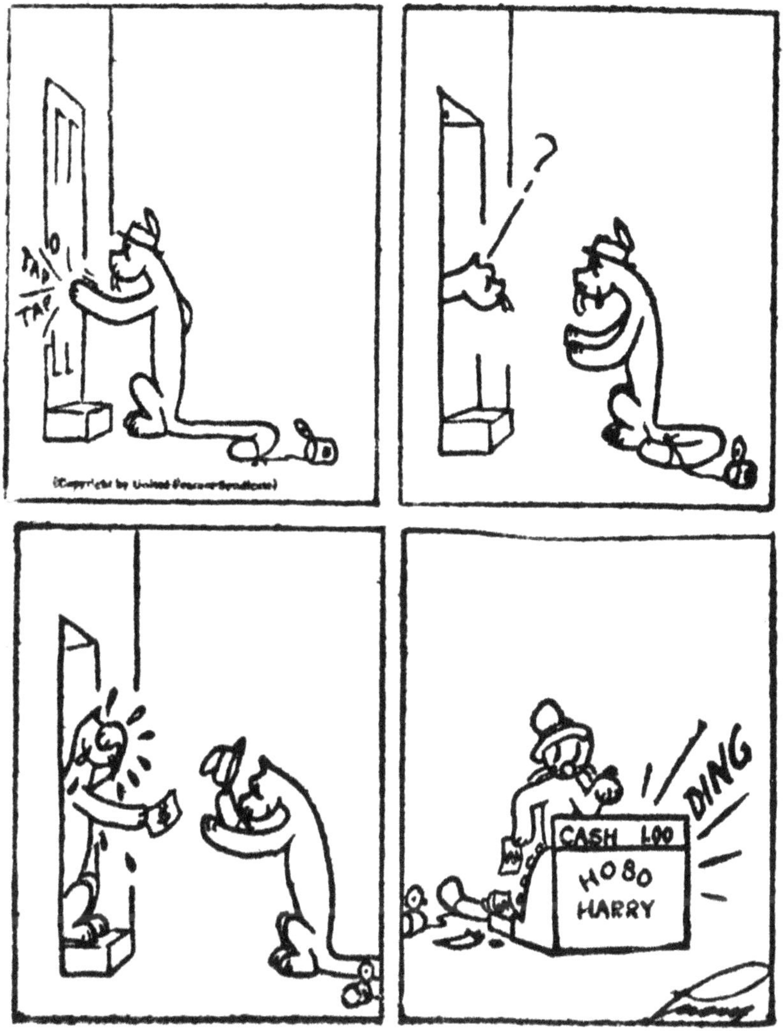
TAP TAP
?
CASH LOO
HOBO HARRY
DING

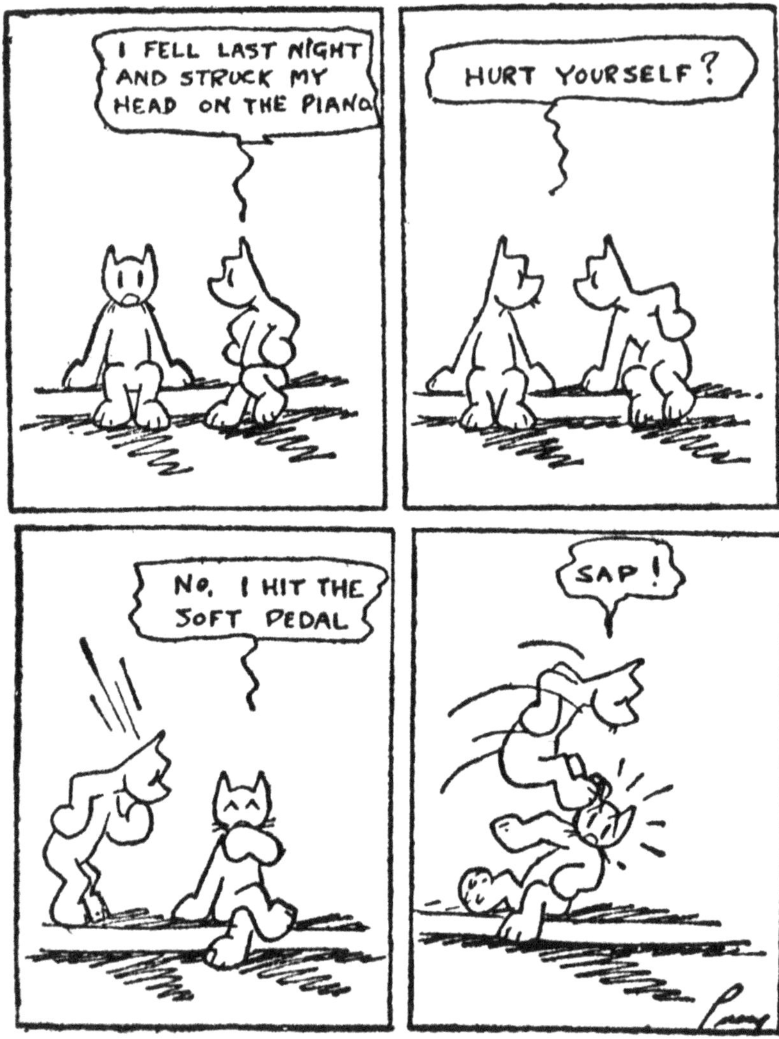
I FELL LAST NIGHT AND STRUCK MY HEAD ON THE PIANO
HURT YOURSELF?
NO, I HIT THE SOFT PEDAL
SAP!

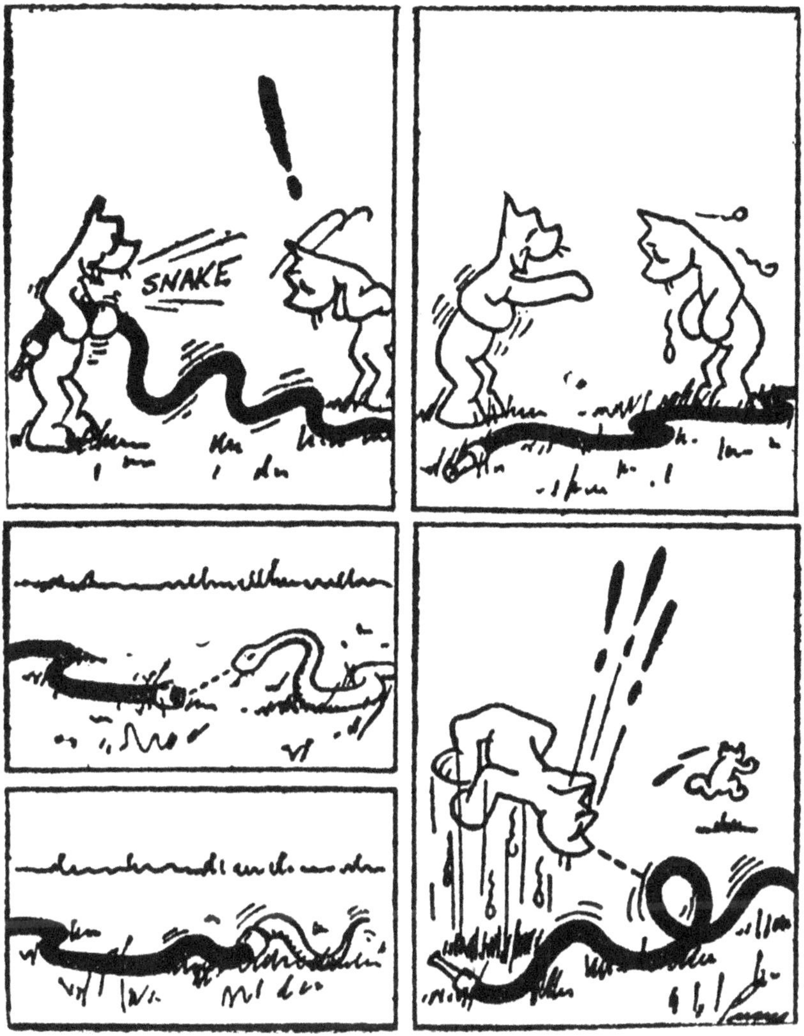
!
SNAKE
!!!

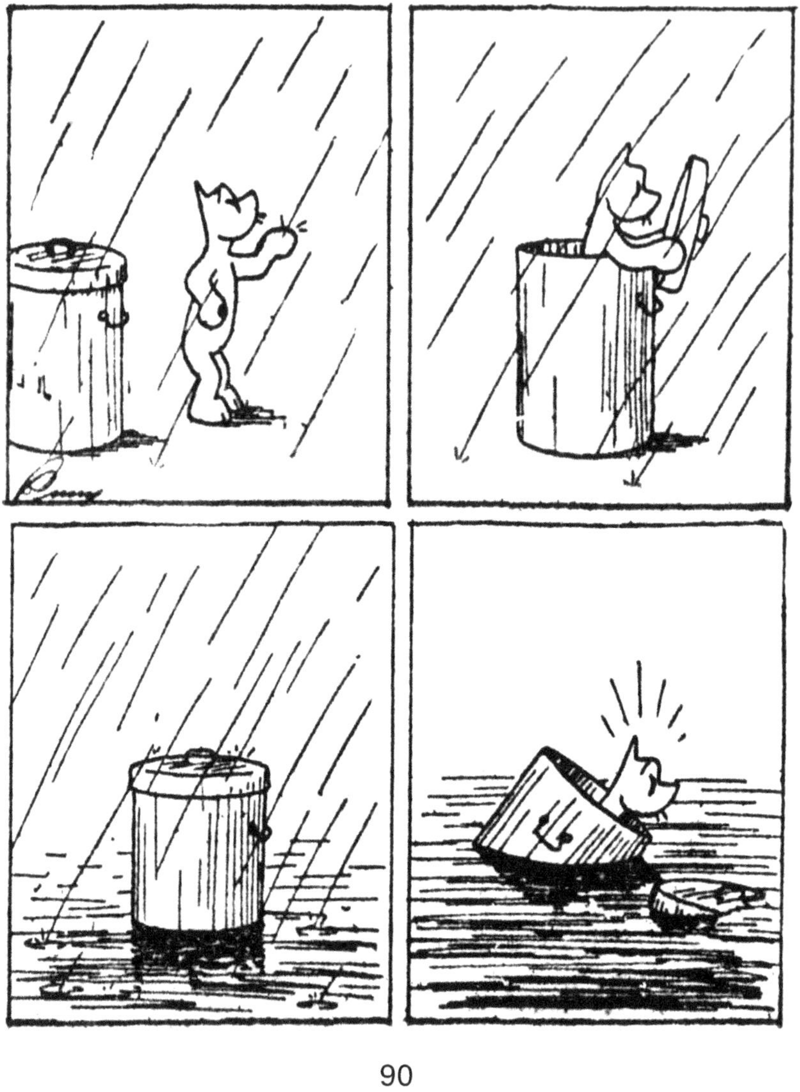

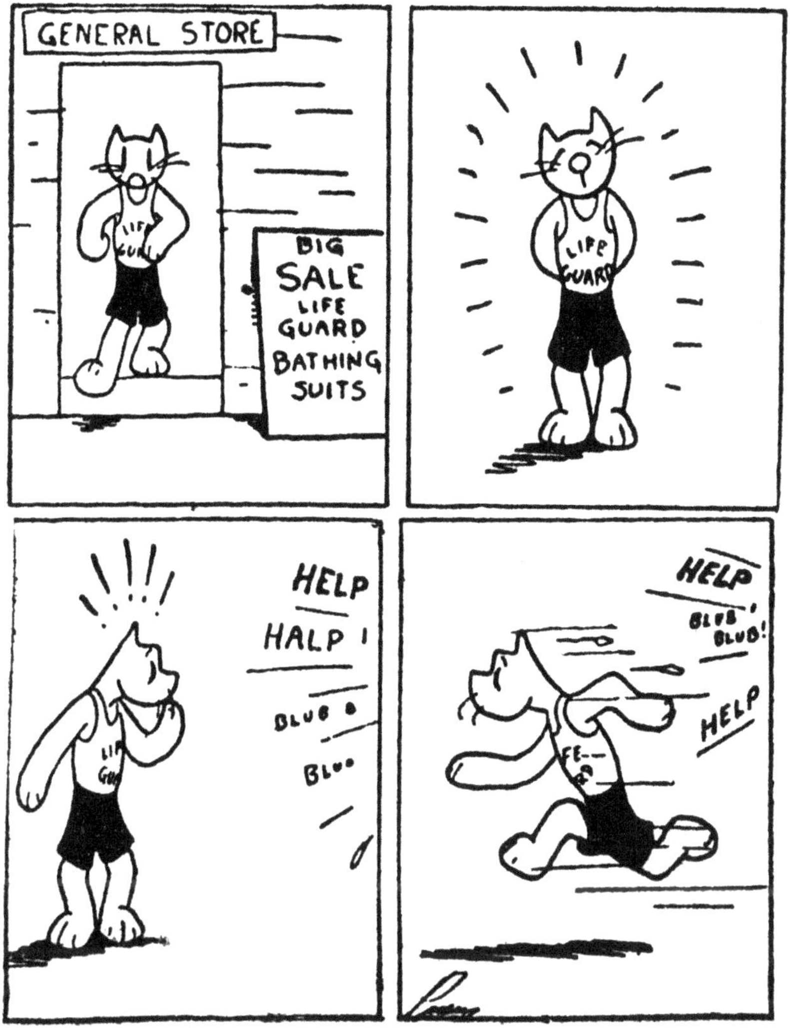
GENERAL STORE
LIFE GUARD
BIG SALE LIFE GUARD BATHING SUITS
LIFE GUARD
HELP
HALP !
BLUB
BLUB
HELP
BLUB BLUB!
HELP

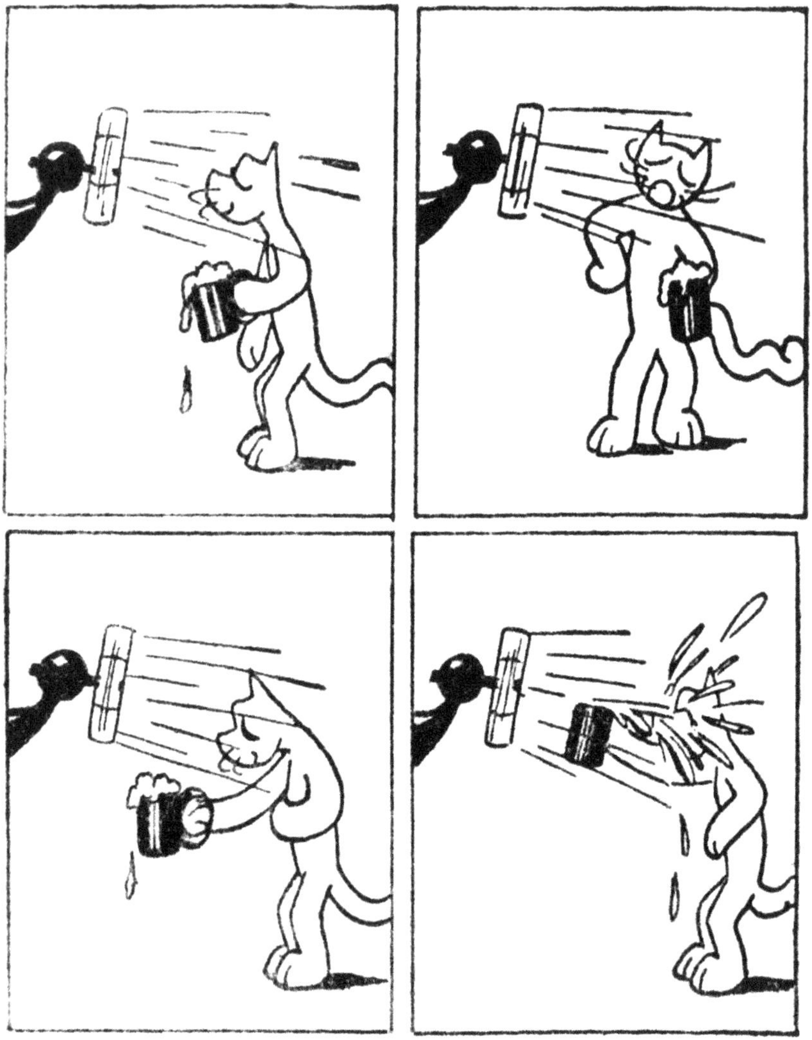

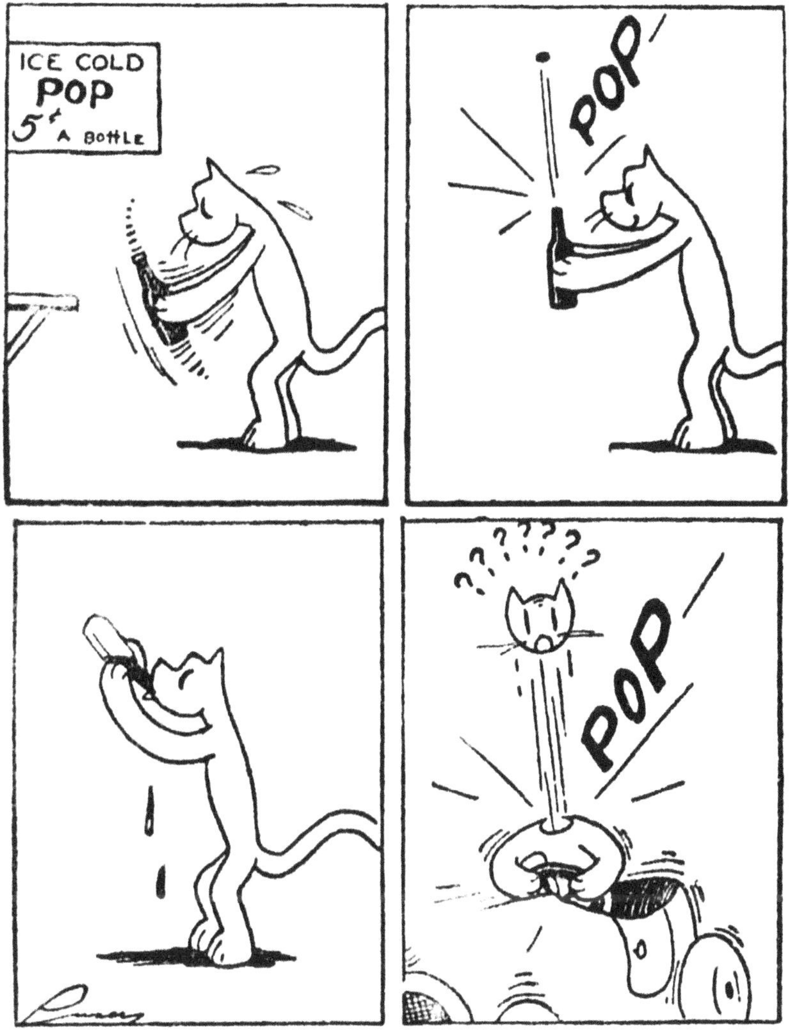
ICE COLD
POP
5¢ A BOTTLE
POP
POP

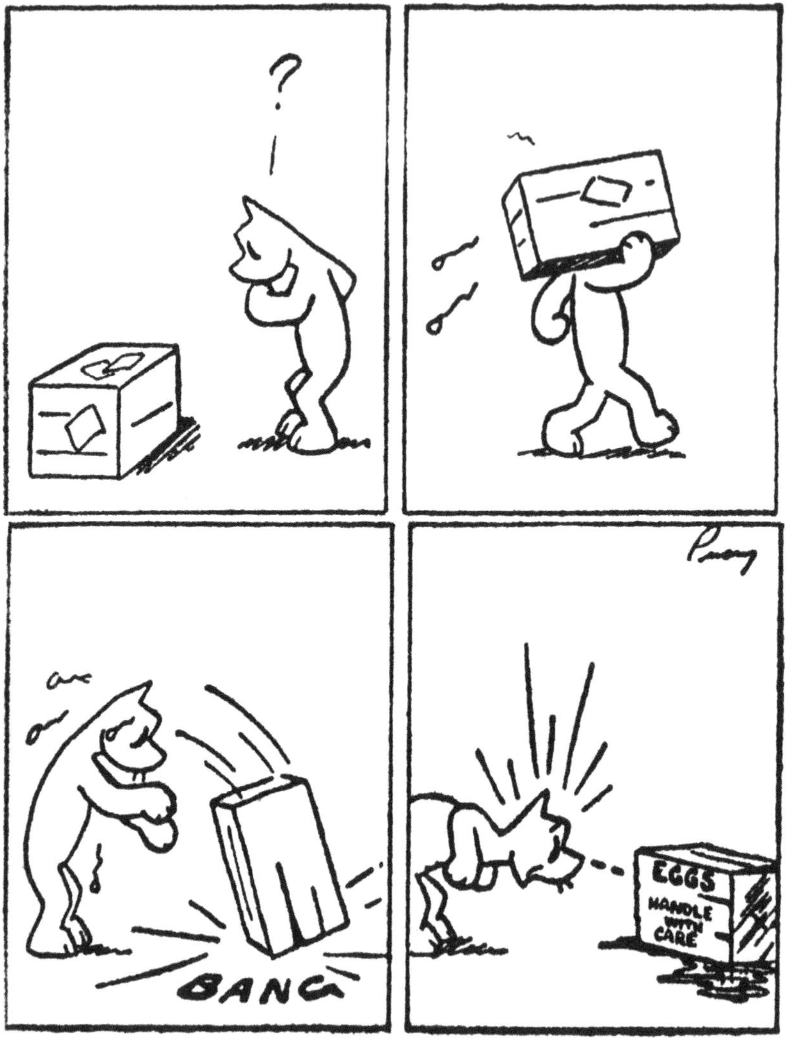
?
BANG
EGGS
HANDLE WITH CARE

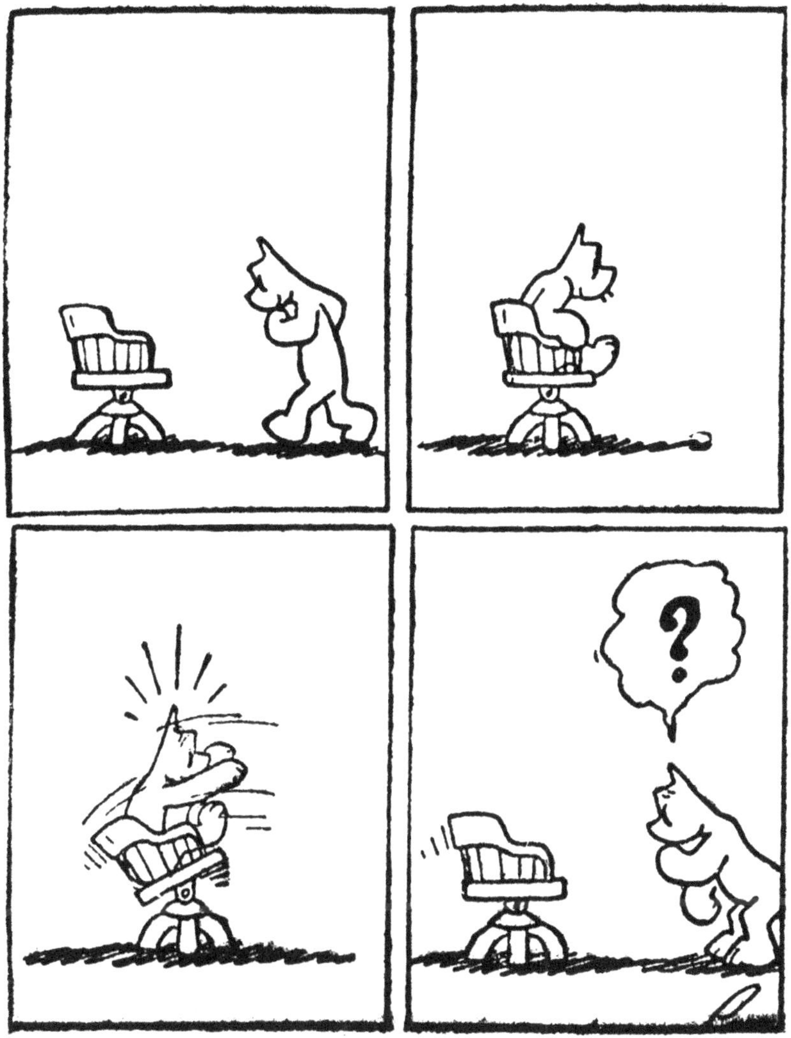
?

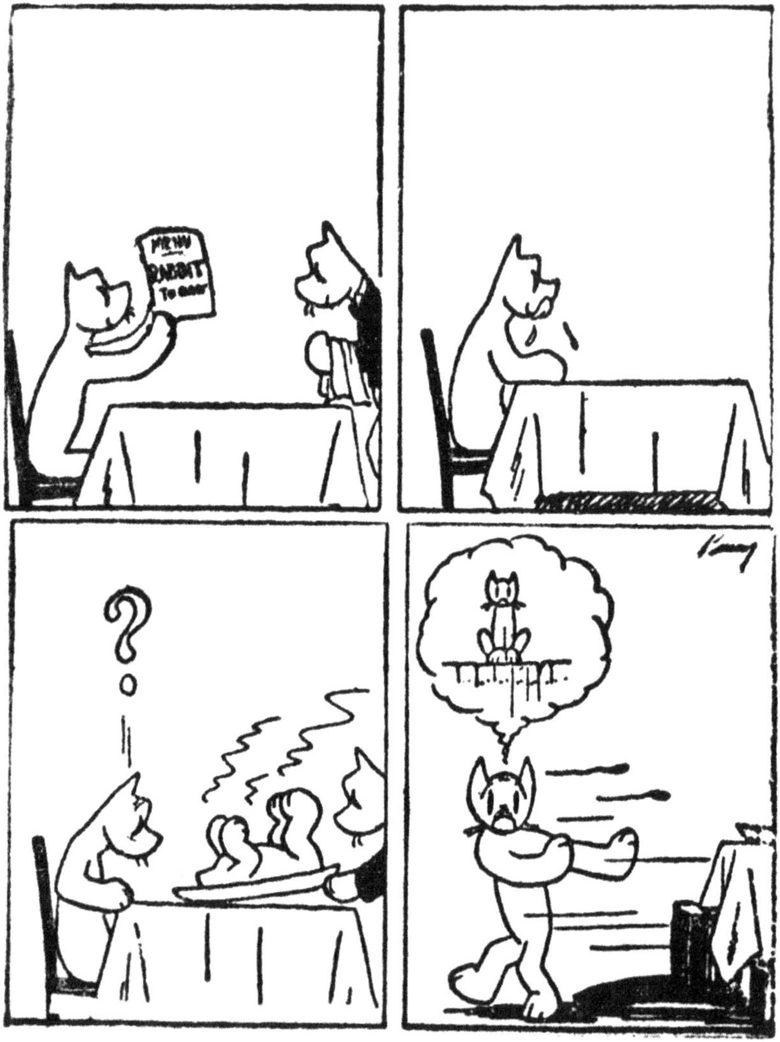
MENU
RABBIT

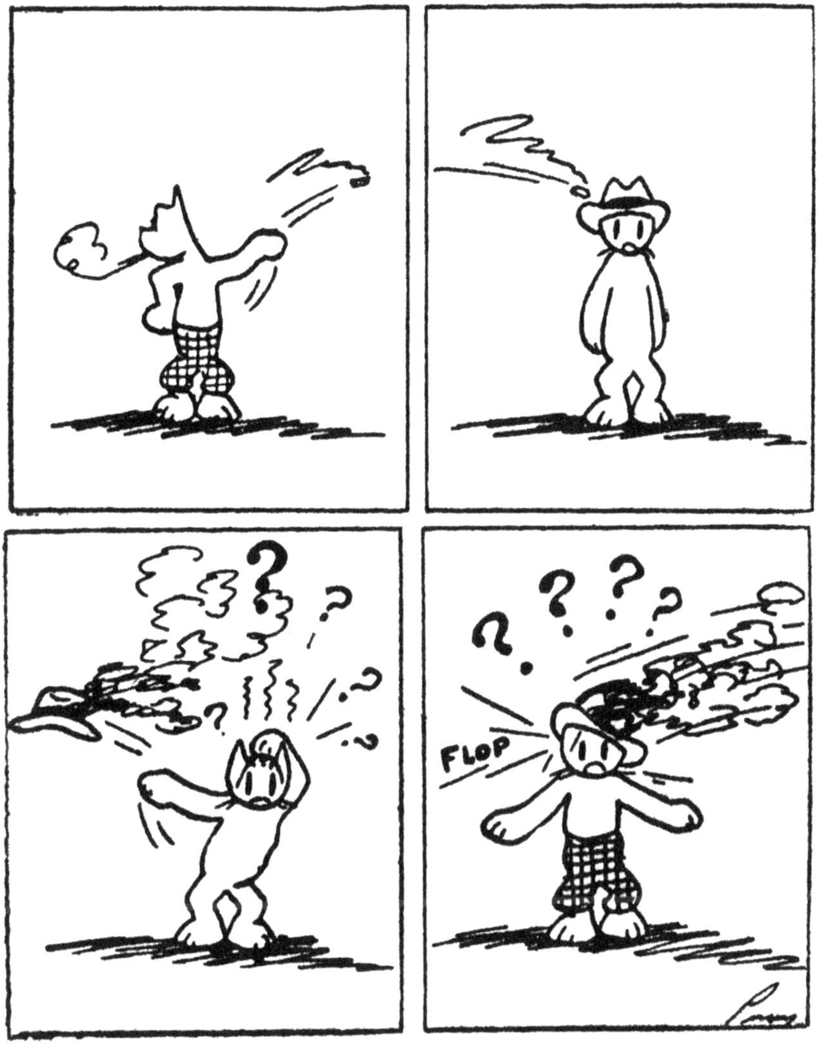
FLOP

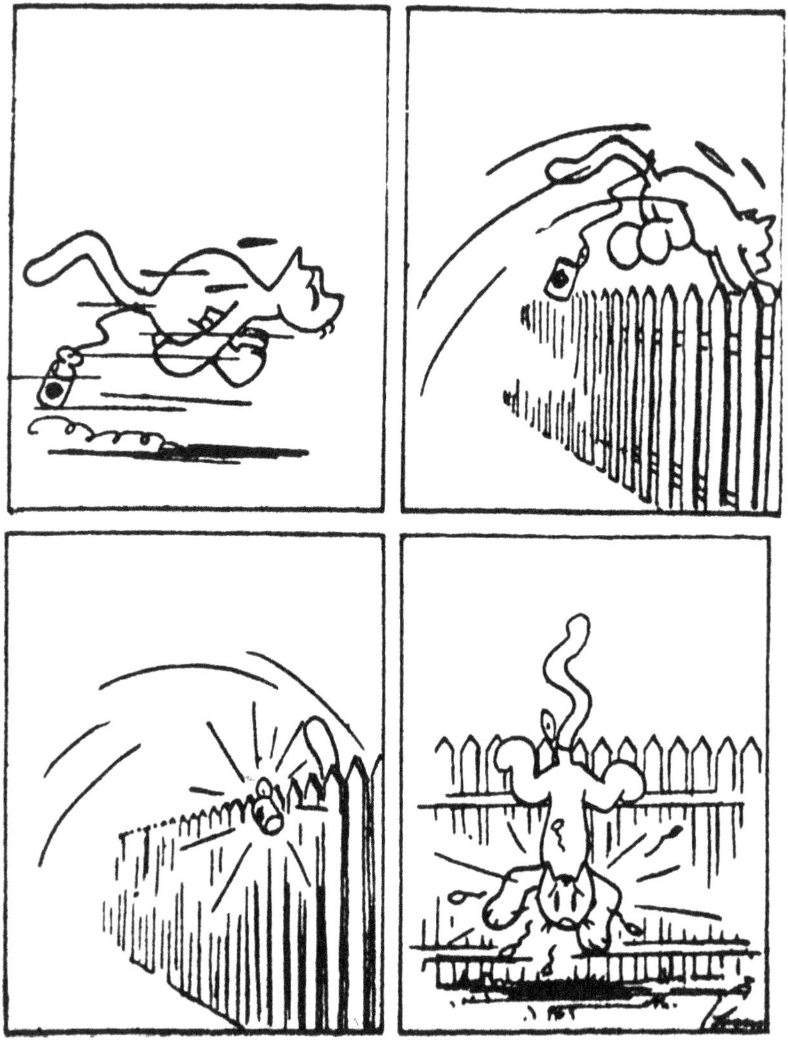

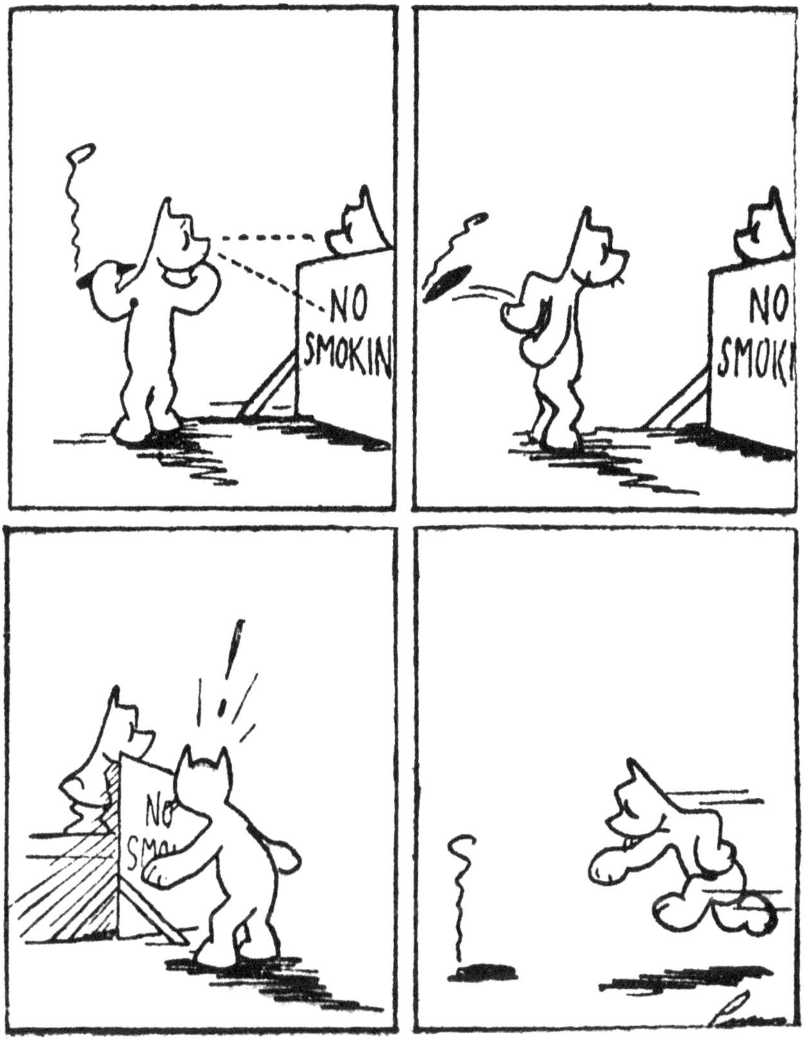
NO SMOKIN
NO SMOK
NO SMO

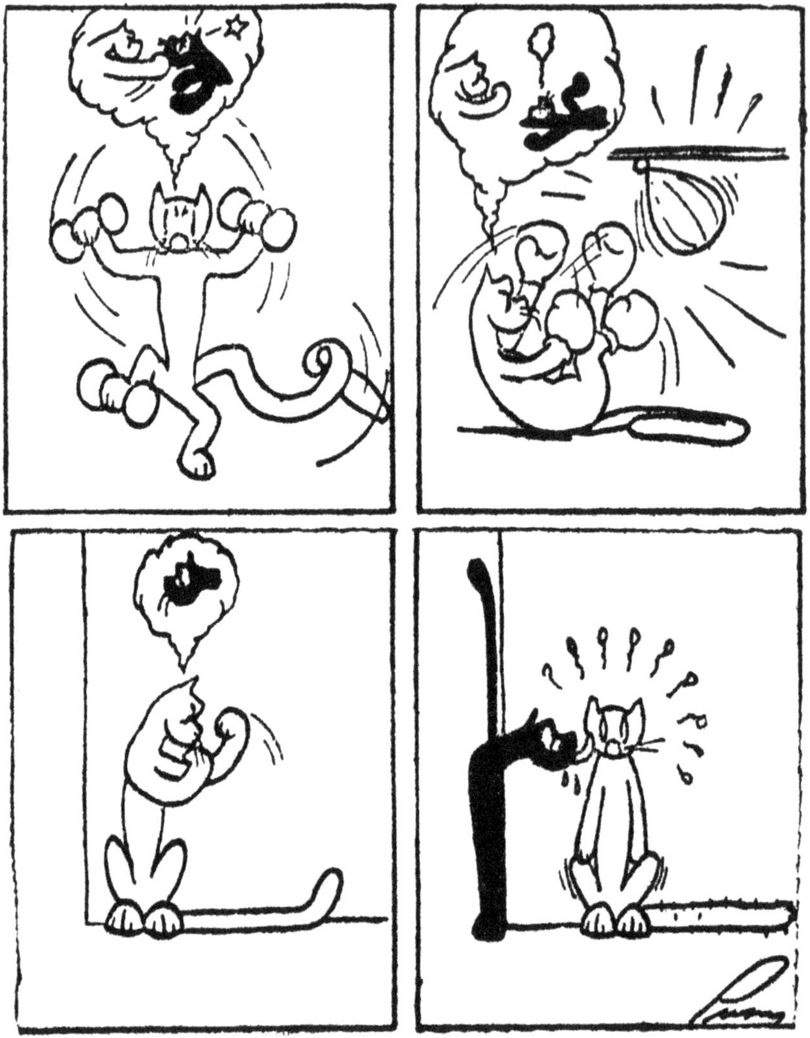

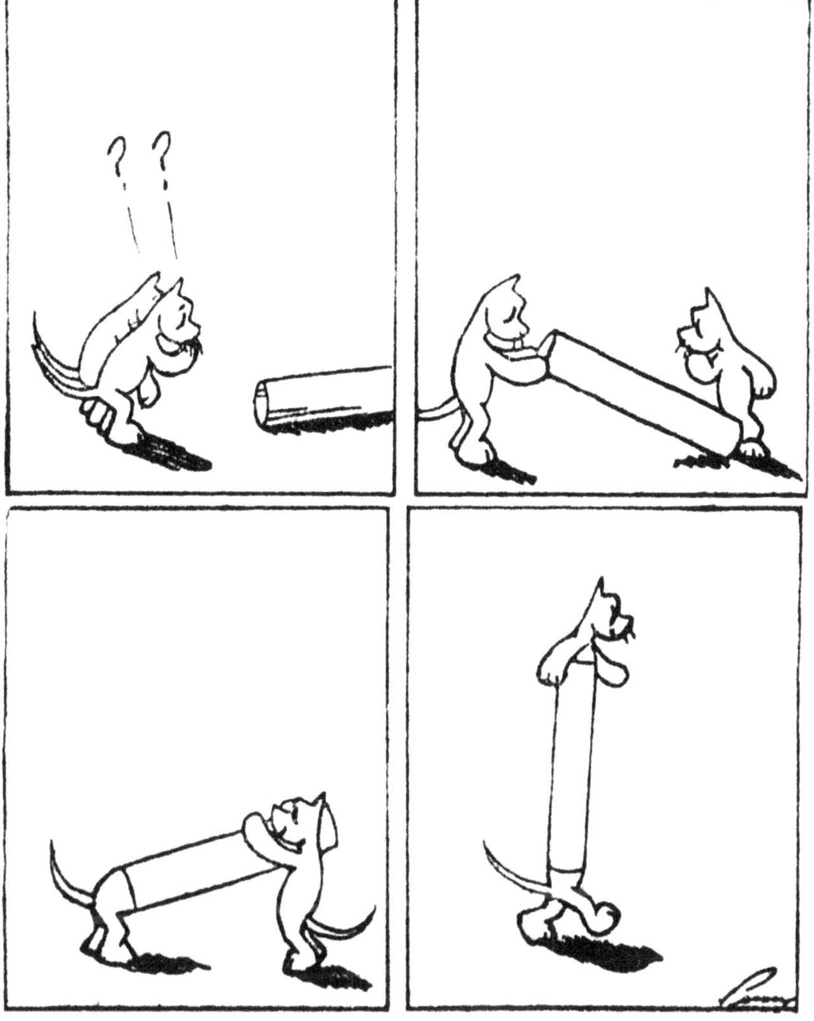
? ?

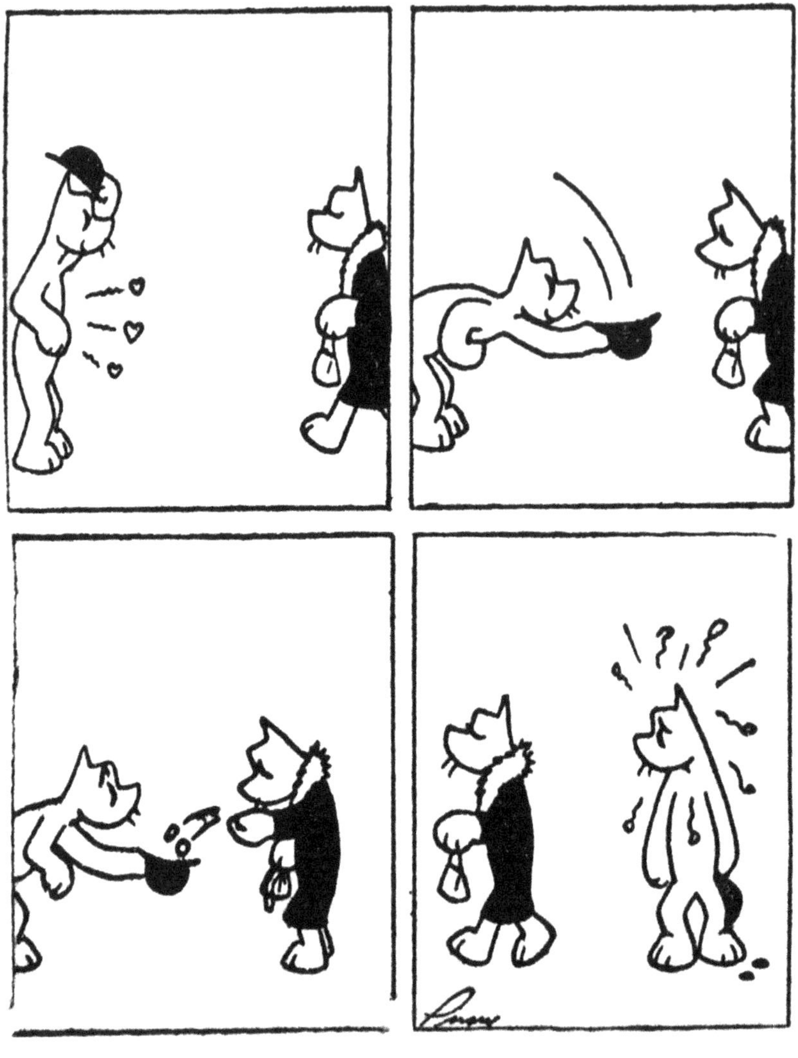

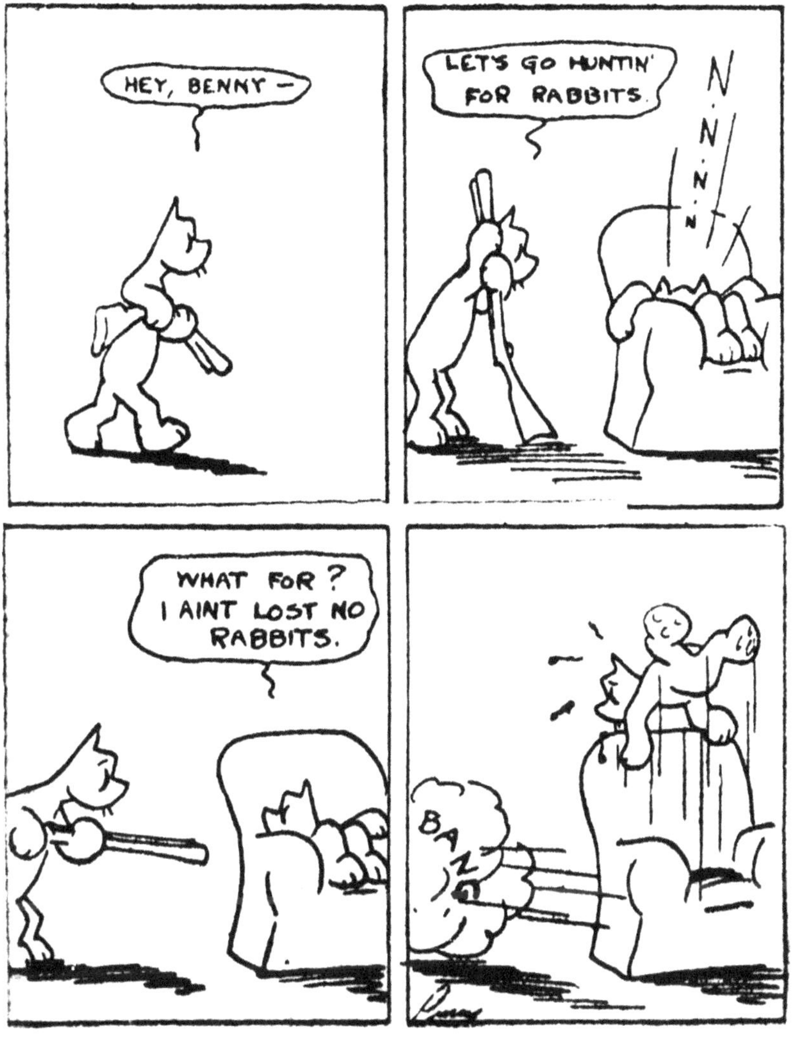
HEY, BENNY —
LET'S GO HUNTIN' FOR RABBITS.
N.N.N.N
WHAT FOR? I AINT LOST NO RABBITS.
BANG

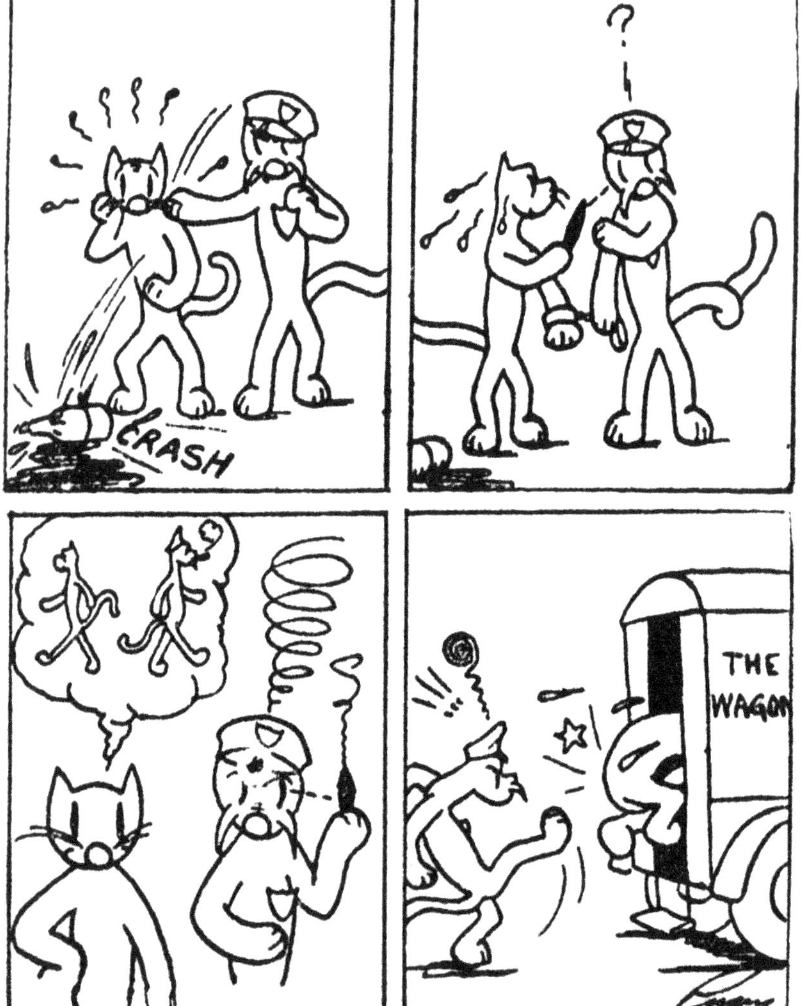
CRASH
THE
WAGON

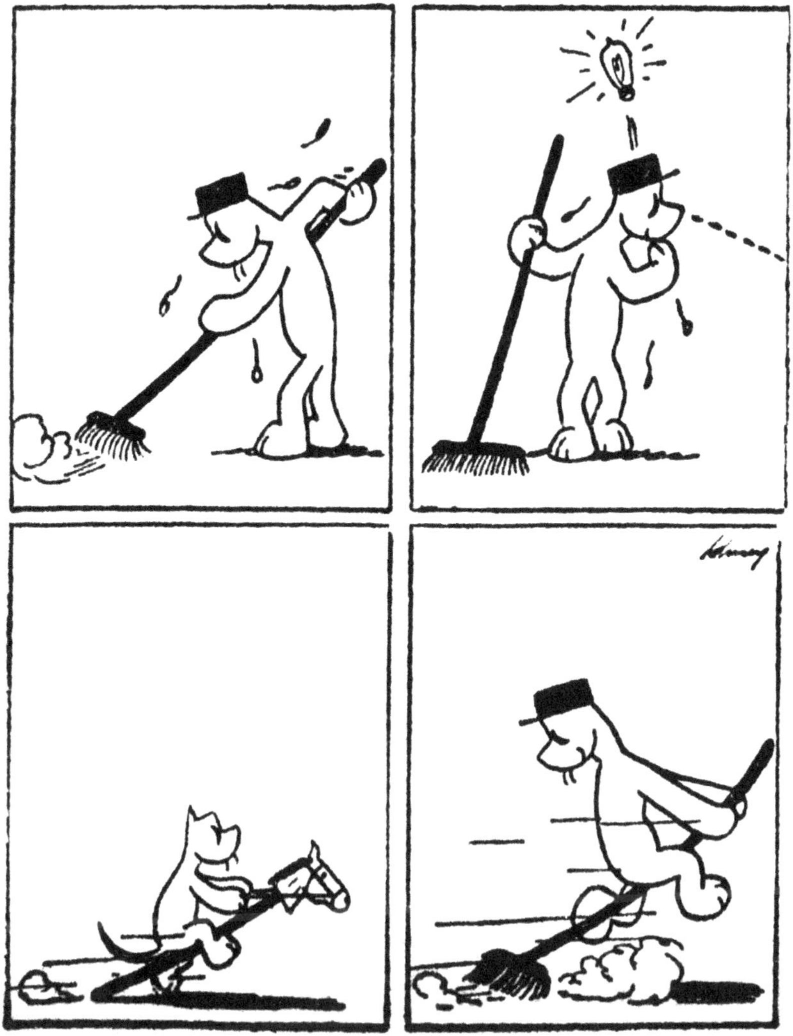

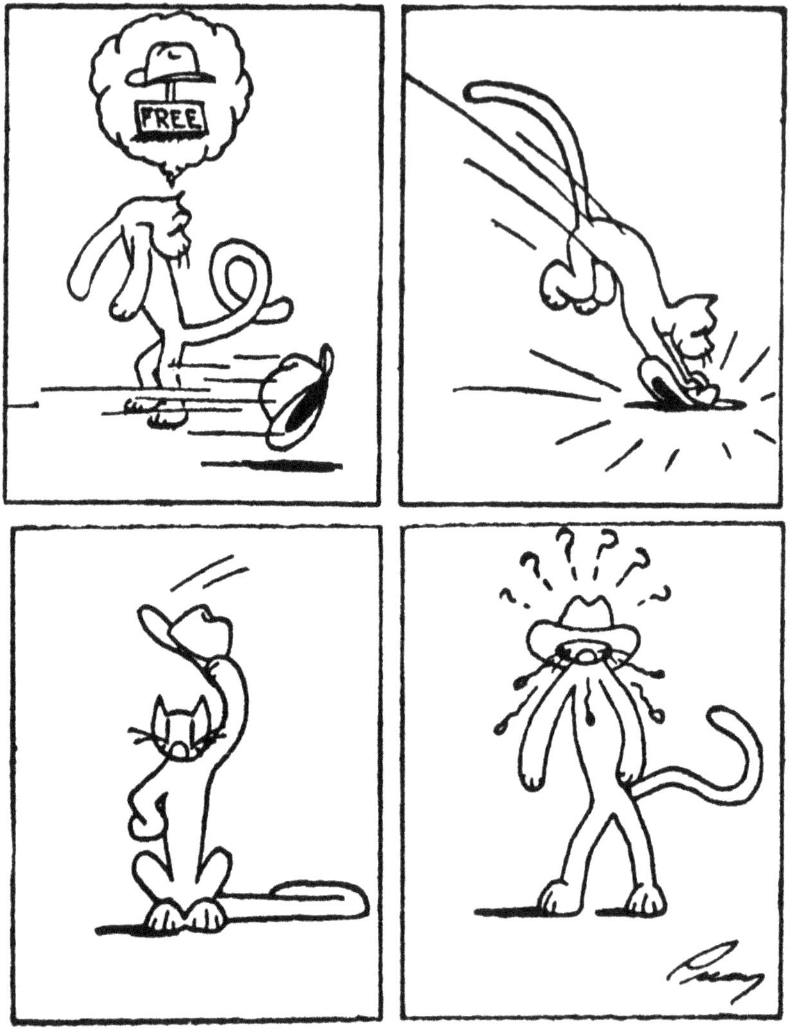
FREE

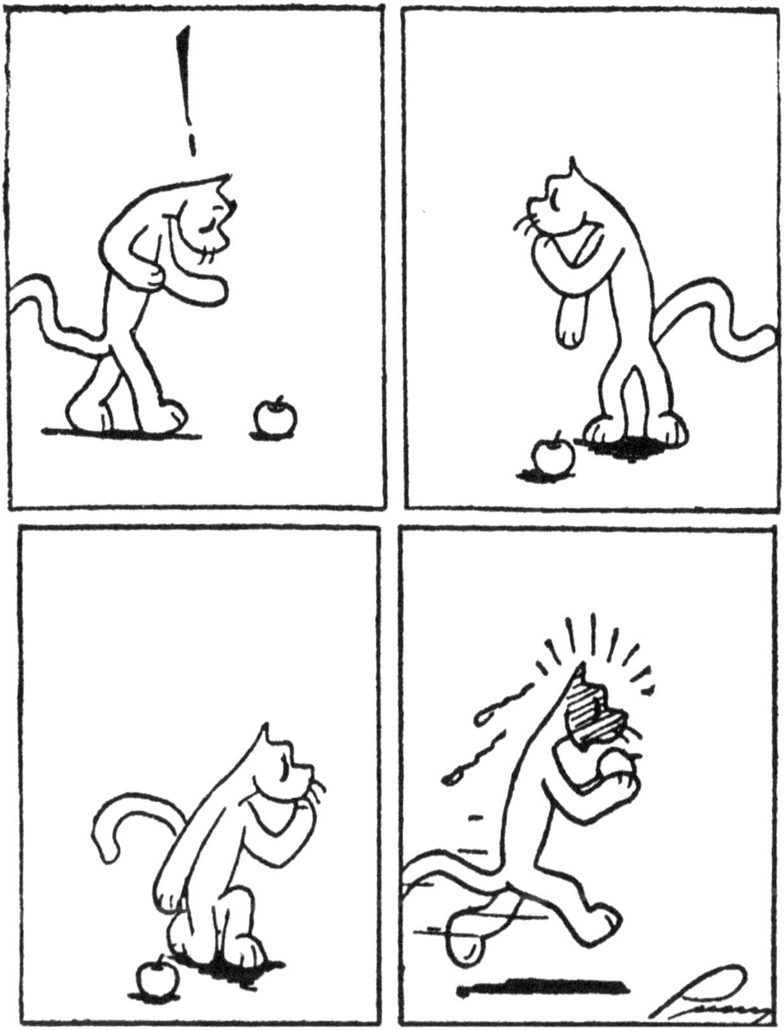
!

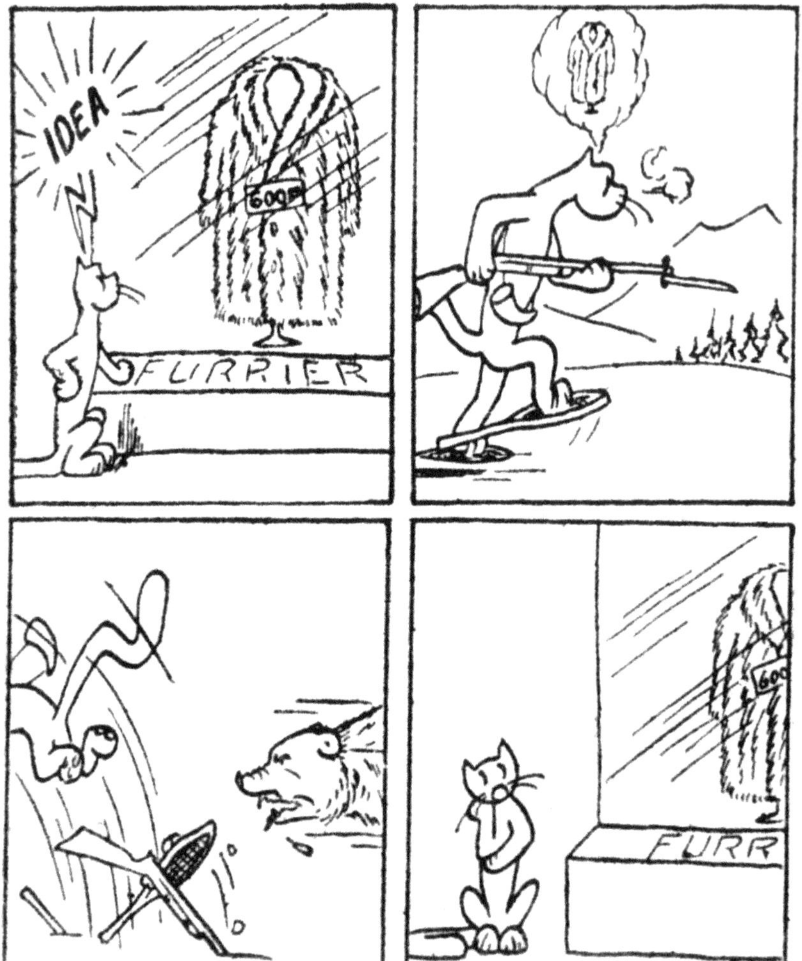
IDEA
FURRIER
FURR

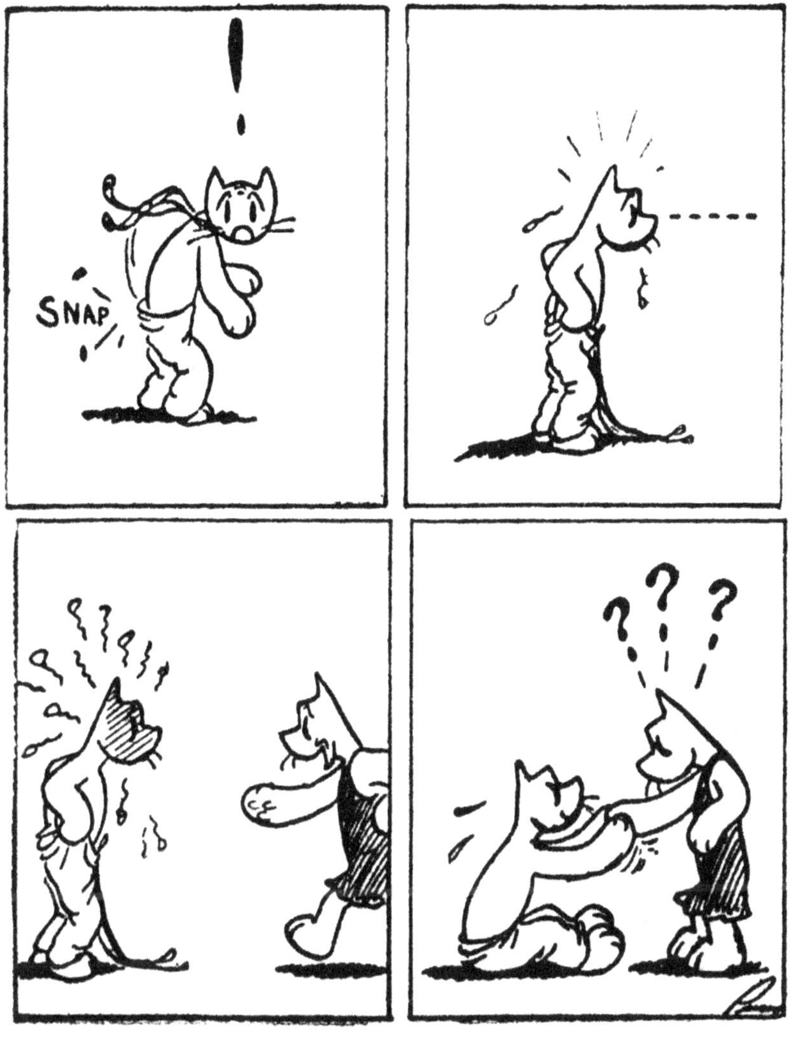
!
SNAP

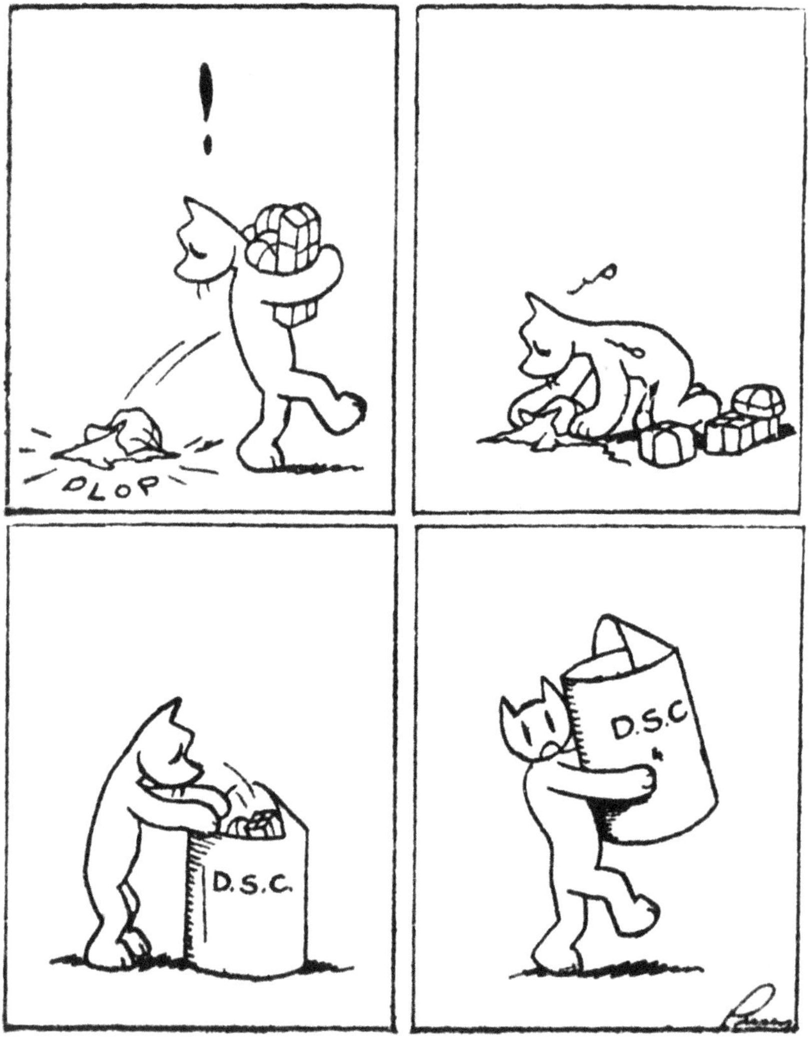
!
PLOP
D.S.C.
D.S.C

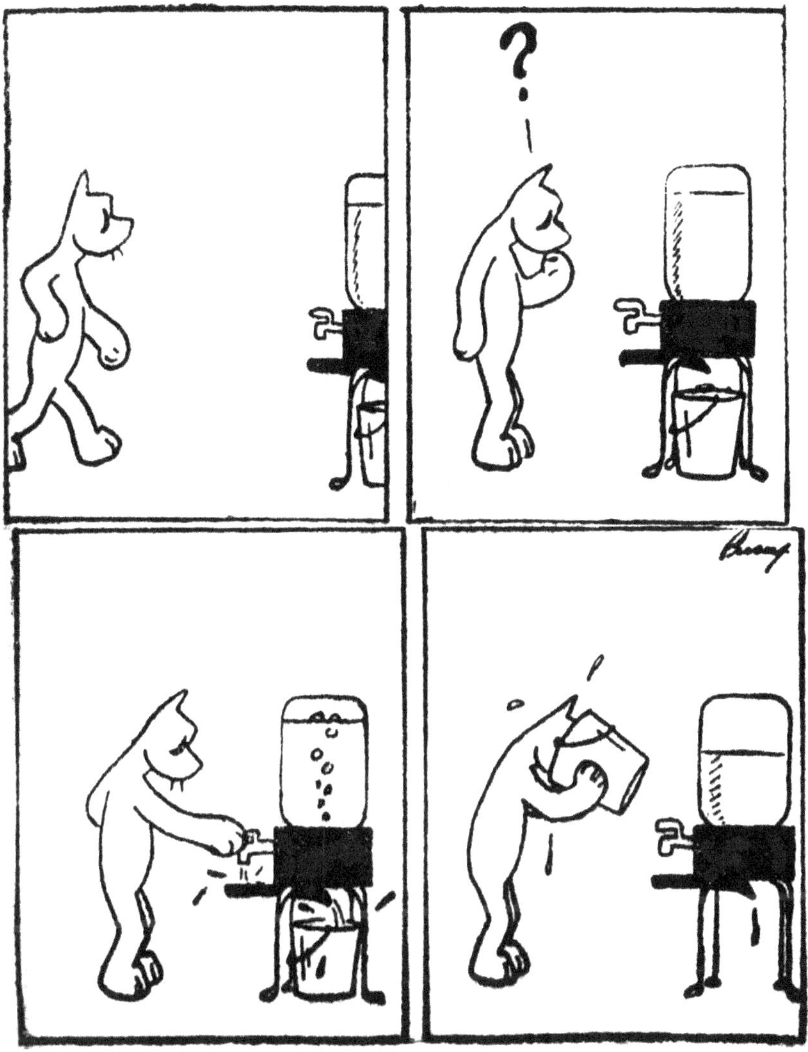
?

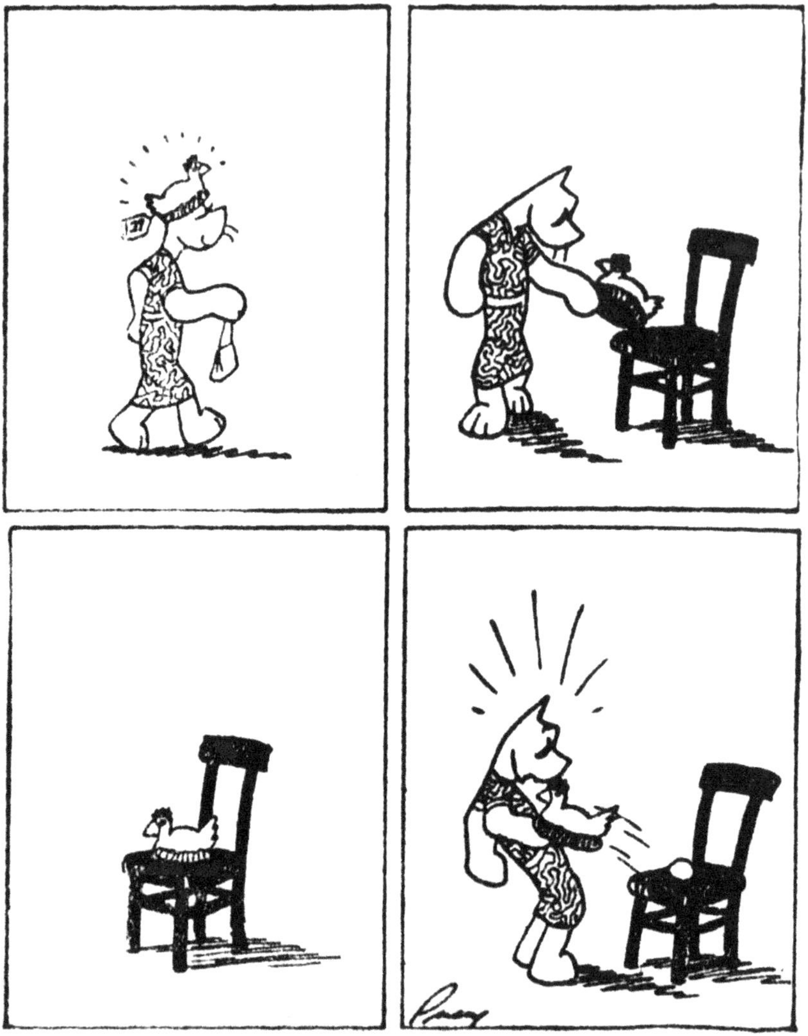

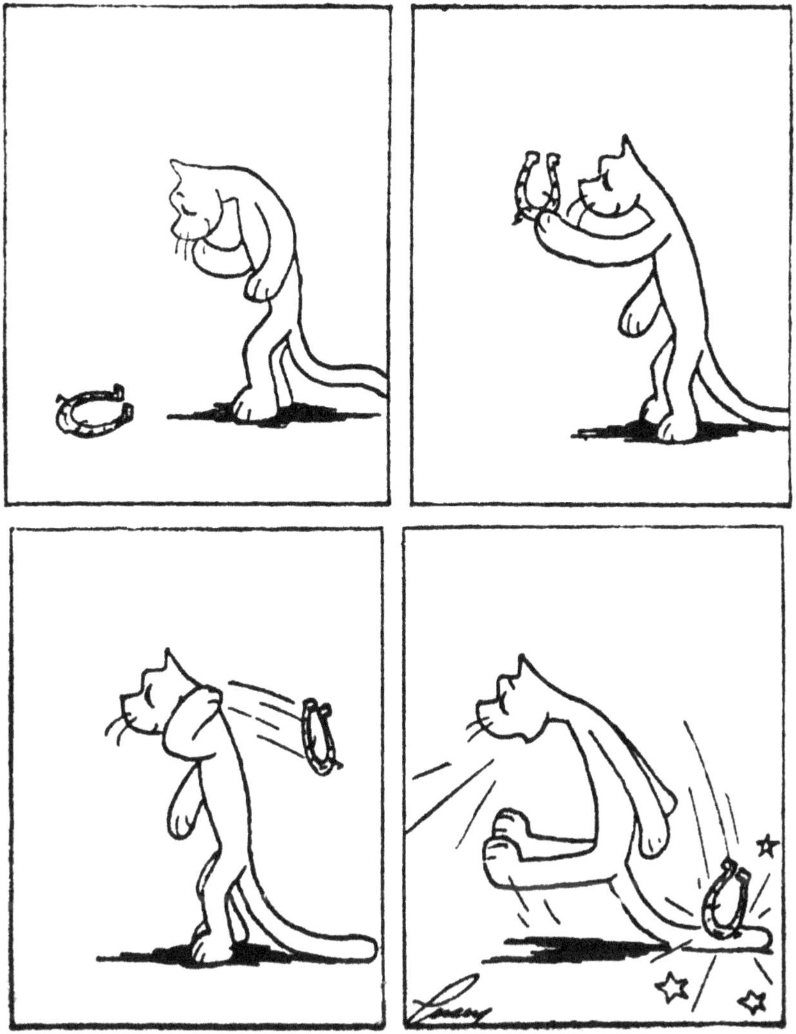

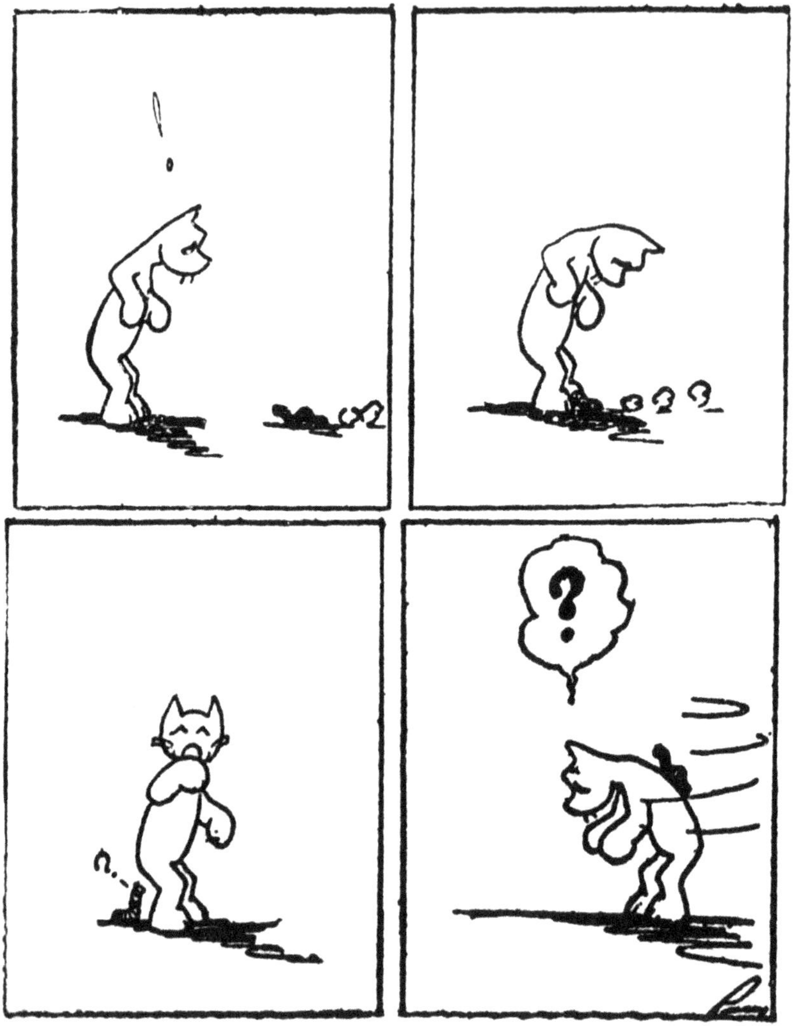
!
?

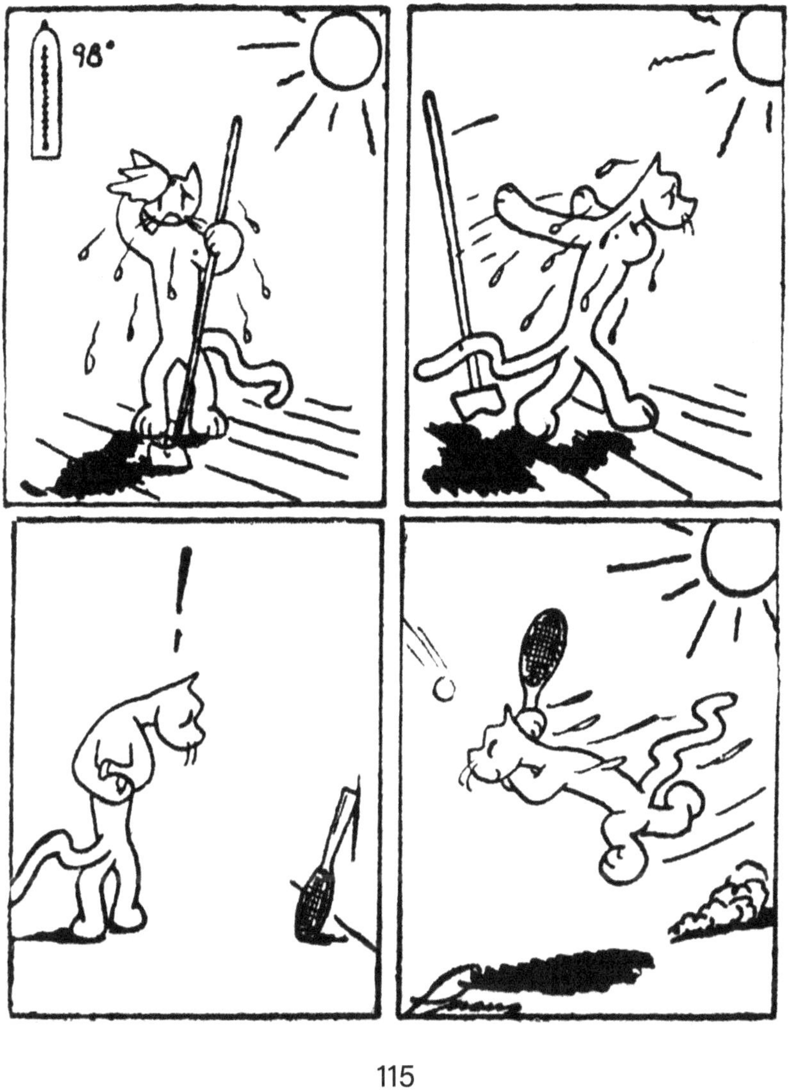
98°
!

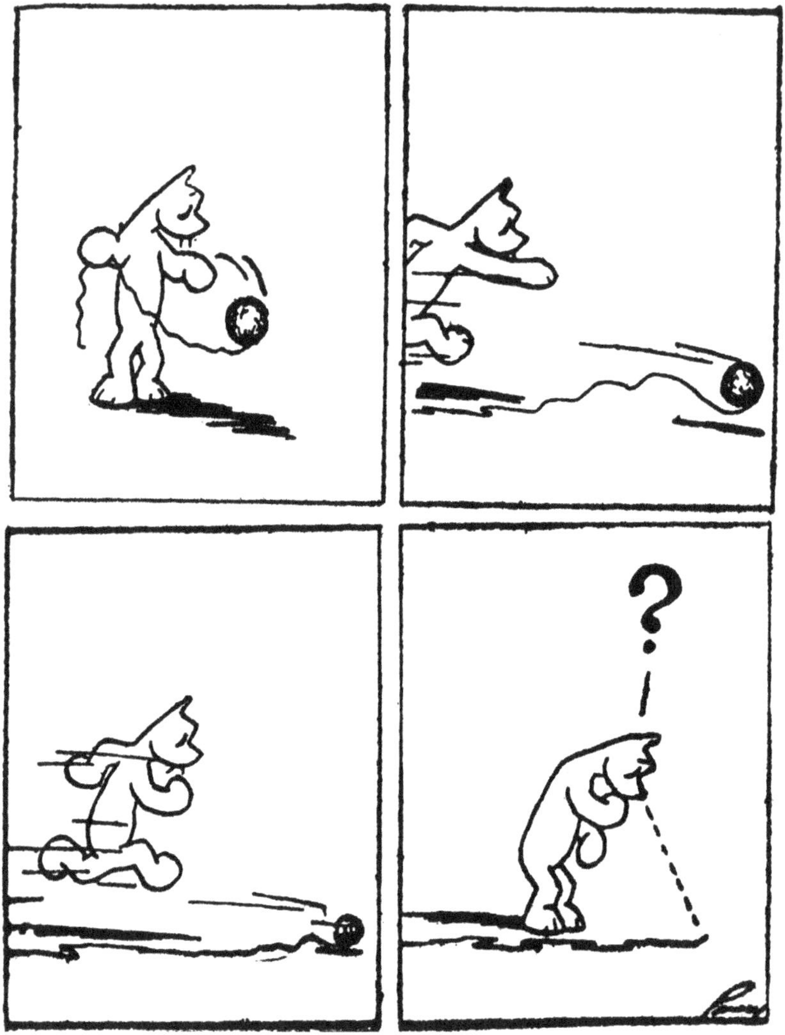
?

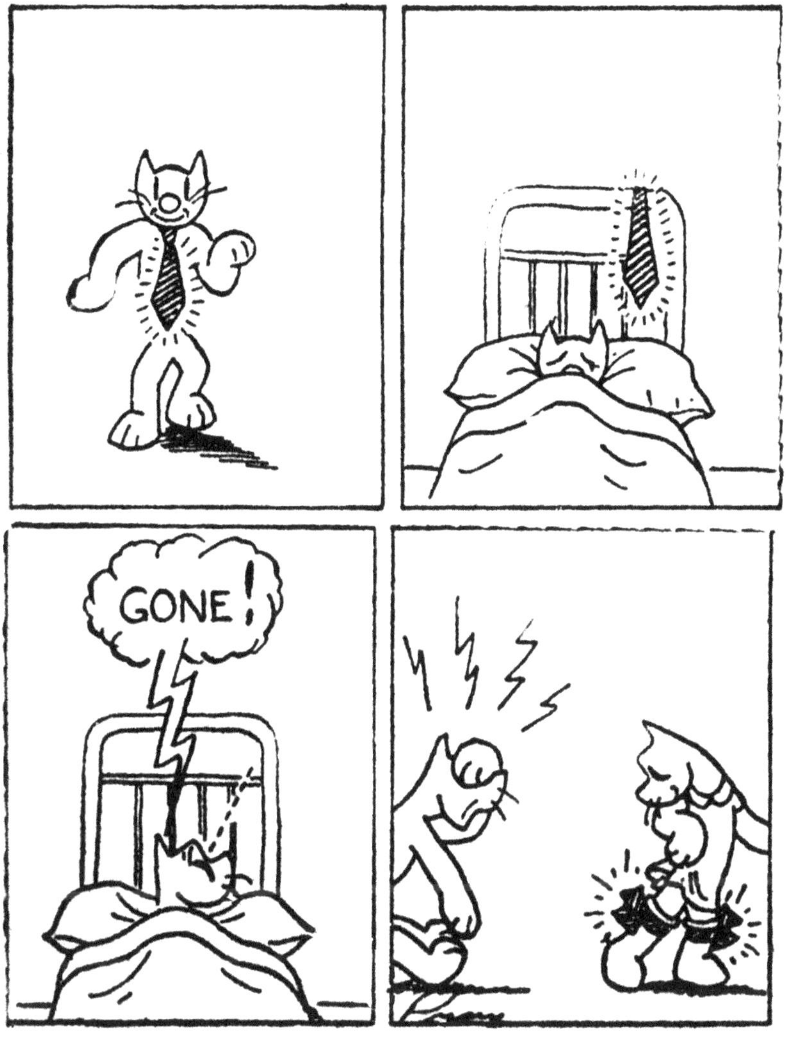
GONE!

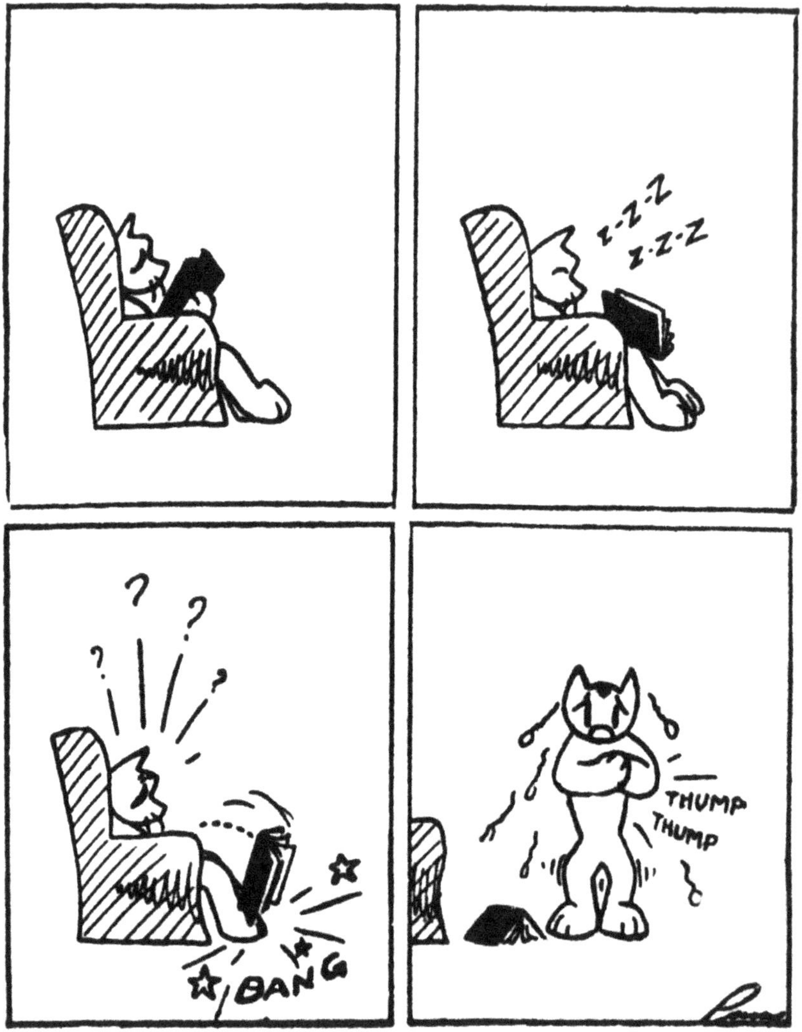
Z-Z-Z
Z-Z-Z
BANG
THUMP
THUMP

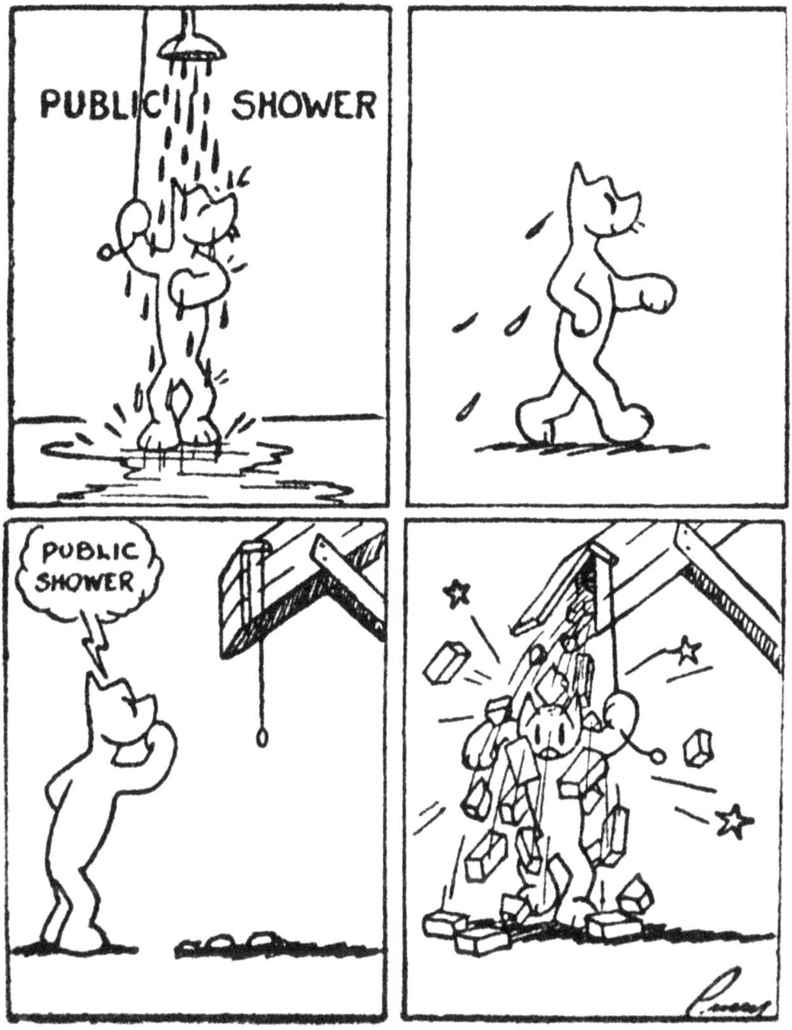
PUBLIC SHOWER
PUBLIC SHOWER

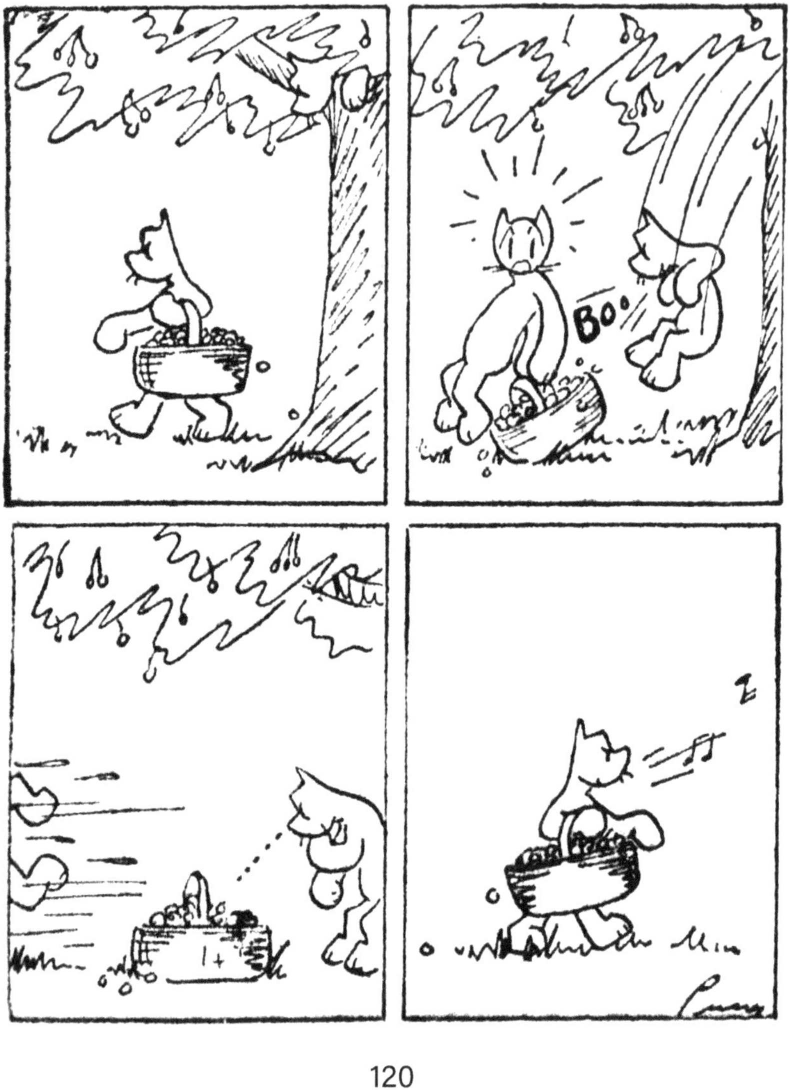
BOO
Z

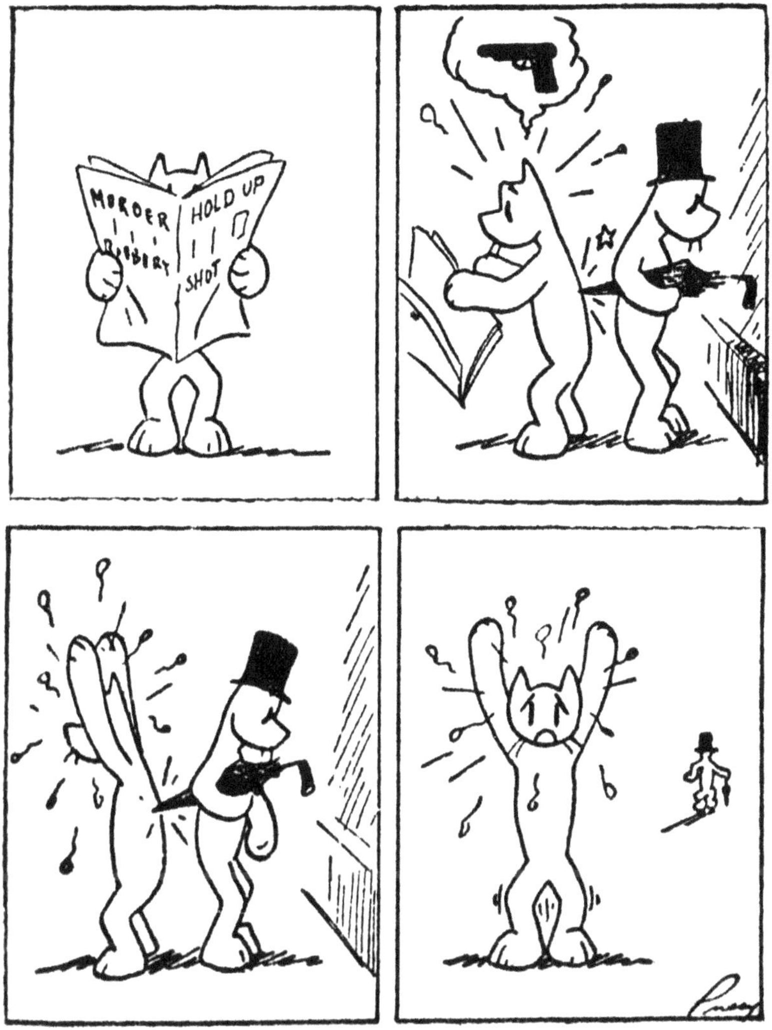
MURDER
ROBBERY
HOLD UP
SHOT

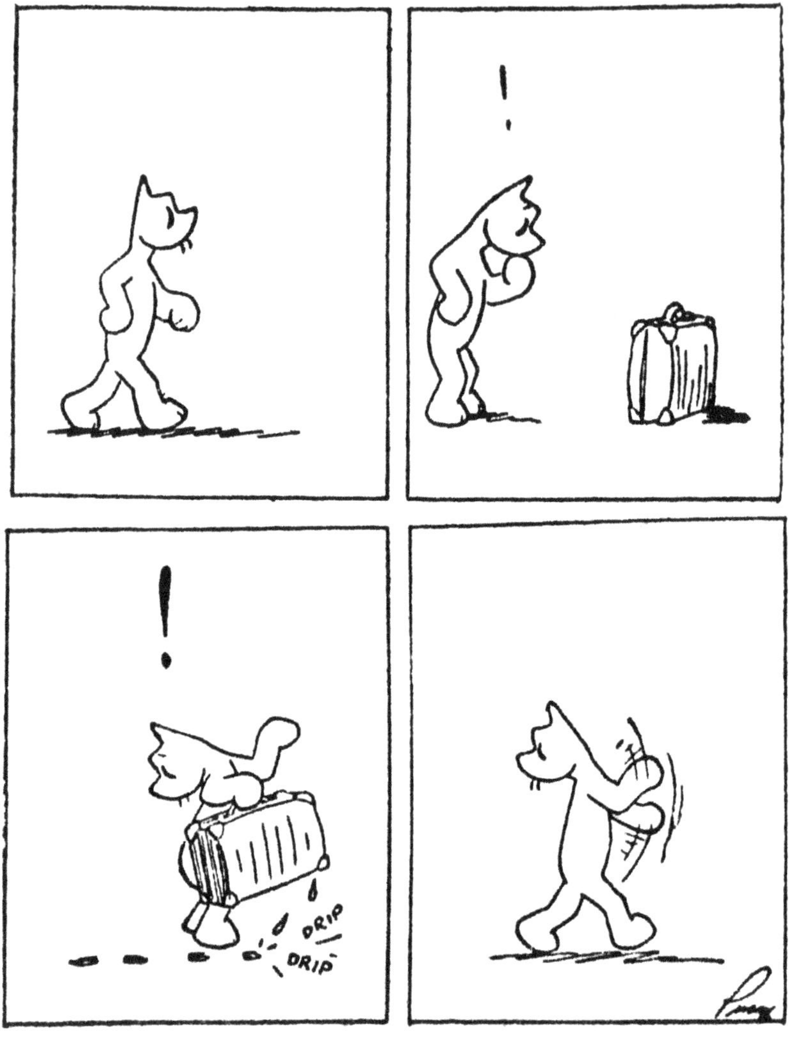
!
!
DRIP
DRIP

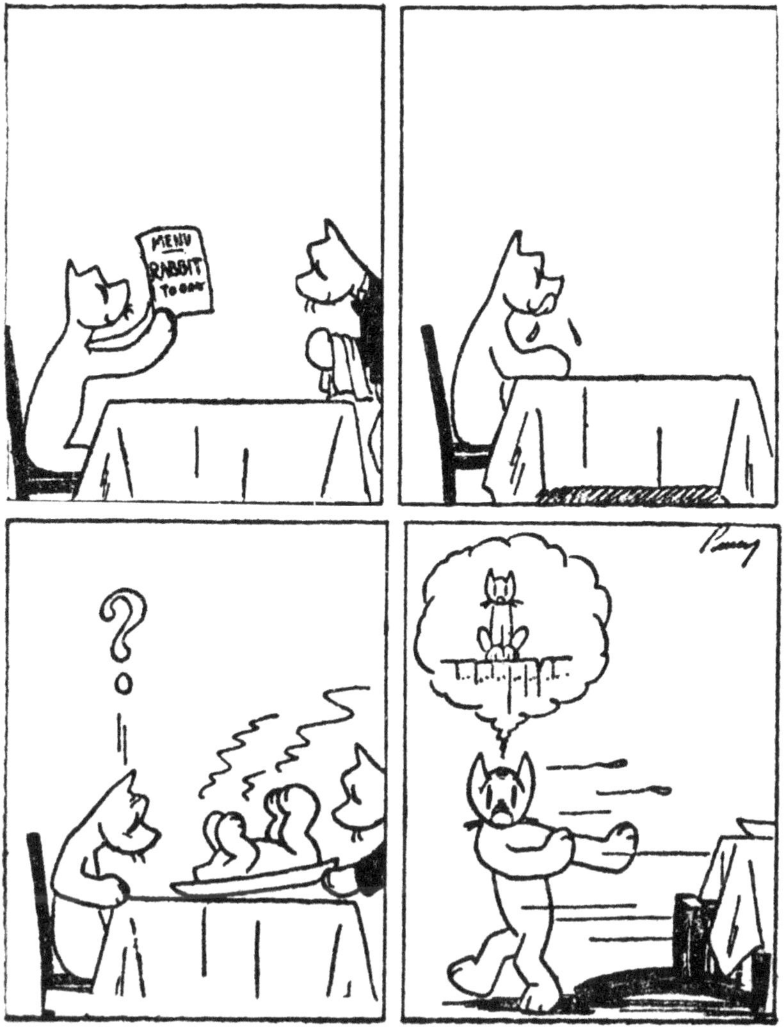
MENU
RABBIT

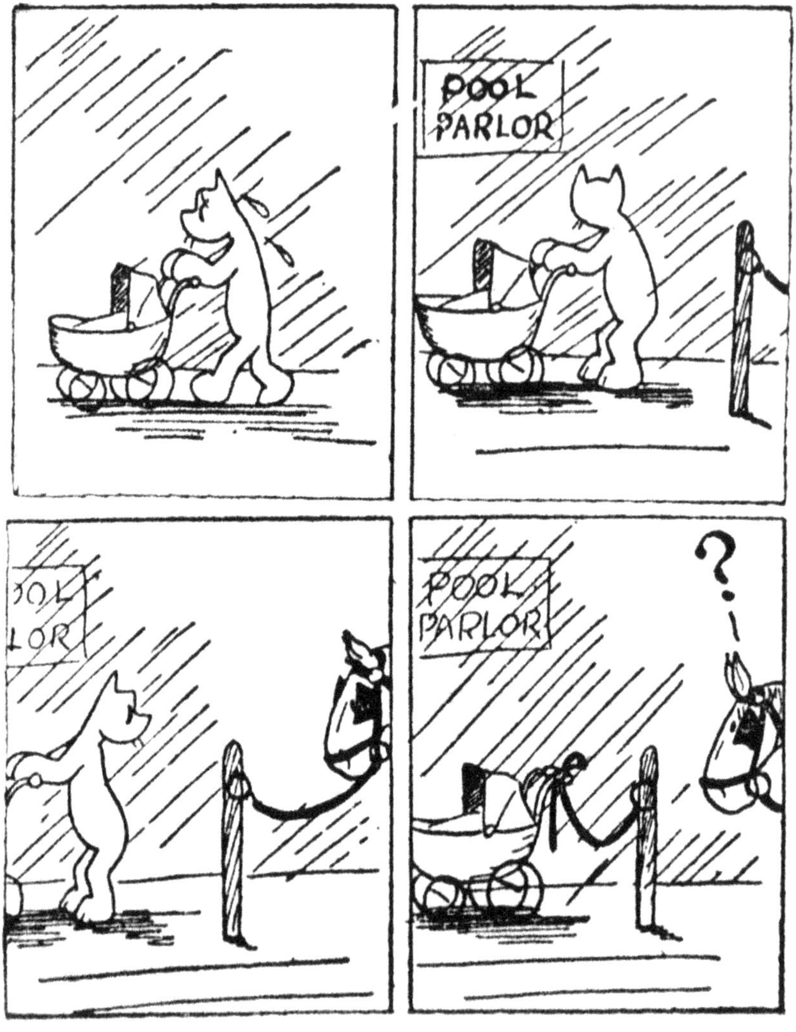
POOL
PARLOR
OOL
LOR
POOL
PARLOR
?

ANY OLD BONES, RAGS, PAPERS—
THE ALL NITE CLUB
THE ALL NITE CLUB
ANY EMPTY BOTTLES

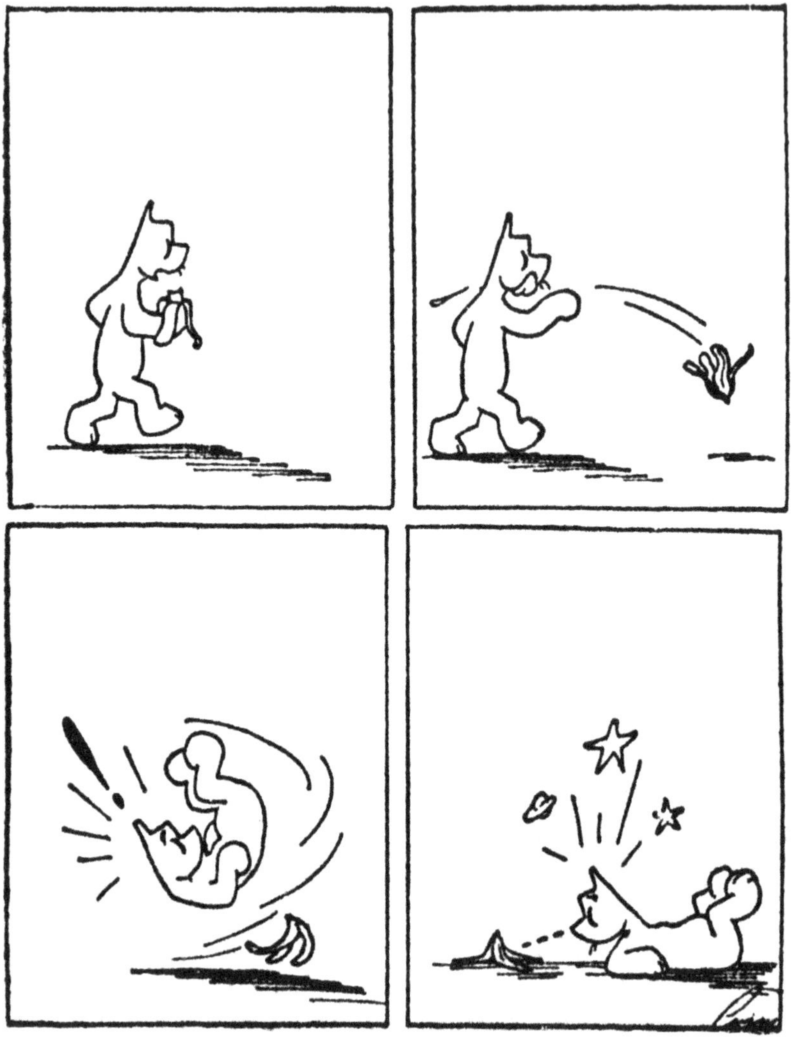
!

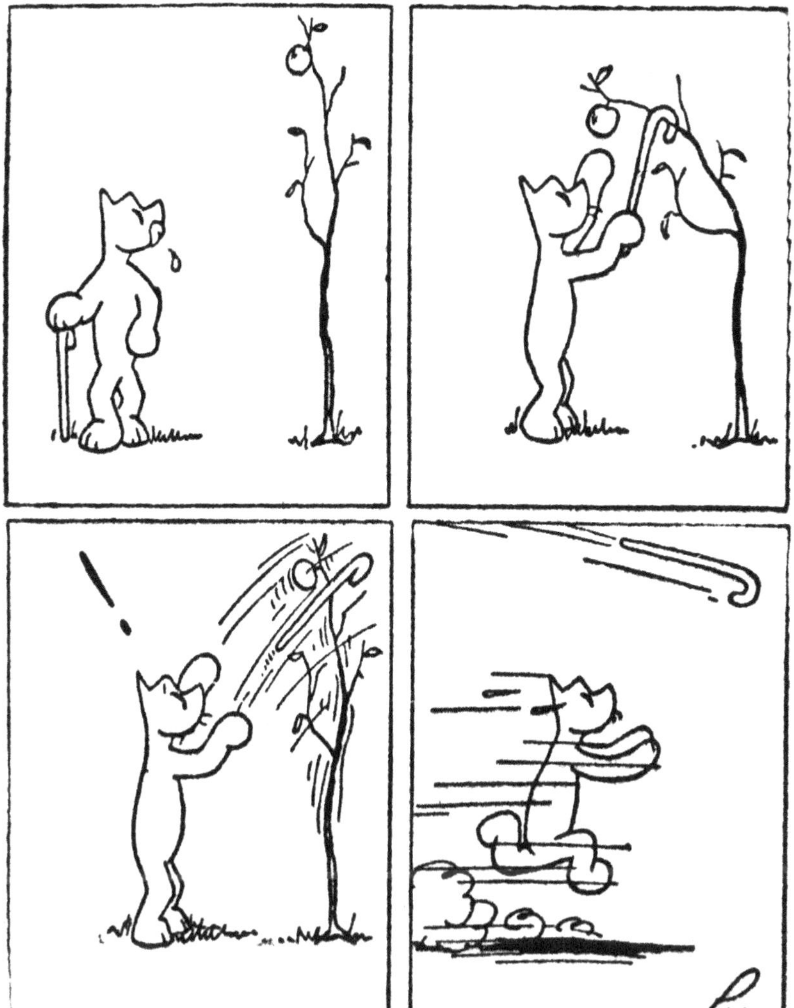
!

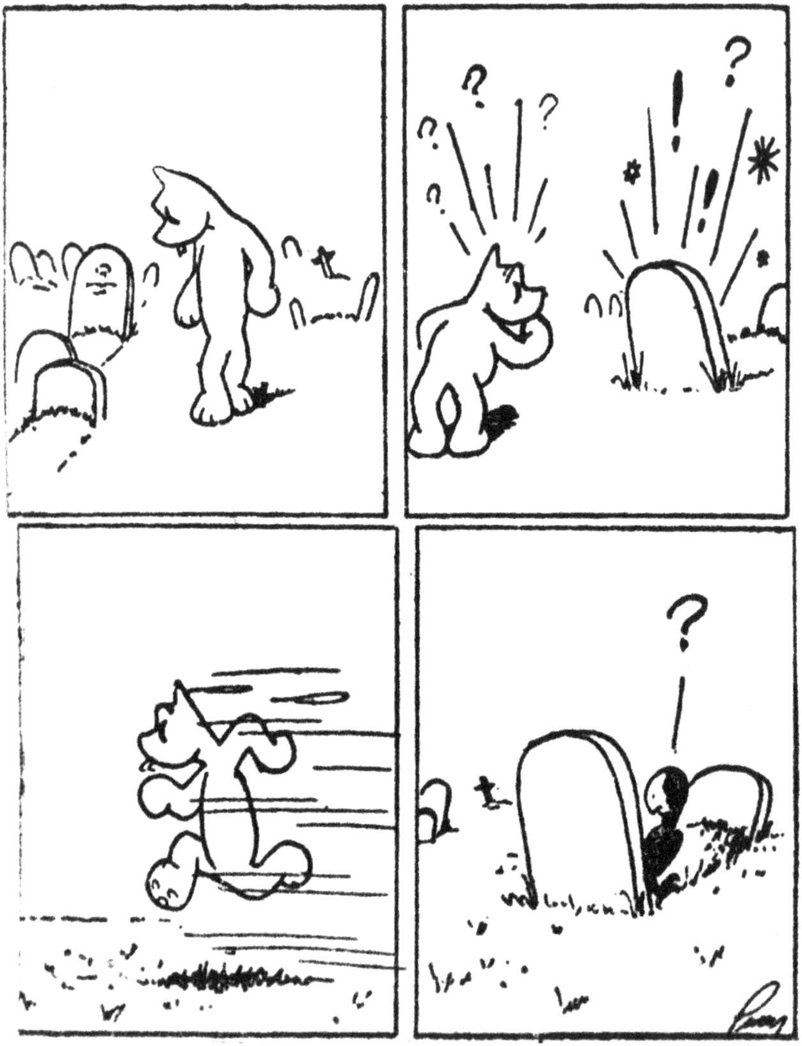

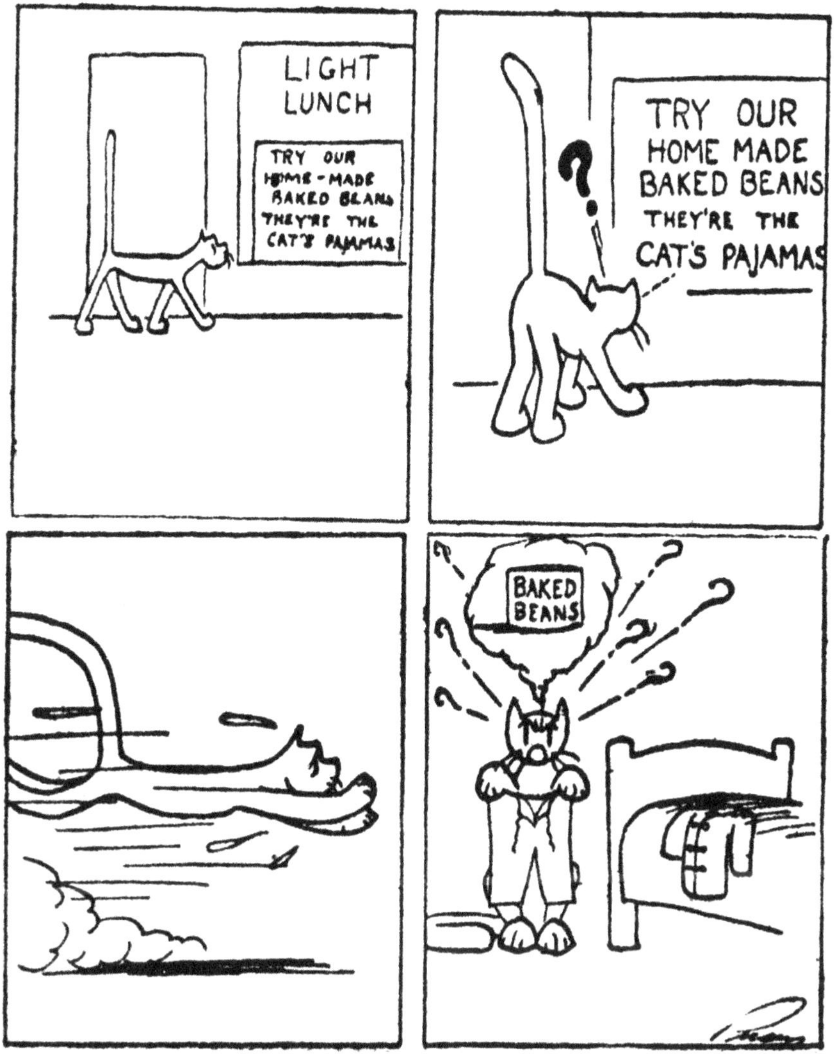
LIGHT LUNCH
TRY OUR HOME-MADE BAKED BEANS THEY'RE THE CAT'S PAJAMAS
TRY OUR HOME MADE BAKED BEANS THEY'RE THE CAT'S PAJAMAS
BAKED BEANS

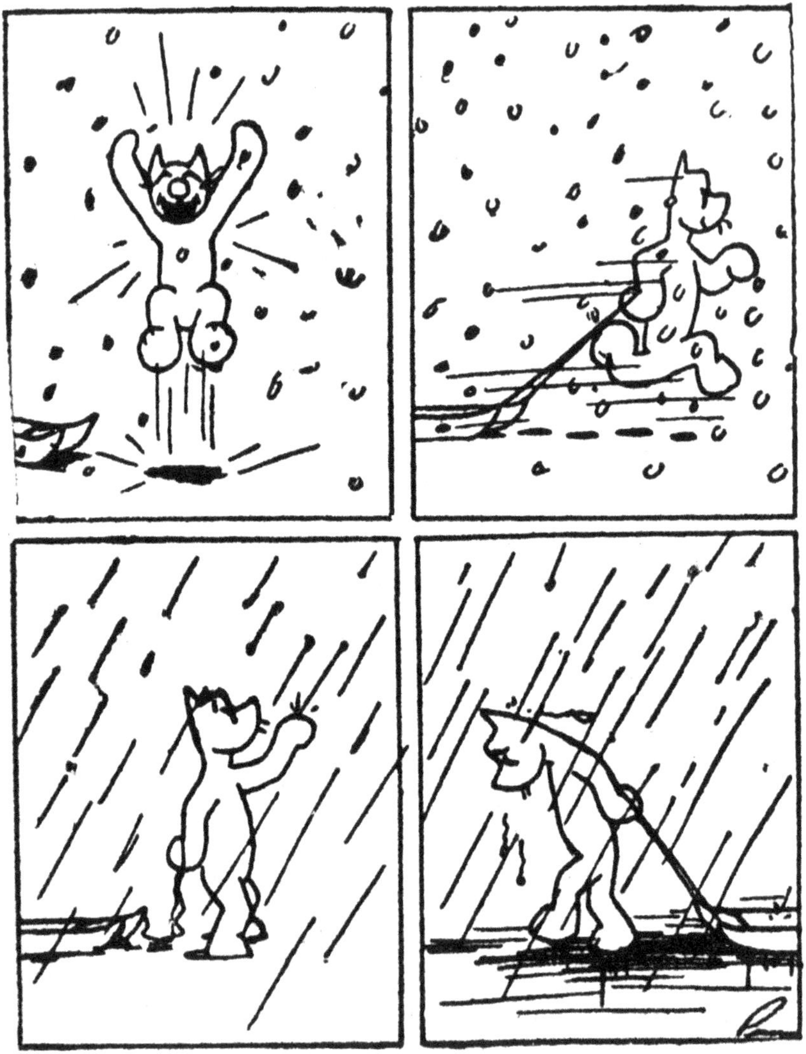

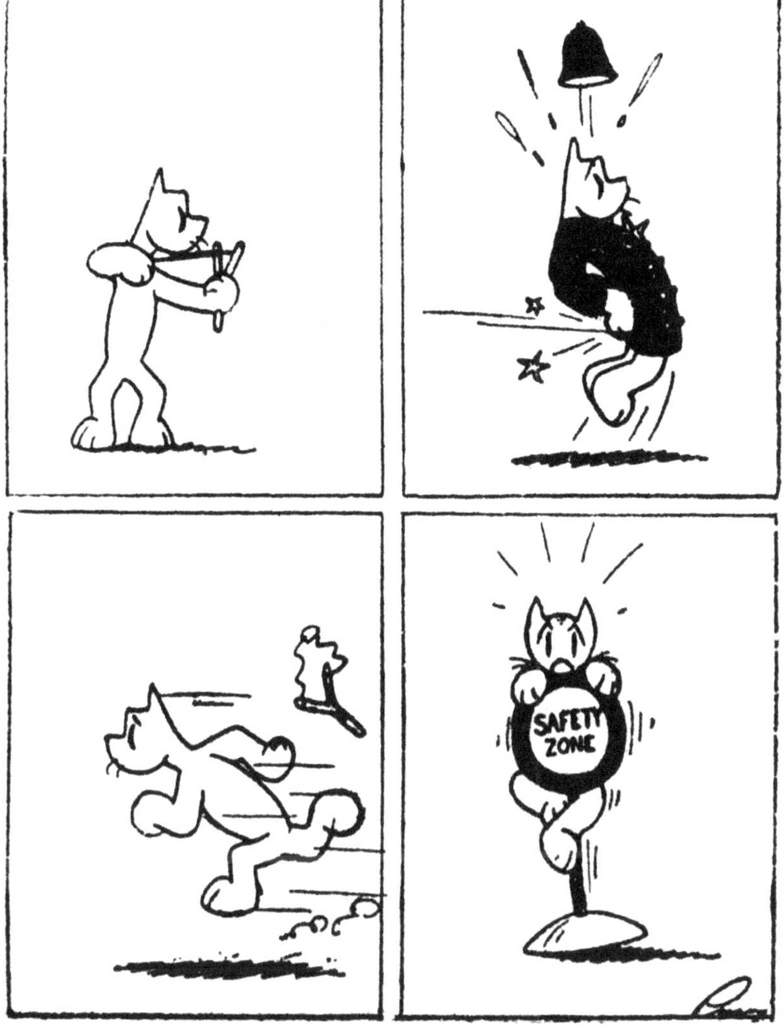
SAFETY
ZONE

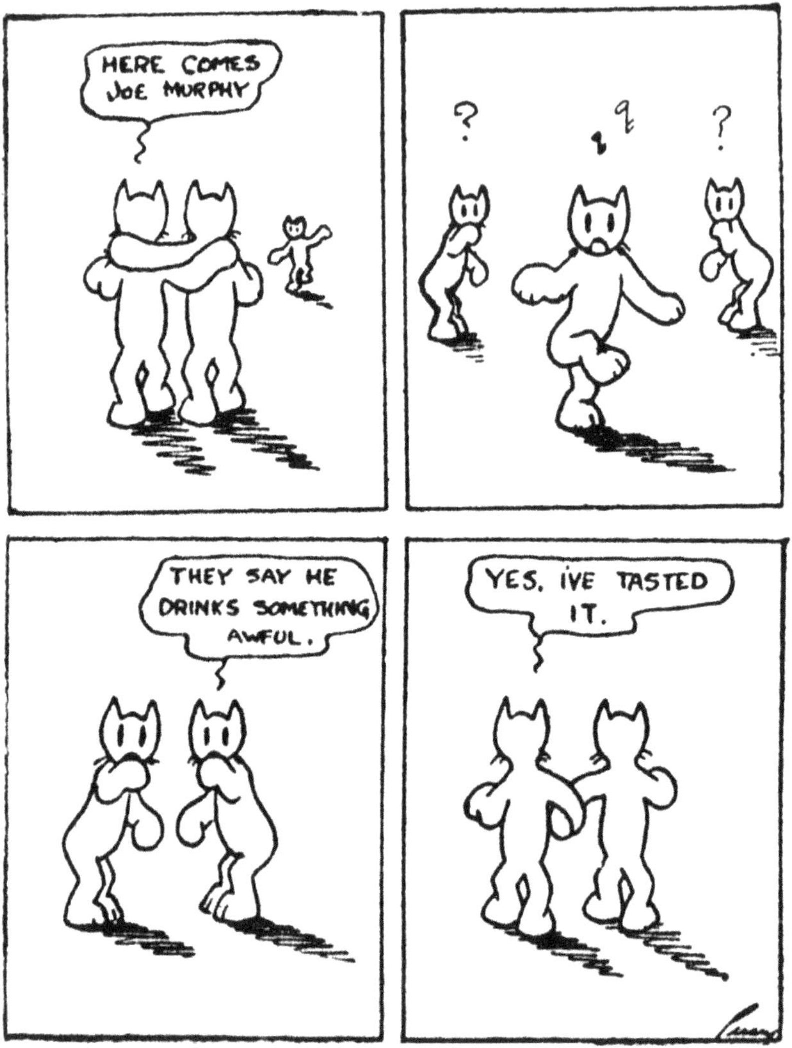
HERE COMES JOE MURPHY
THEY SAY HE DRINKS SOMETHING AWFUL.
YES, IVE TASTED IT.

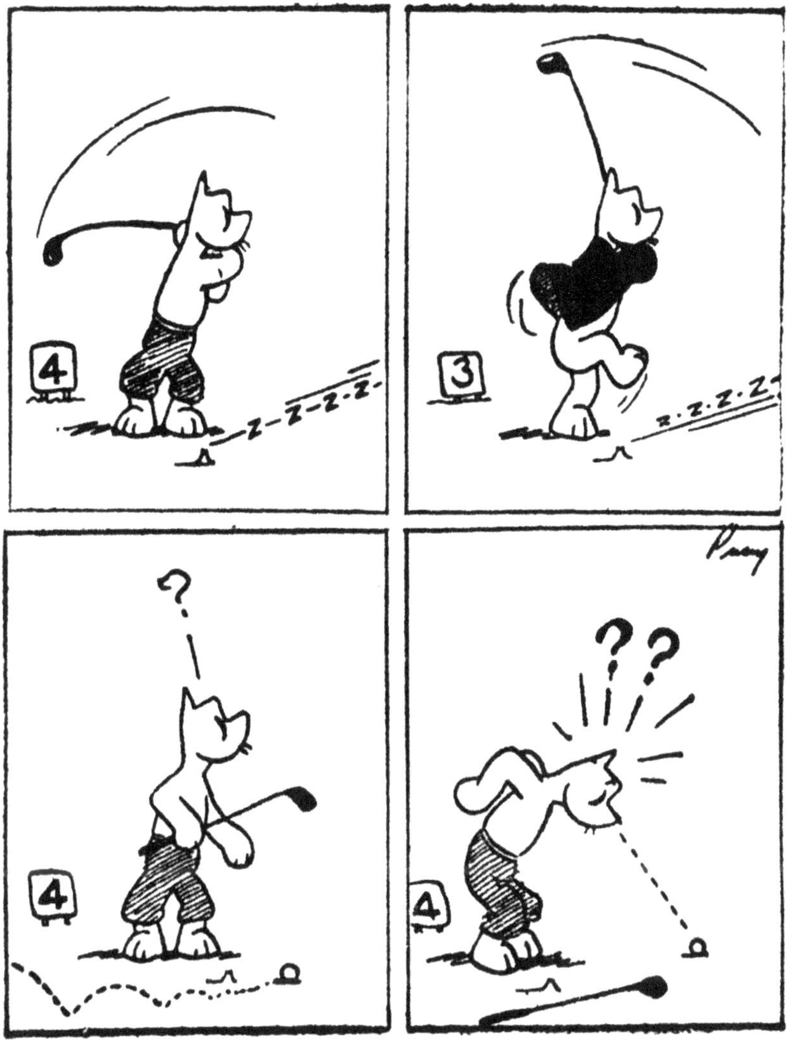
4
Z-Z-Z-Z
3
Z-Z-Z-Z
?
4
??
4

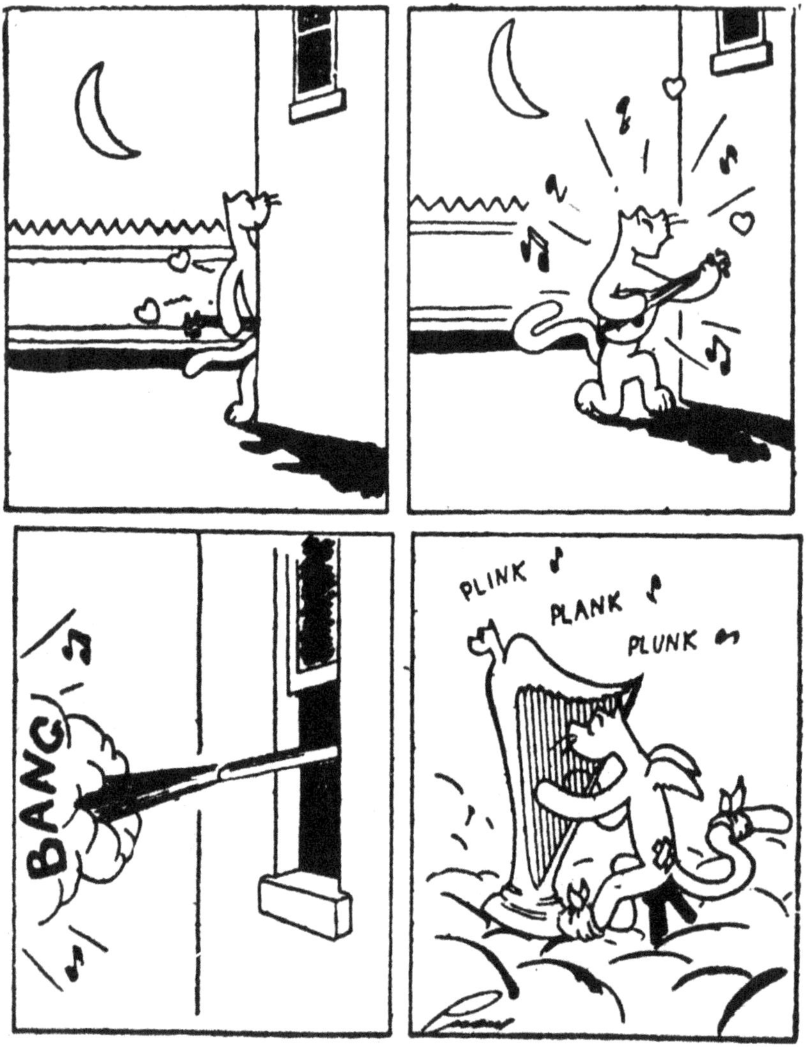
BANG
PLINK
PLANK
PLUNK

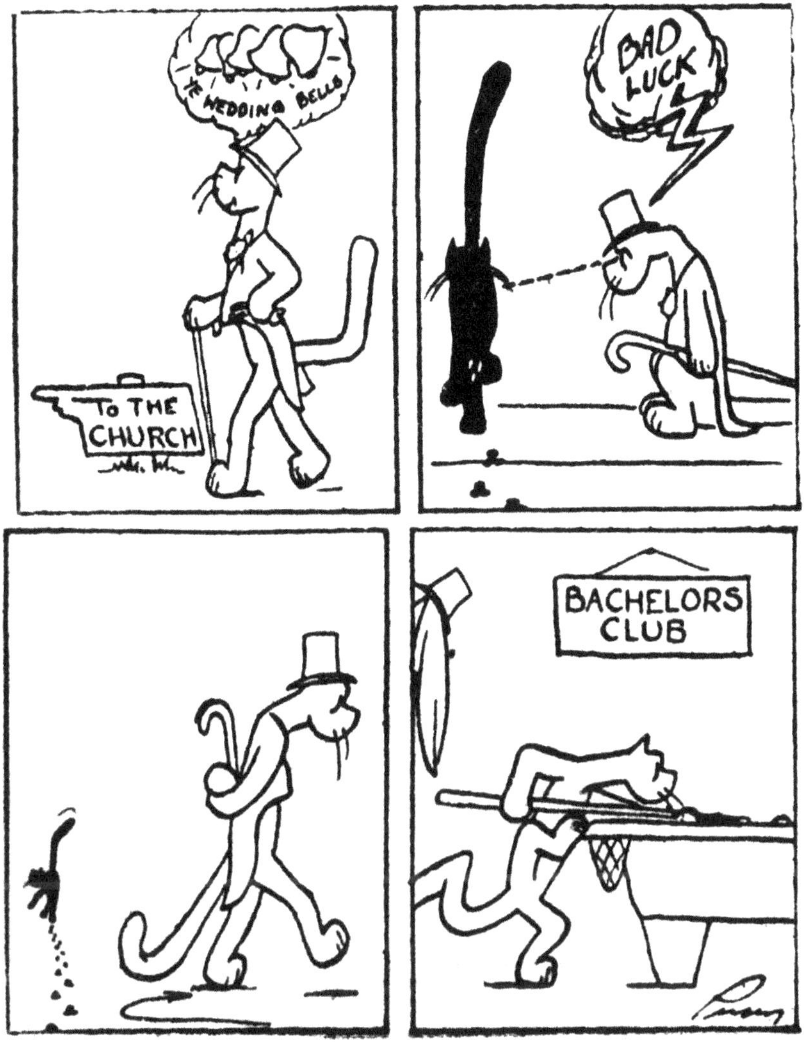

YE WEDDING BELLS
TO THE CHURCH
BAD LUCK
BACHELORS CLUB

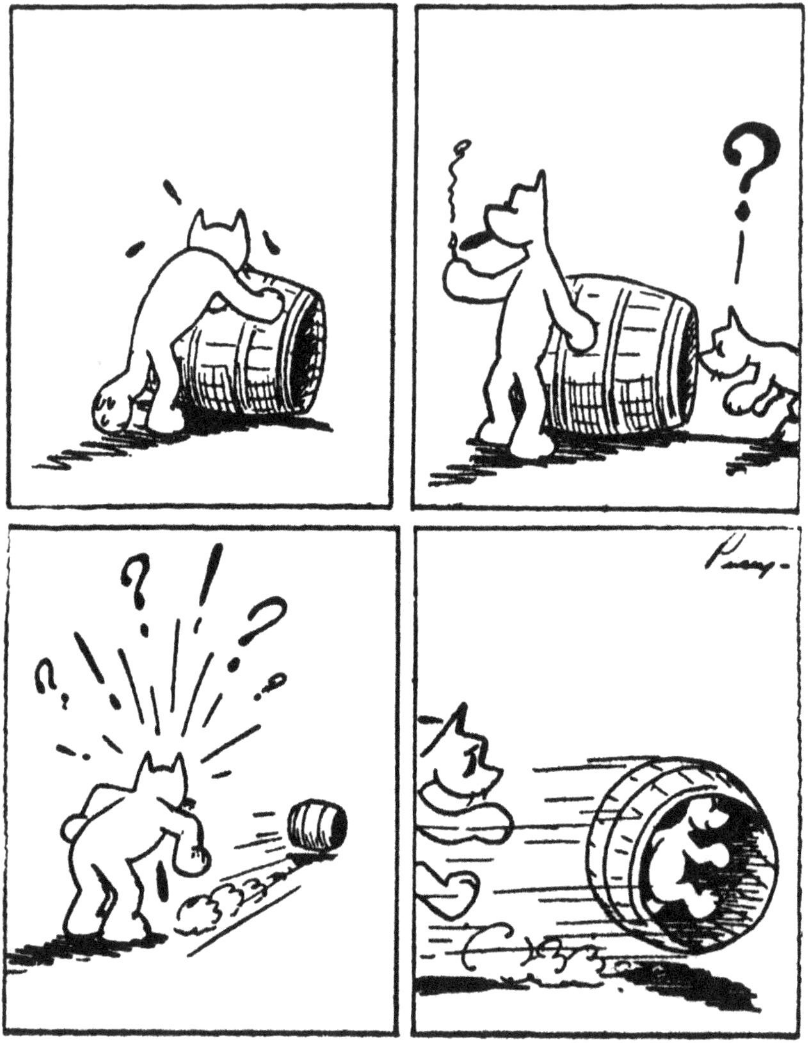

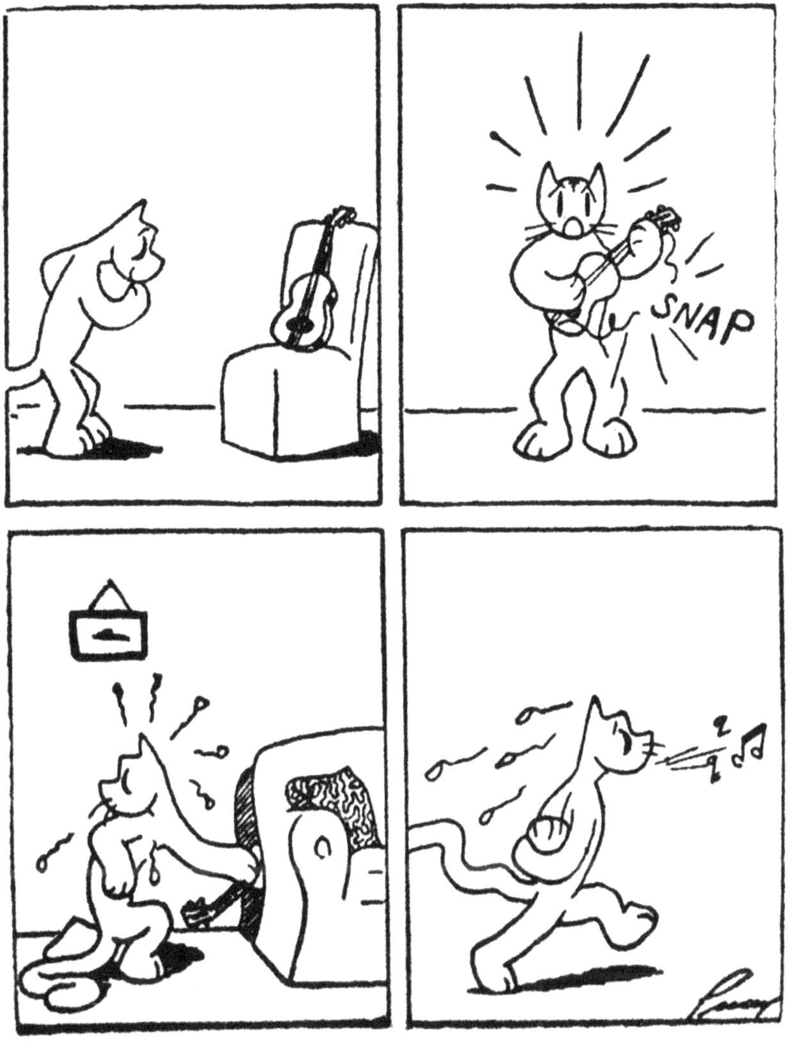
SNAP

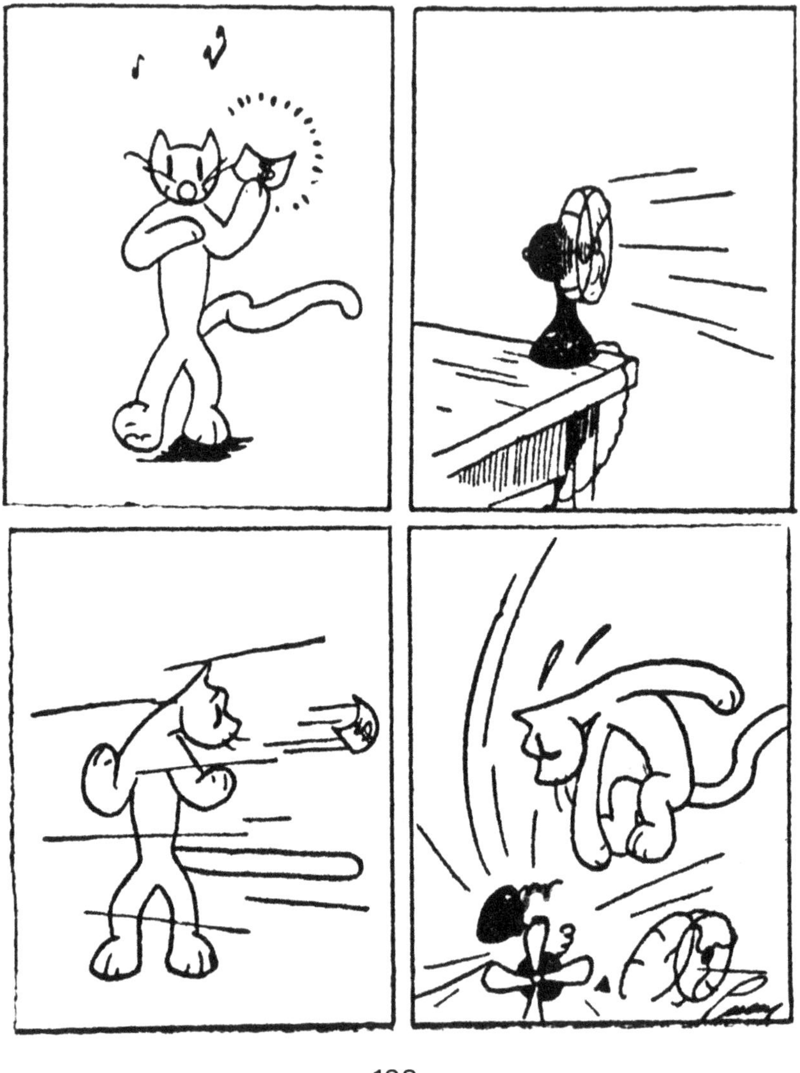

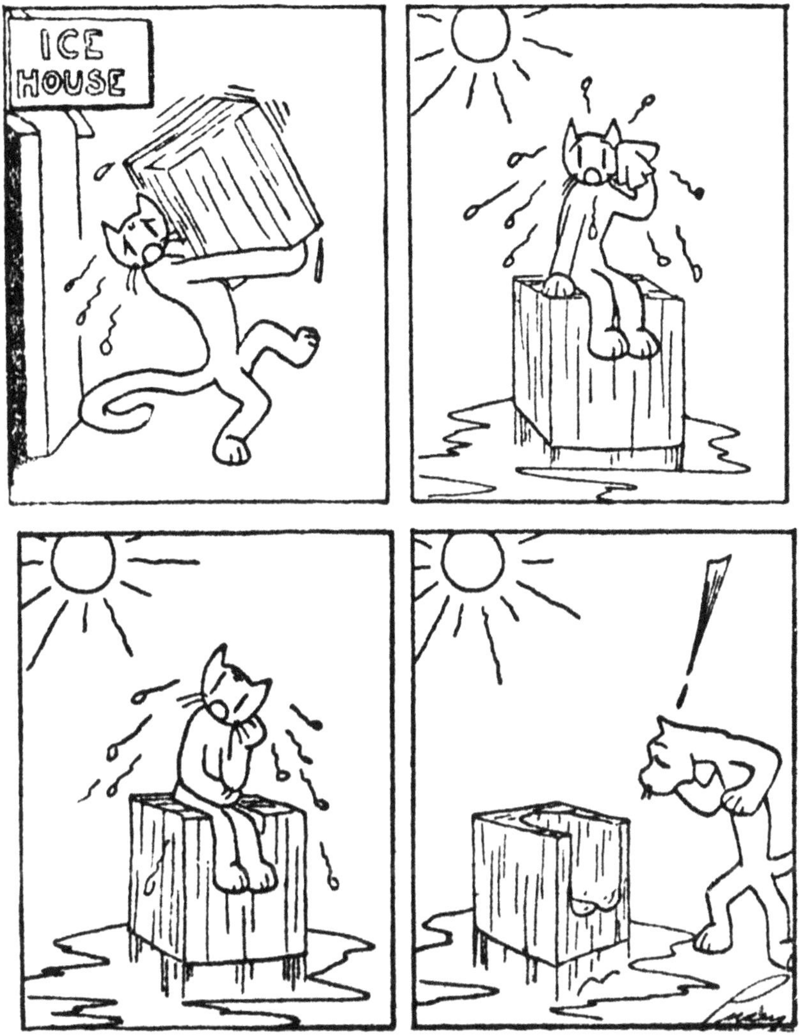
ICE
HOUSE

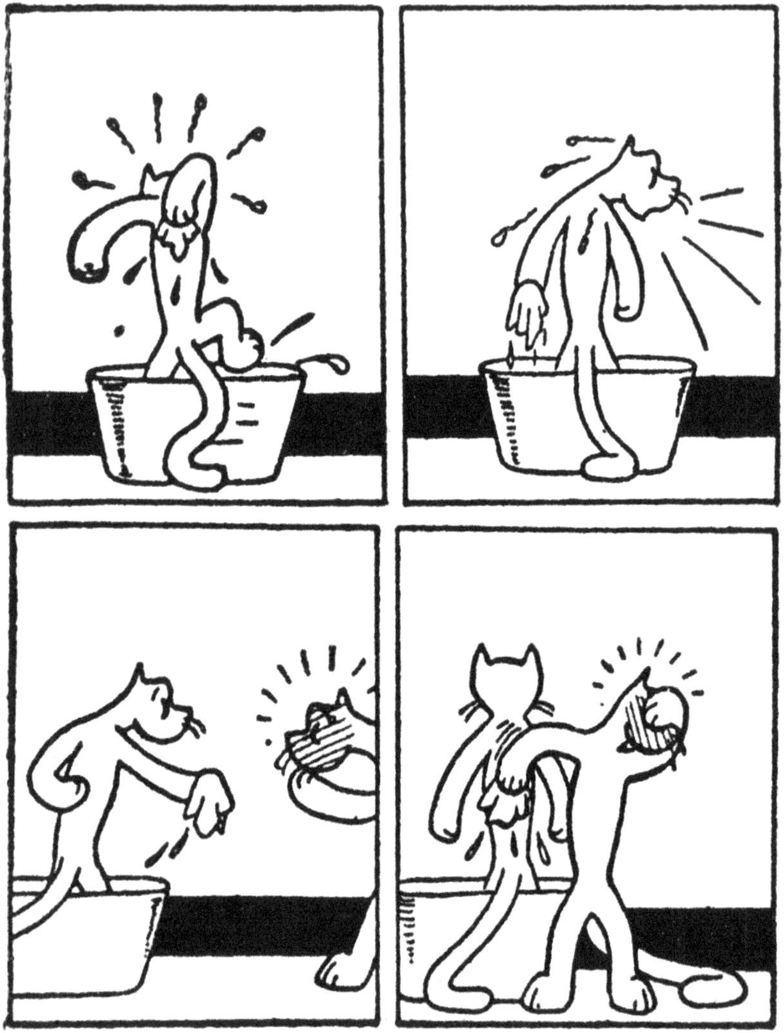

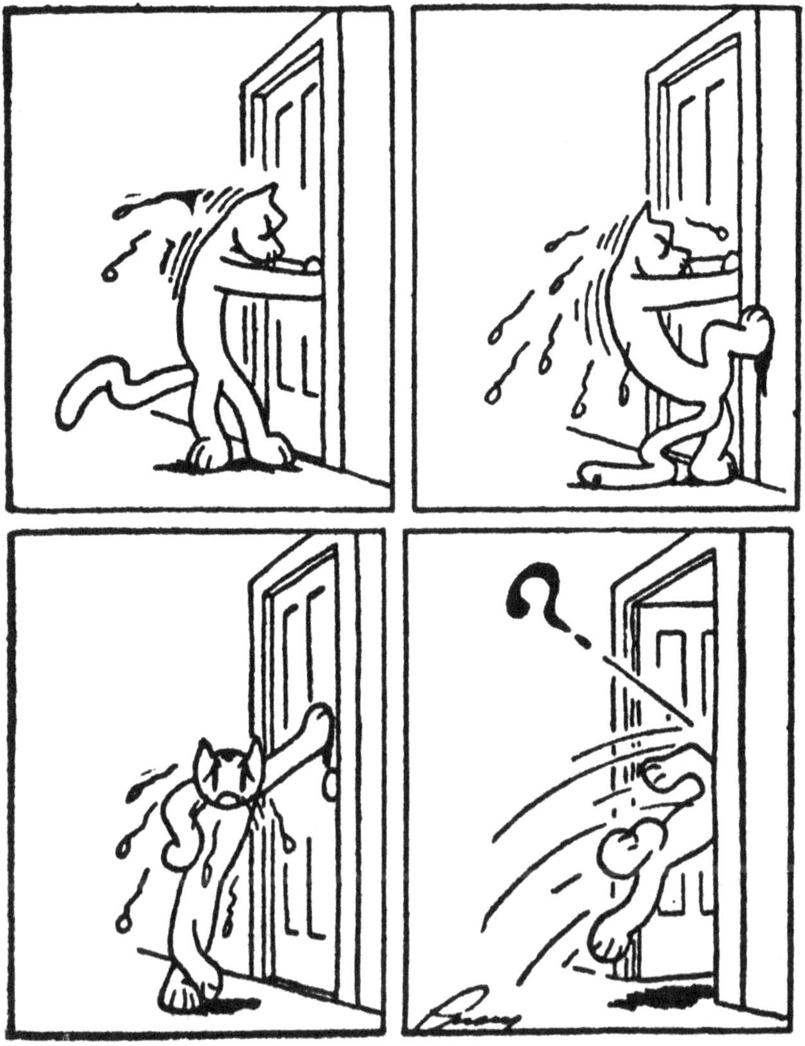

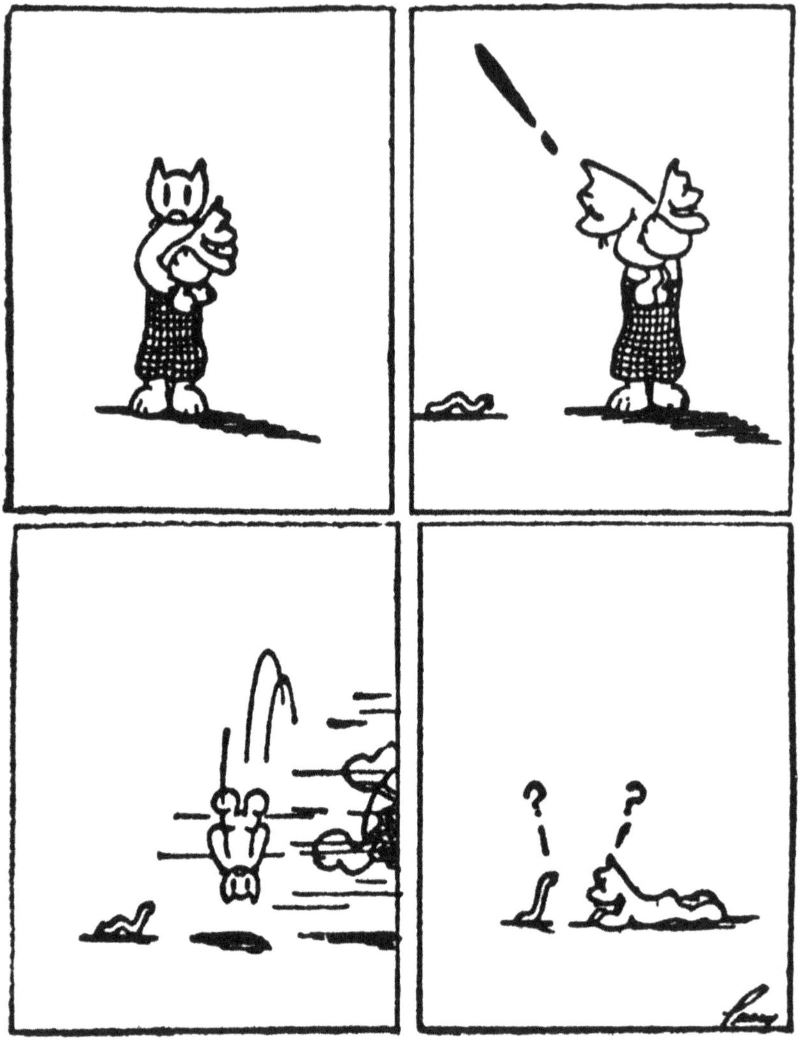

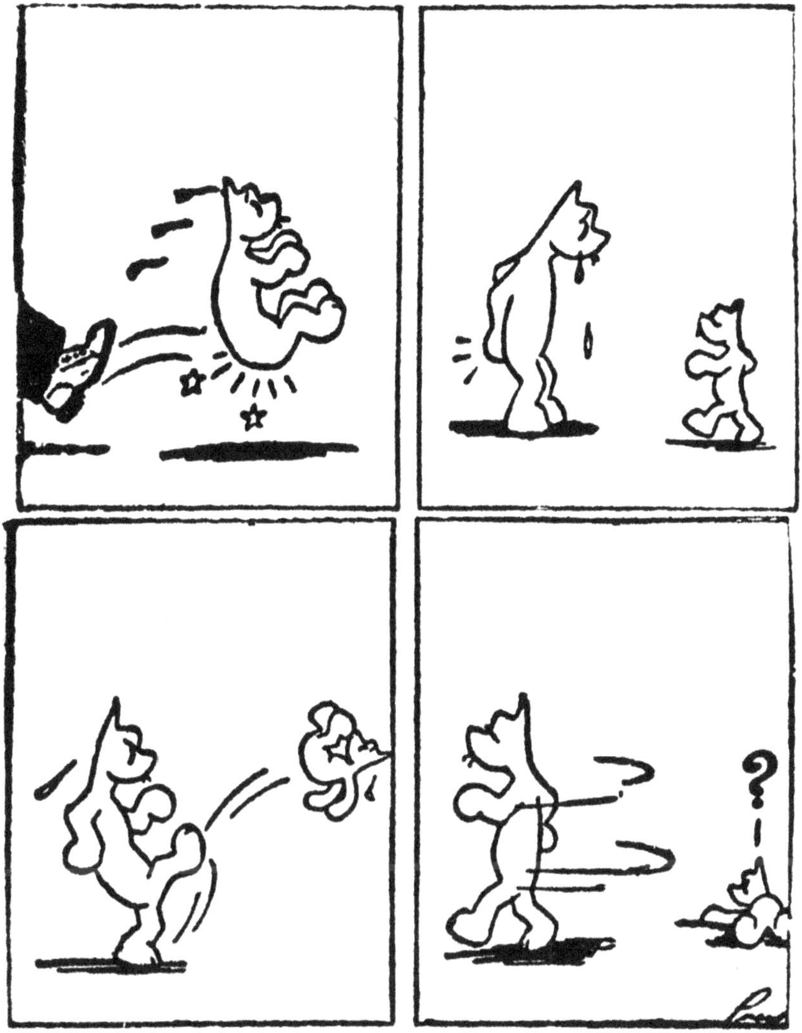
?

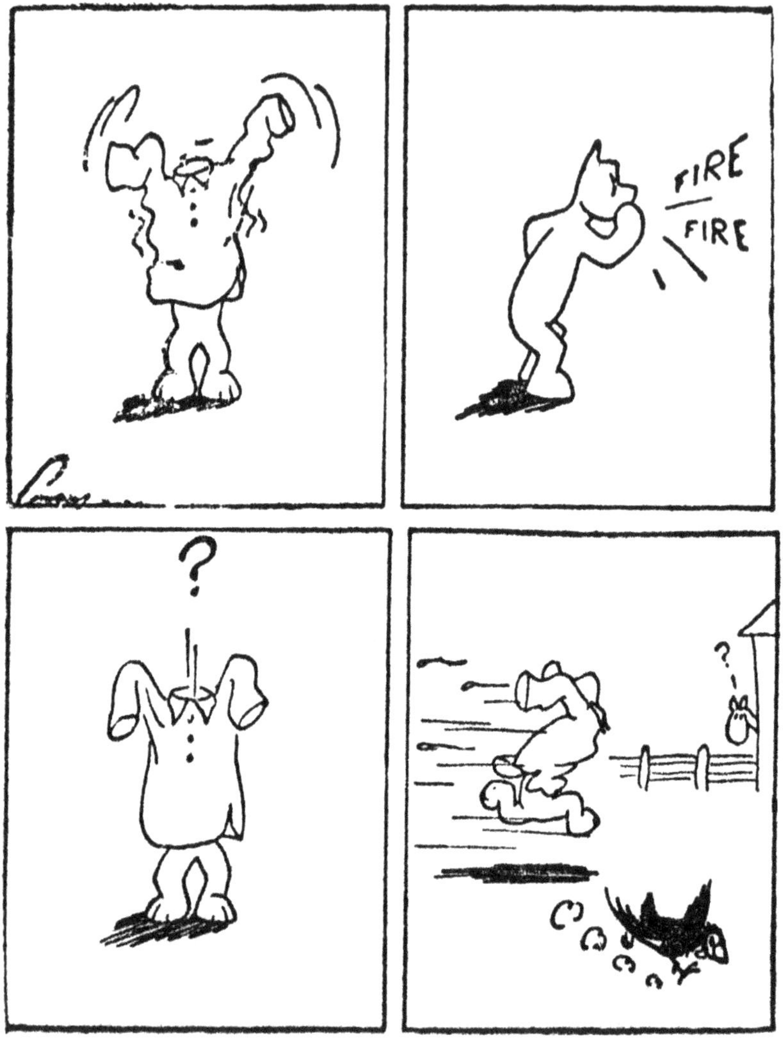
FIRE
FIRE
?
?

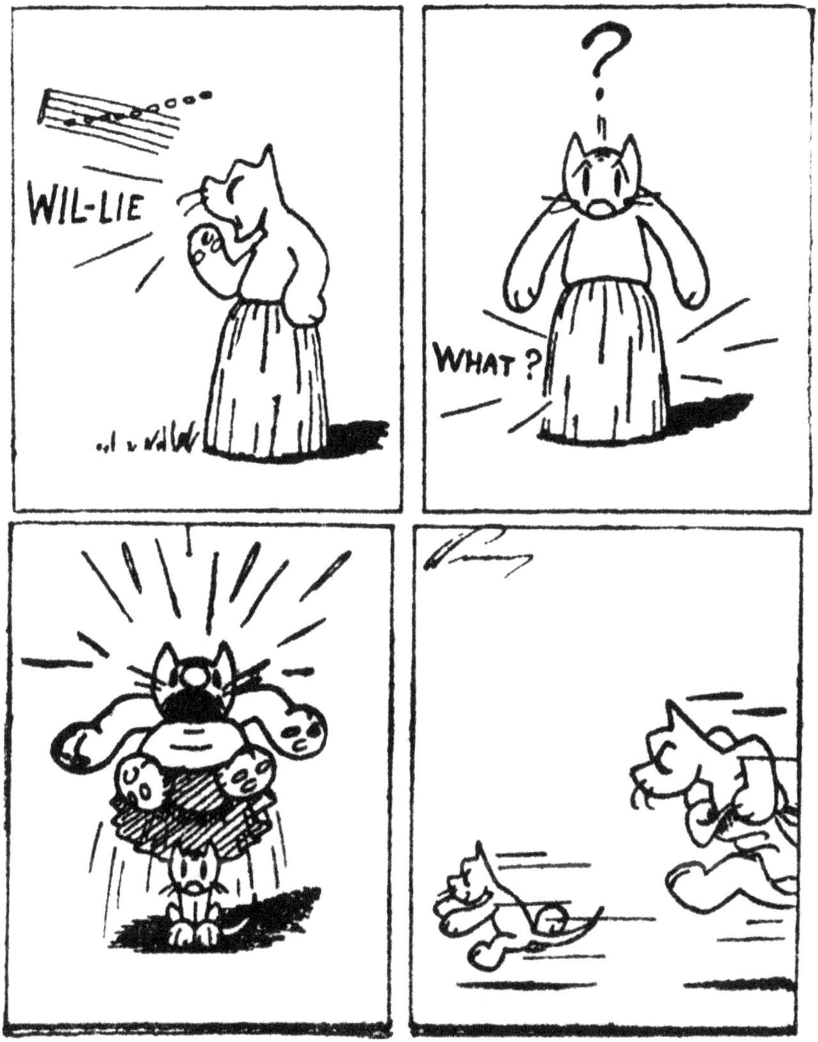
WIL-LIE
WHAT ?
?

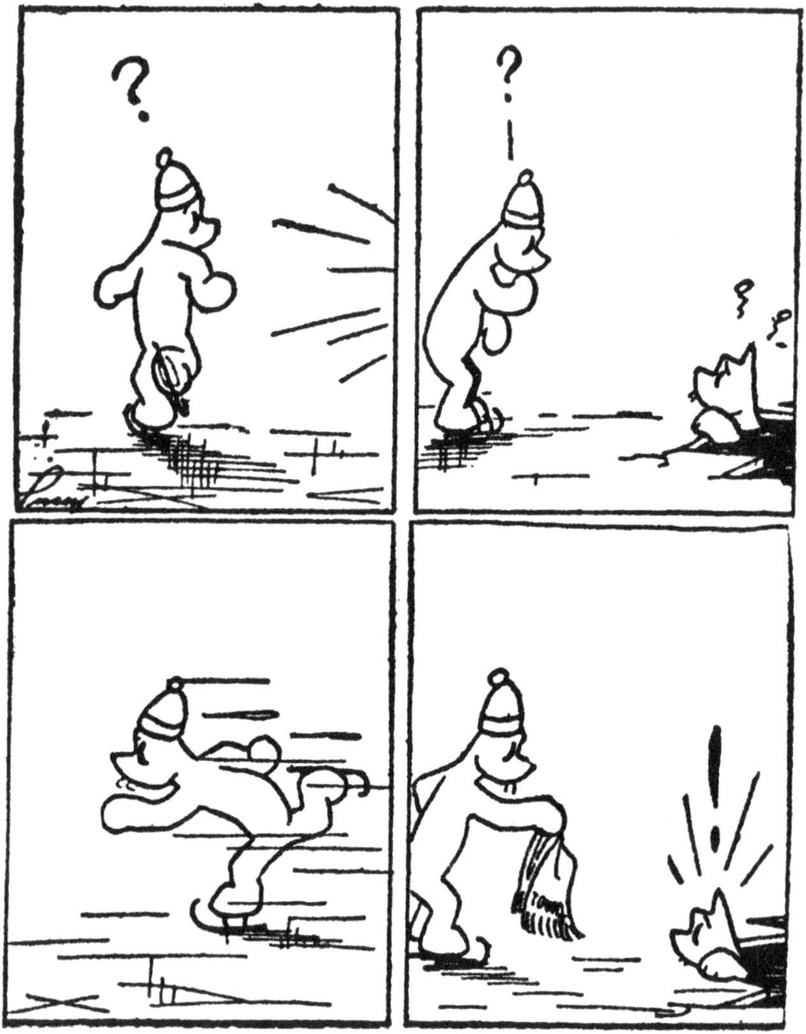

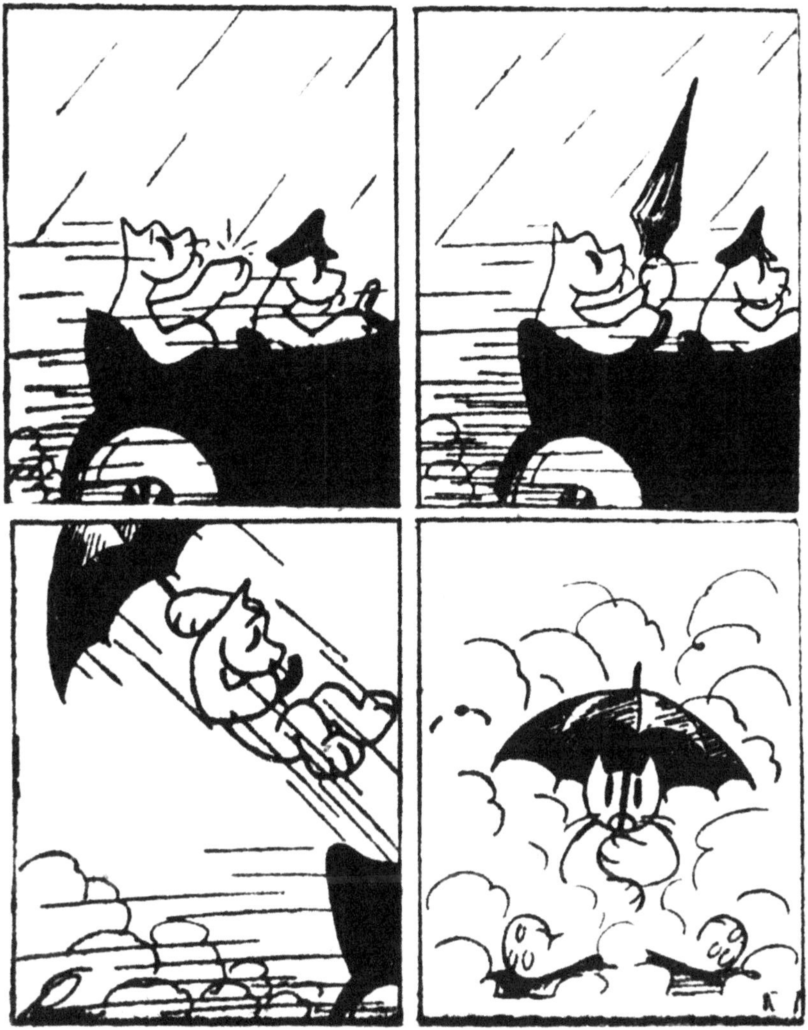

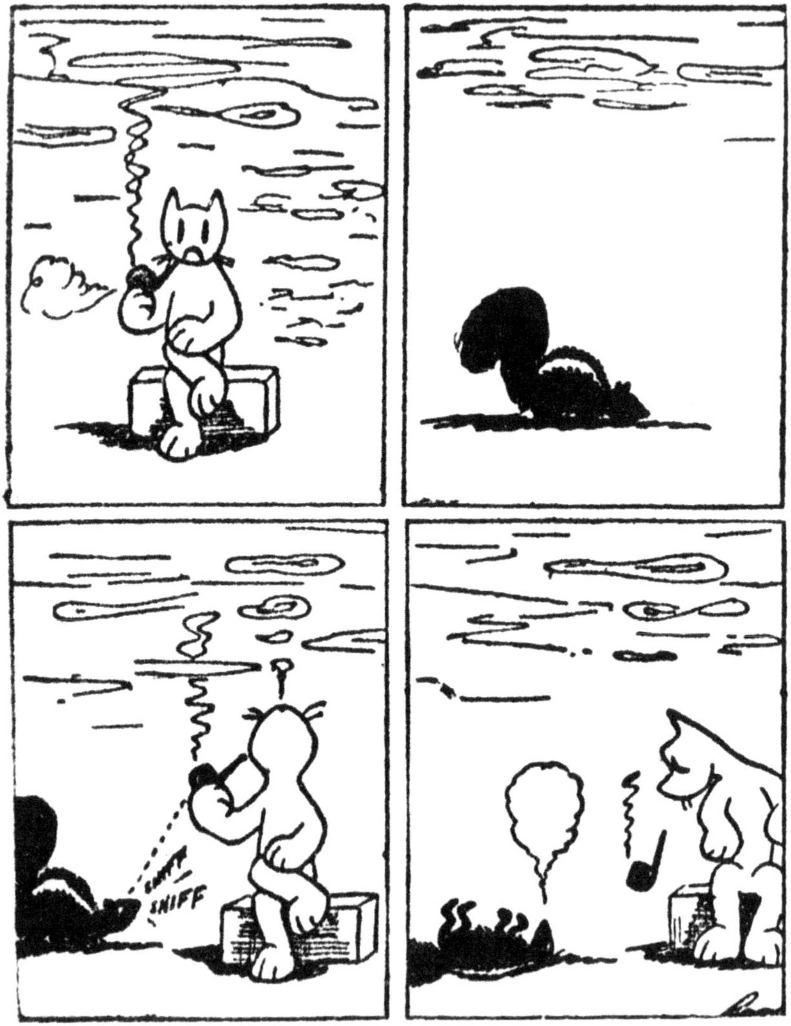
SNIFF

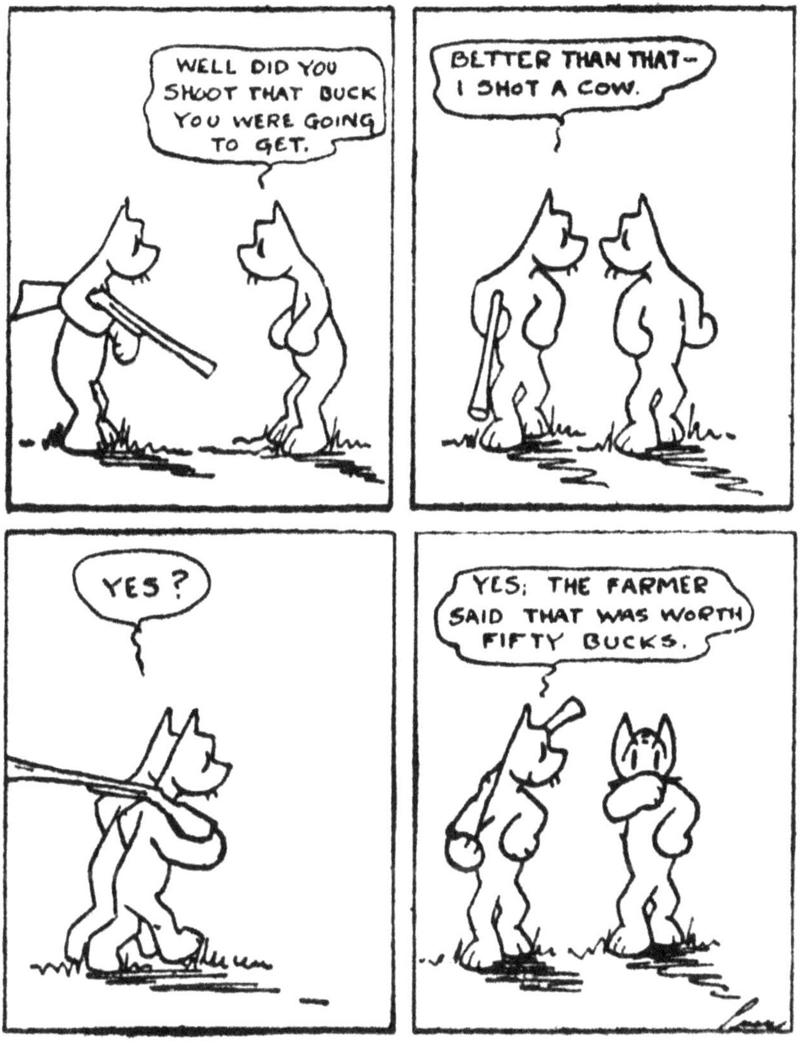
WELL DID YOU SHOOT THAT BUCK YOU WERE GOING TO GET.
BETTER THAN THAT— I SHOT A COW.
YES?
YES; THE FARMER SAID THAT WAS WORTH FIFTY BUCKS.

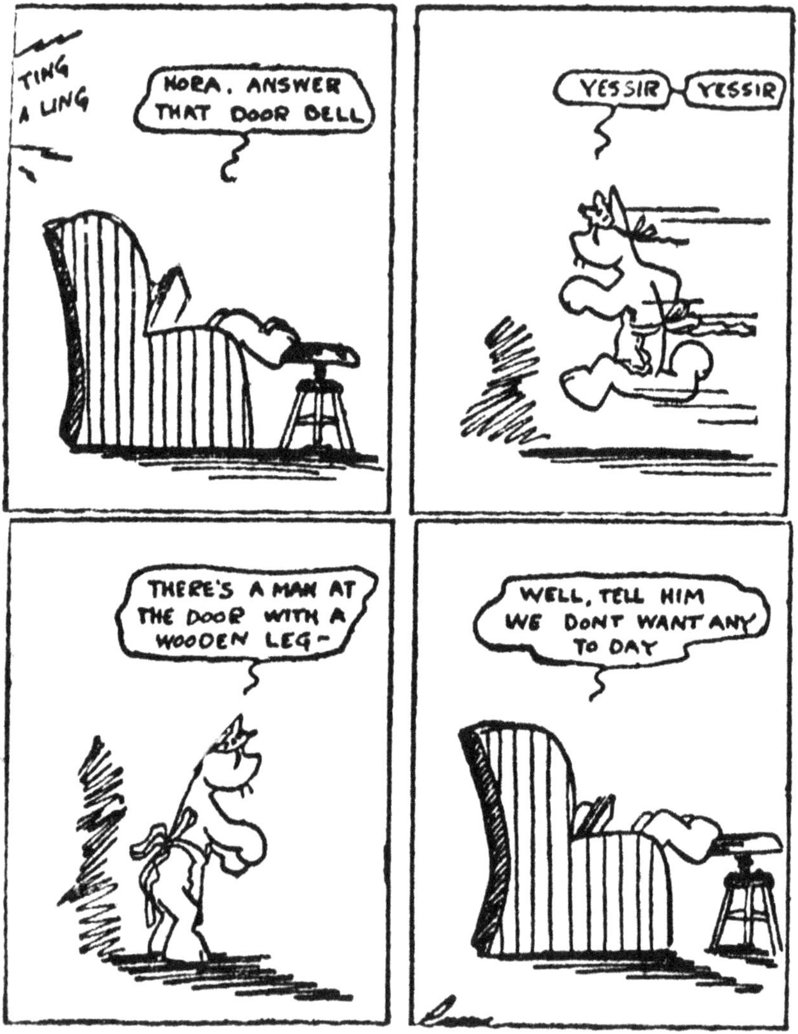
TING A LING
NORA, ANSWER THAT DOOR BELL
YESSIR
YESSIR
THERE'S A MAN AT THE DOOR WITH A WOODEN LEG-
WELL, TELL HIM WE DONT WANT ANY TO DAY

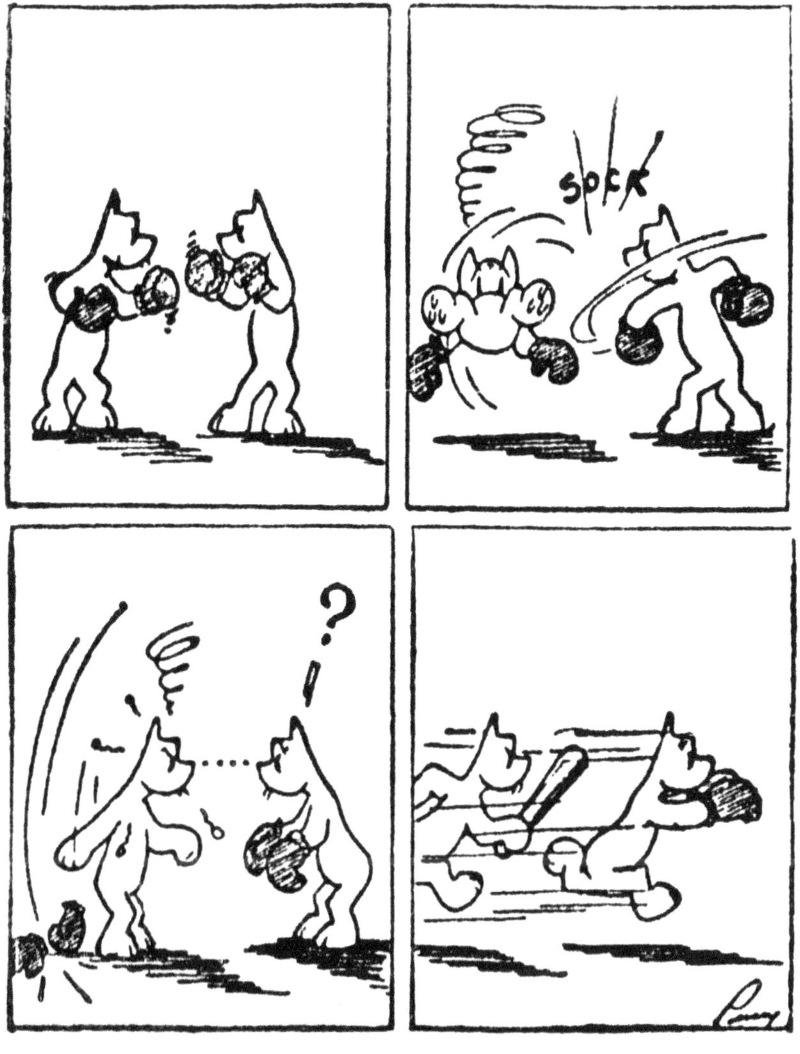
SOCK
?

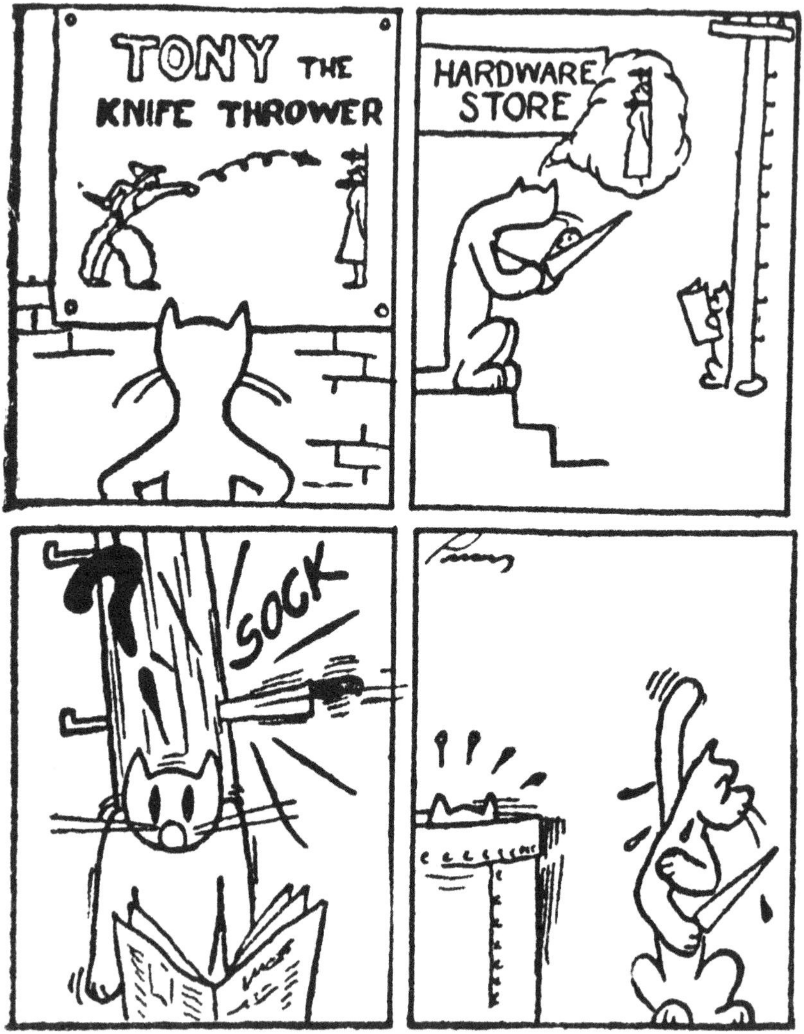
TONY THE
KNIFE THROWER
HARDWARE
STORE
SOCK

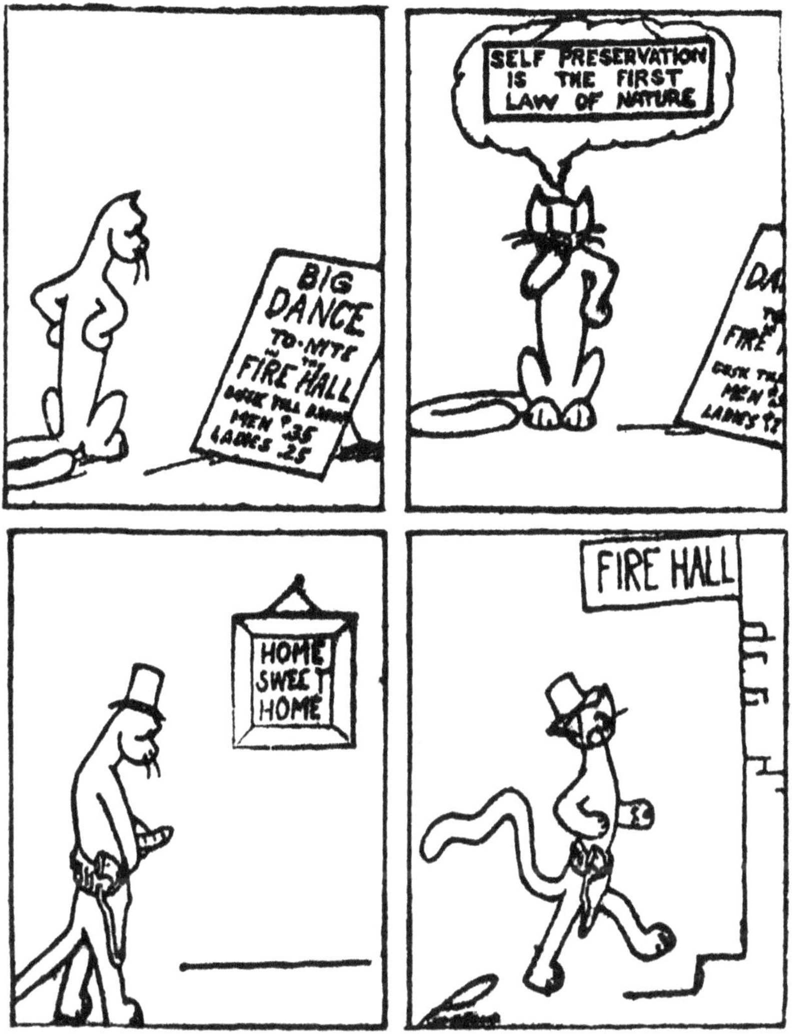
BIG
DANCE
TO-NITE
FIRE HALL
MEN .35
LADIES .25
SELF PRESERVATION
IS THE FIRST
LAW OF NATURE
HOME
SWEET
HOME
FIRE HALL

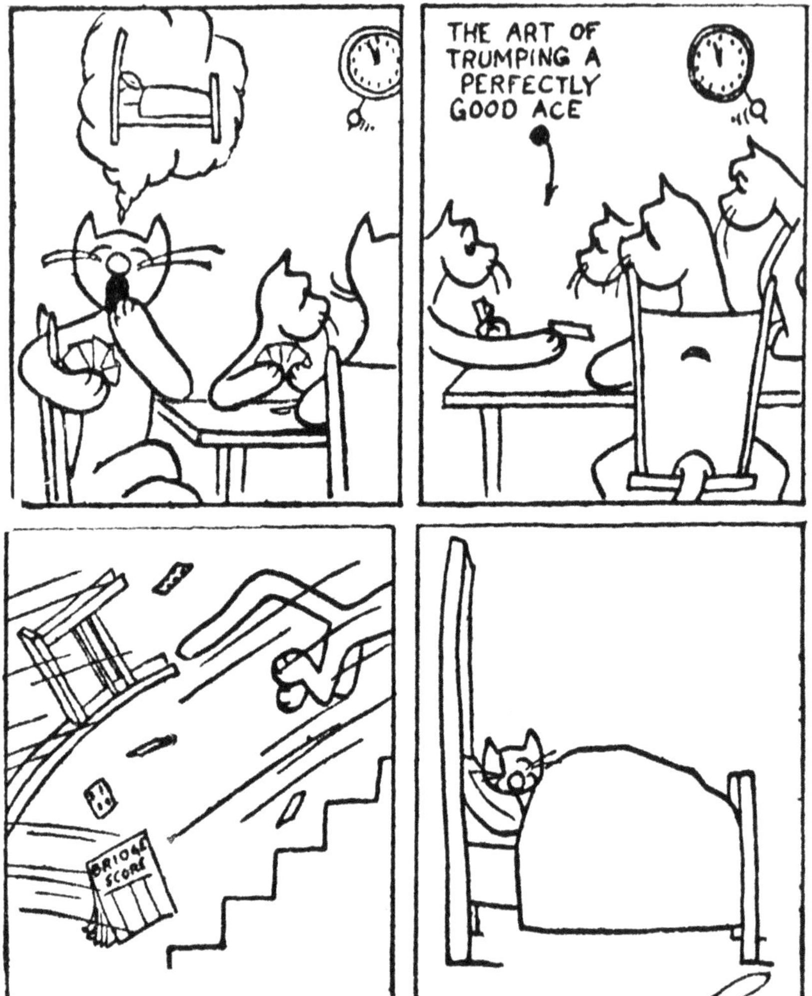
THE ART OF TRUMPING A PERFECTLY GOOD ACE
BRIDGE SCORE

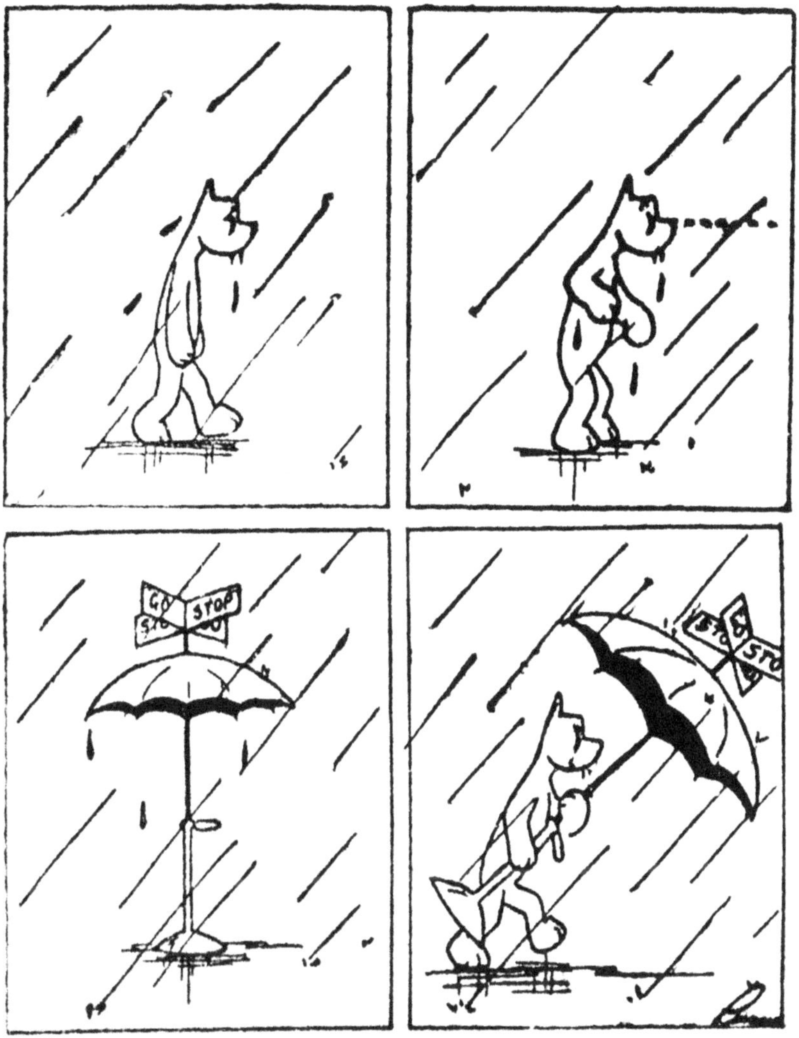
GO
STOP

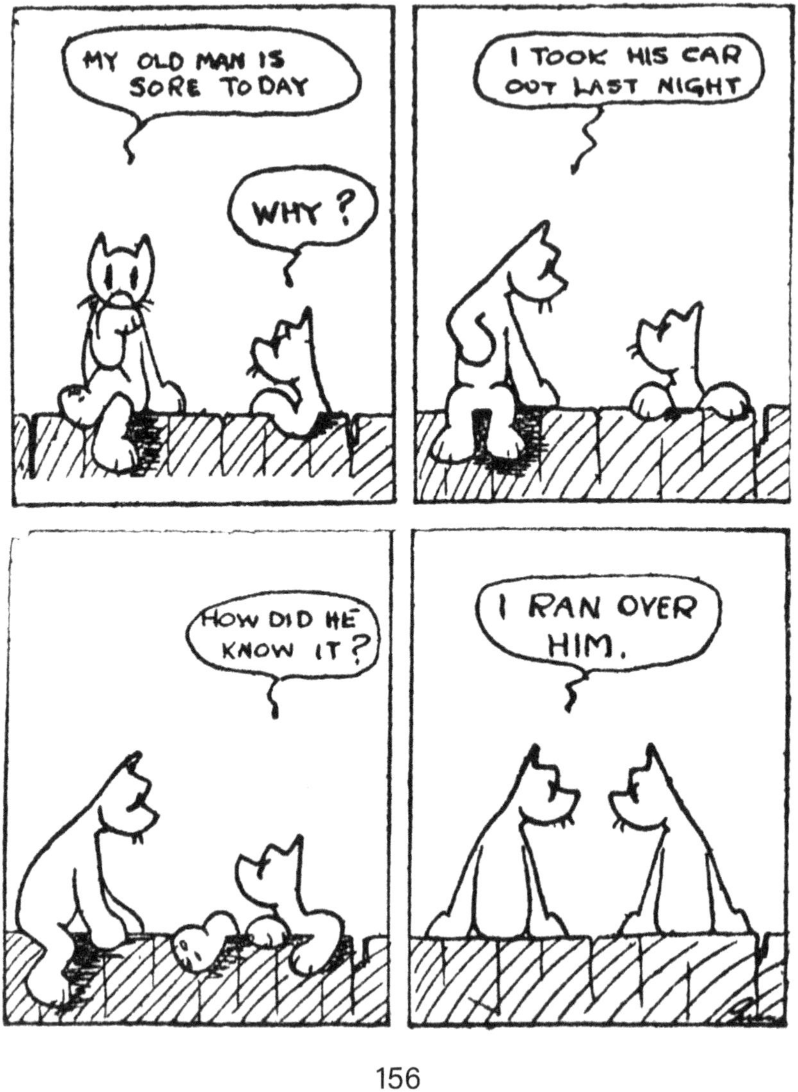
MY OLD MAN IS SORE TODAY
WHY?
I TOOK HIS CAR OUT LAST NIGHT
HOW DID HE KNOW IT?
I RAN OVER HIM.

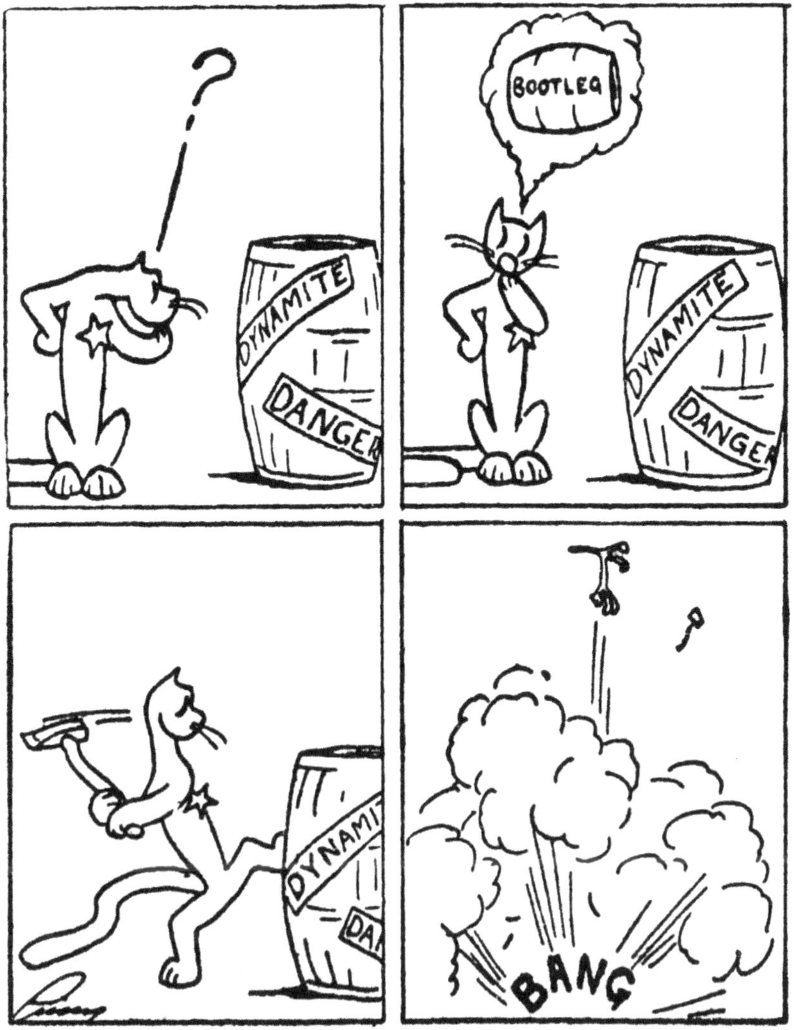
?
BOOTLEG
DYNAMITE
DANGER
DYNAMITE
DANGER
BANG

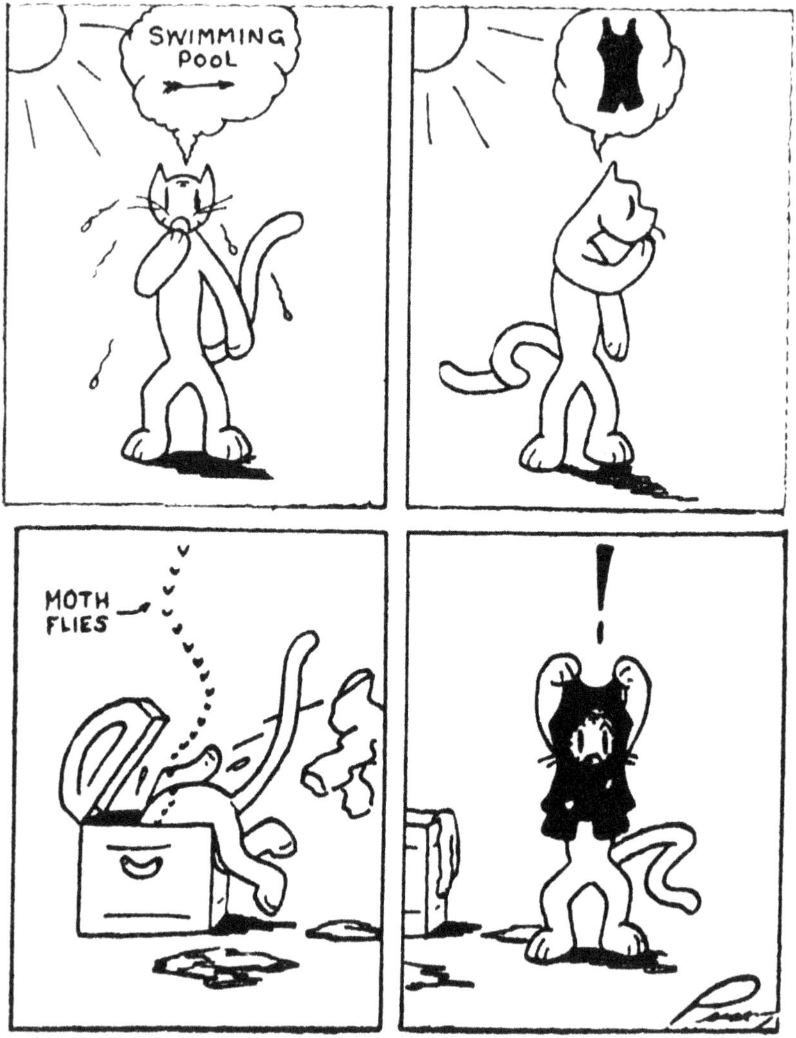
SWIMMING
POOL
MOTH
FLIES
!

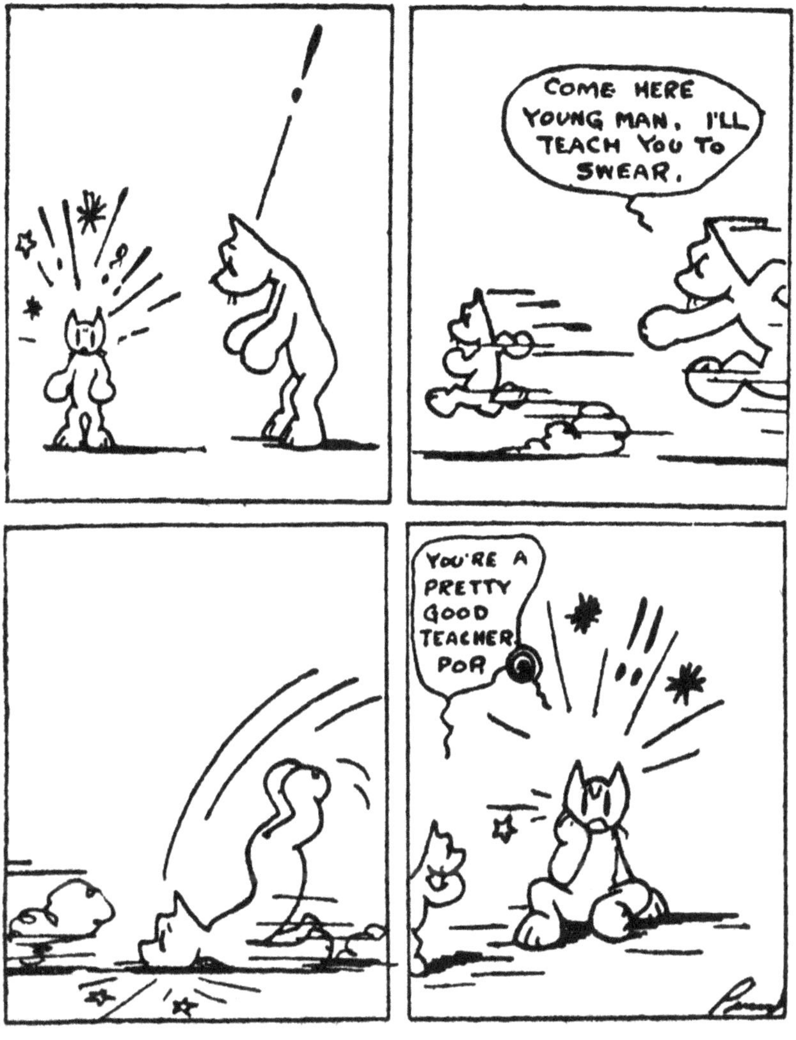
COME HERE YOUNG MAN, I'LL TEACH YOU TO SWEAR.
YOU'RE A PRETTY GOOD TEACHER POP

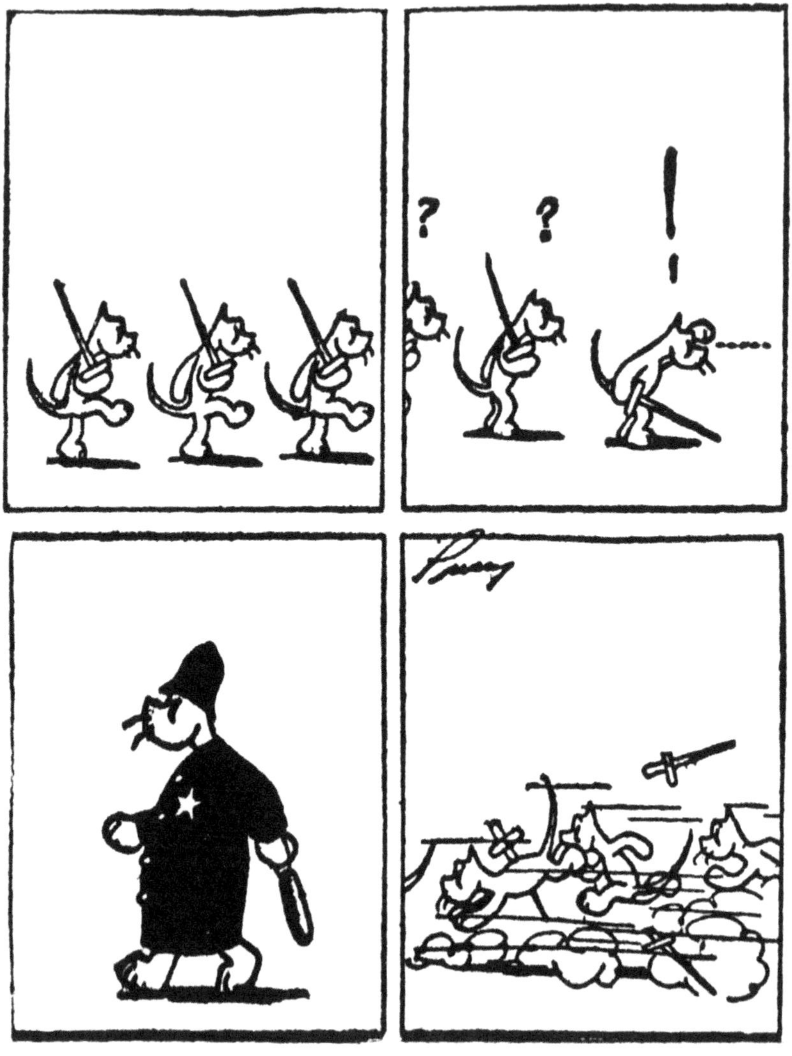
?
?
!

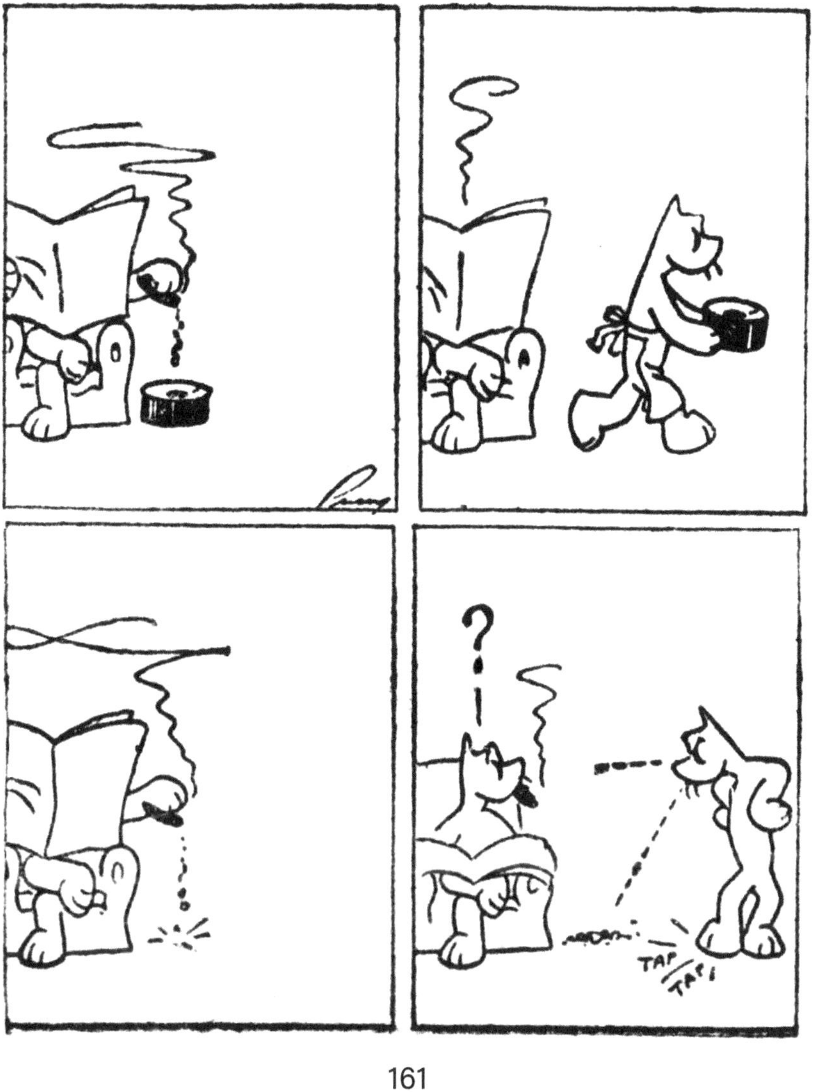
?
TAP
TAP!

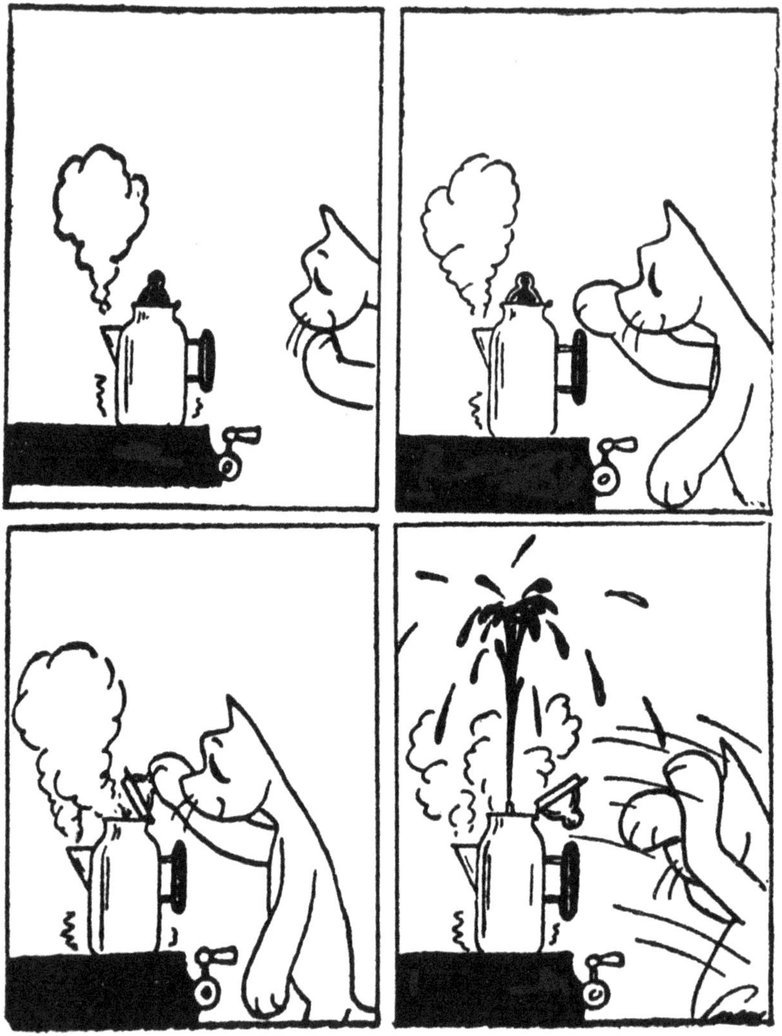

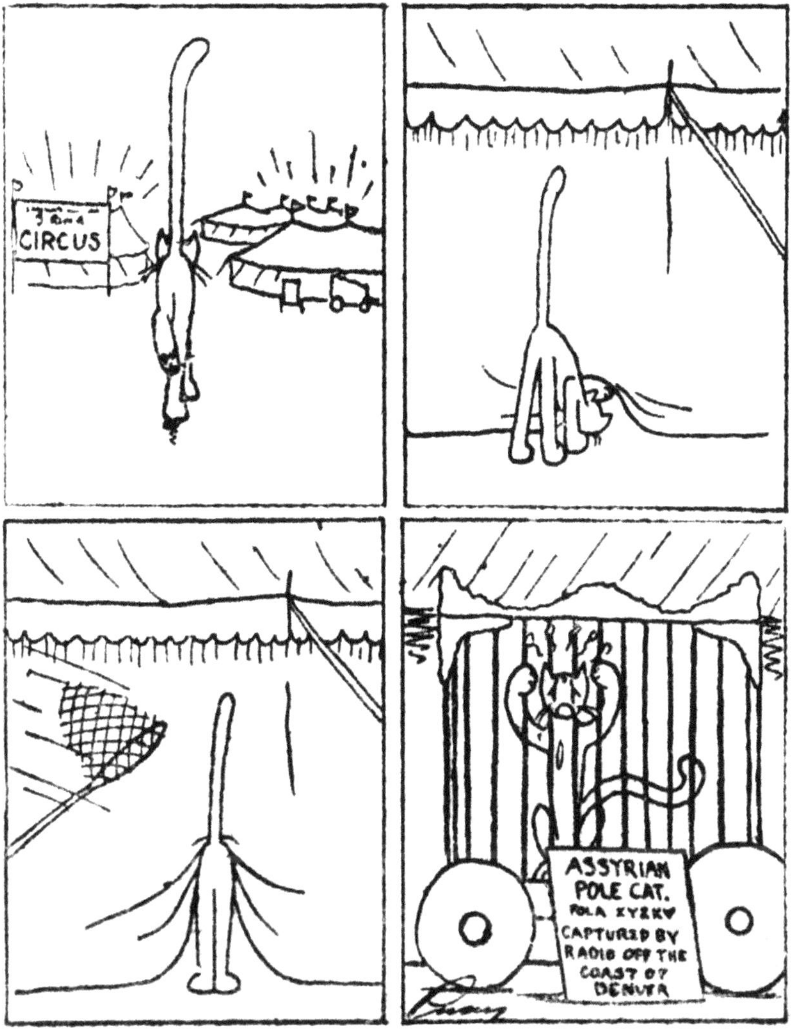
CIRCUS
ASSYRIAN
POLE CAT.
CAPTURED BY
RADIO OFF THE
COAST OF
DENVER

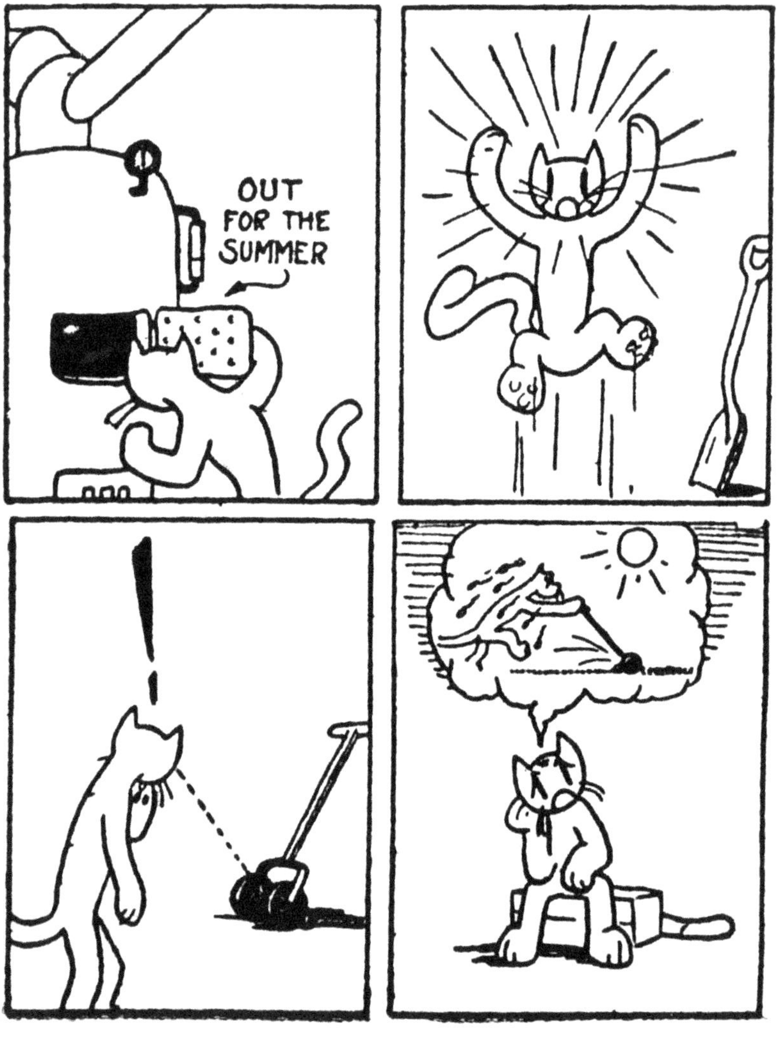
OUT FOR THE SUMMER
!

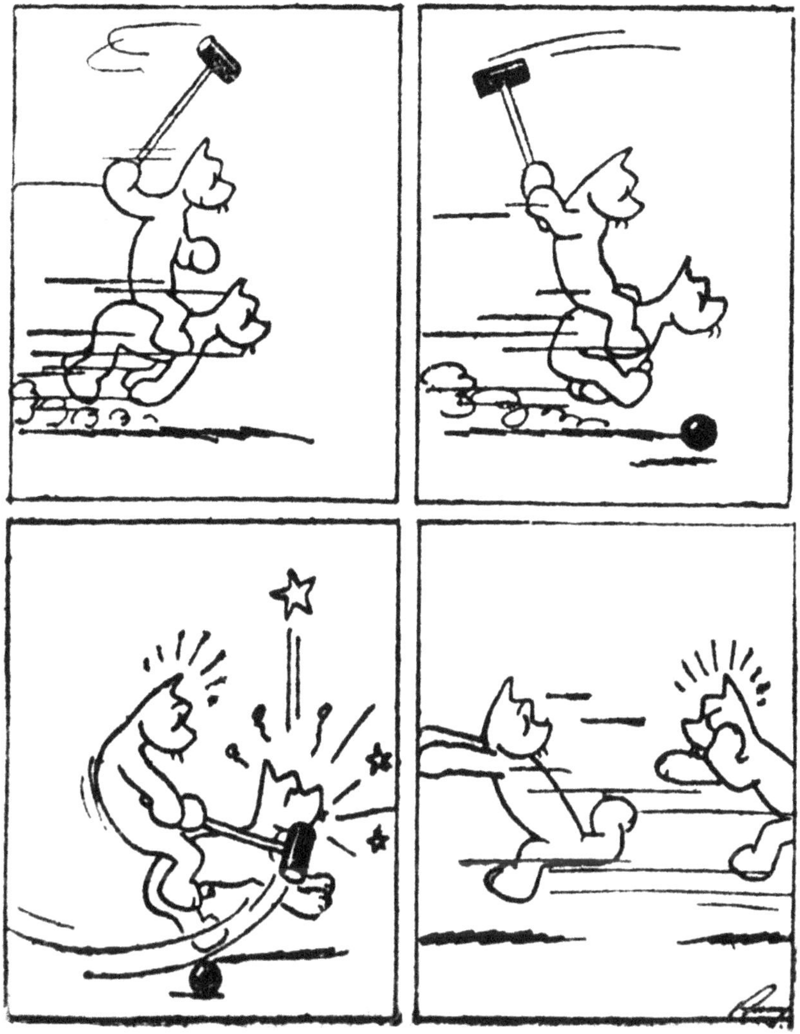

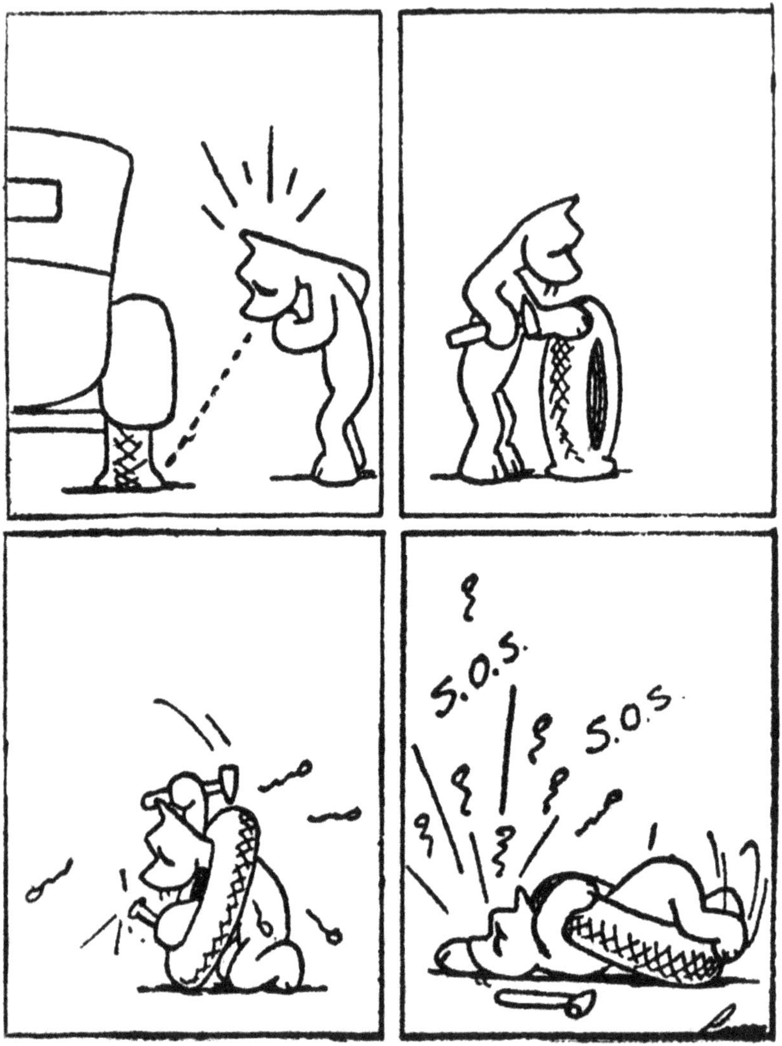
S.O.S.
S.O.S.

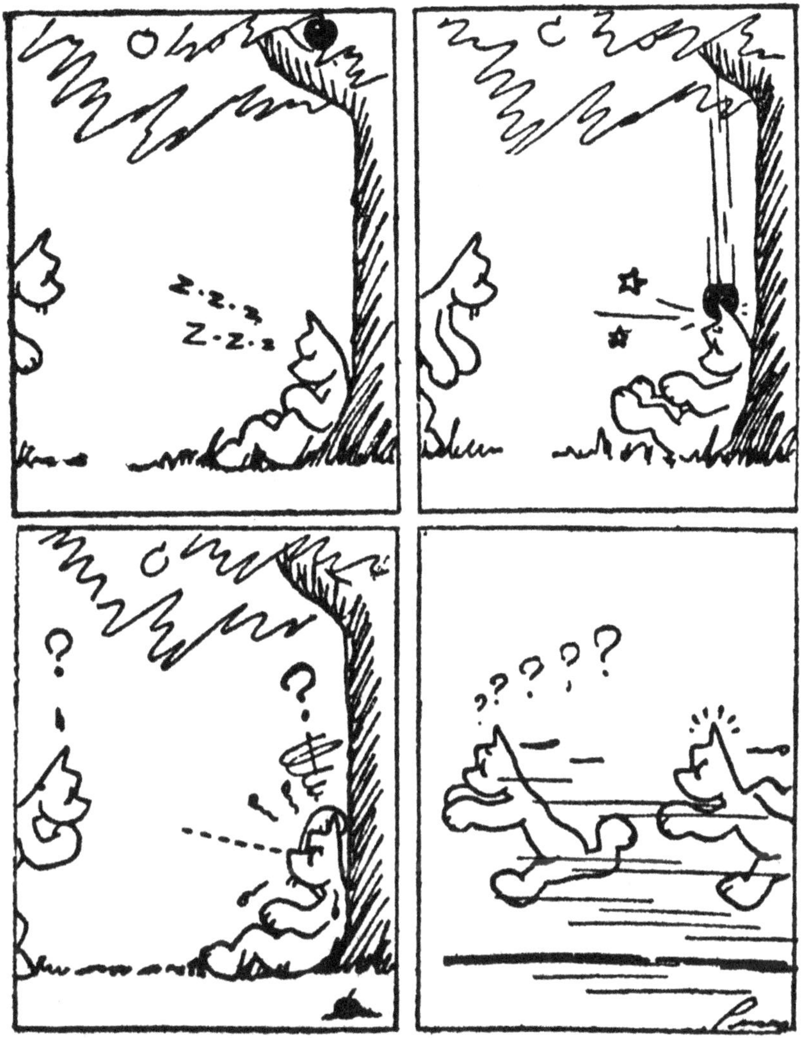
Z-Z-Z
Z-Z-Z

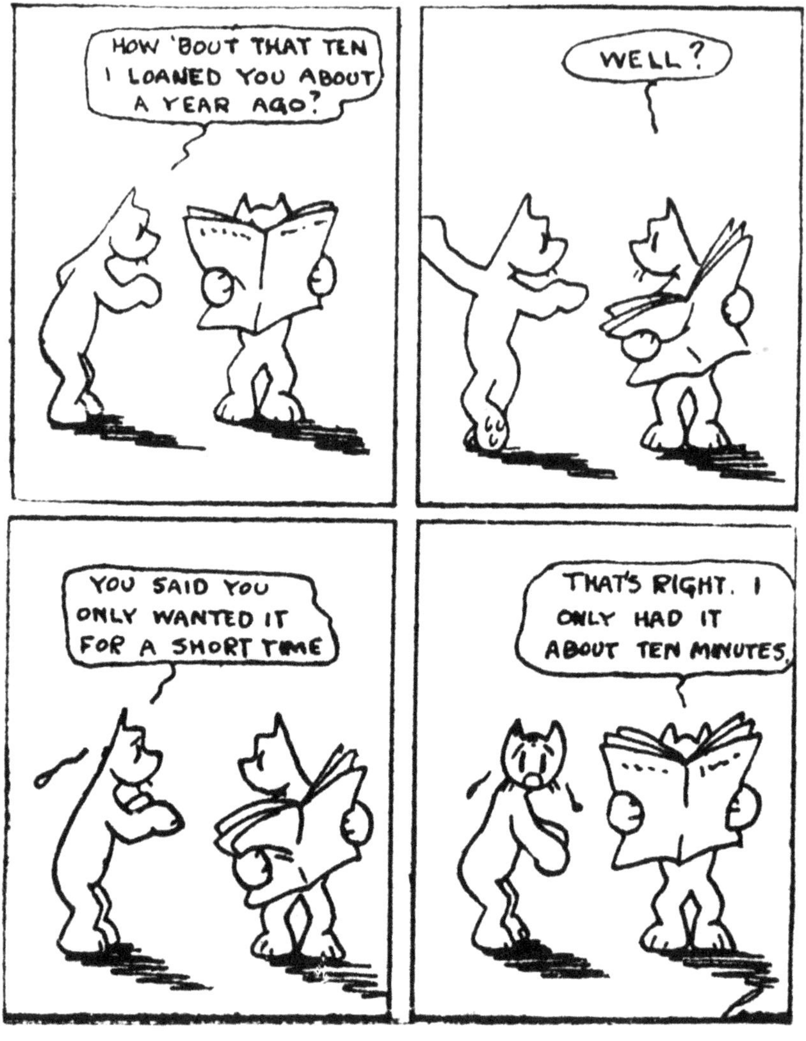
HOW 'BOUT THAT TEN I LOANED YOU ABOUT A YEAR AGO?
WELL?
YOU SAID YOU ONLY WANTED IT FOR A SHORT TIME
THAT'S RIGHT. I ONLY HAD IT ABOUT TEN MINUTES.

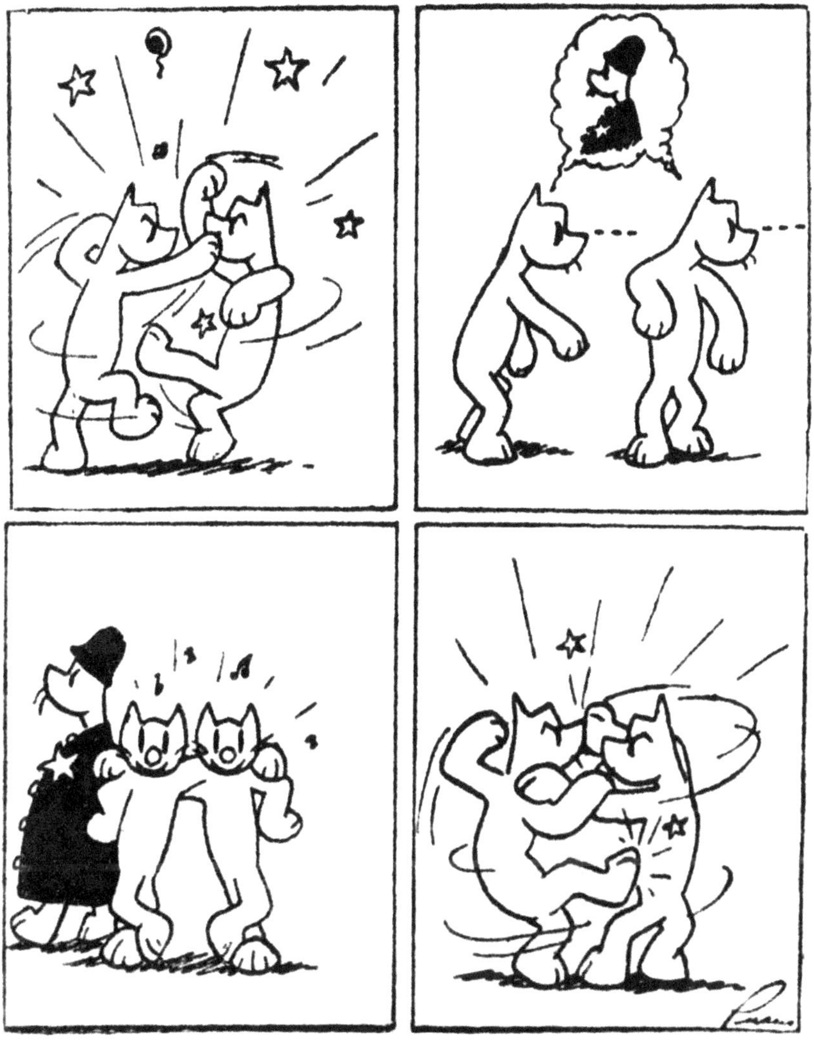

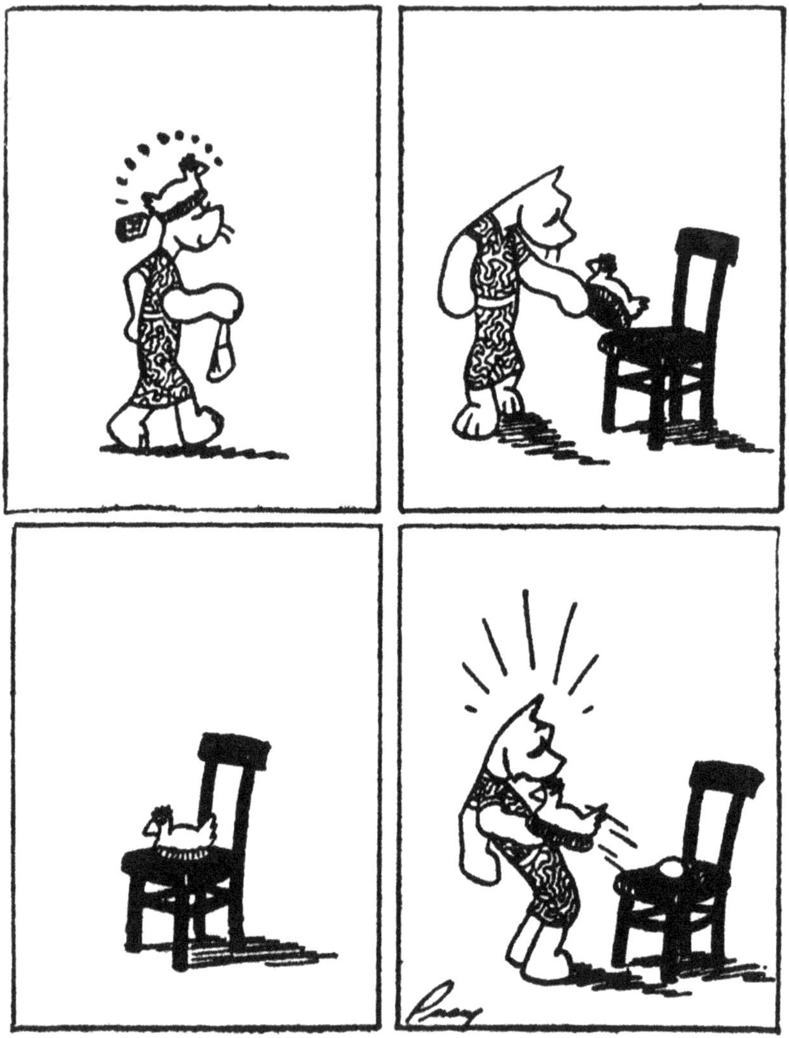

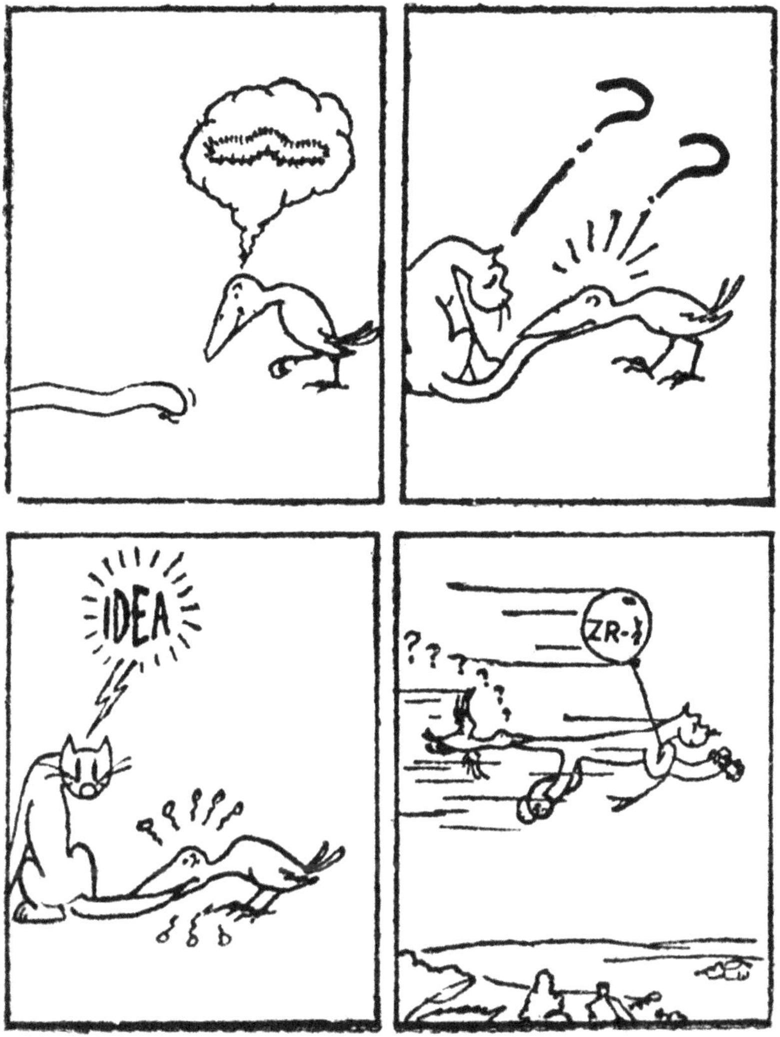
IDEA
ZR-1

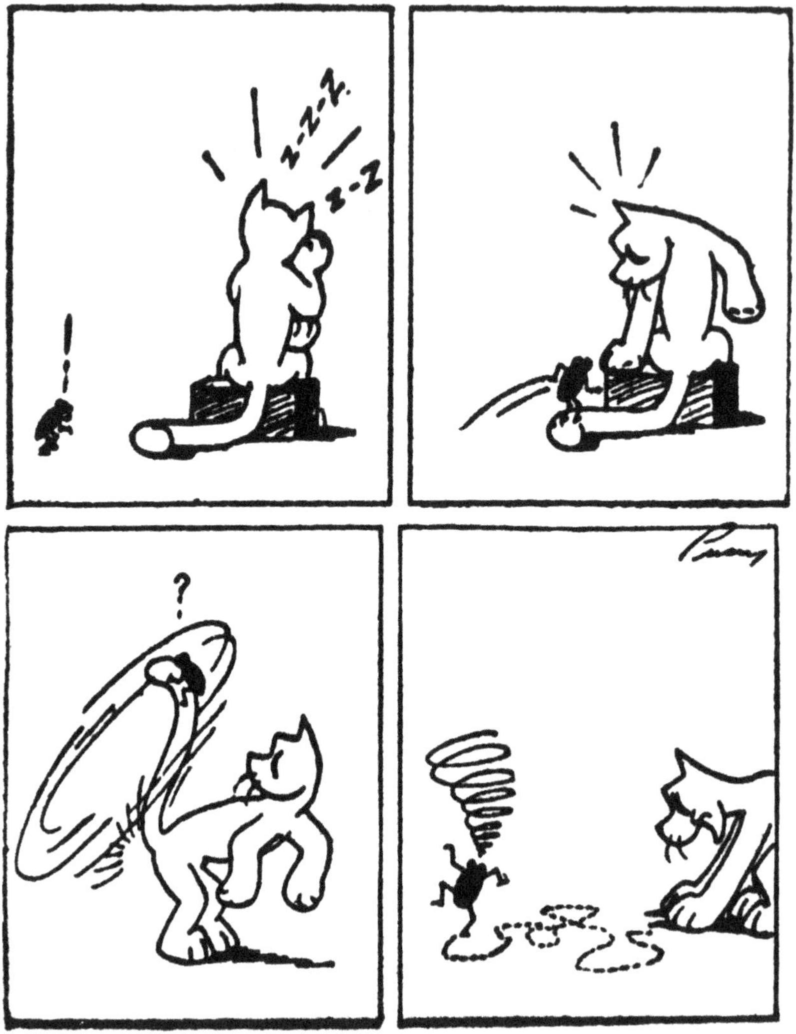
z-z-z.
z-z
!
?

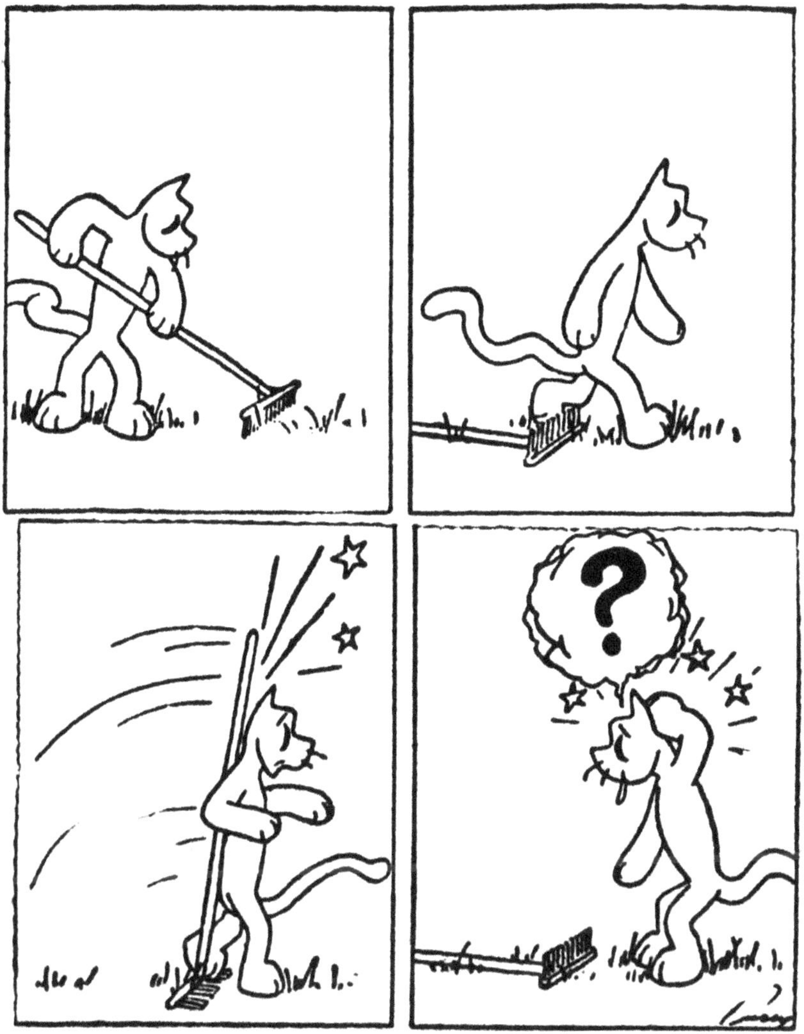
?

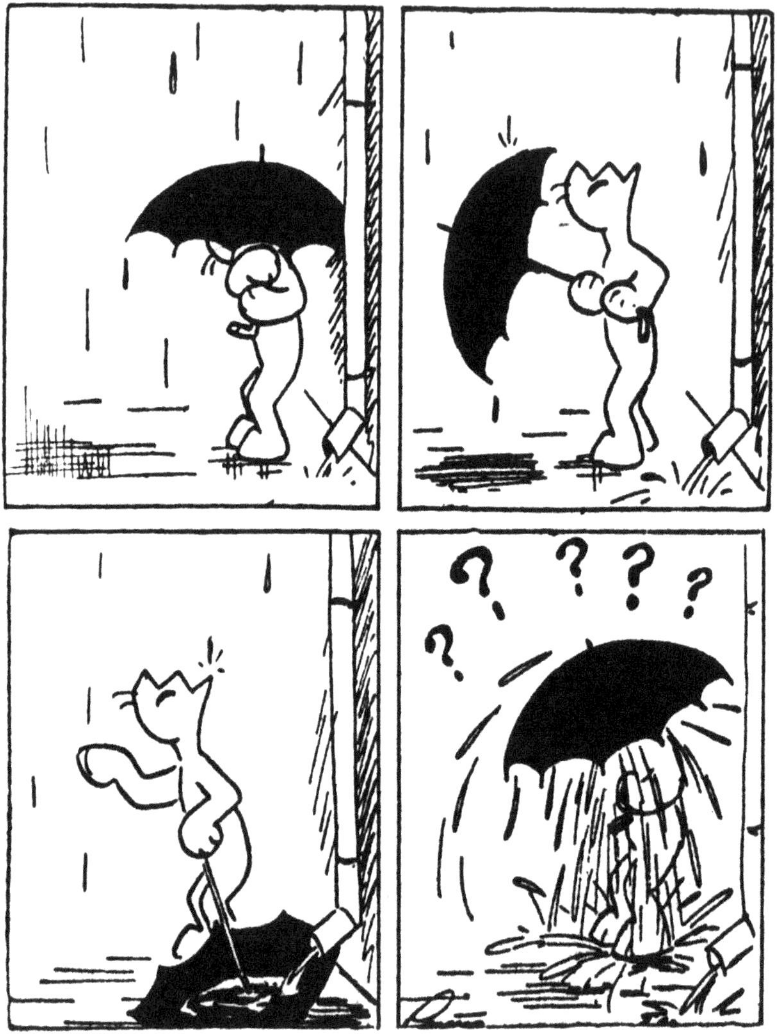
? ? ? ? ?

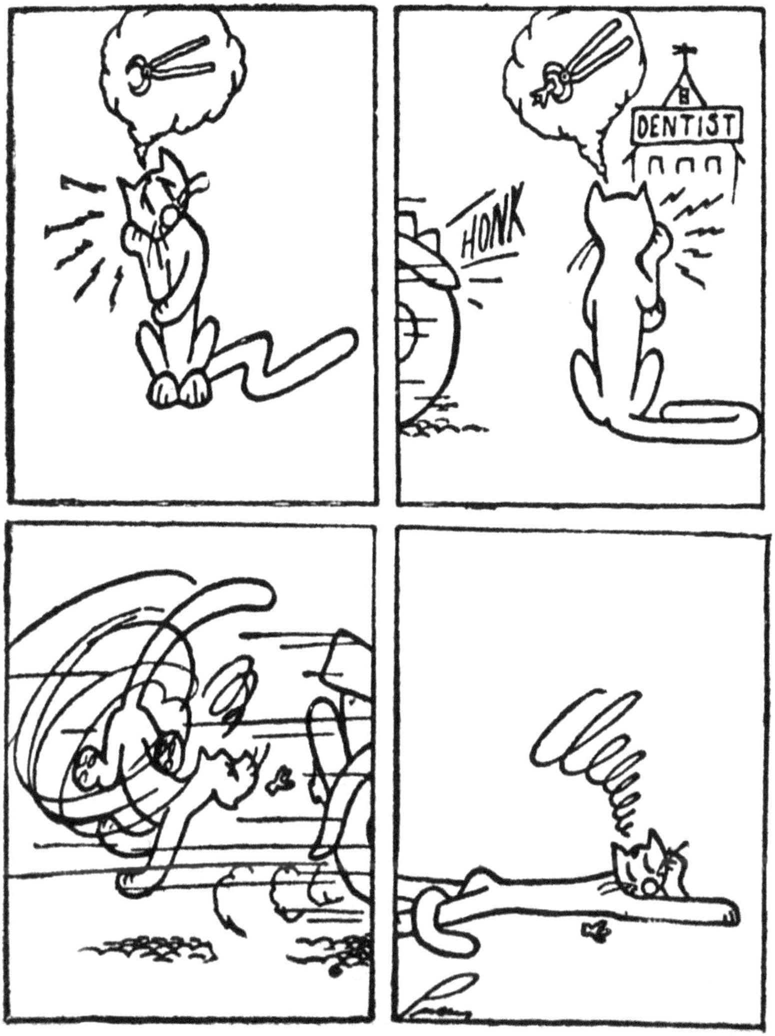
HONK
DENTIST

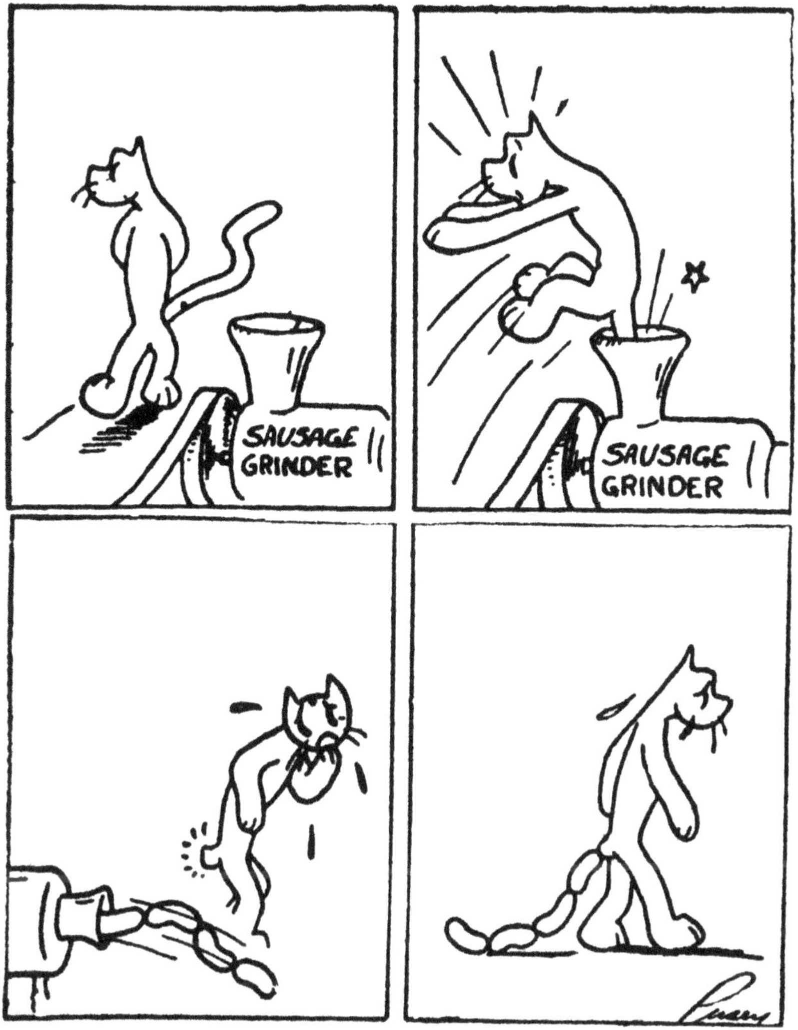
SAUSAGE
GRINDER
SAUSAGE
GRINDER

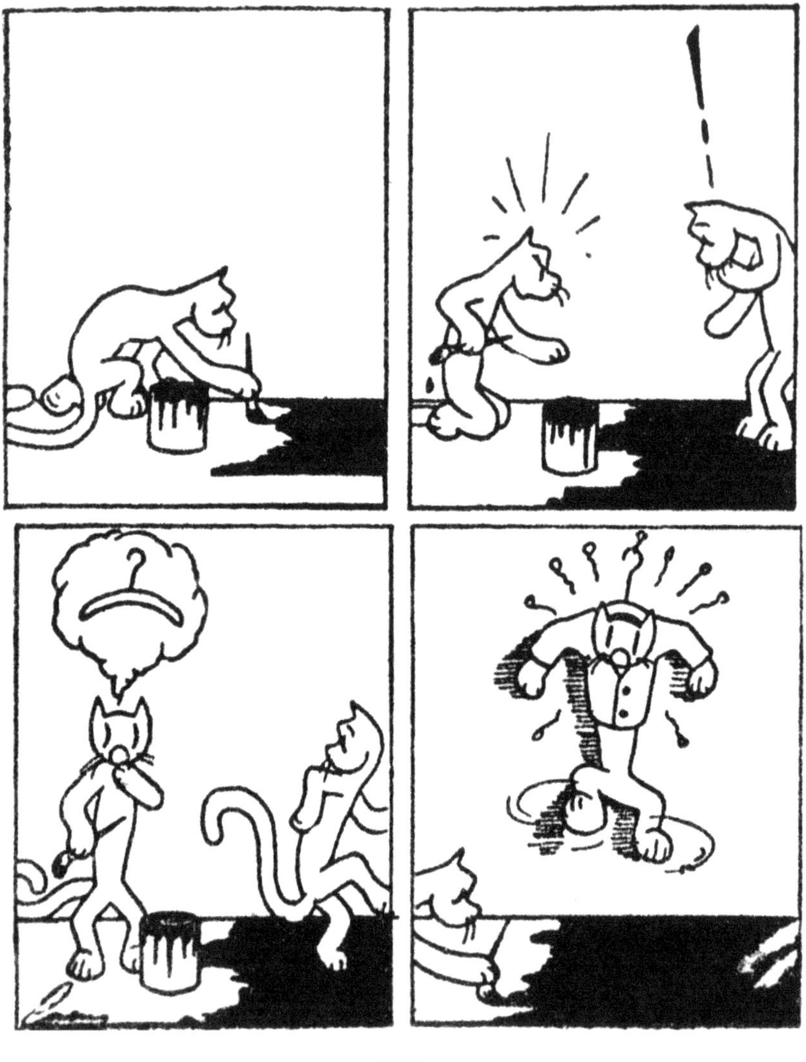

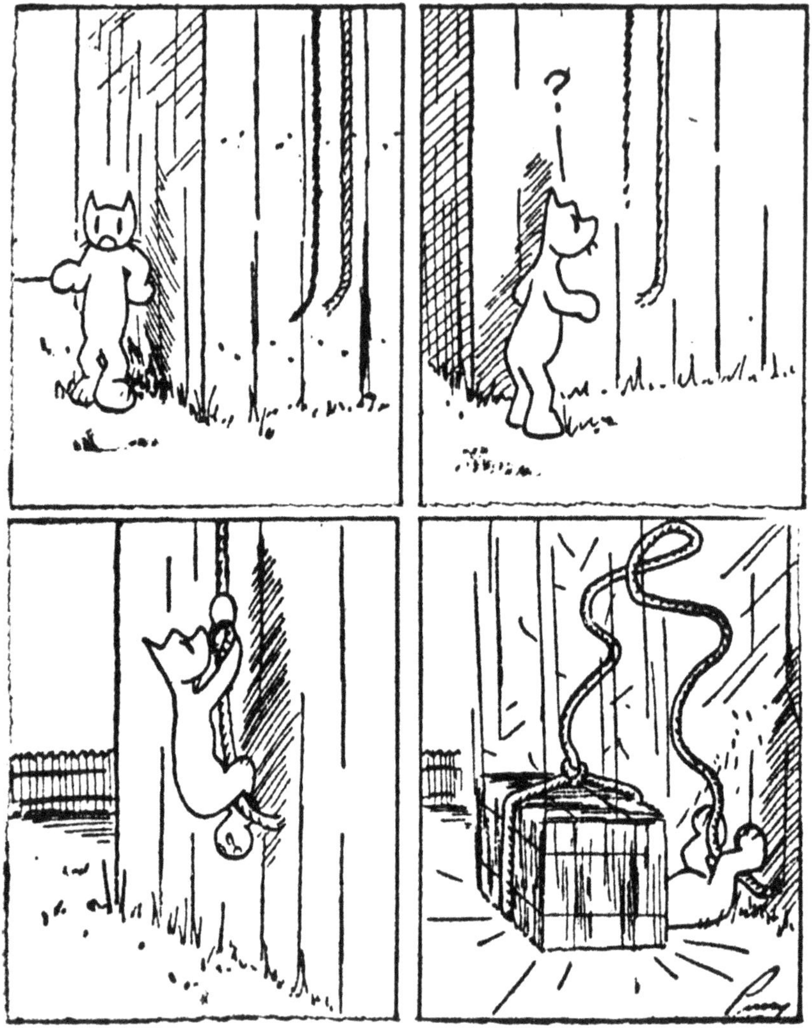
?

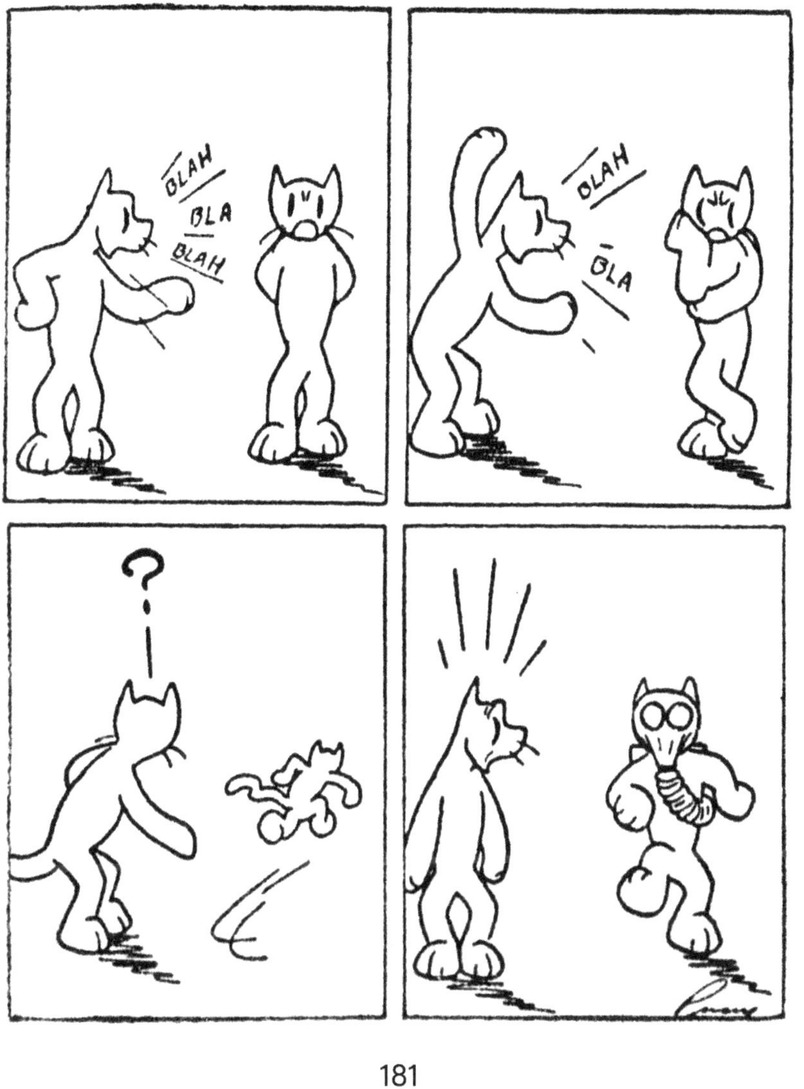
BLAH
BLA
BLAH
BLAH
BLA
?

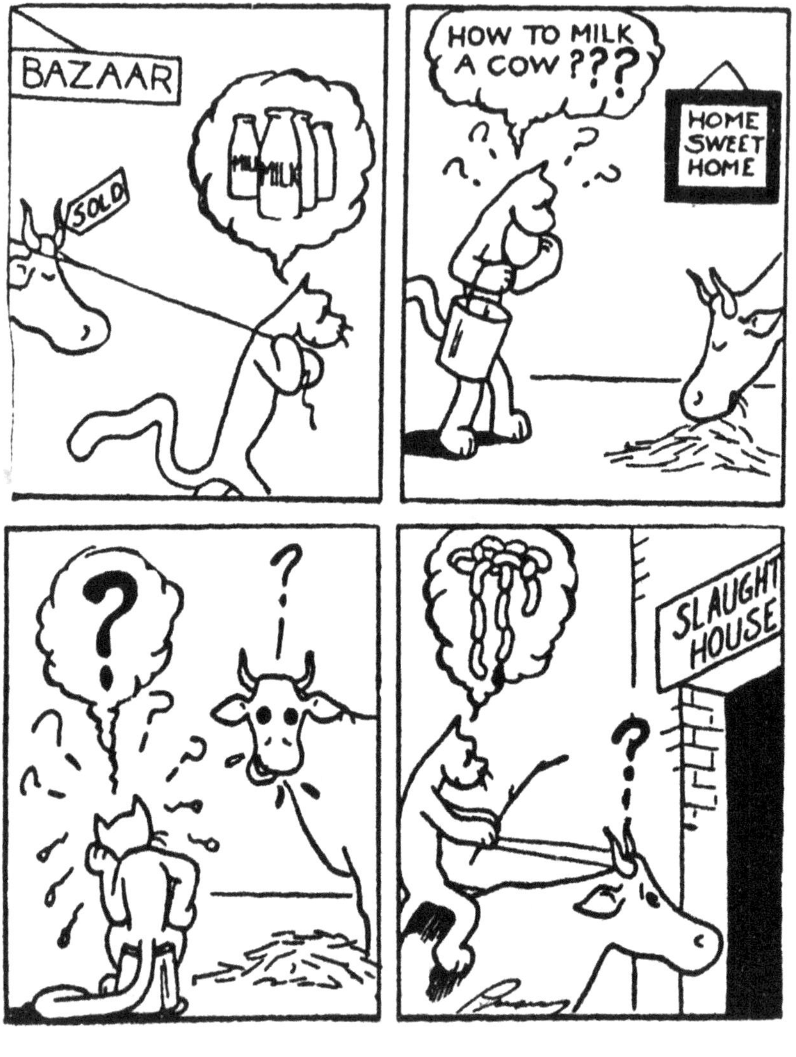
BAZAAR
SOLD
MILK
MILK
HOW TO MILK A COW???
HOME SWEET HOME
SLAUGHT HOUSE

KKK

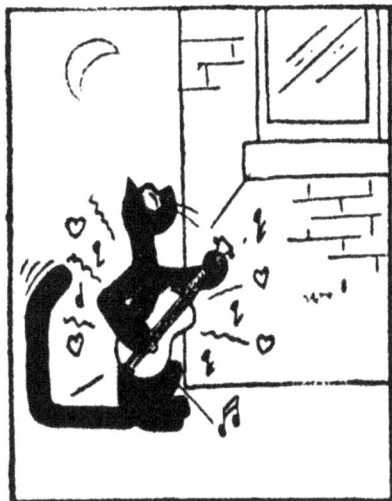

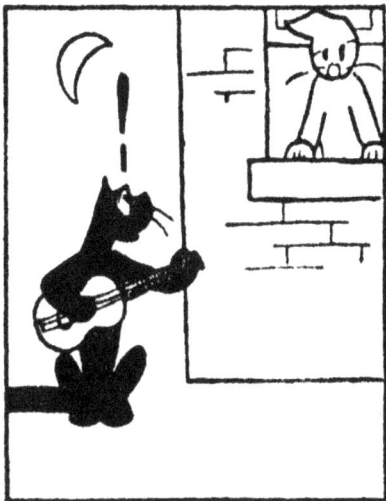

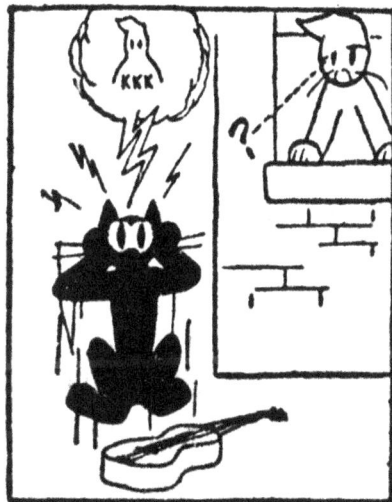

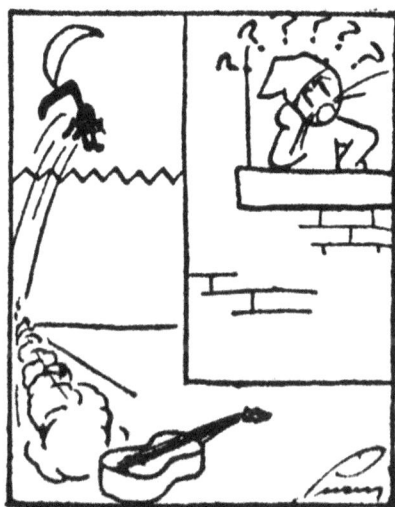

BALLOON TIRES
?

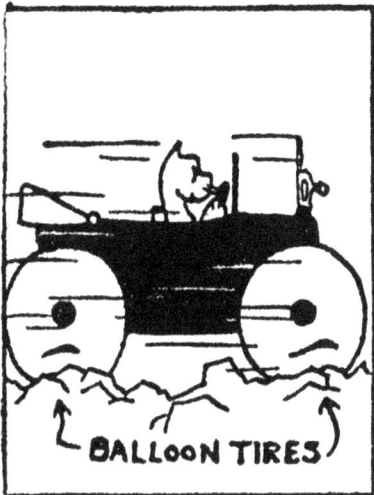

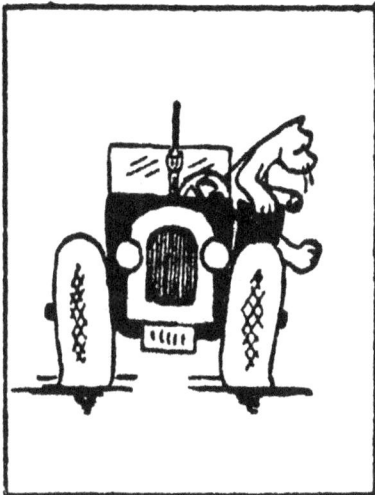

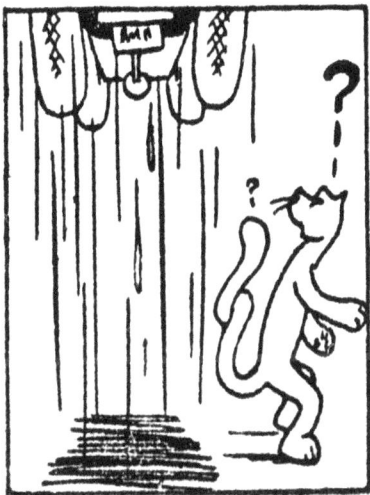

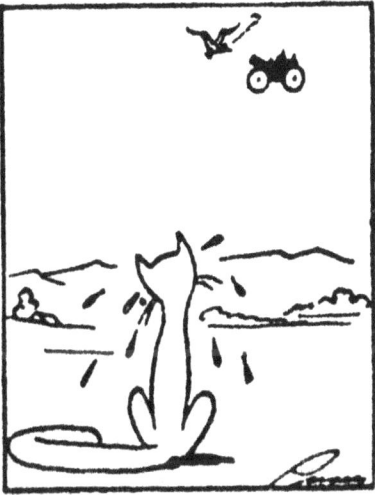

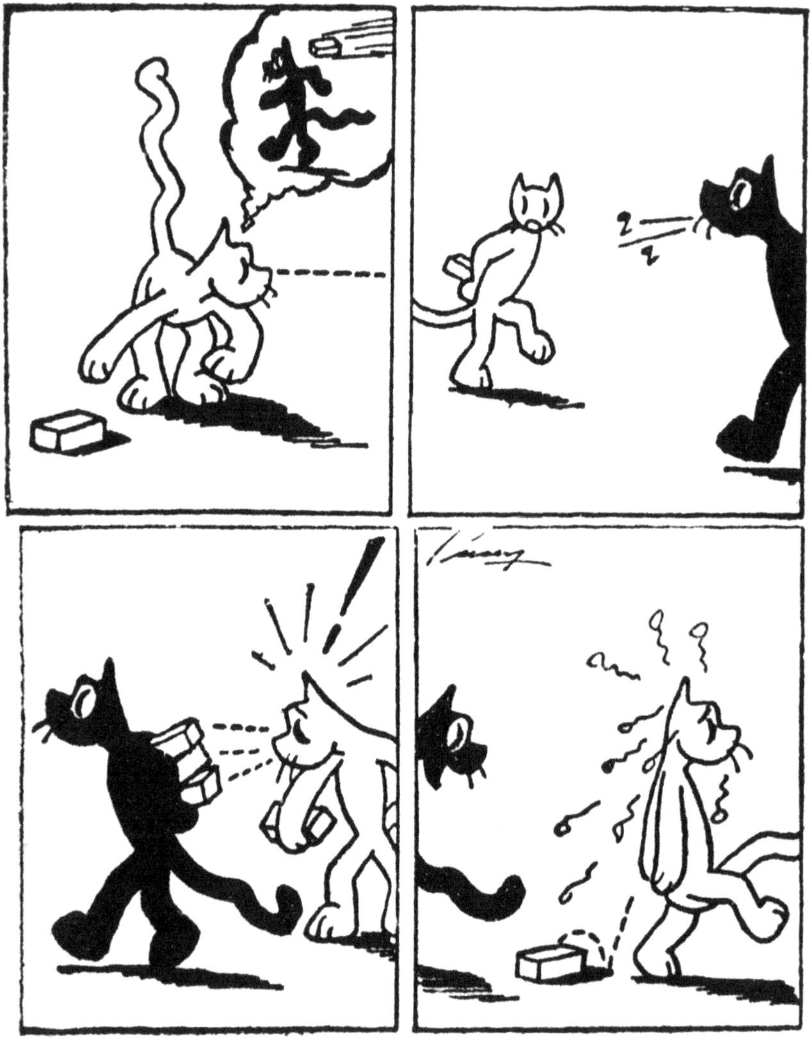

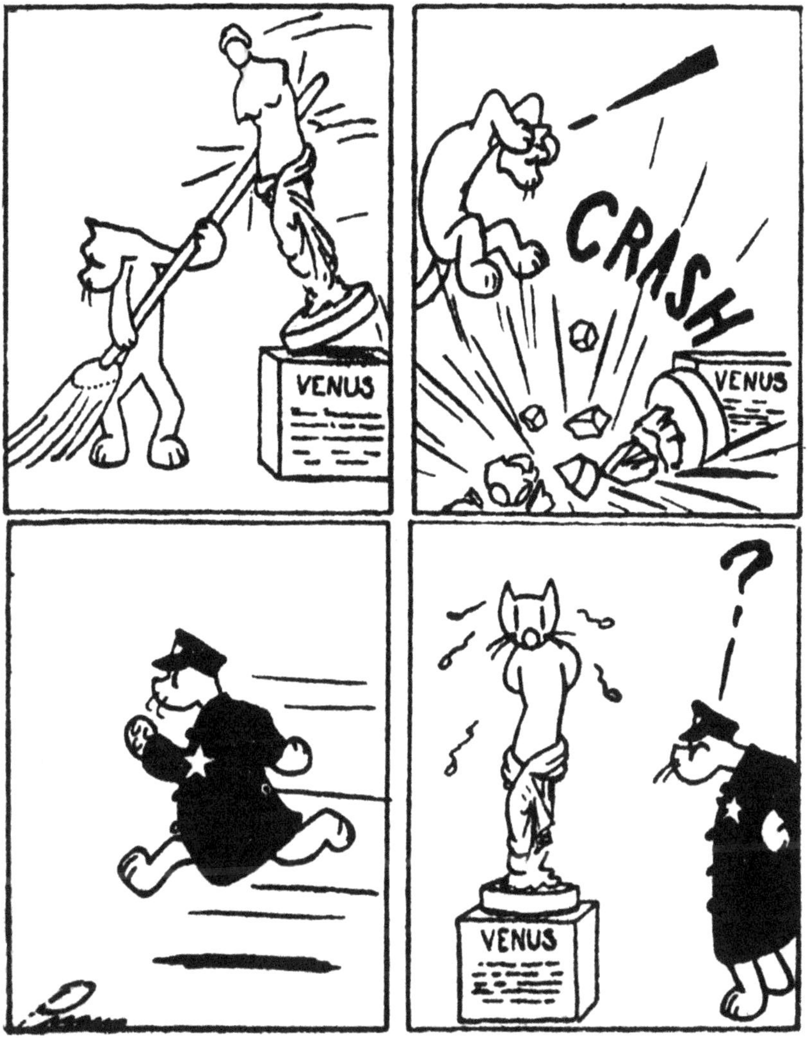
VENUS
CRASH
VENUS
?
VENUS

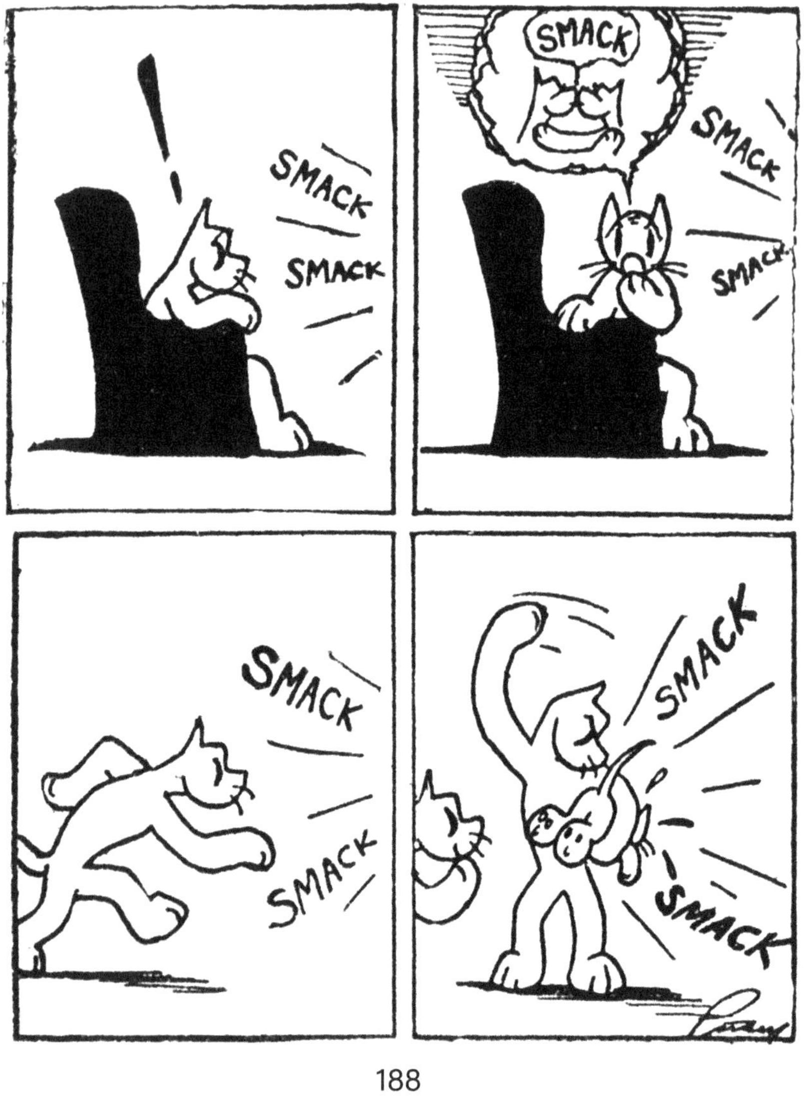
!
SMACK
SMACK
SMACK
SMACK
SMACK
SMACK
SMACK
SMACK
SMACK

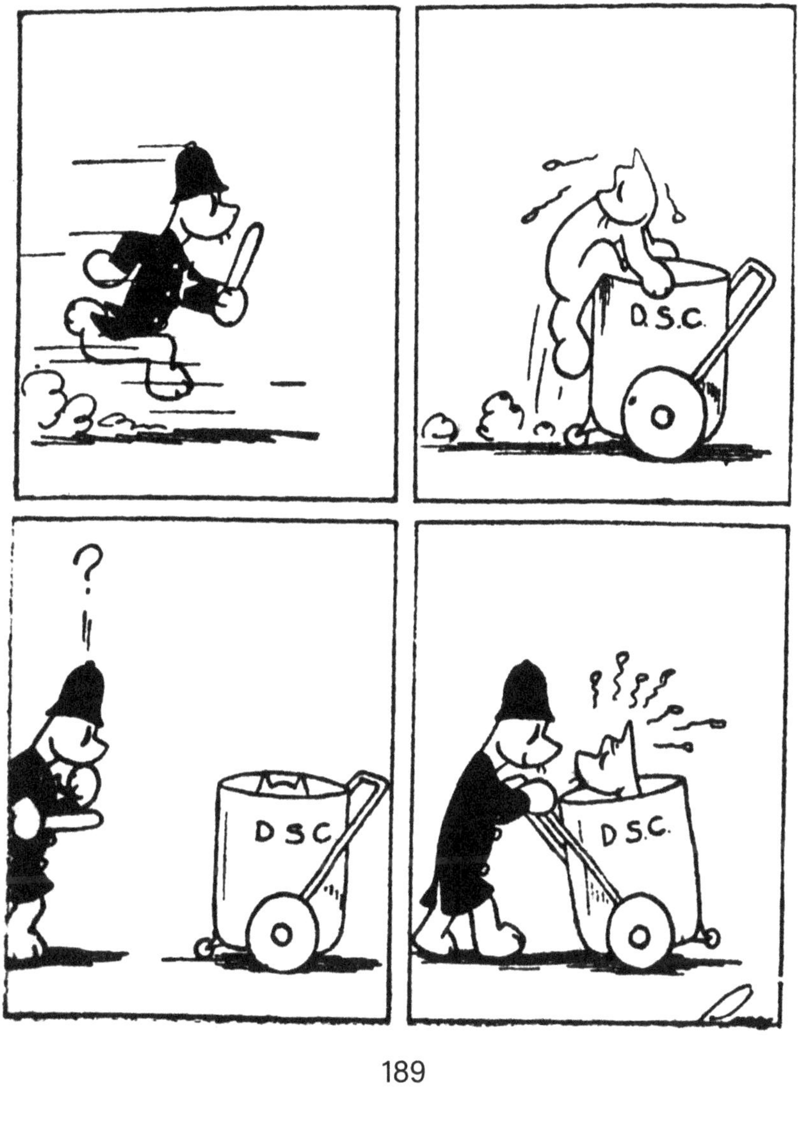
D.S.C.
?
DSC.
DSC.

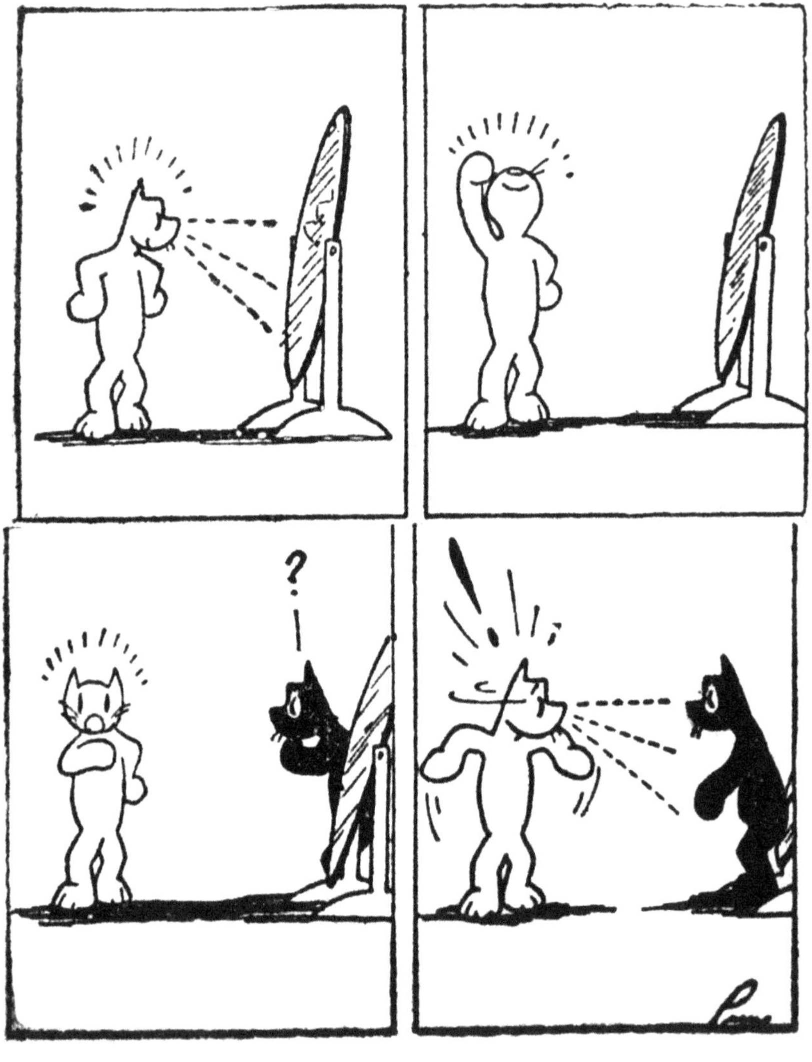

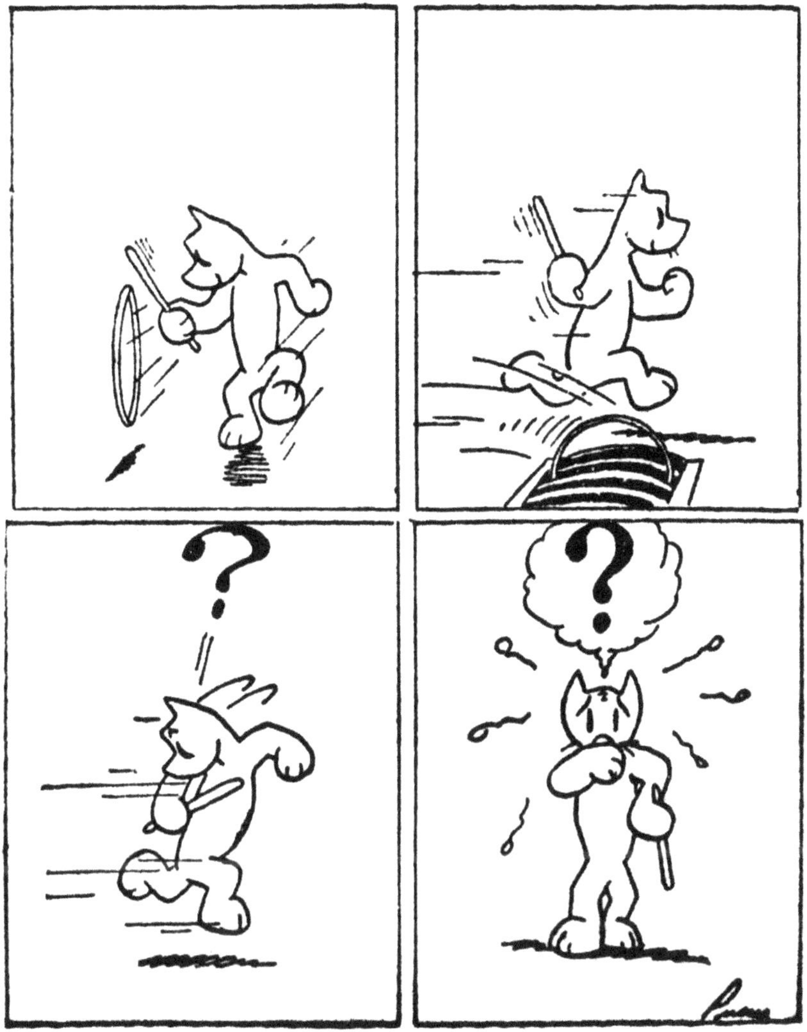

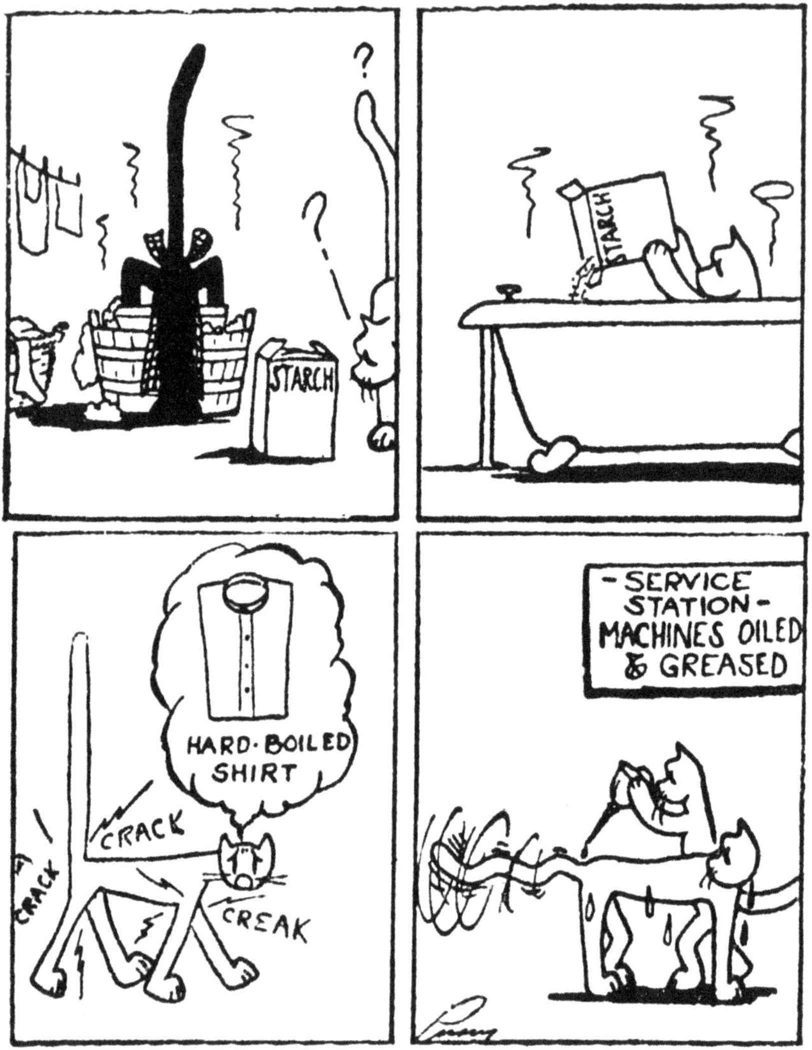
?
?
STARCH
STARCH
HARD·BOILED SHIRT
CRACK
CRACK
CREAK
-SERVICE STATION-
MACHINES OILED & GREASED

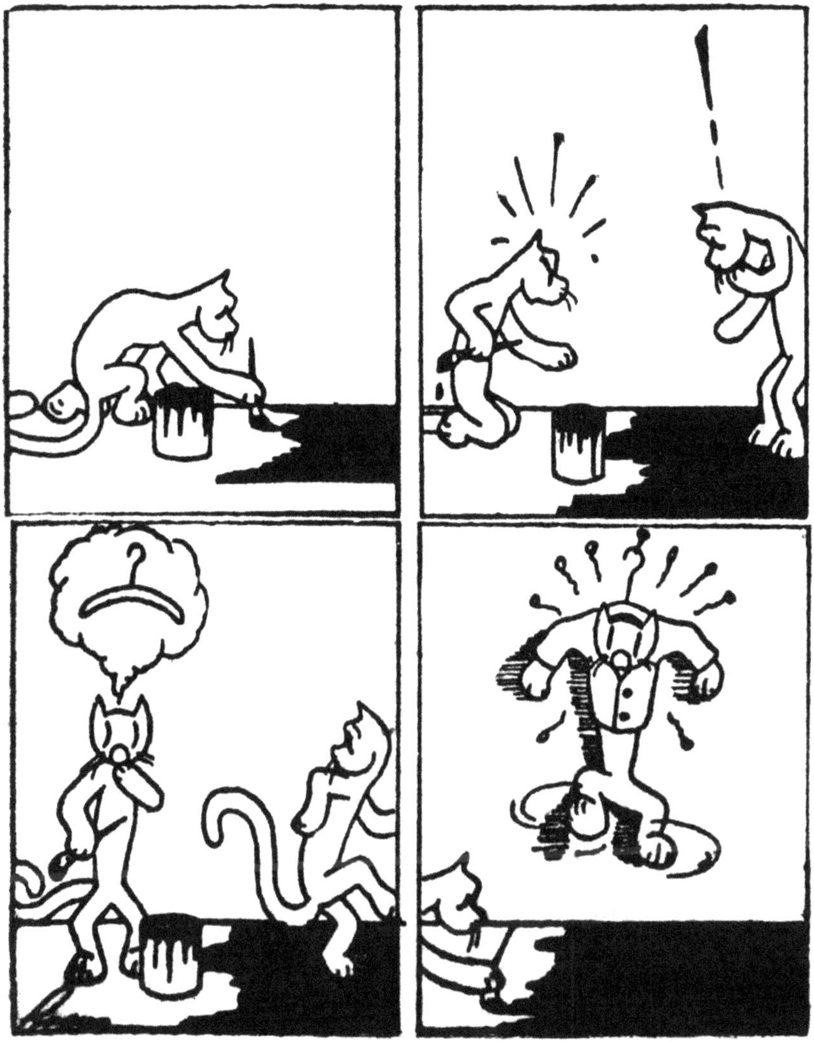

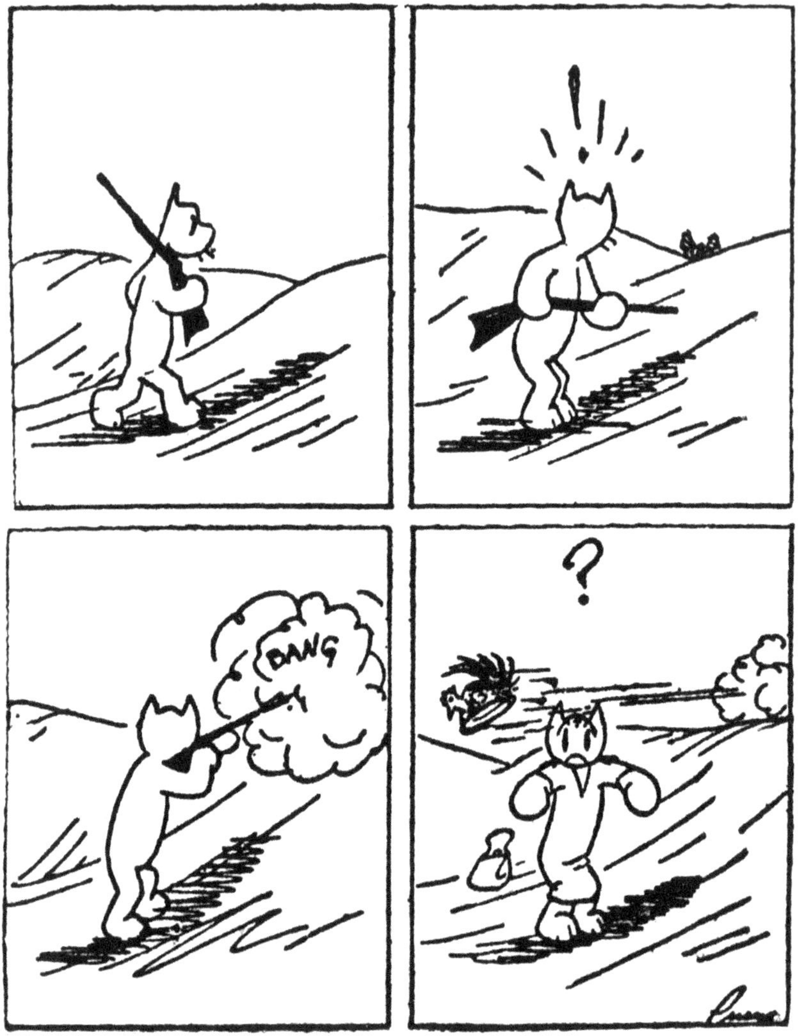
!
DANG
?

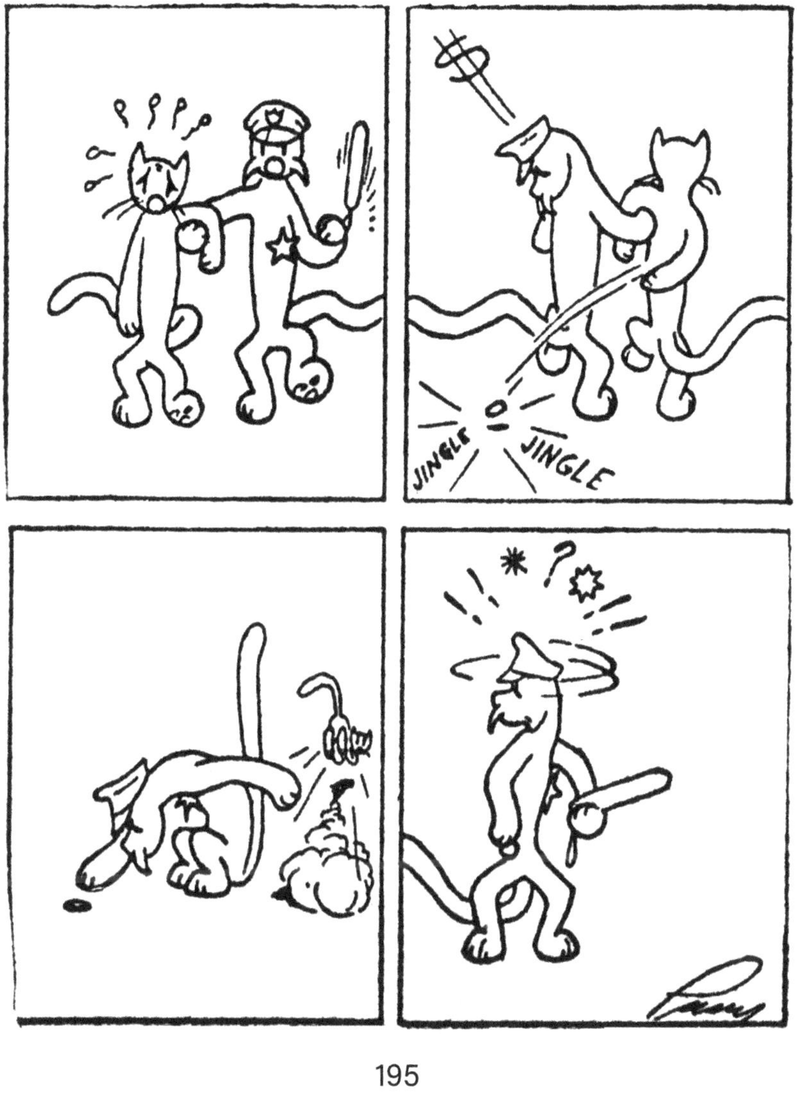
JINGLE
JINGLE

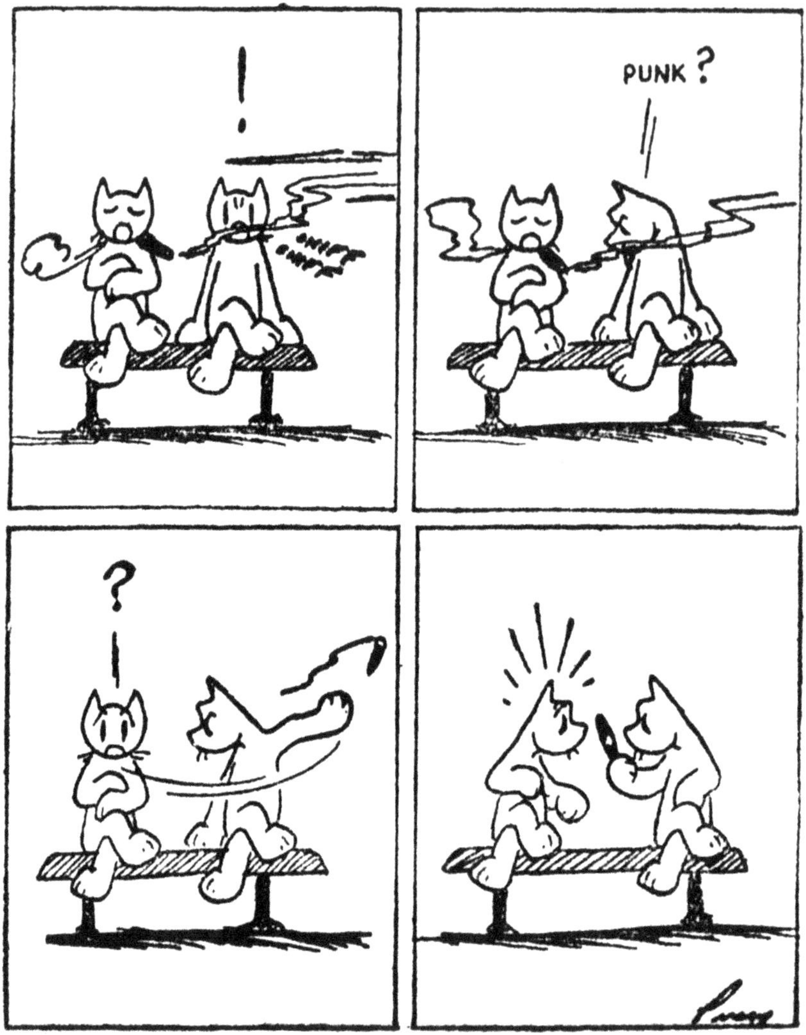
!
PUNK?
?

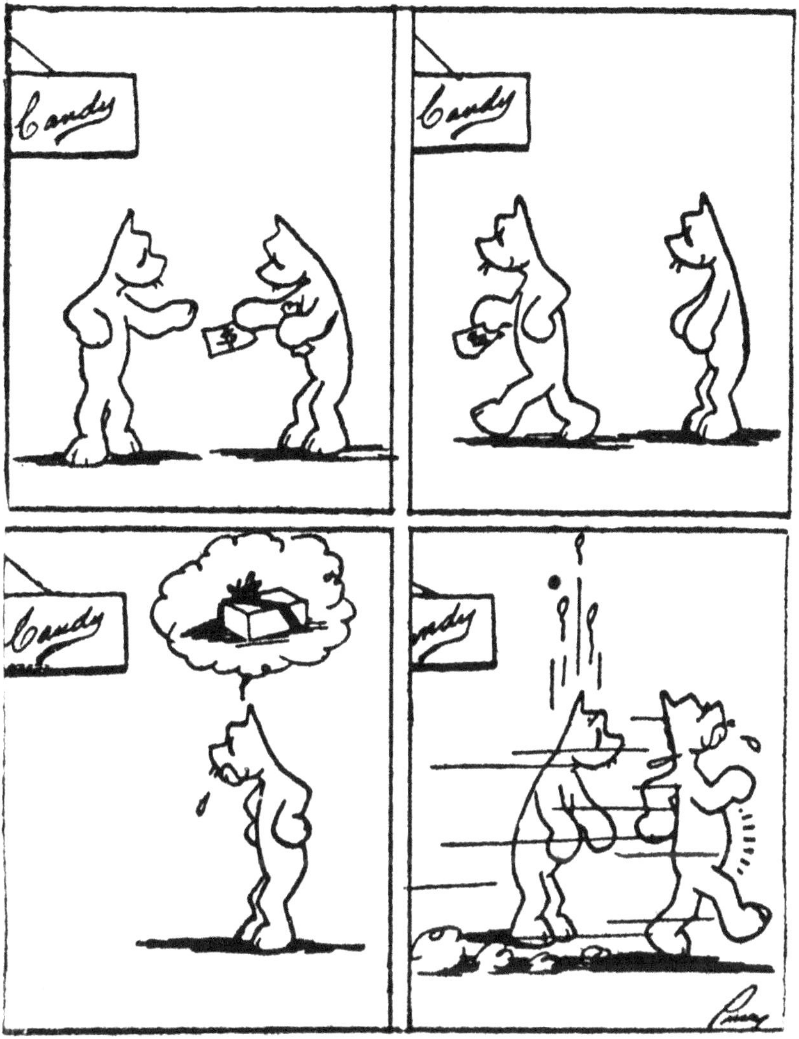
Candy
$
Candy
Candy

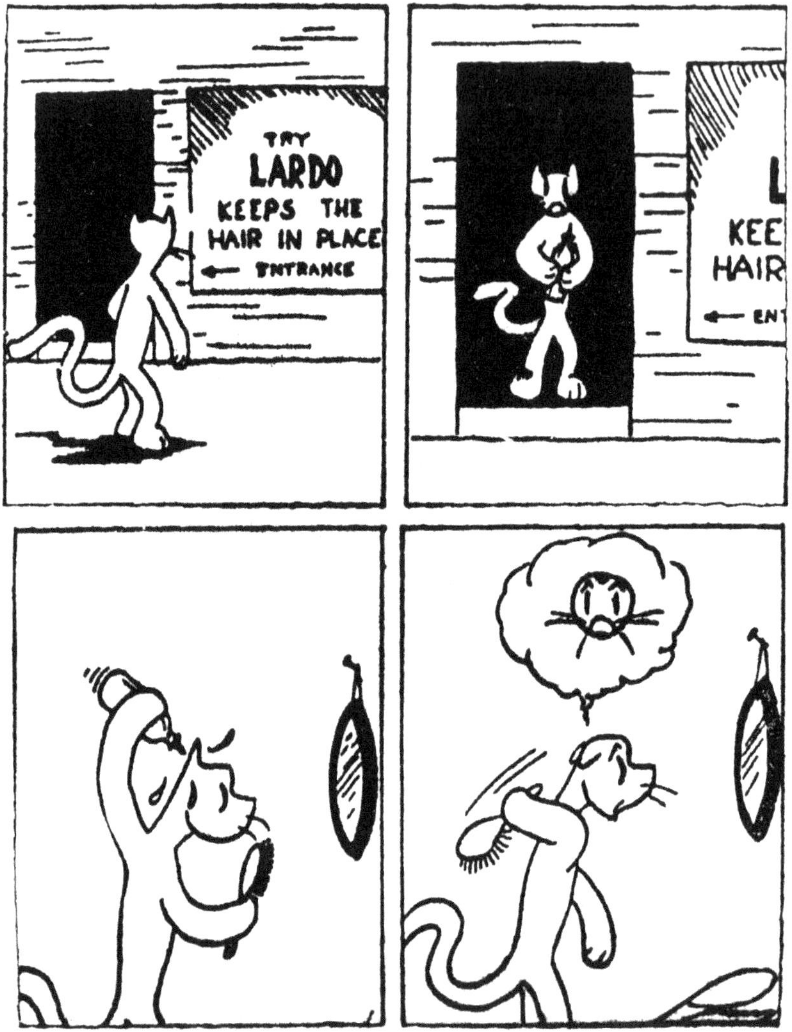
TRY
LARDO
KEEPS THE
HAIR IN PLACE
← ENTRANCE
KEE
HAIR
← EN

ICE
CREAM
ICE
CREAM
!!!!

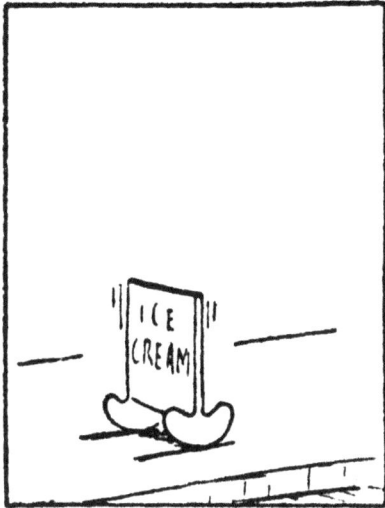

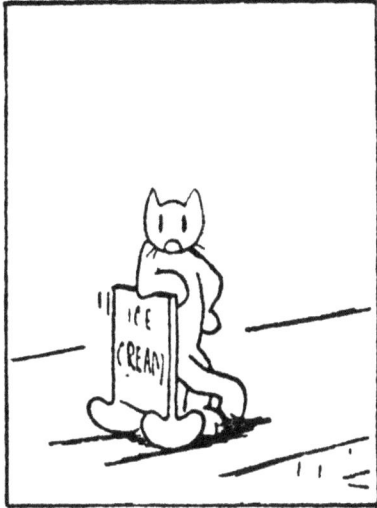

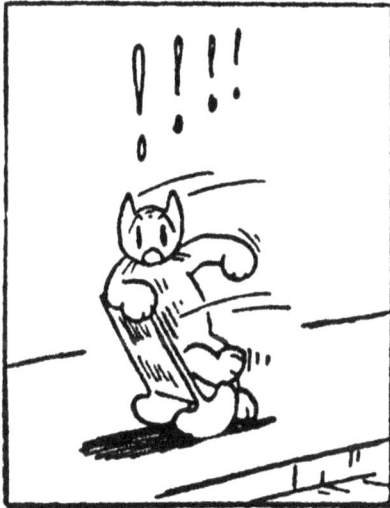

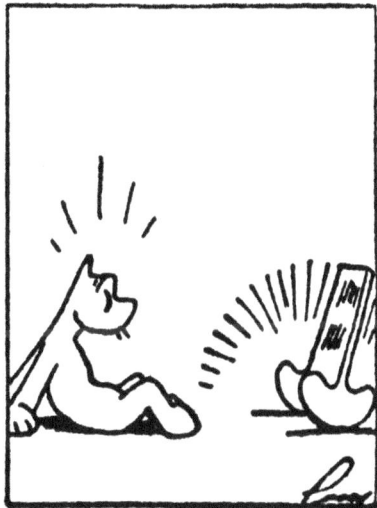

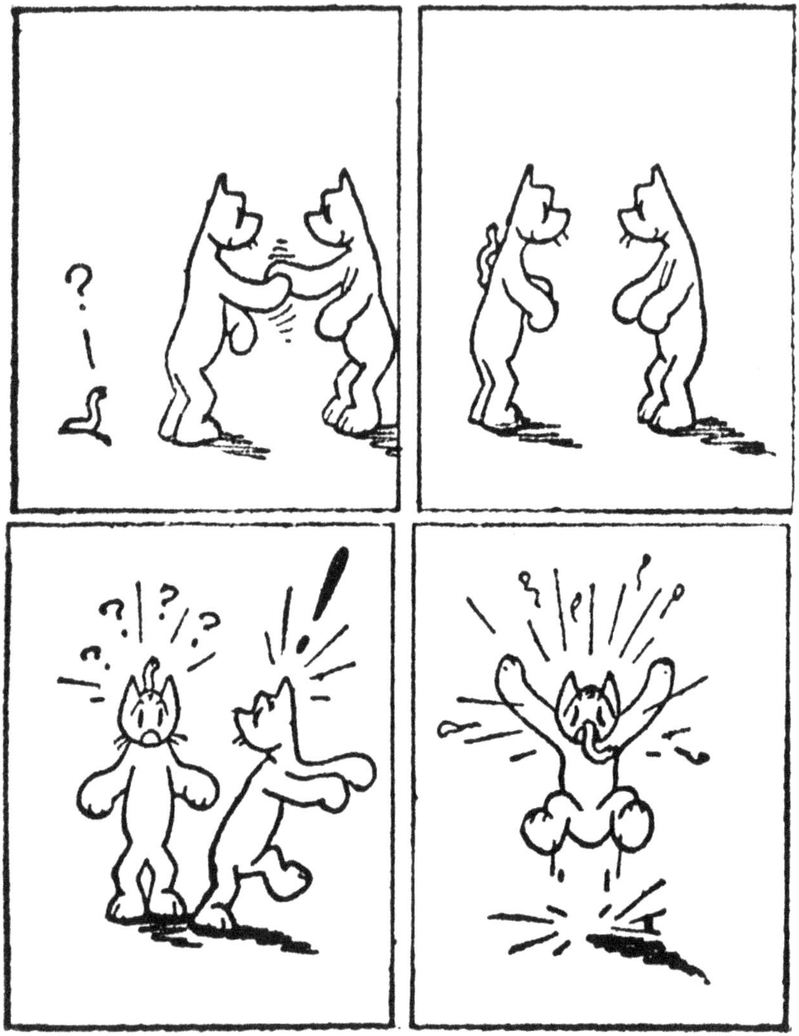
?
?
?
?
?
!

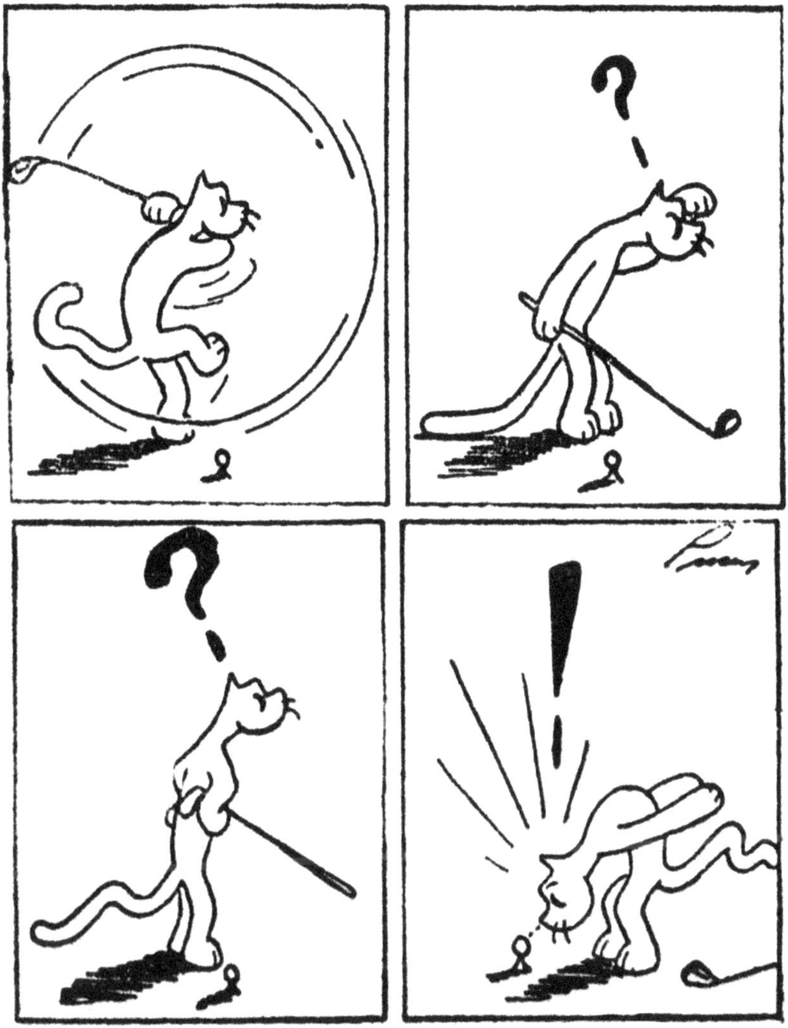

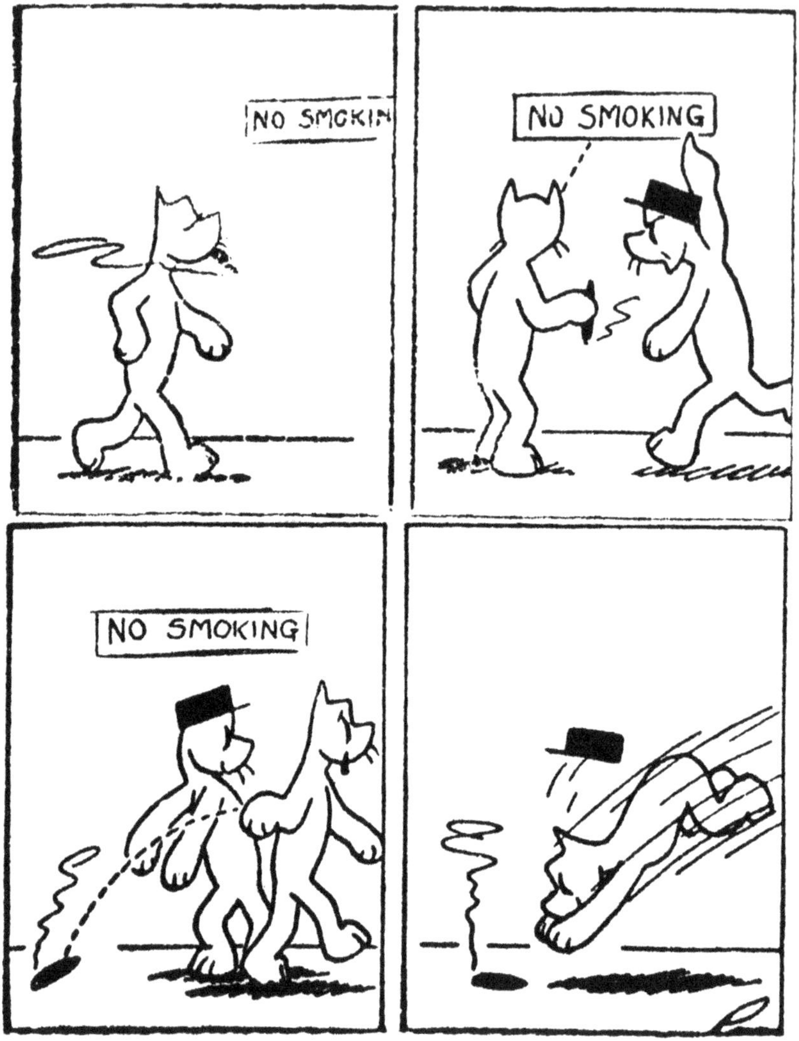
NO SMOKIN
NO SMOKING
NO SMOKING

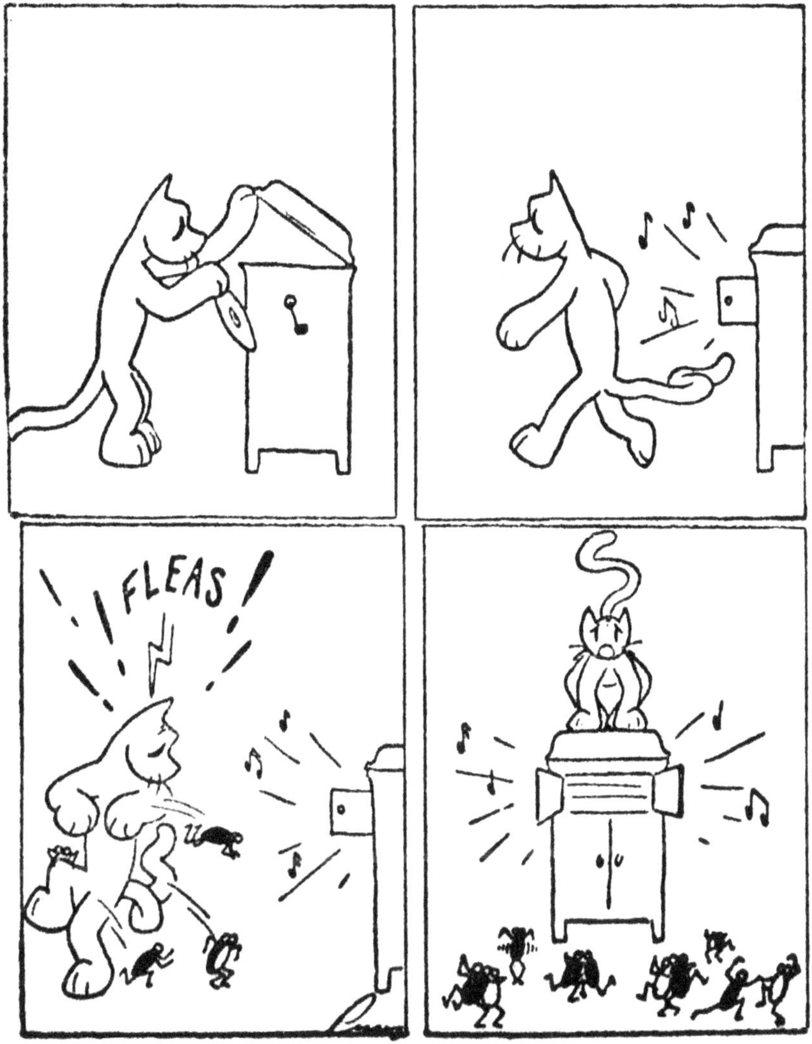
FLEAS!

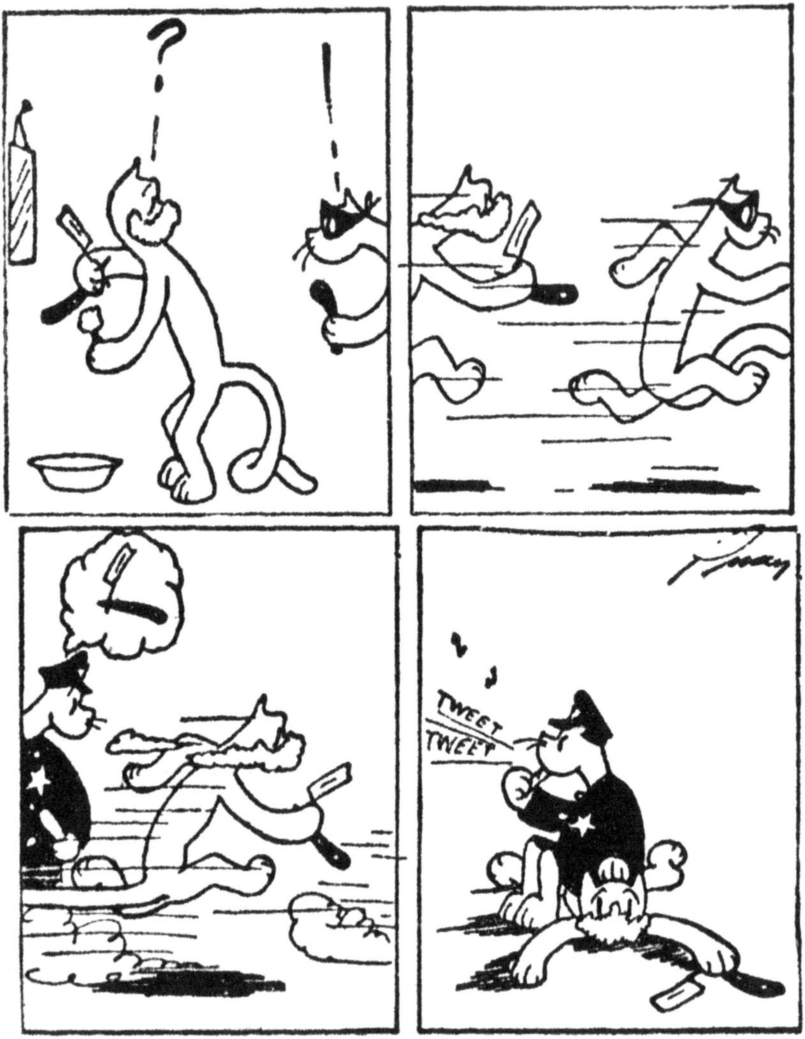
?
!
TWEET
TWEET

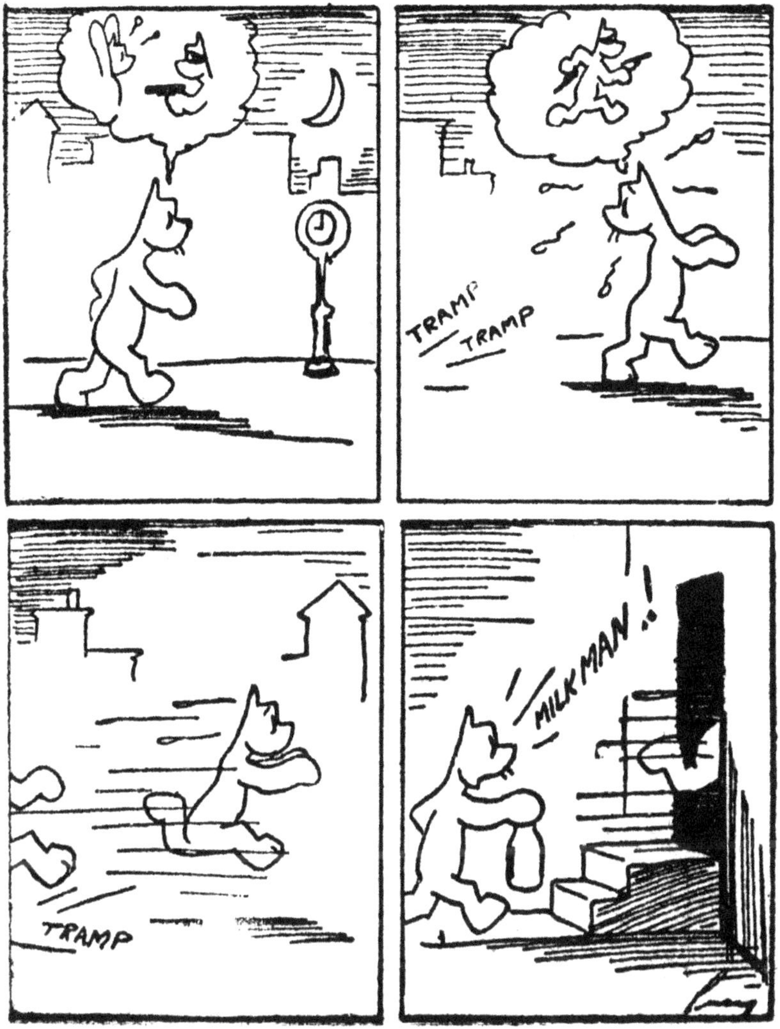
TRAMP
TRAMP
TRAMP
MILKMAN!

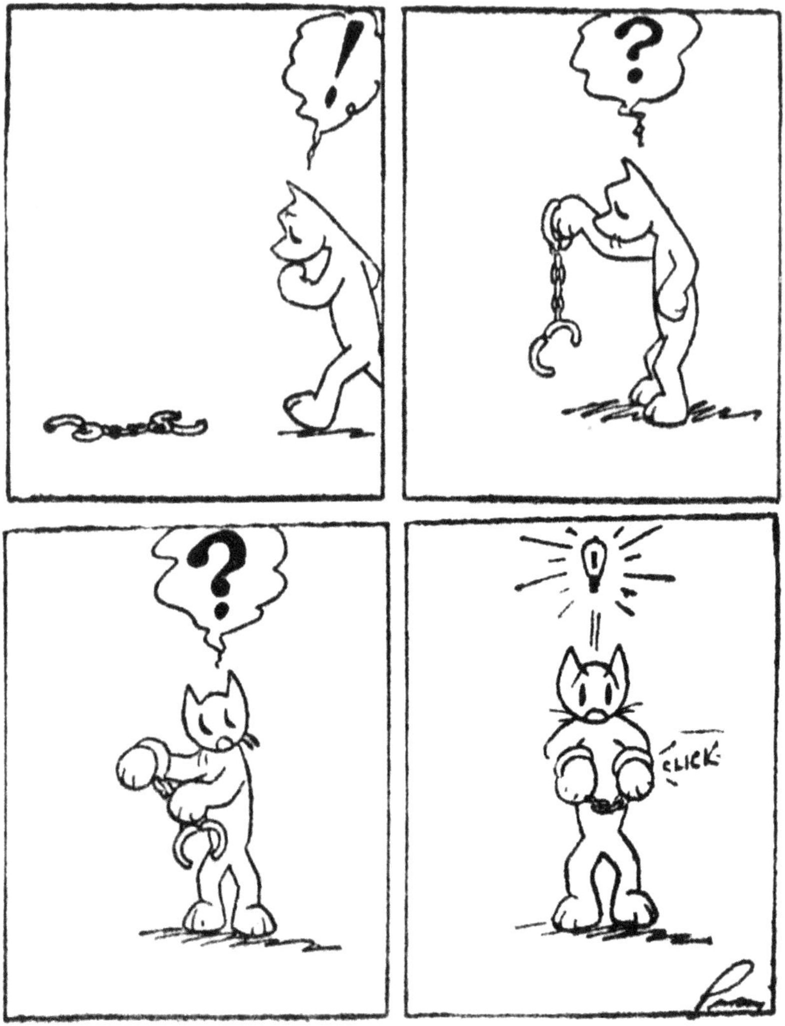
!
?
?
CLICK

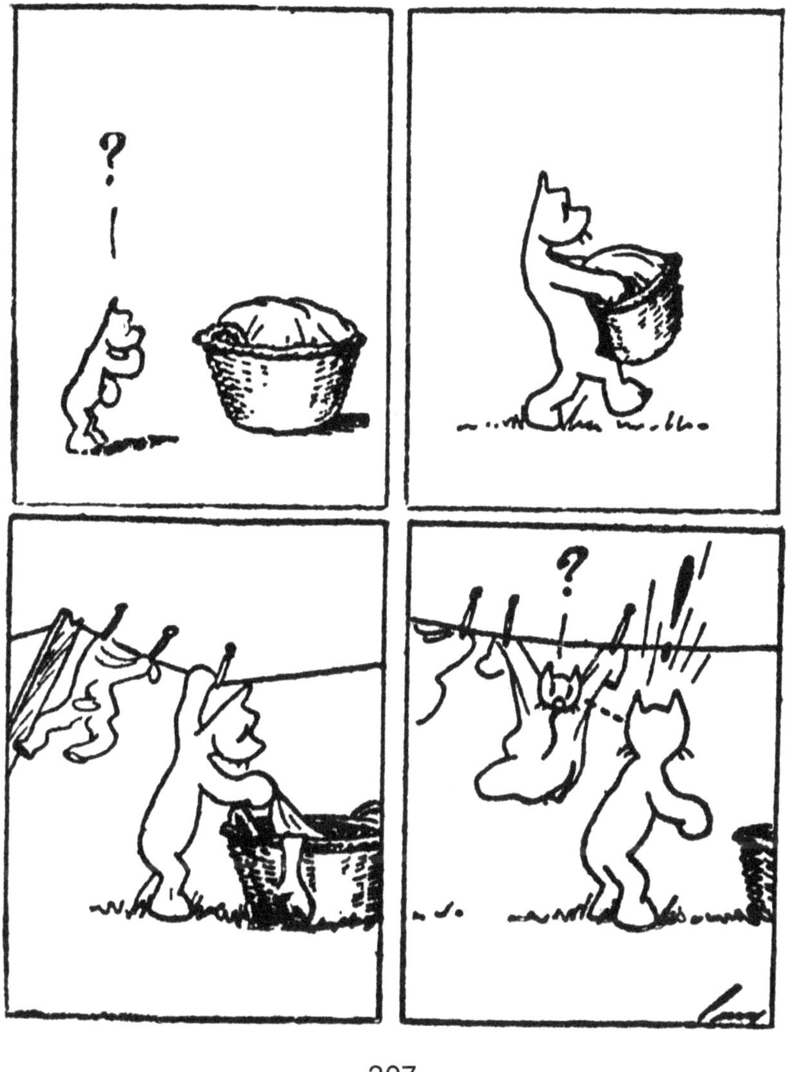

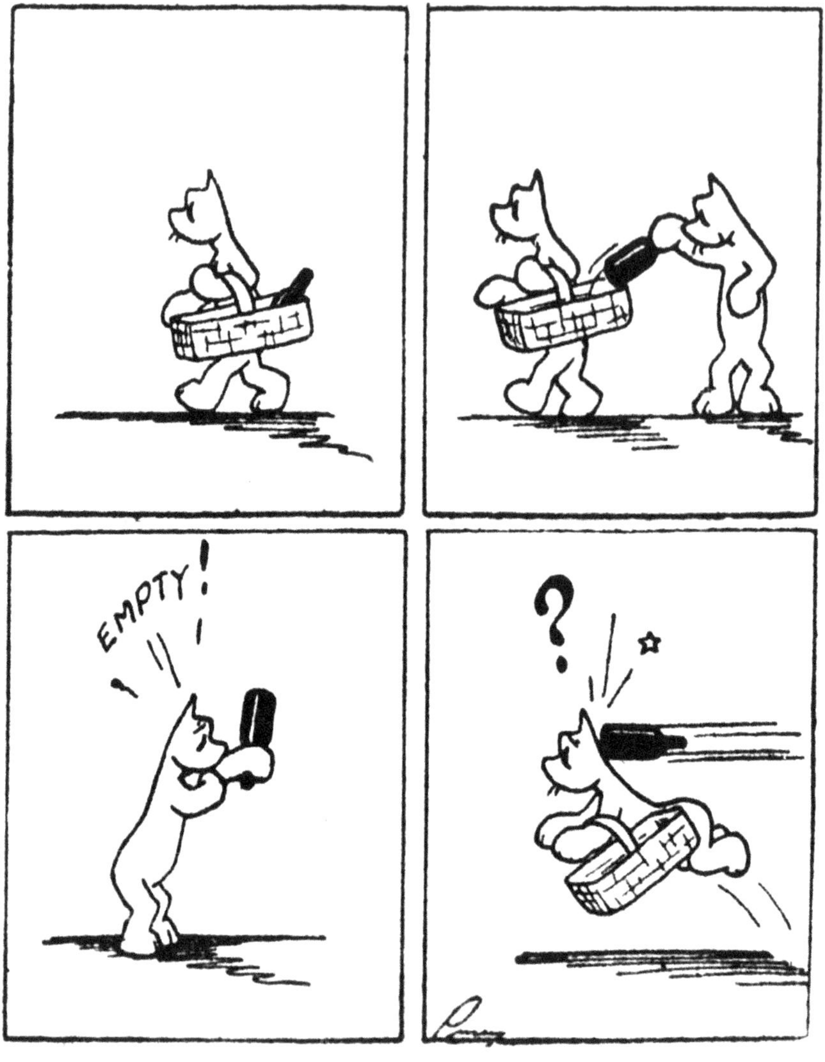
EMPTY!
?

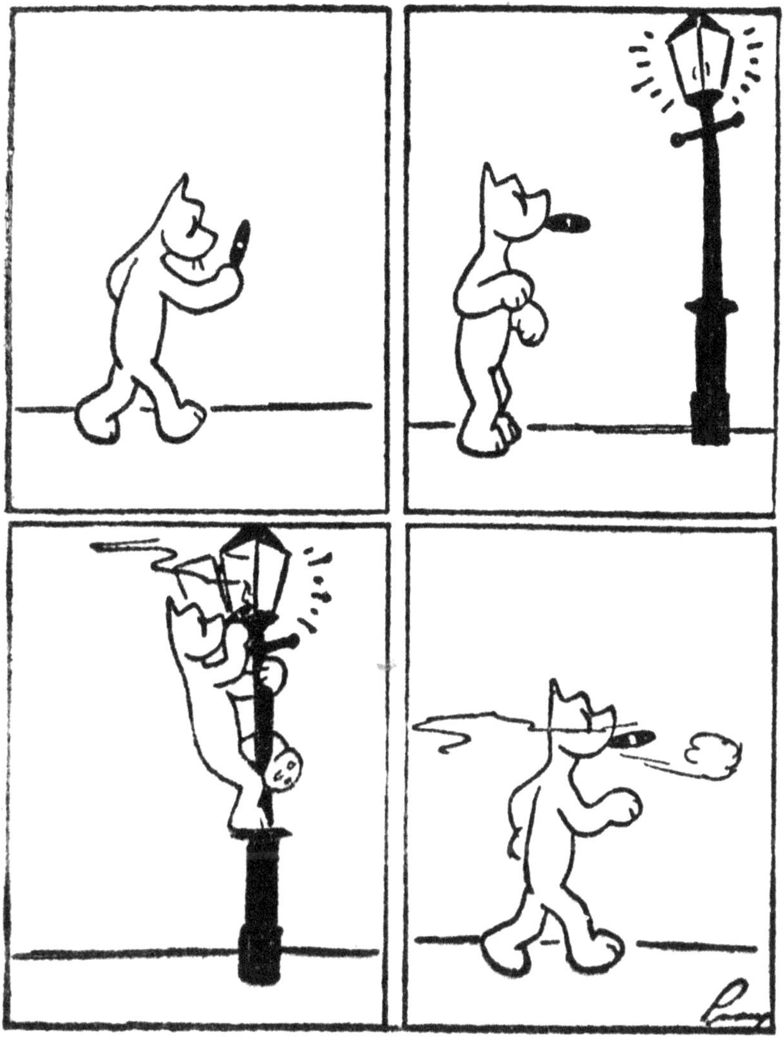

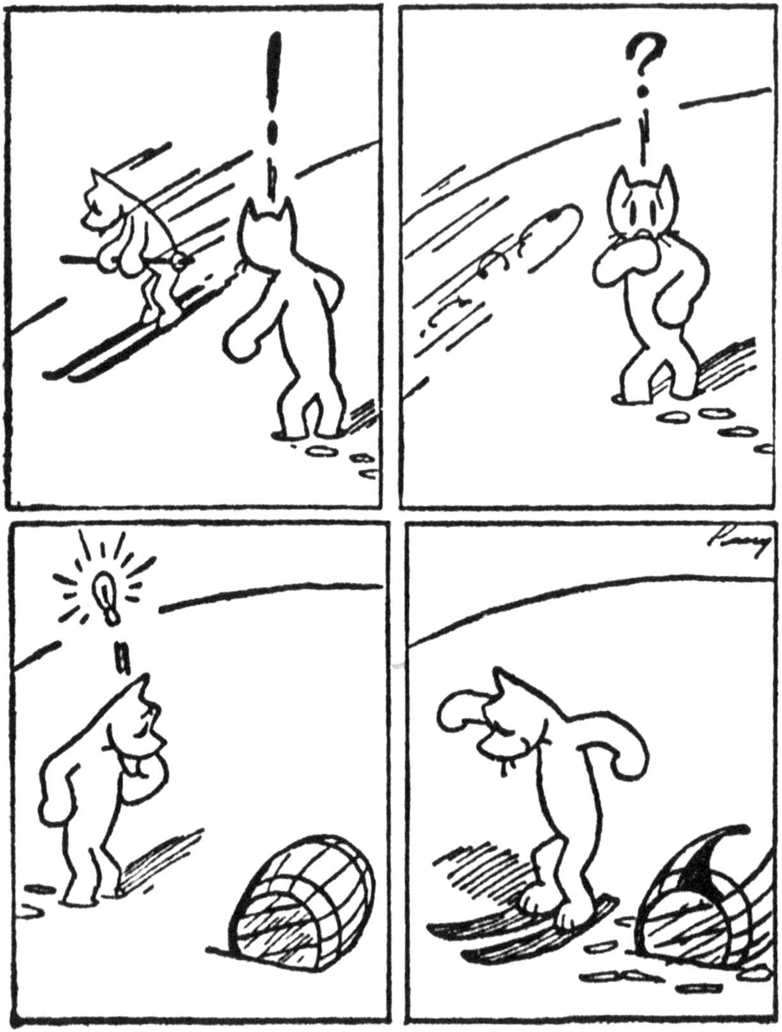
!
?

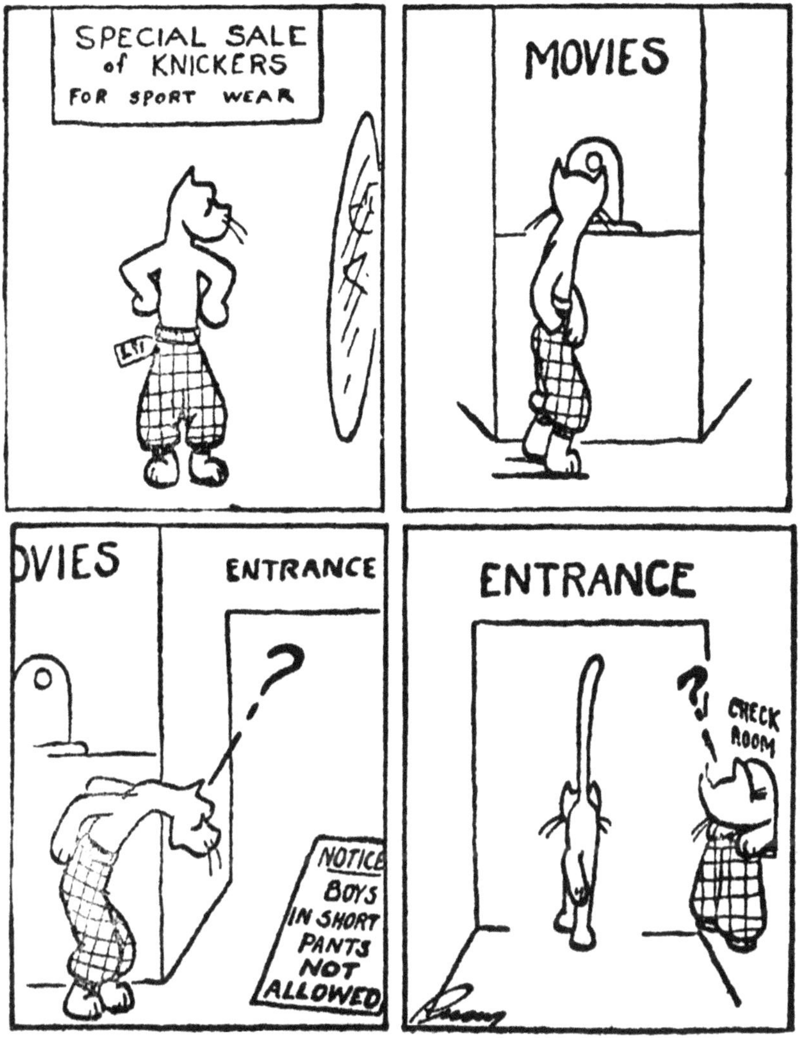
SPECIAL SALE
of KNICKERS
FOR SPORT WEAR
MOVIES
OVIES
ENTRANCE
?
NOTICE
BOYS
IN SHORT
PANTS
NOT
ALLOWED
ENTRANCE
?
CHECK
ROOM

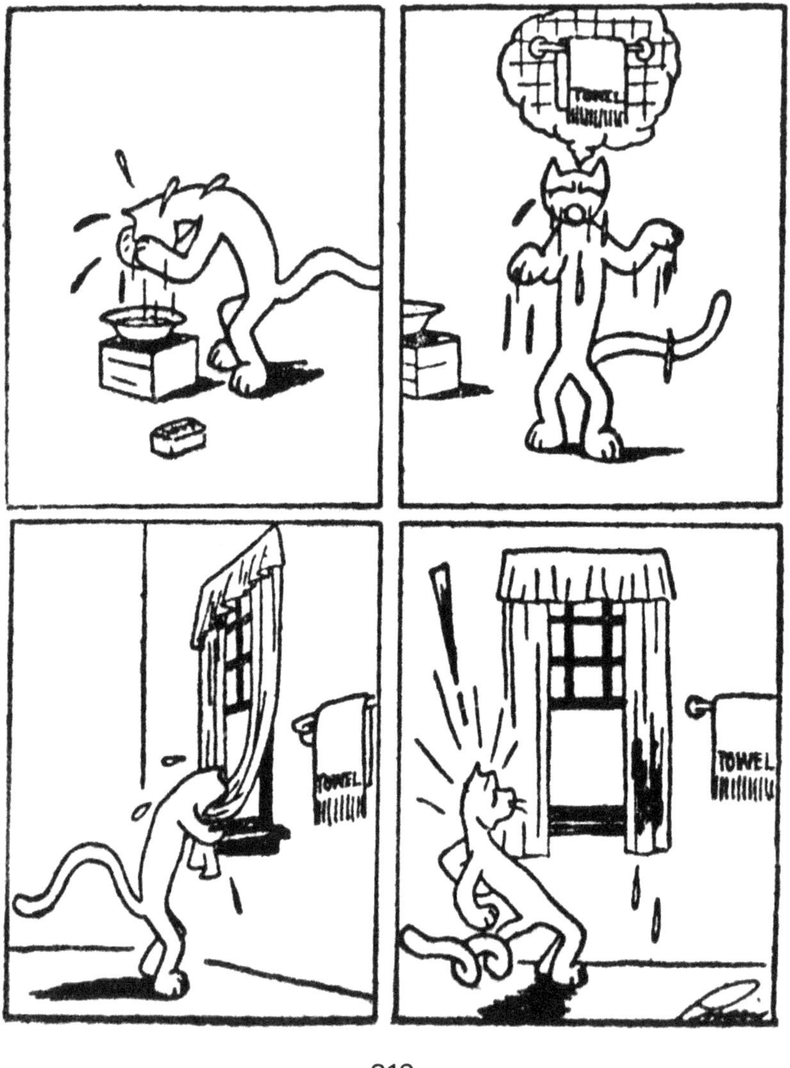
TOWEL
TOWEL
TOWEL

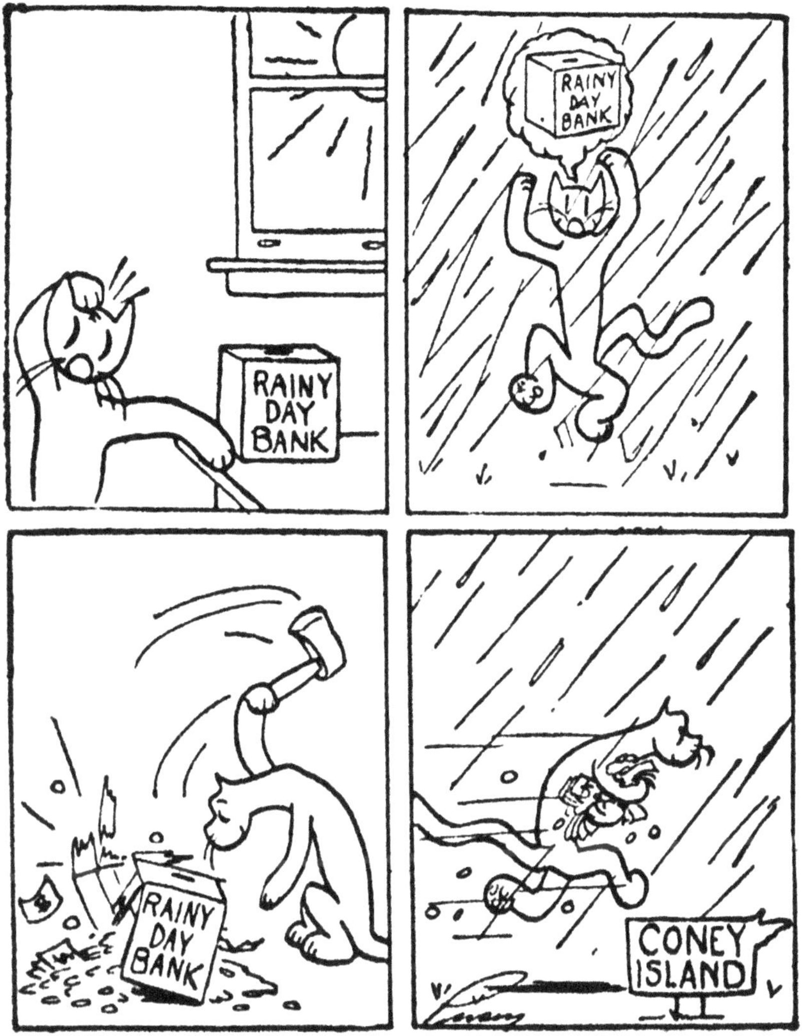
RAINY DAY BANK
RAINY DAY BANK
RAINY DAY BANK
CONEY ISLAND

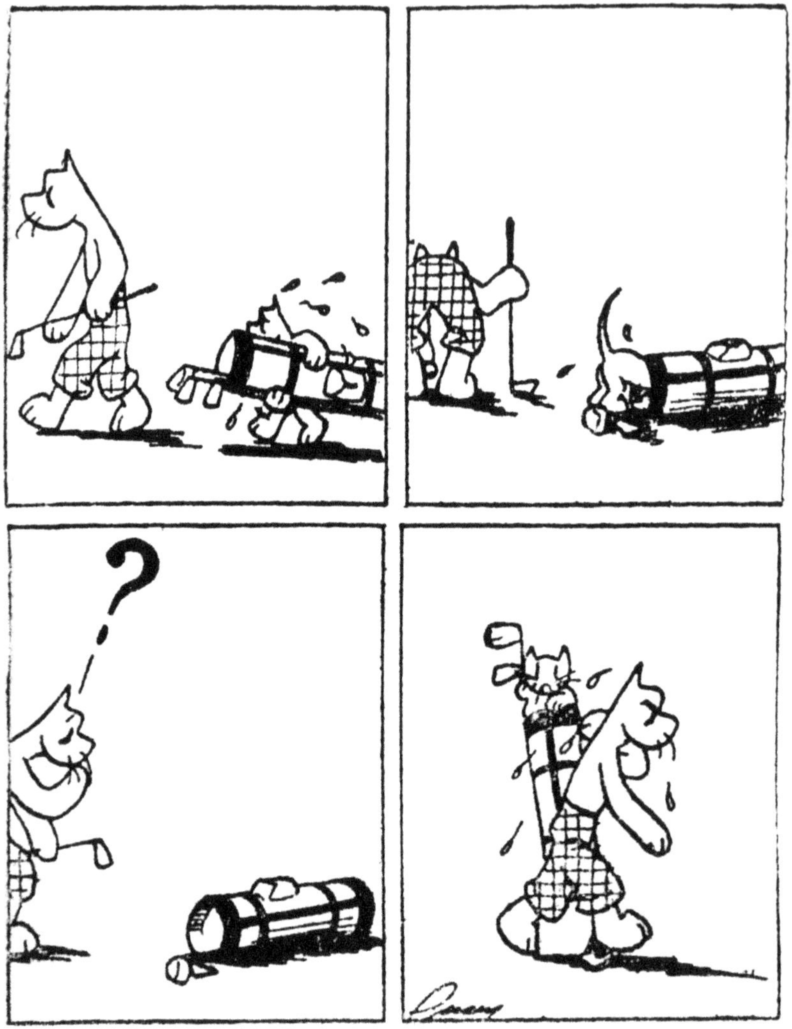

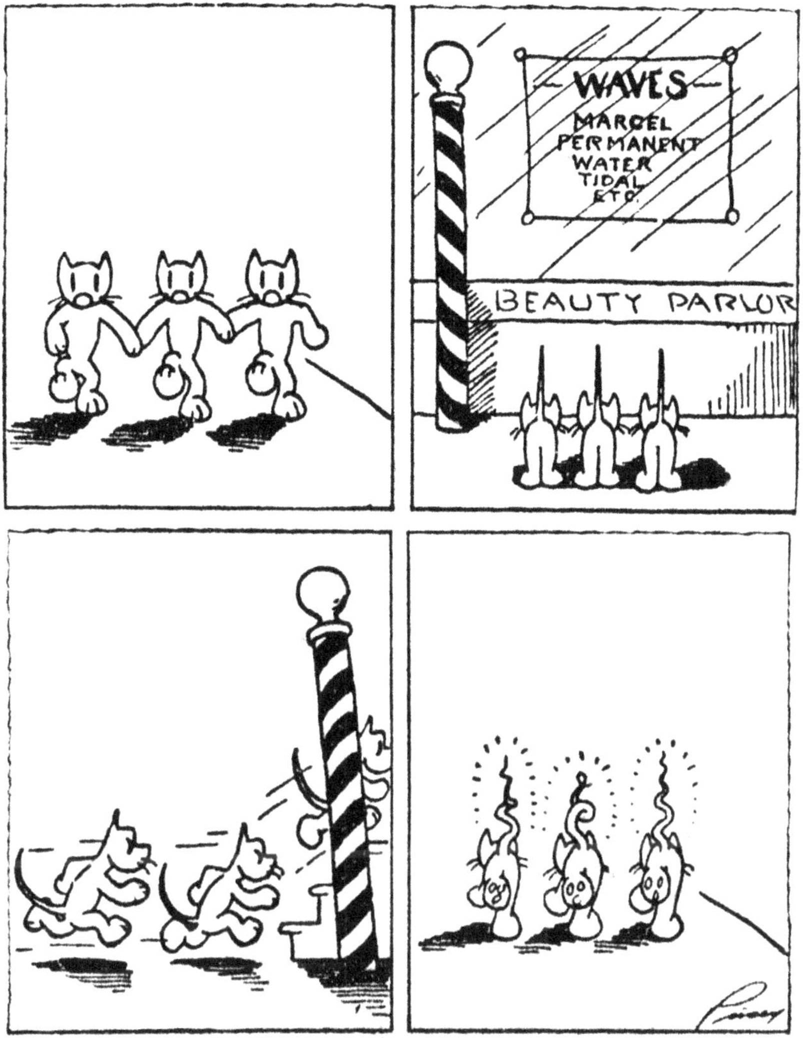
WAVES
MARCEL
PERMANENT
WATER
TIDAL
ETC.
BEAUTY PARLOR

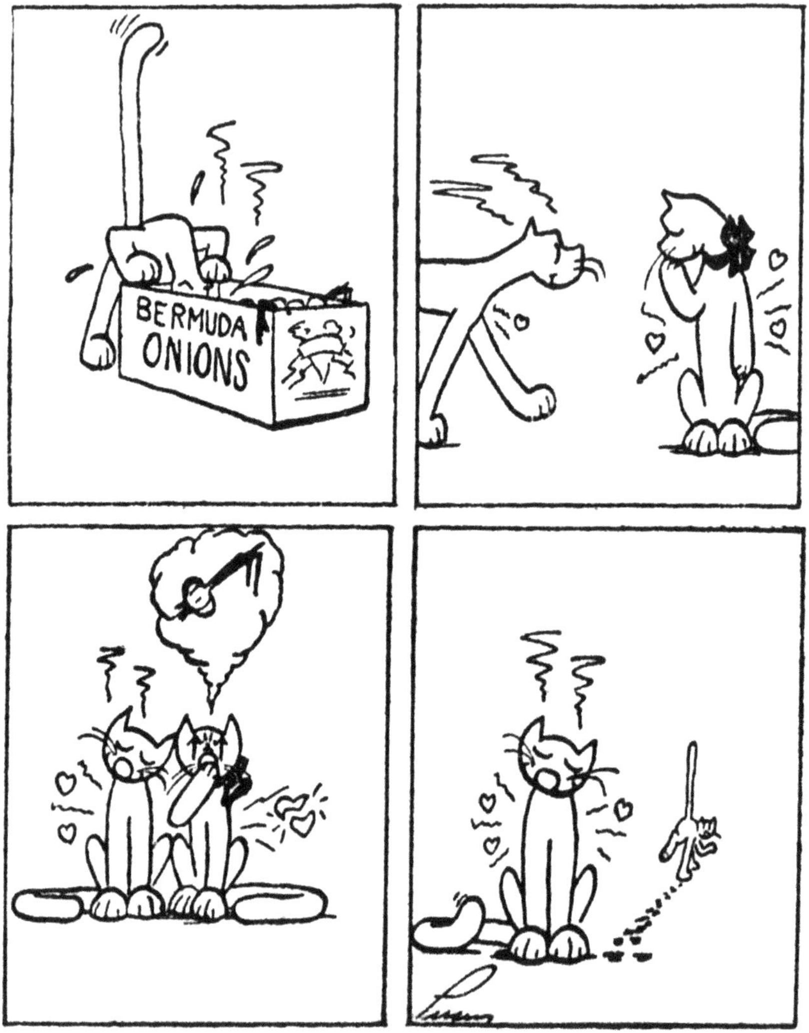
BERMUDA
ONIONS

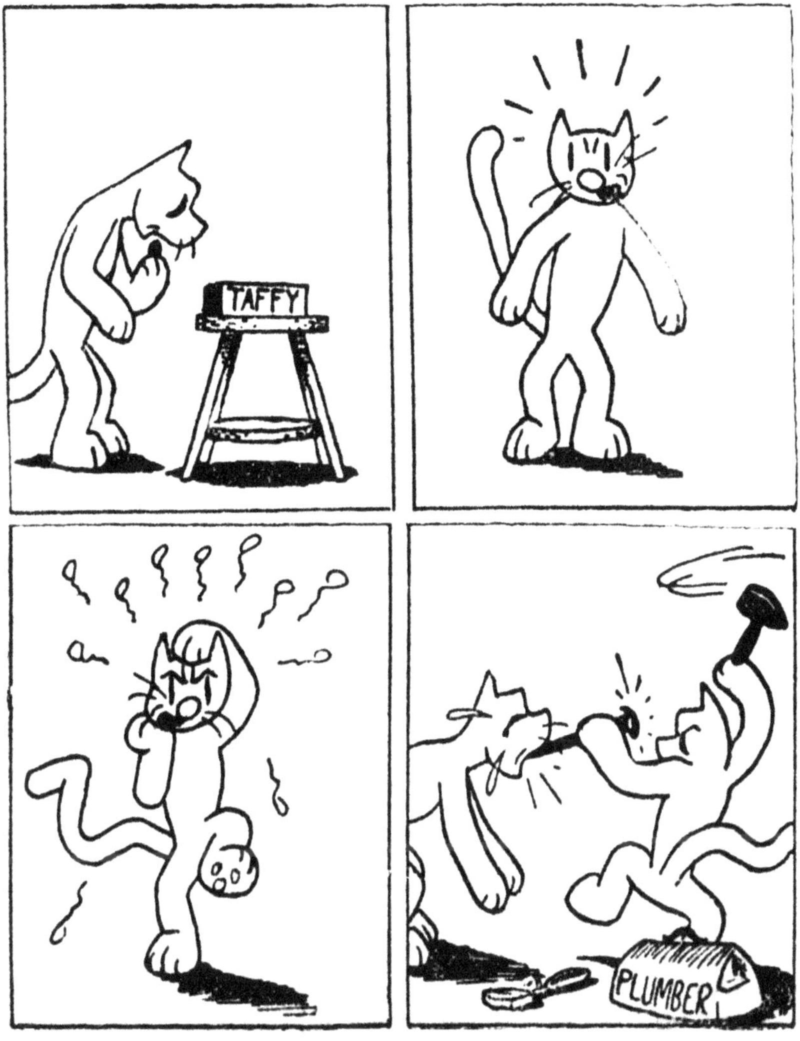
TAFFY
PLUMBER

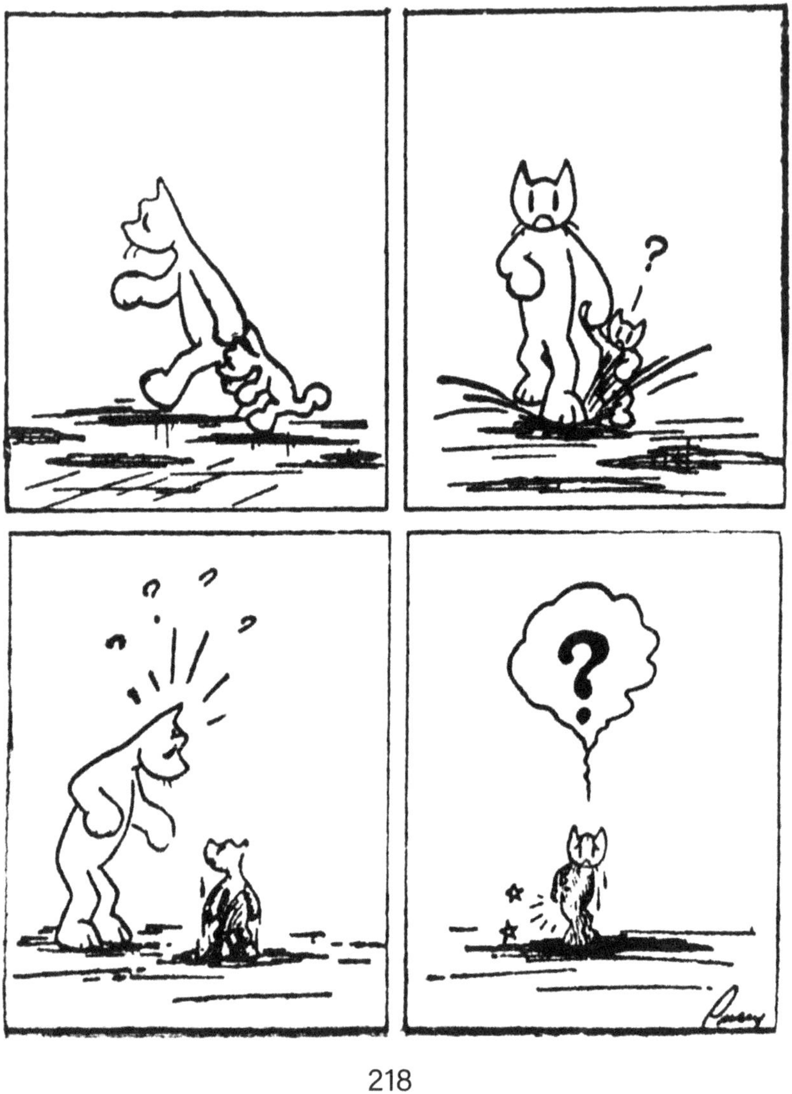

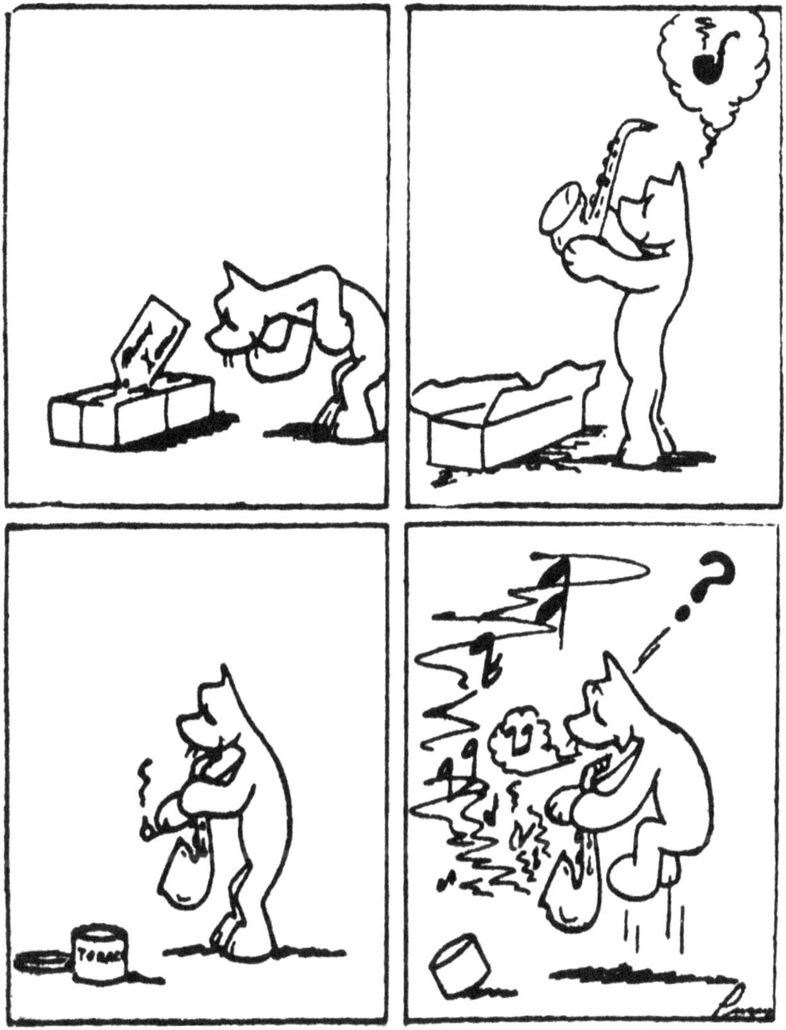

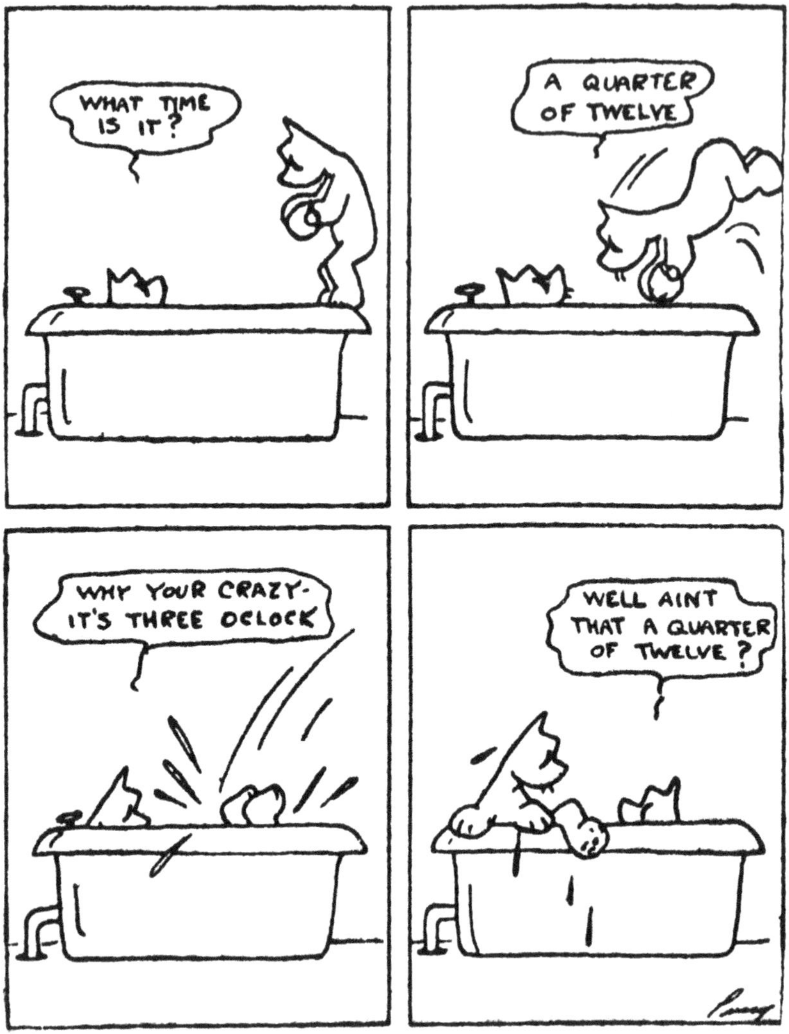
WHAT TIME IS IT?
A QUARTER OF TWELVE
WHY YOUR CRAZY- IT'S THREE OCLOCK
WELL AINT THAT A QUARTER OF TWELVE?

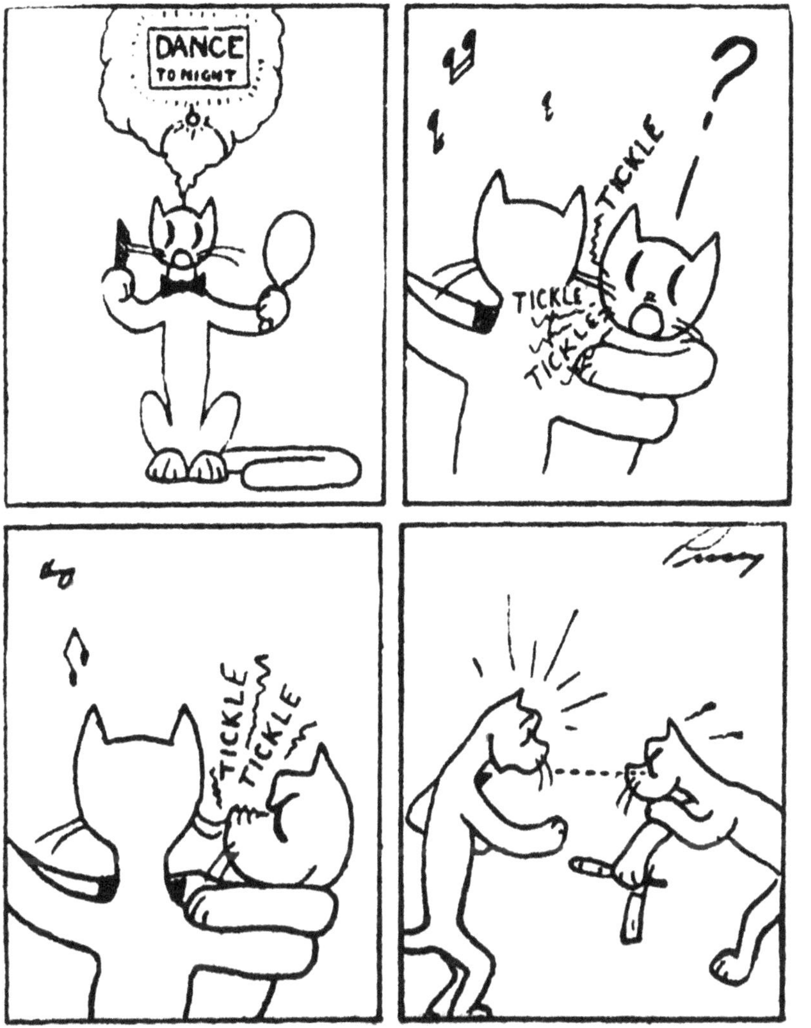
DANCE
TO NIGHT
TICKLE
TICKLE
TICKLE
TICKLE
TICKLE
TICKLE
TICKLE

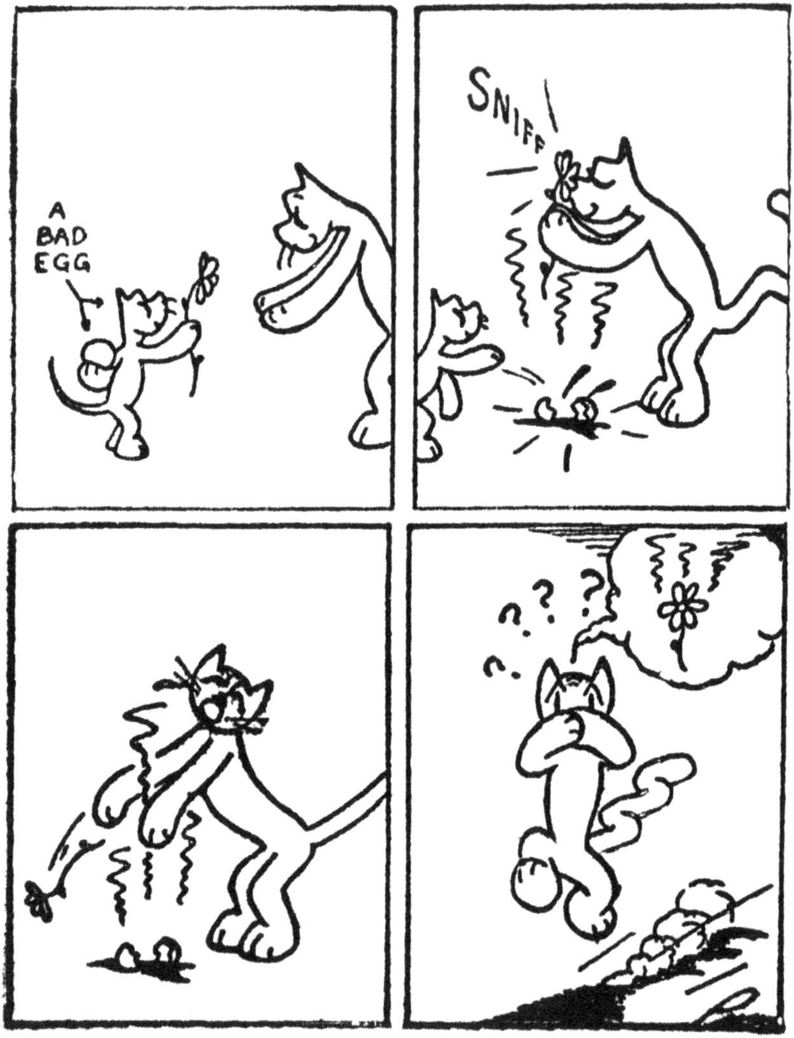
A BAD EGG
SNIFF

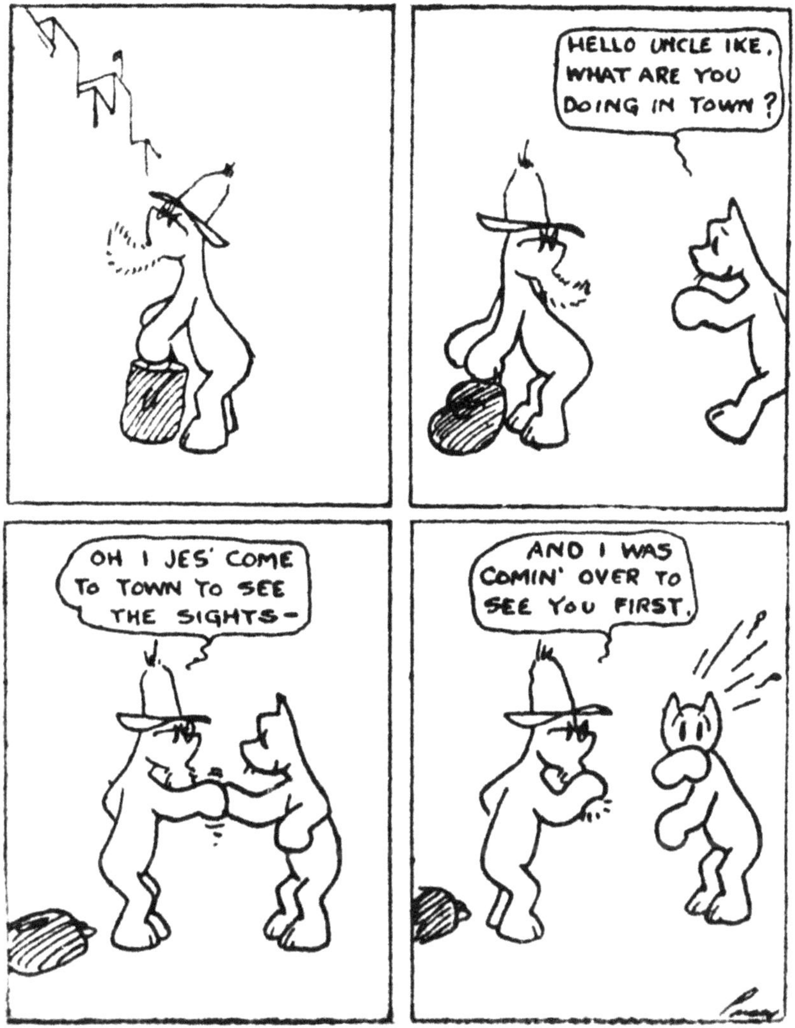
HELLO UNCLE IKE, WHAT ARE YOU DOING IN TOWN?
OH I JES' COME TO TOWN TO SEE THE SIGHTS-
AND I WAS COMIN' OVER TO SEE YOU FIRST.

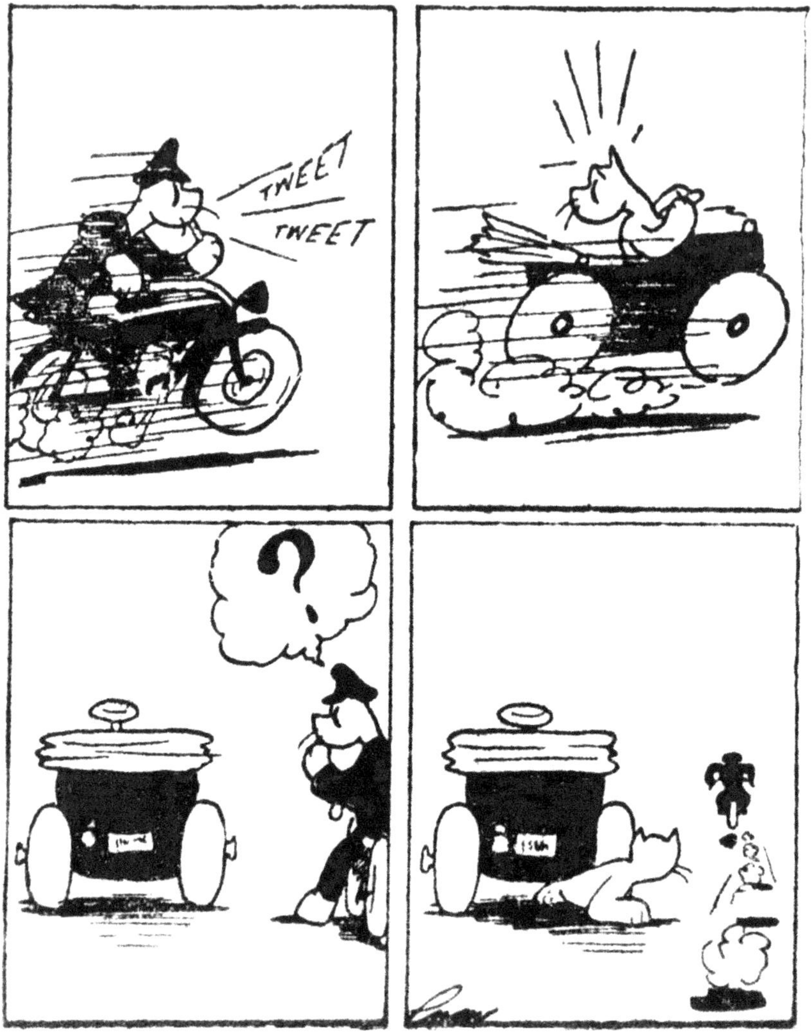
TWEET
TWEET
?

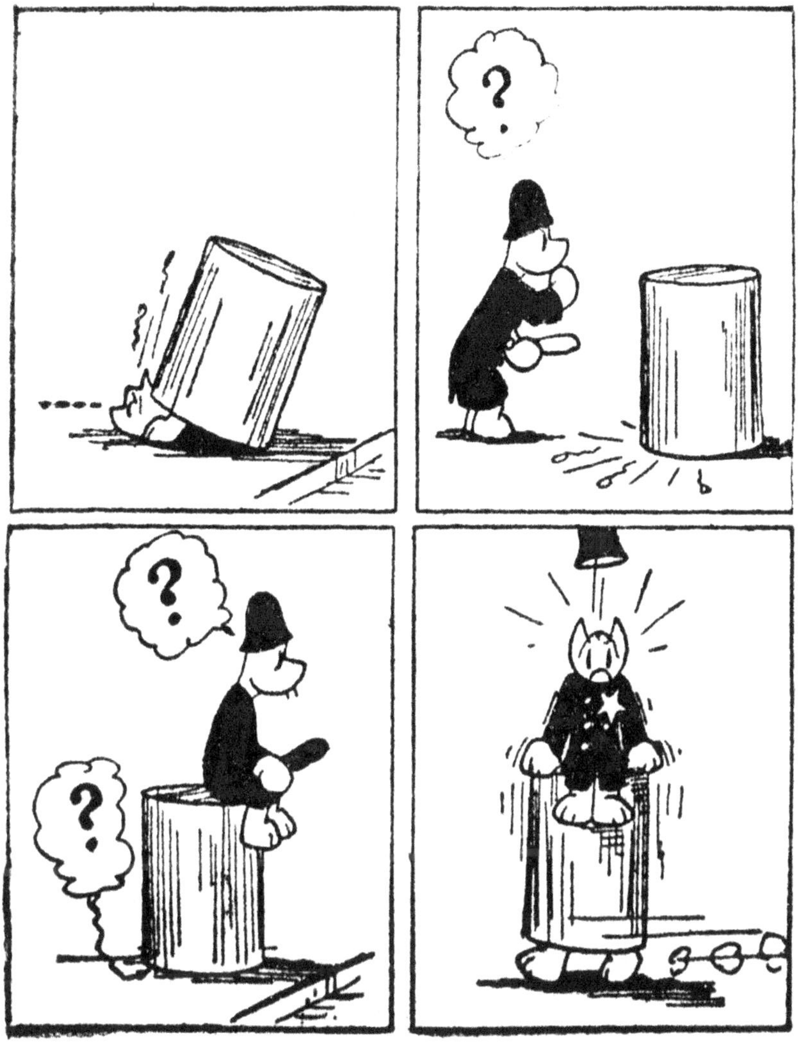
?
?
?

CRACK
CRACK
HELP!
SOS
HALP
HELP!

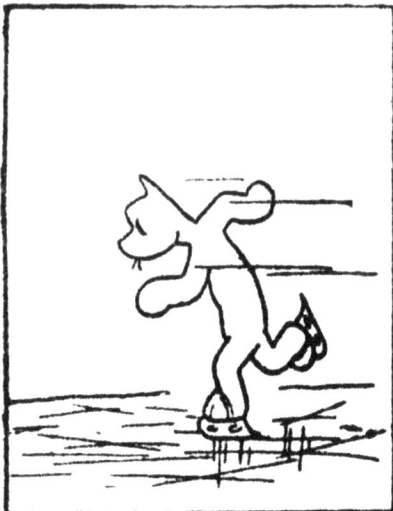

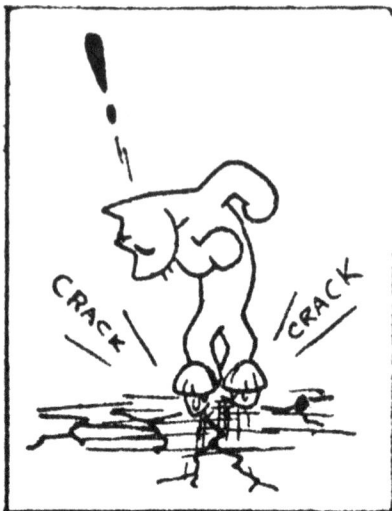

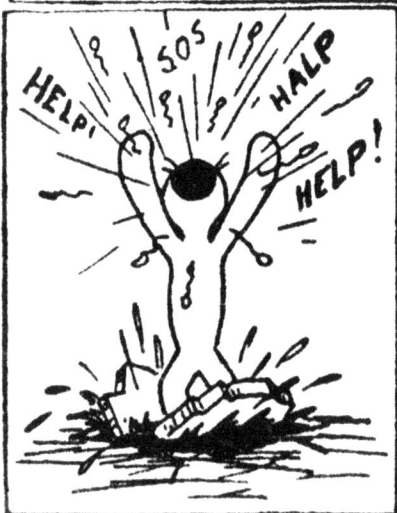

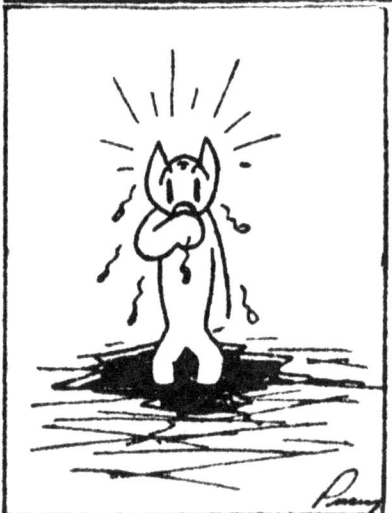

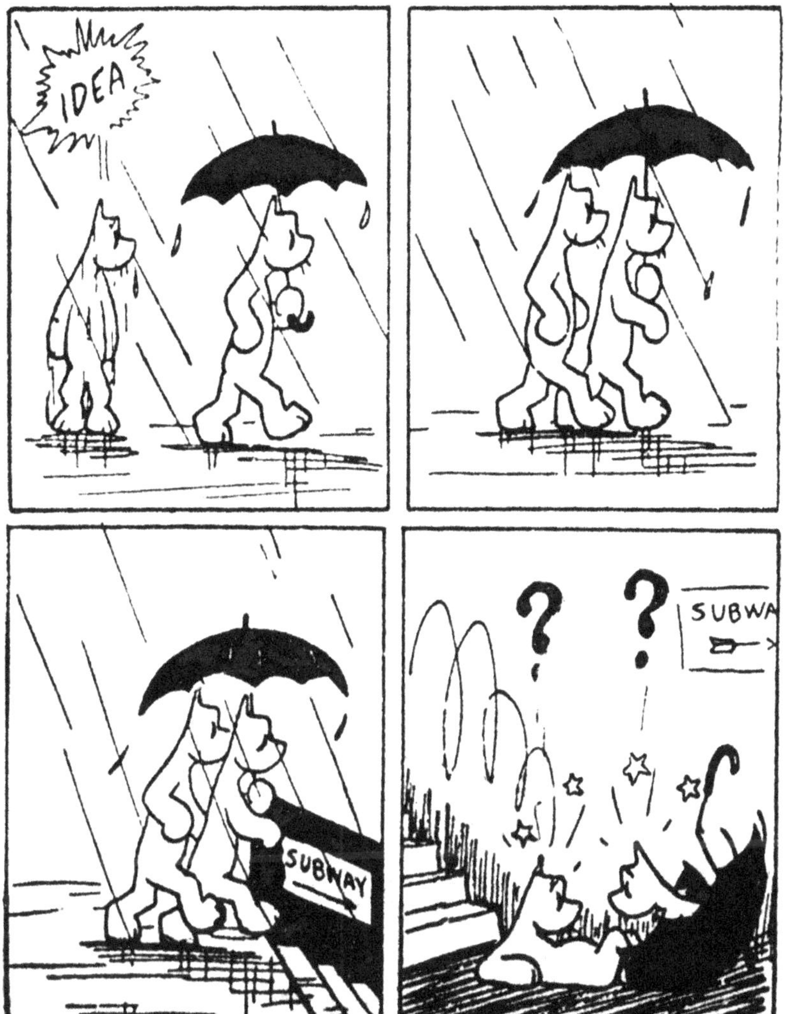
IDEA
SUBWAY
? ?
SUBWA

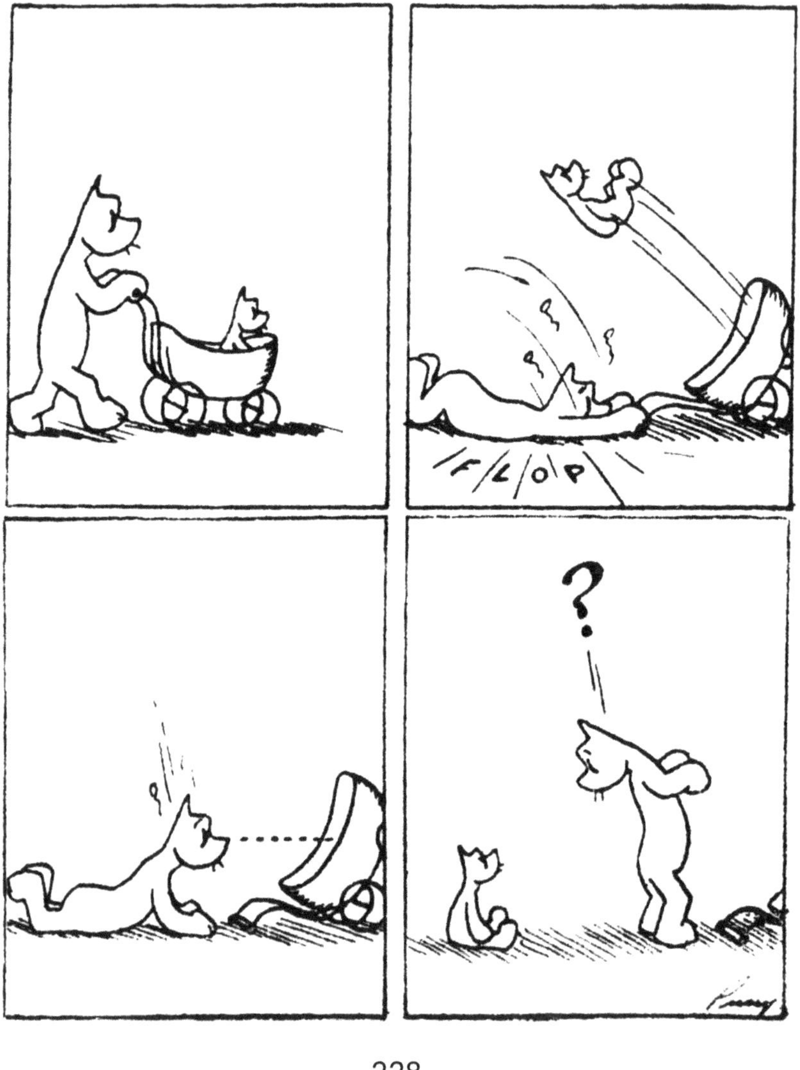
FLOP
?

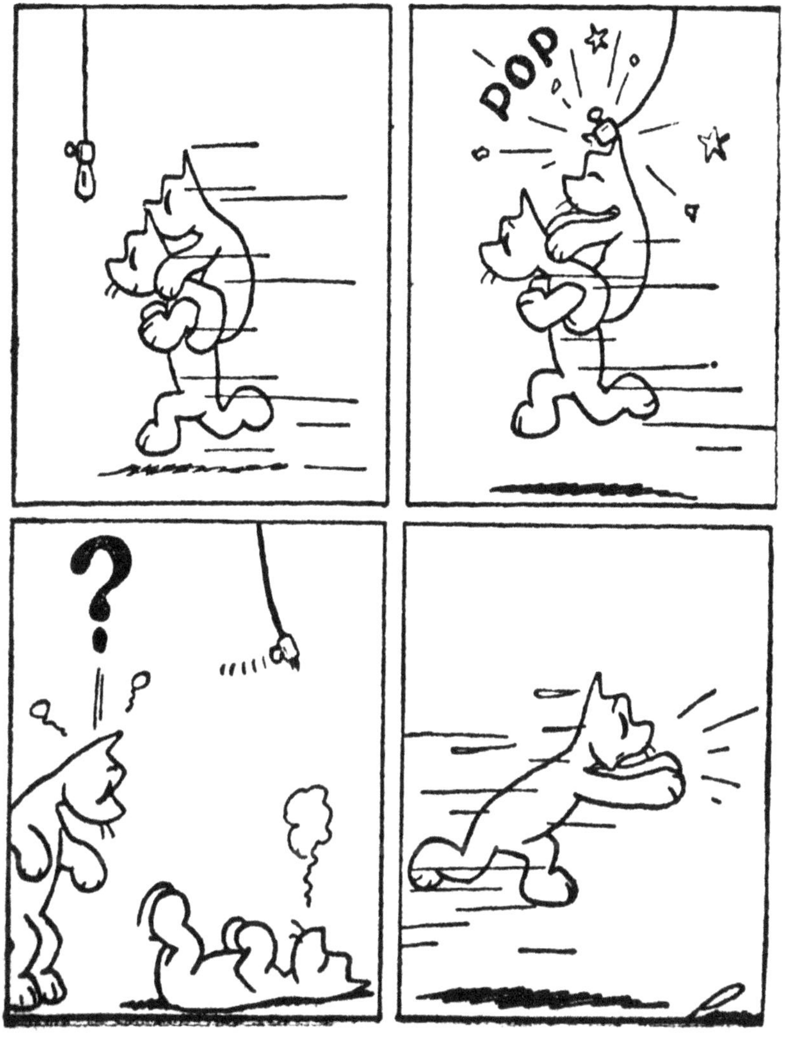
POP
?

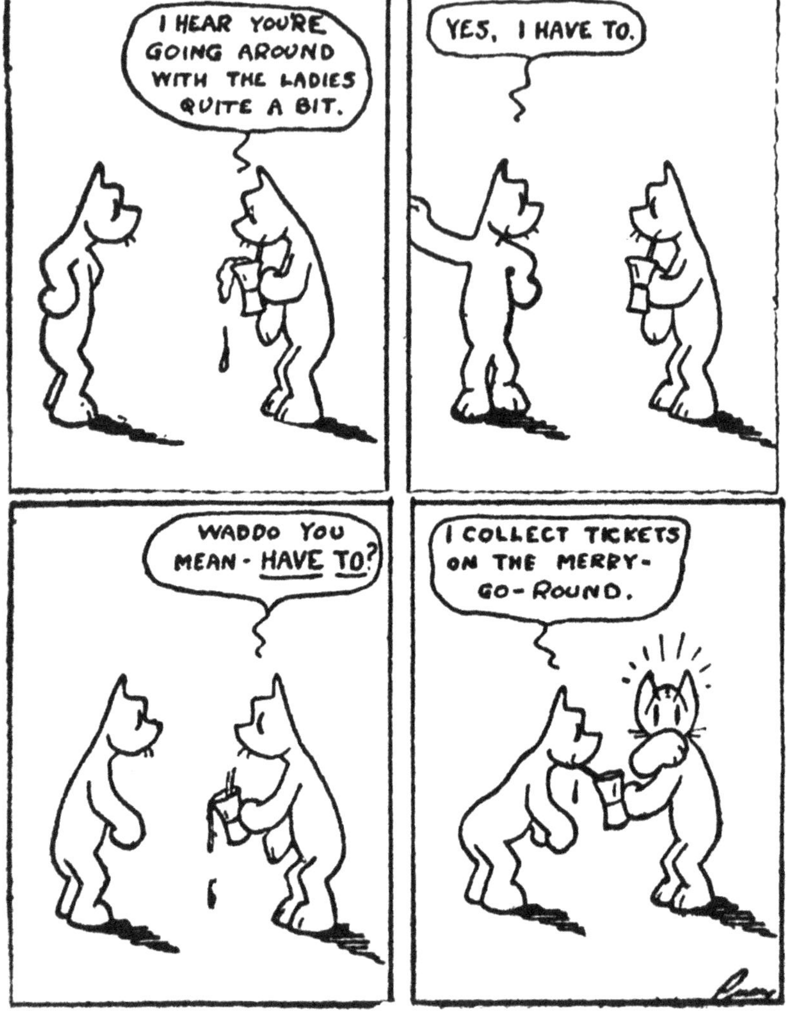
I HEAR YOU'RE GOING AROUND WITH THE LADIES QUITE A BIT.
YES, I HAVE TO.
WADDO YOU MEAN - HAVE TO?
I COLLECT TICKETS ON THE MERRY-GO-ROUND.

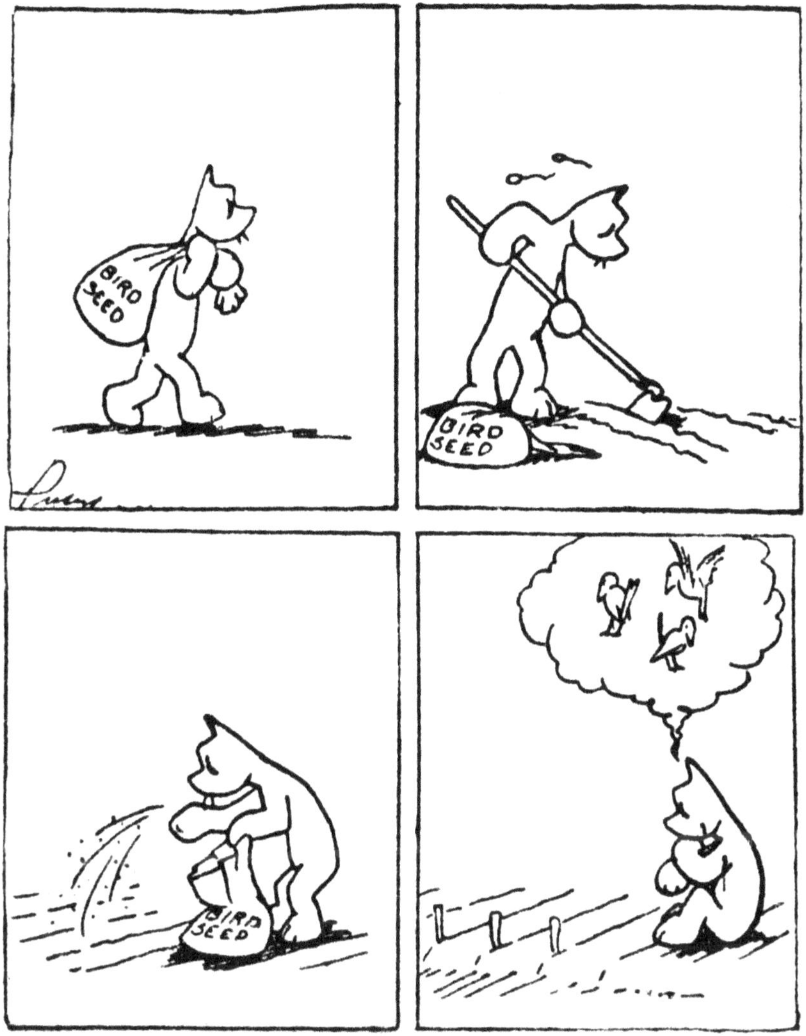
BIRD SEED
BIRD SEED
BIRD SEED

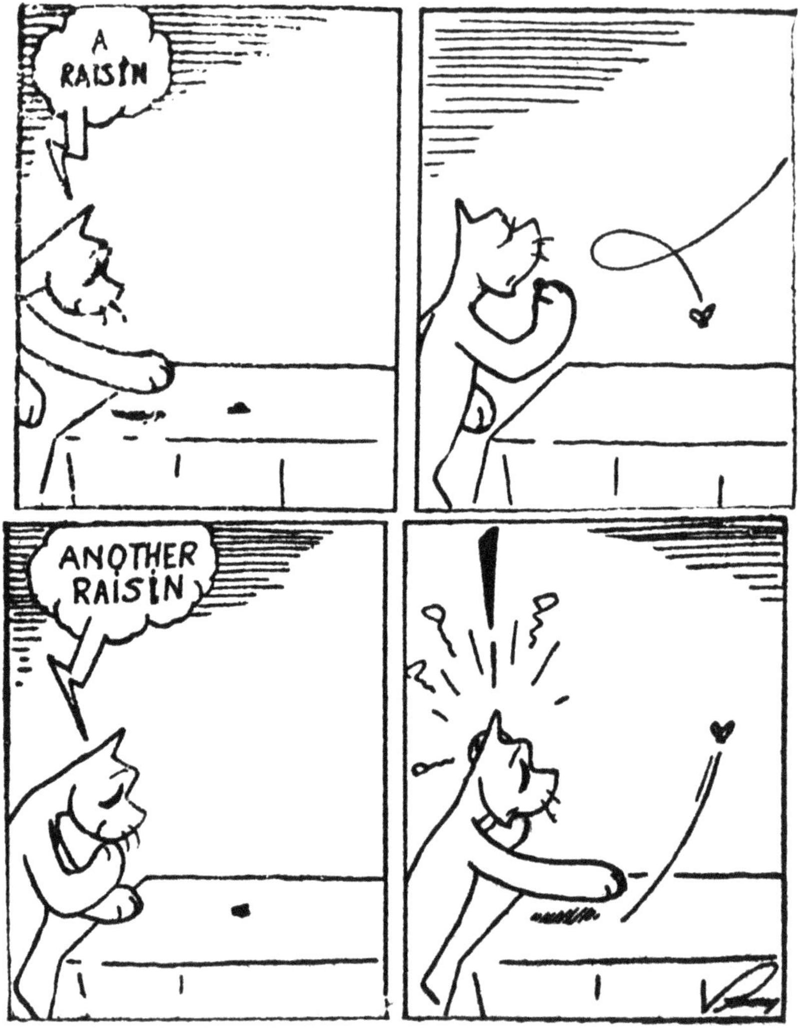
A RAISIN
ANOTHER RAISIN
!

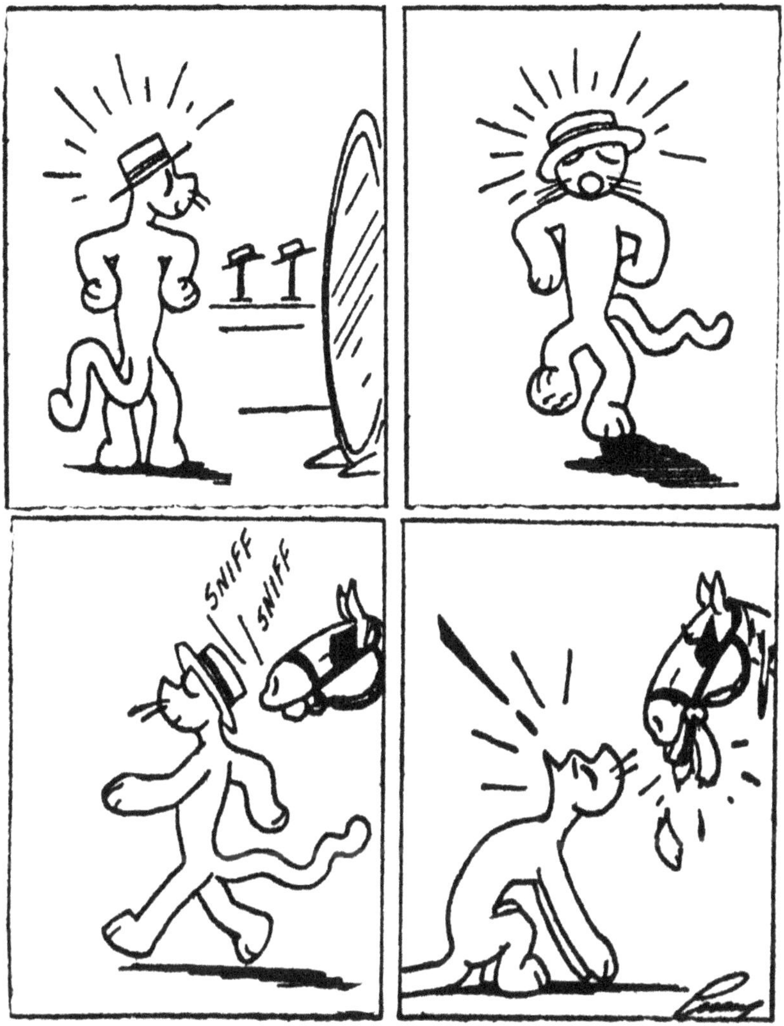
SNIFF
SNIFF

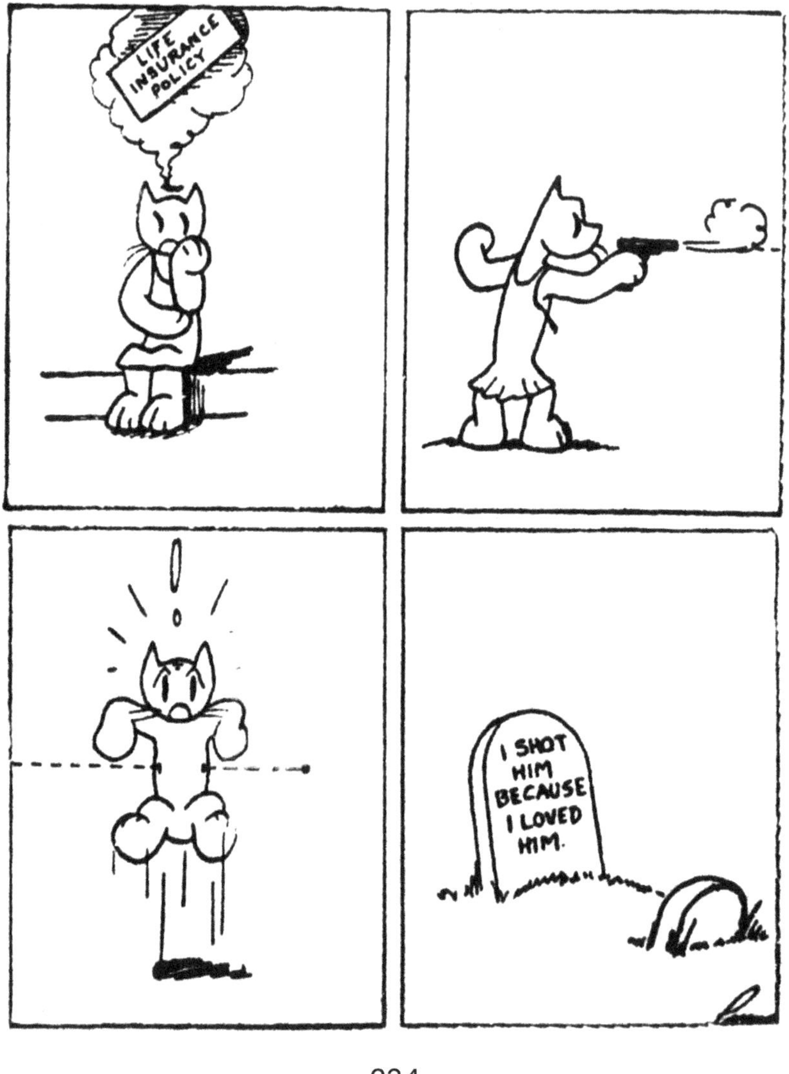
LIFE INSURANCE POLICY
I SHOT HIM BECAUSE I LOVED HIM.

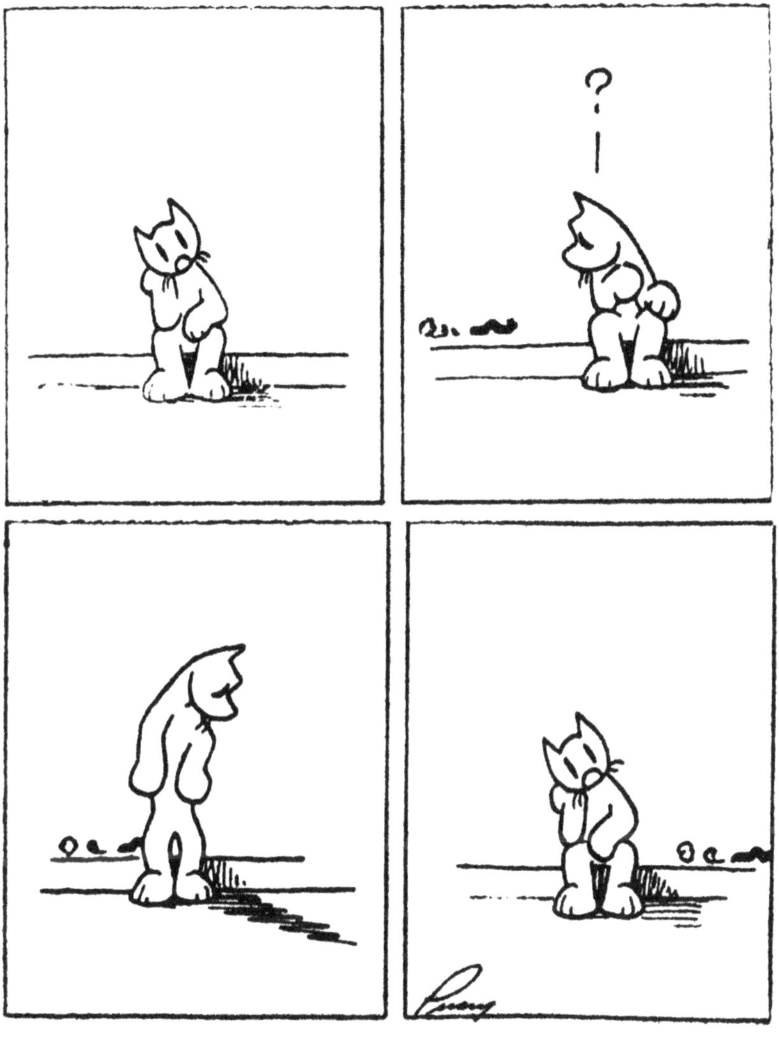
?

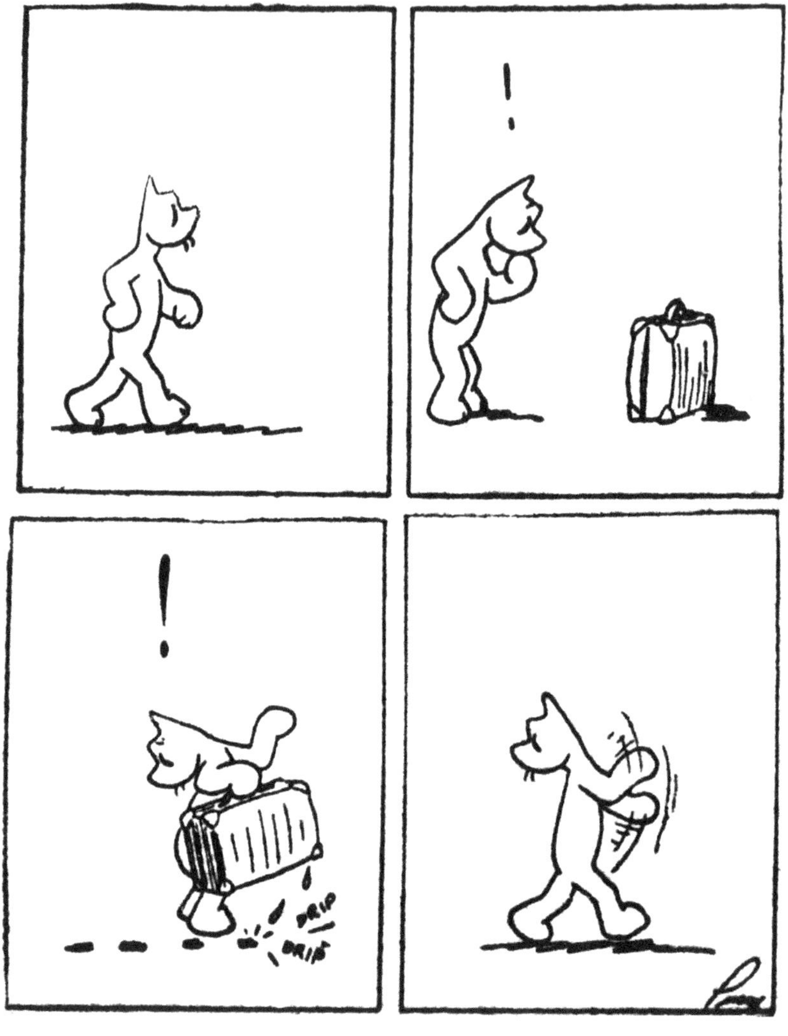
!
!
DRIP
DRIP

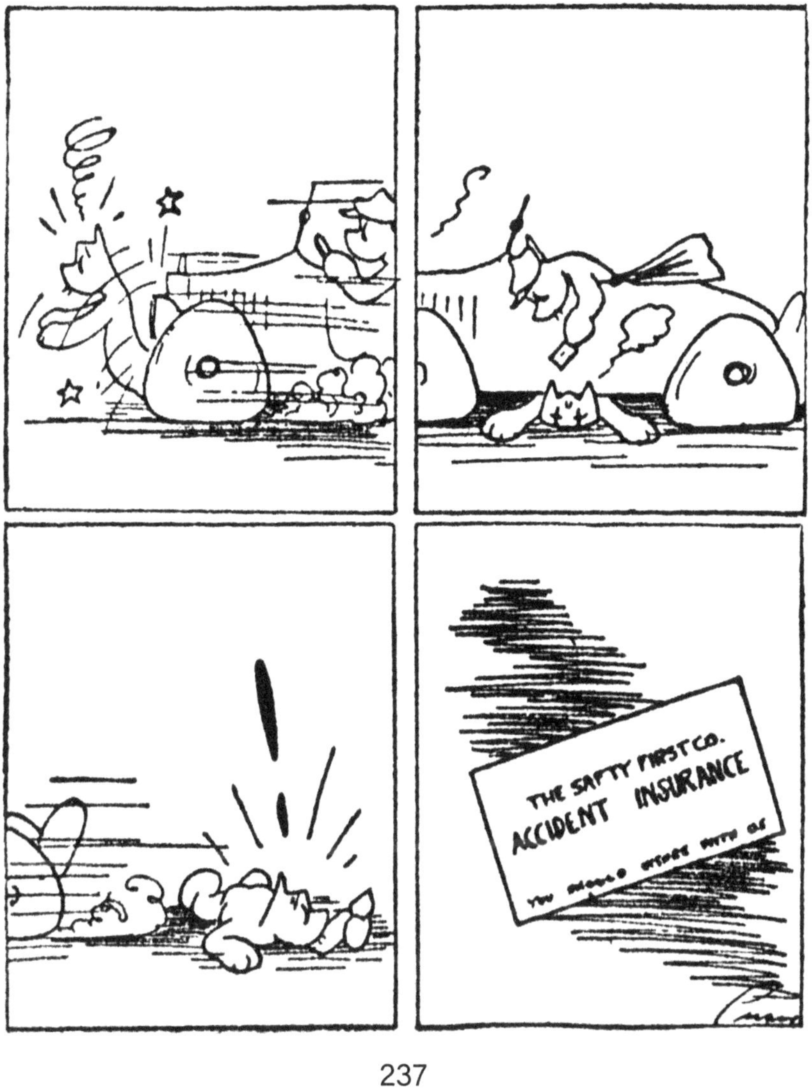
THE SAFTY FIRST CO.
ACCIDENT INSURANCE

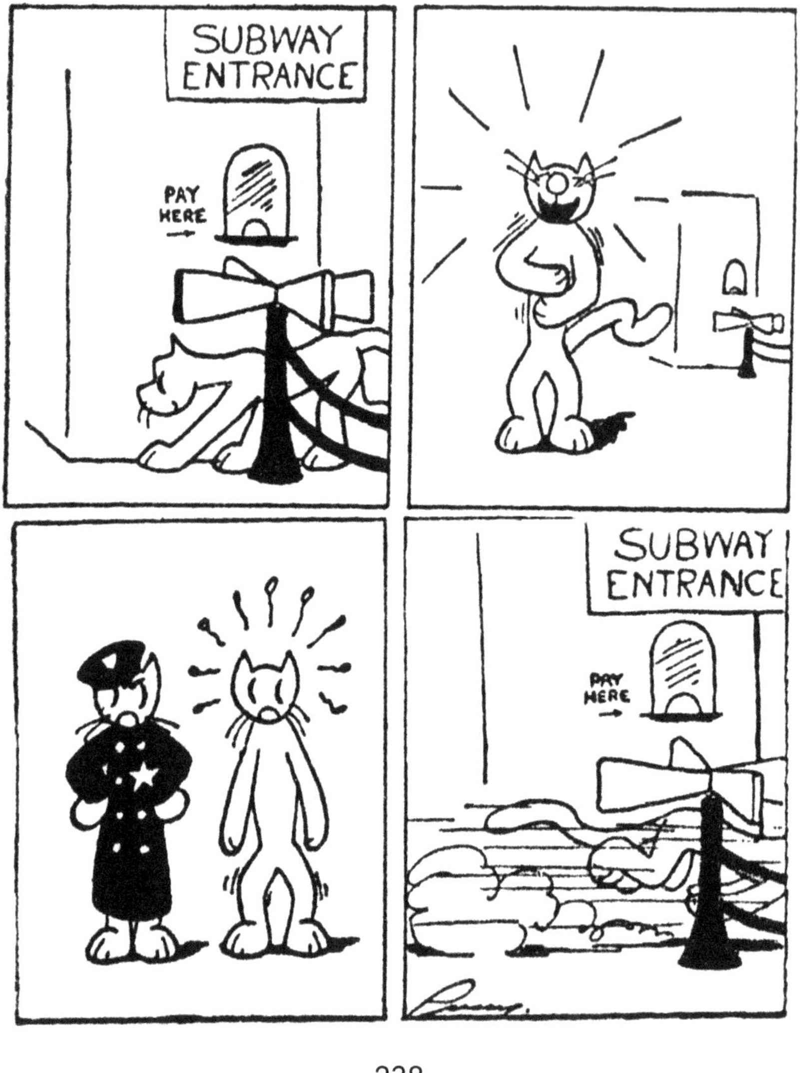
SUBWAY ENTRANCE
PAY HERE
SUBWAY ENTRANCE
PAY HERE

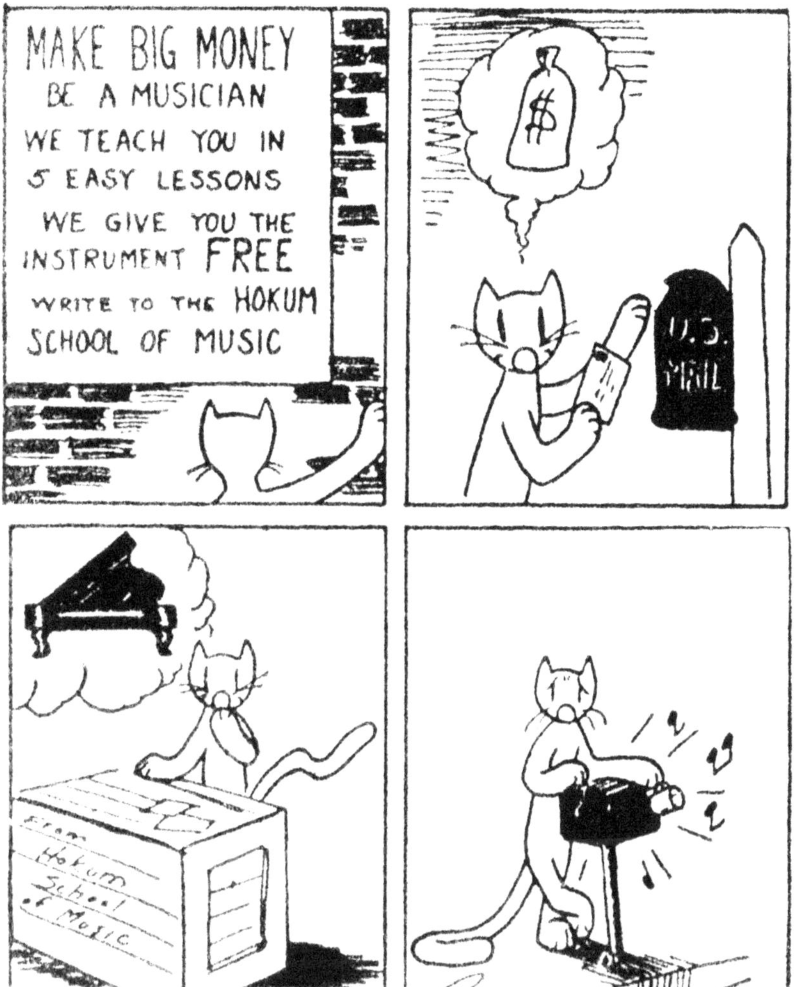
MAKE BIG MONEY
BE A MUSICIAN
WE TEACH YOU IN
5 EASY LESSONS
WE GIVE YOU THE
INSTRUMENT FREE
WRITE TO THE HOKUM
SCHOOL OF MUSIC
U.S. MAIL
From Hokum School of Music

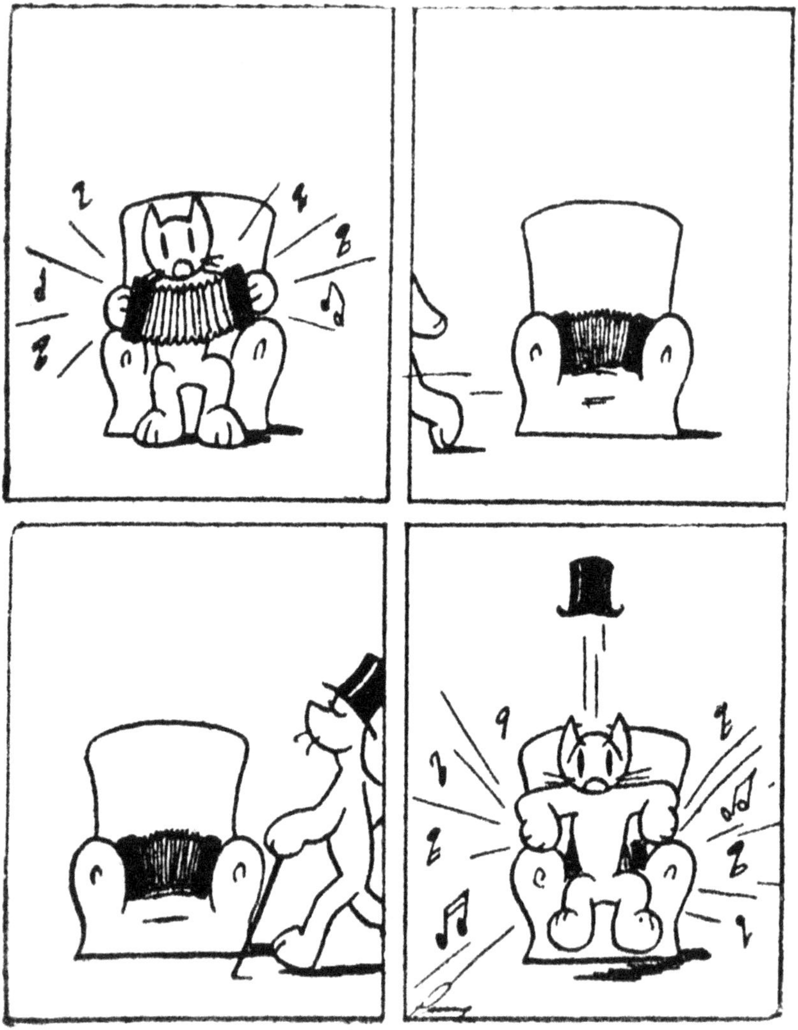

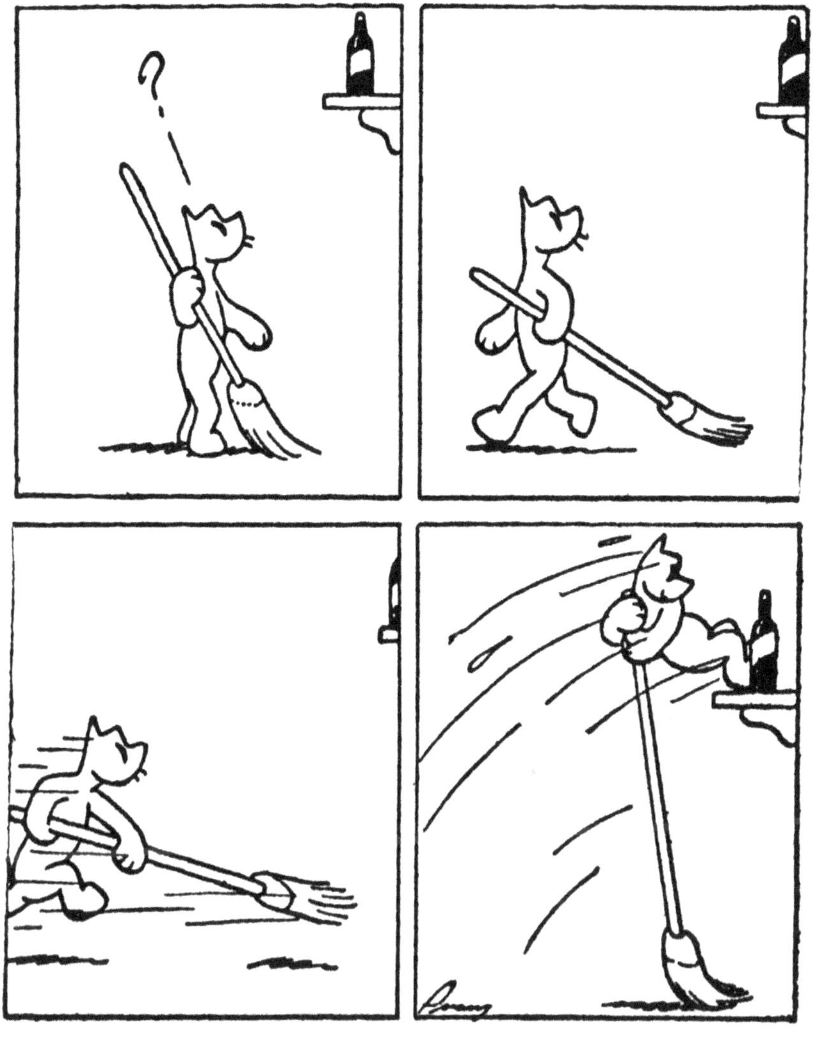
?

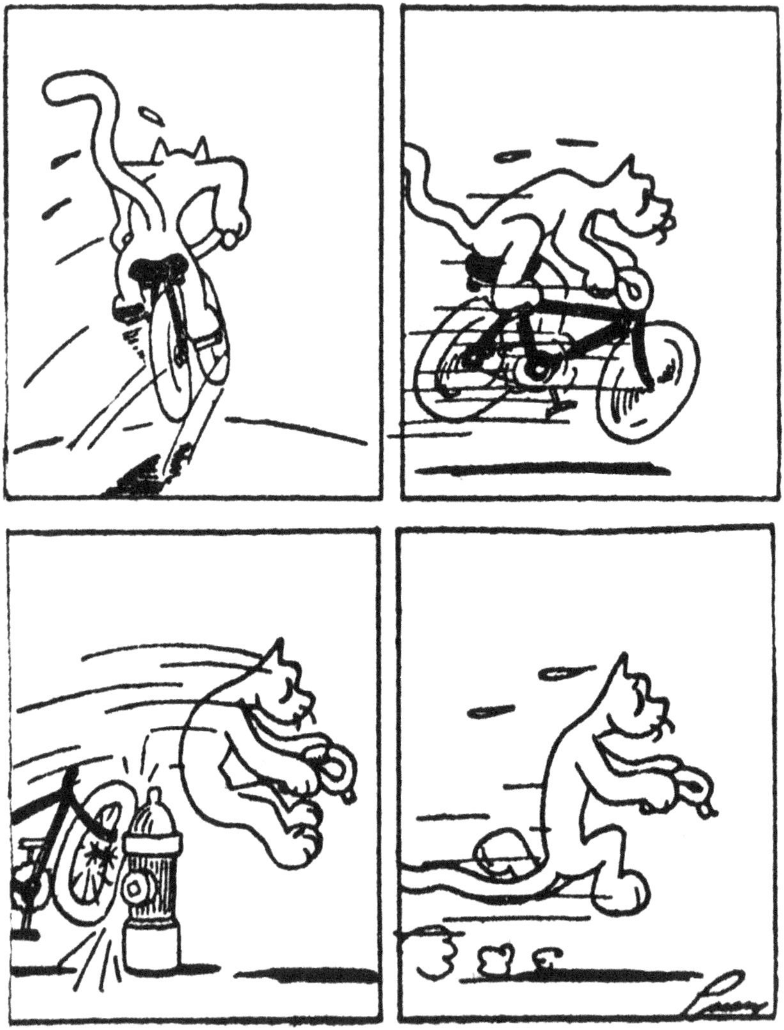

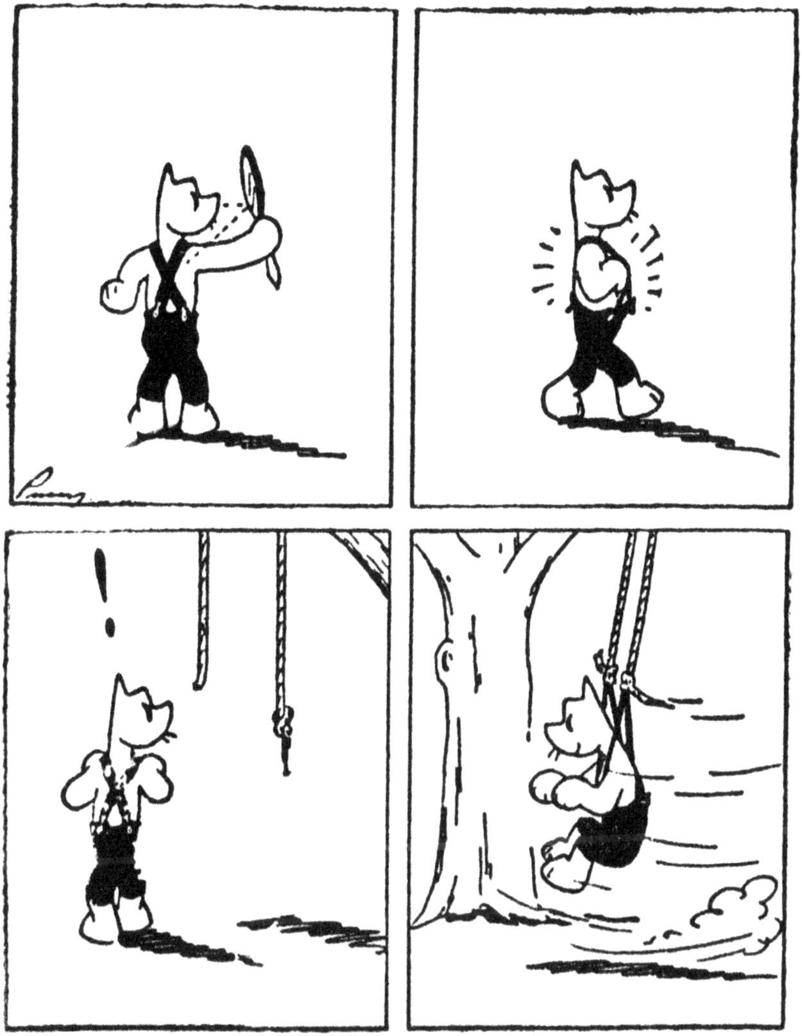
!

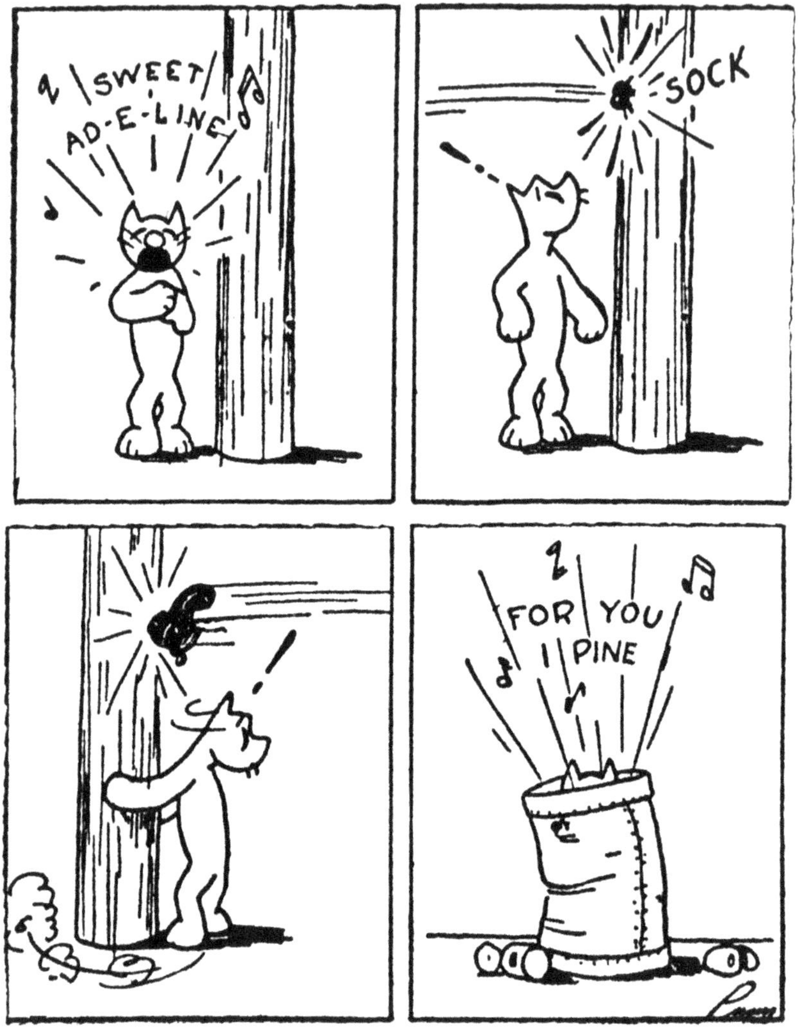
SWEET
AD-E-LINE
SOCK
FOR YOU
I PINE

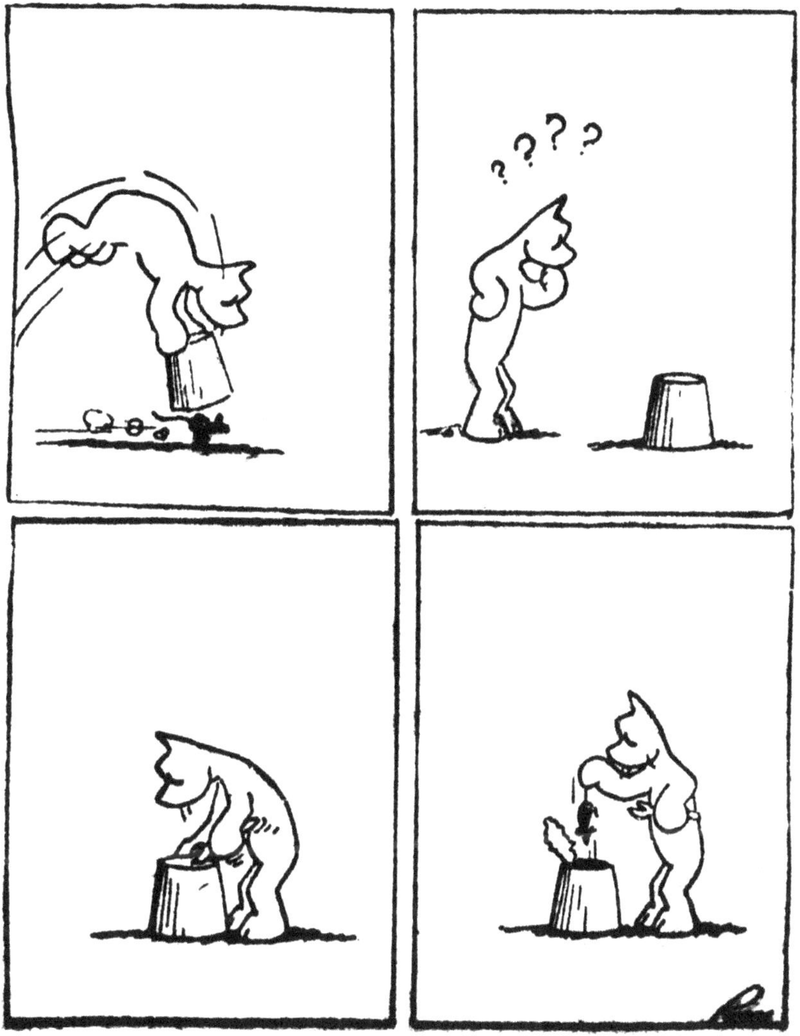
? ? ? ?

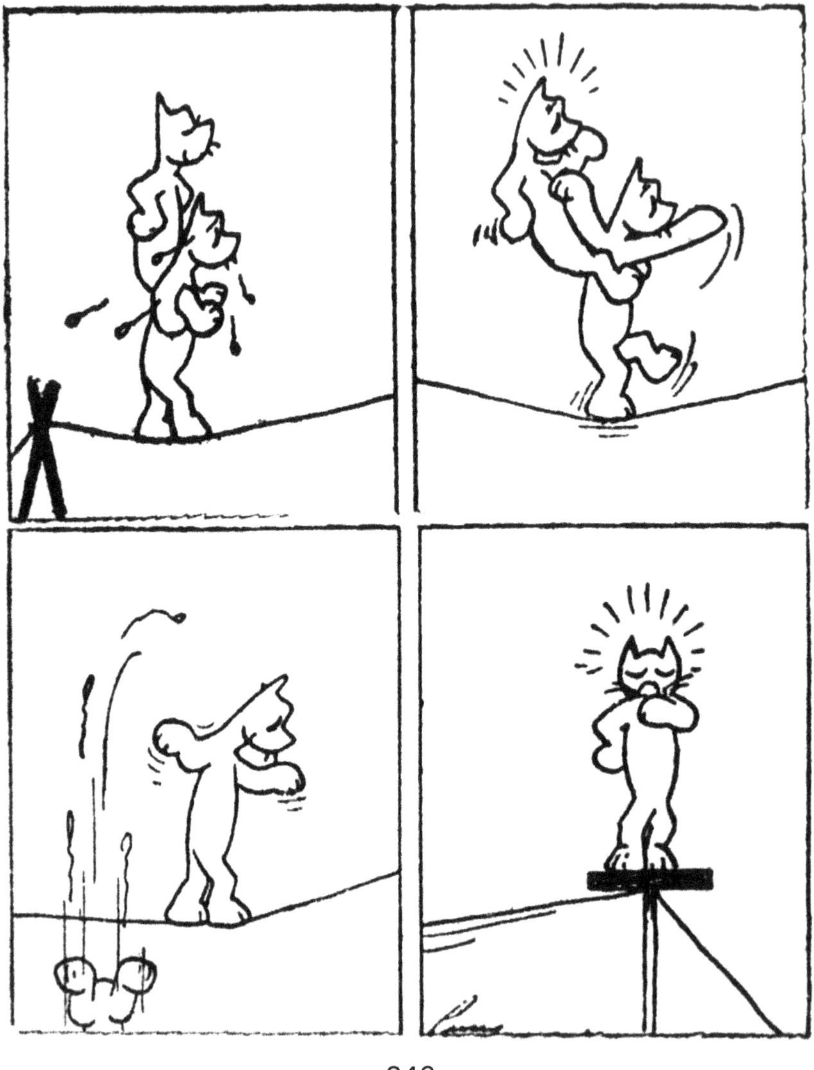

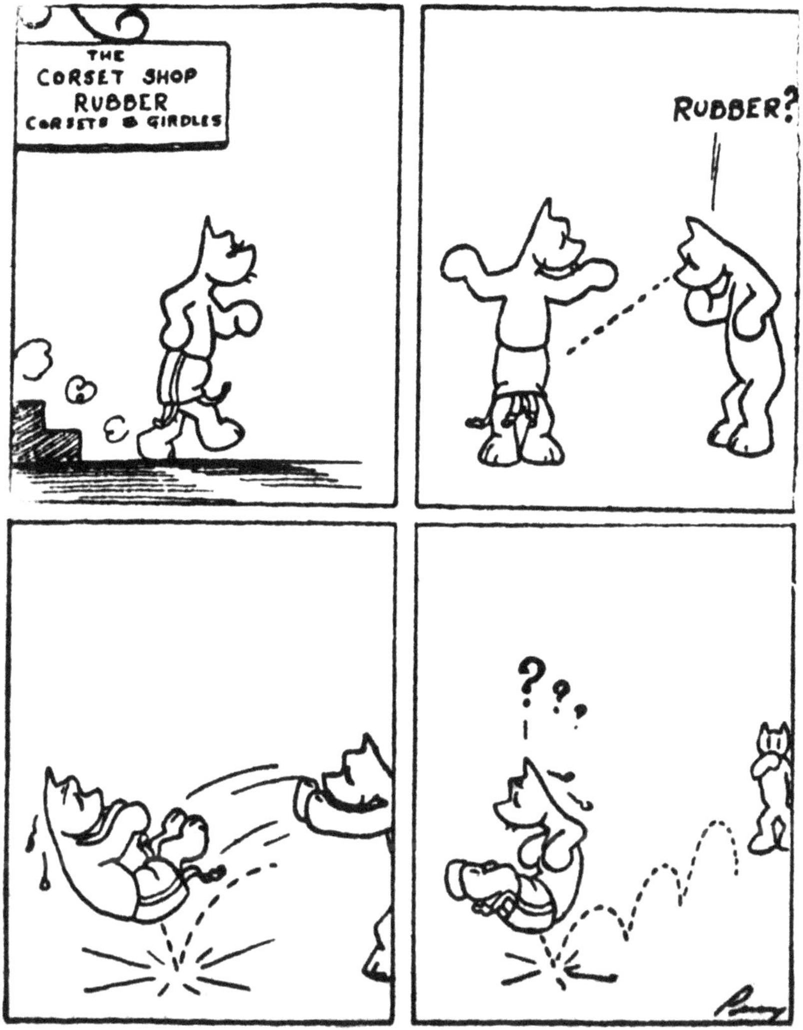
THE
CORSET SHOP
RUBBER
CORSETS & GIRDLES
RUBBER?
? ? ?

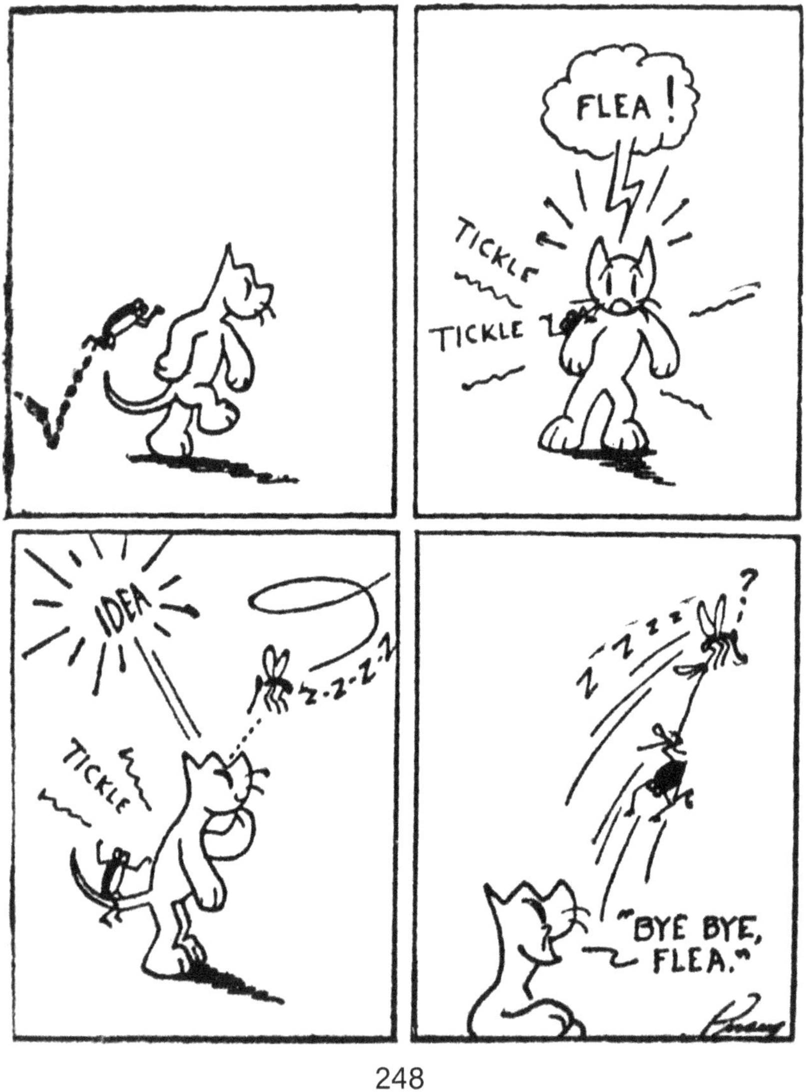
FLEA!
TICKLE
TICKLE
IDEA
TICKLE
Z-Z-Z-Z
Z Z Z Z Z
?
"BYE BYE, FLEA."

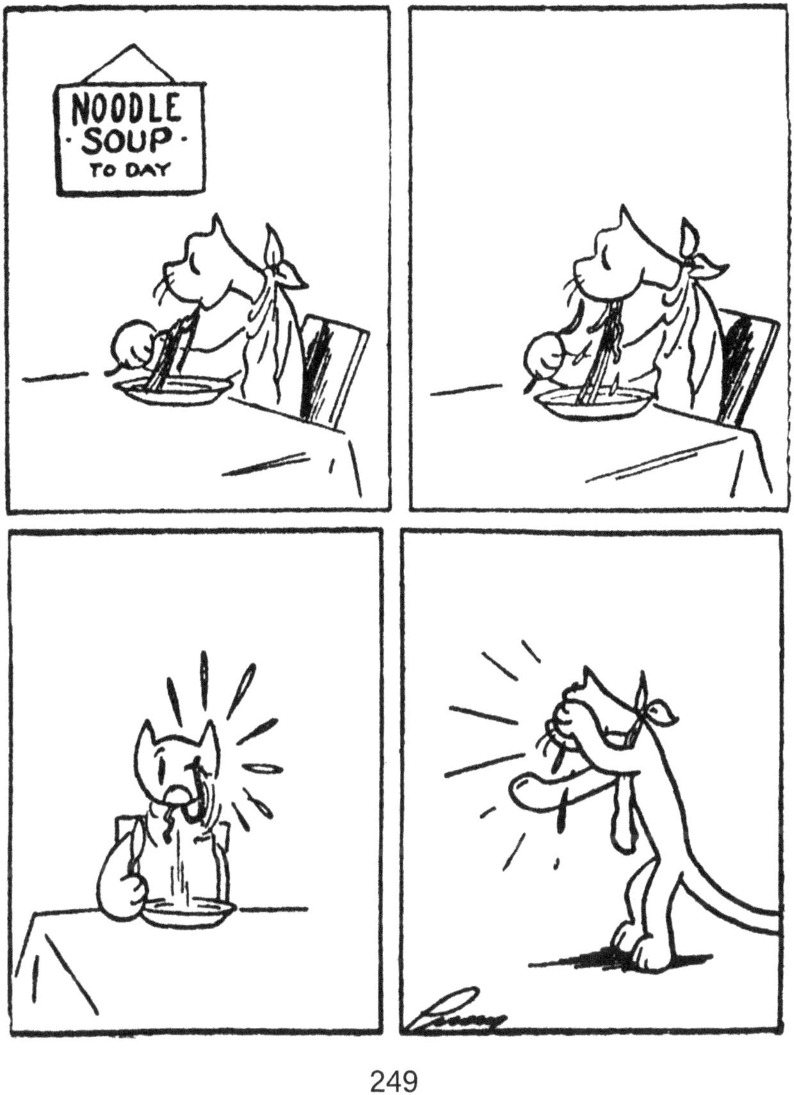
NOODLE
·SOUP·
TO DAY

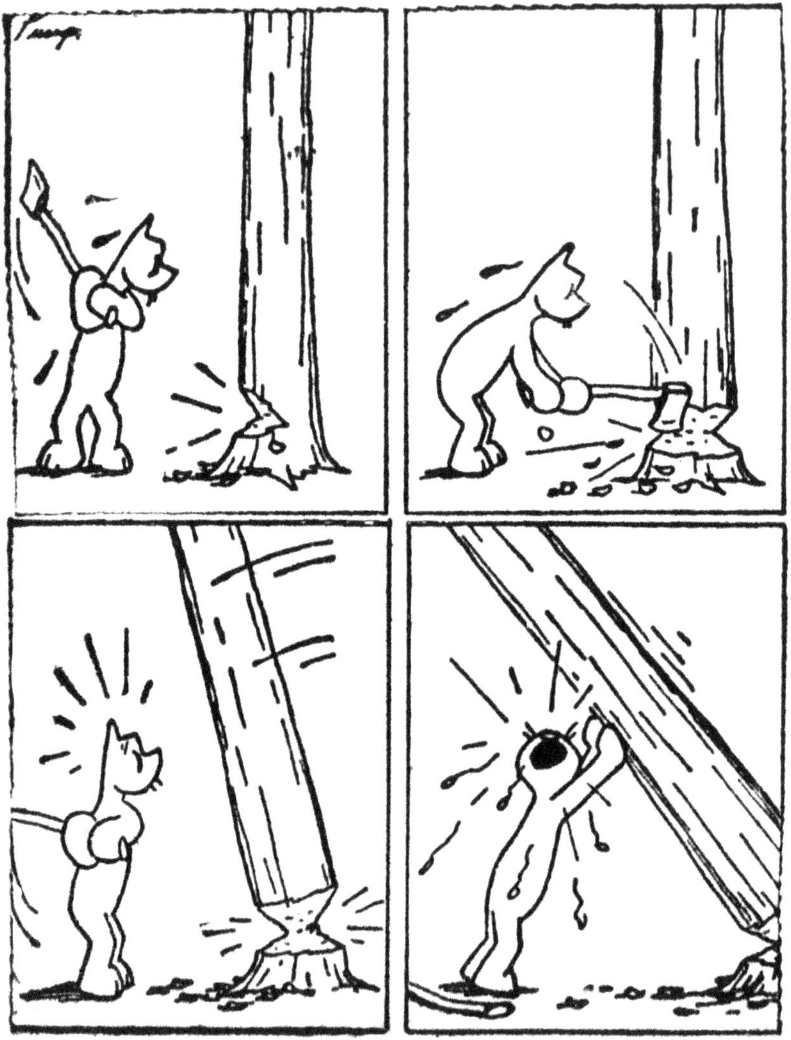

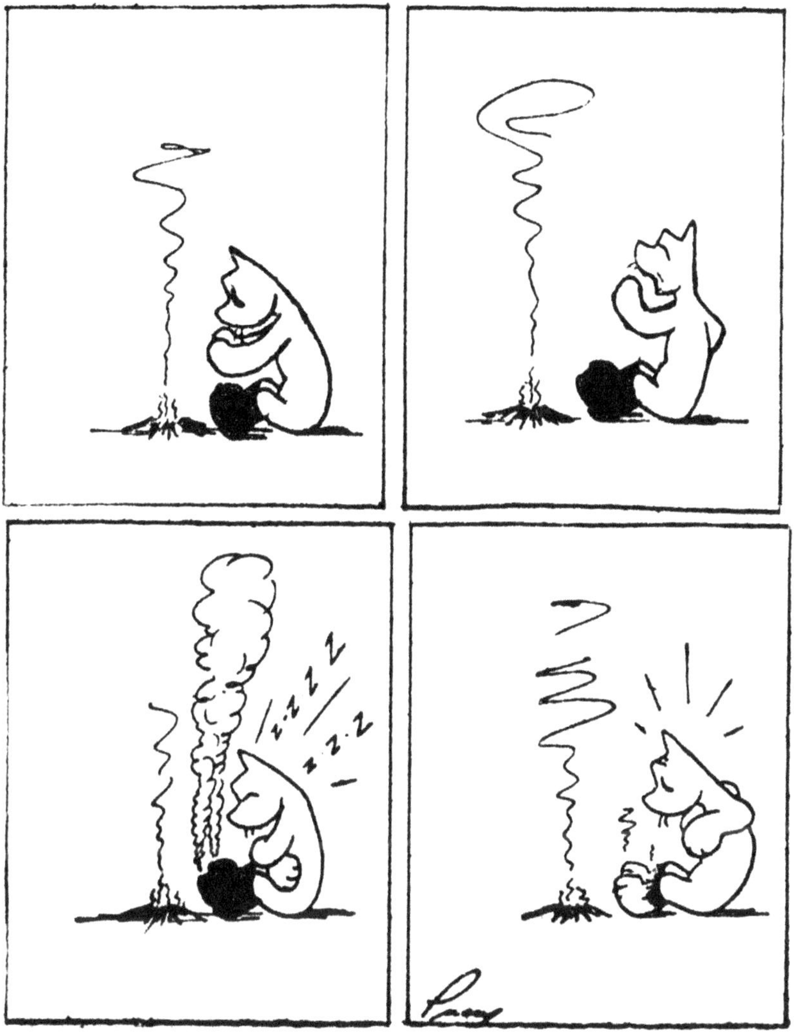

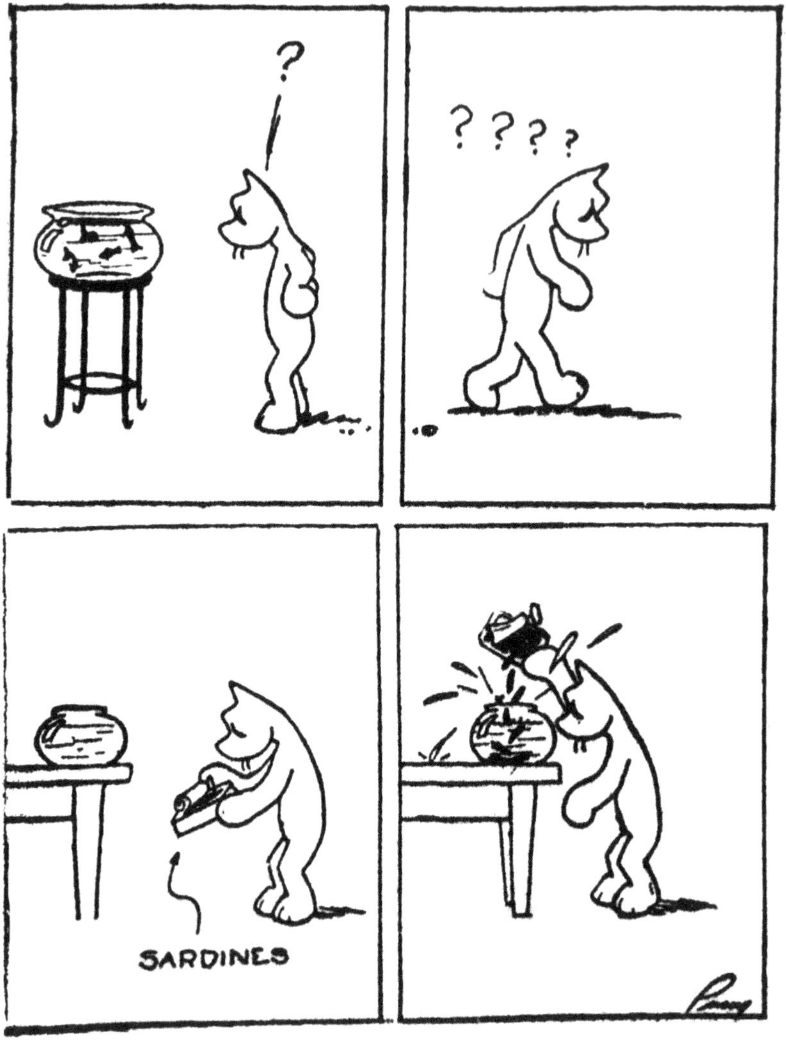
?
????
SARDINES

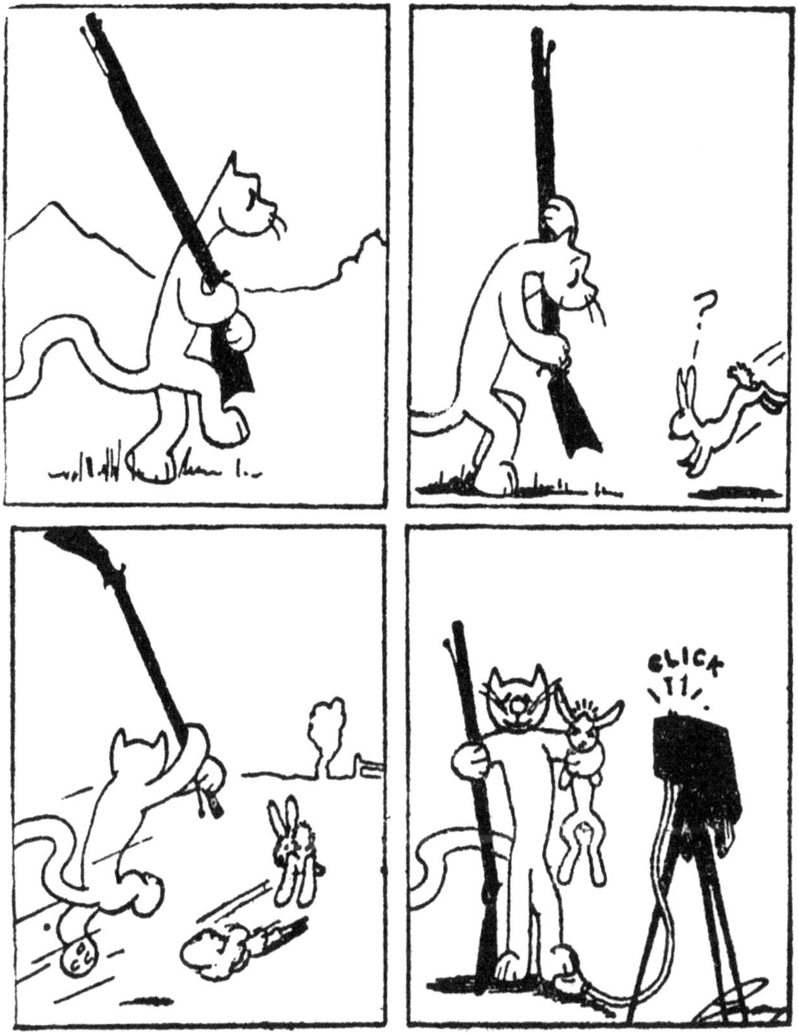
?
CLICK

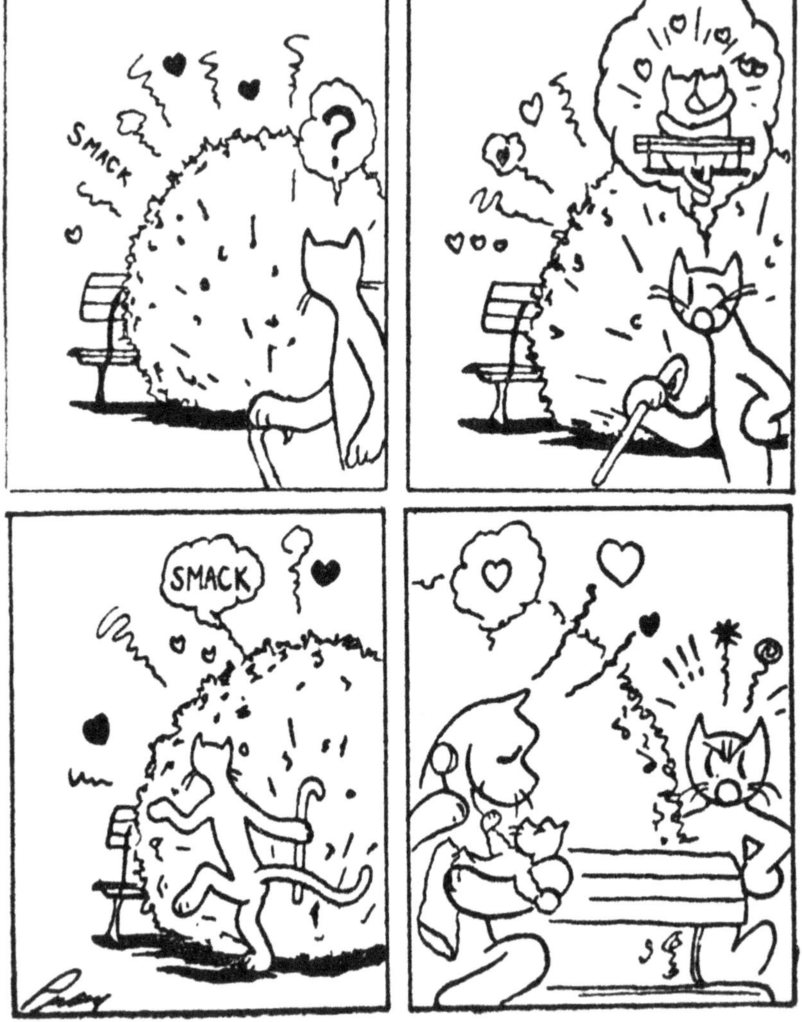
SMACK
SMACK

WELCOME
KNOCK
KNOCK
?
SLAM
BEAT IT

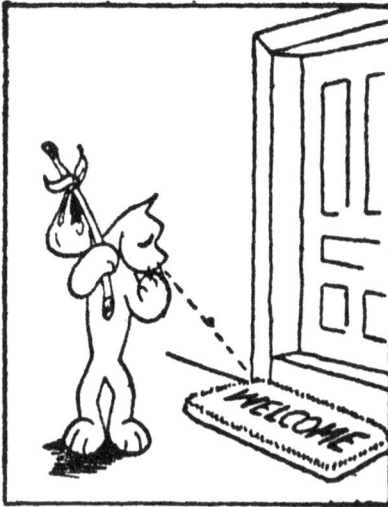

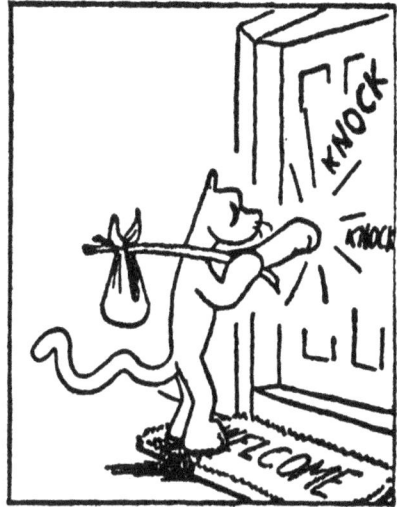

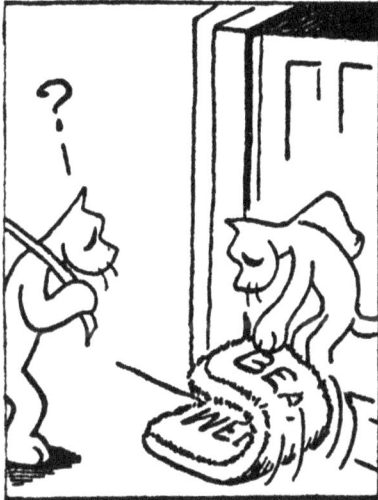

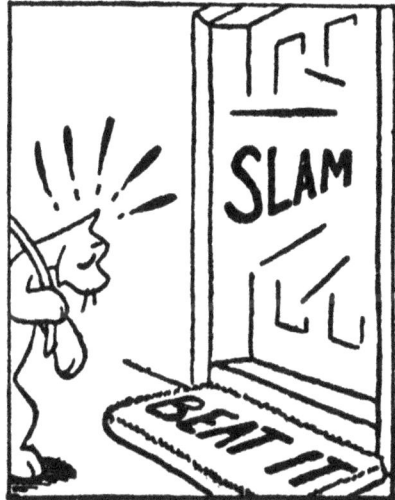

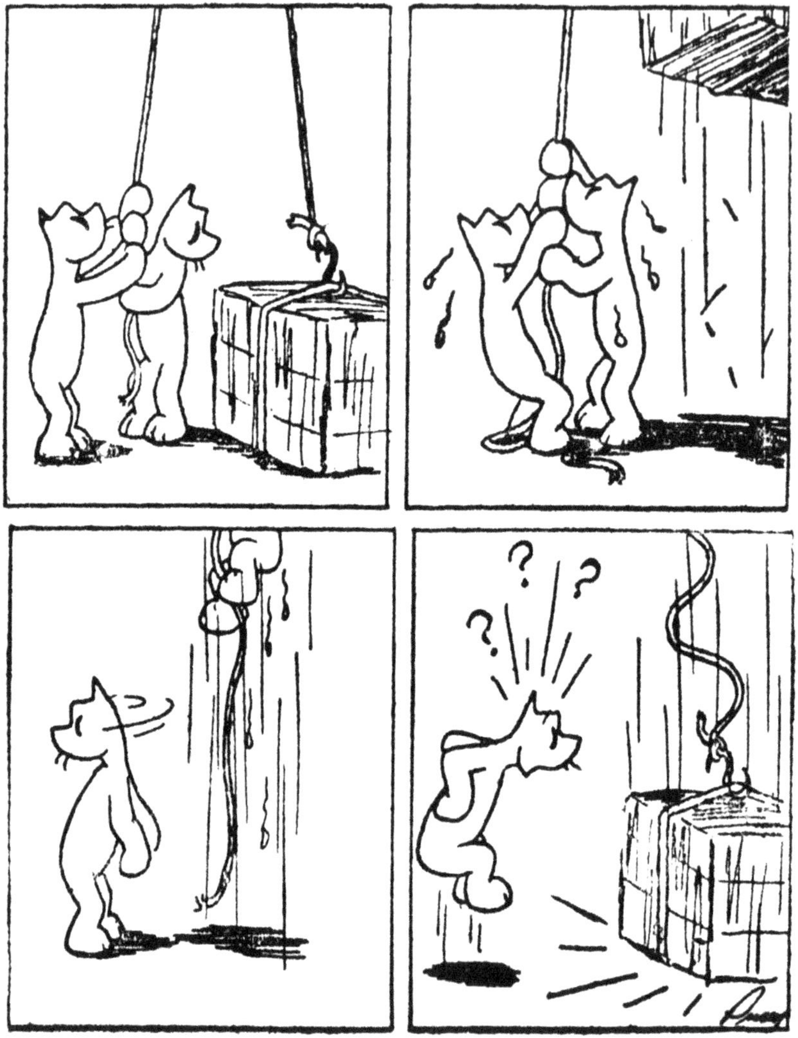

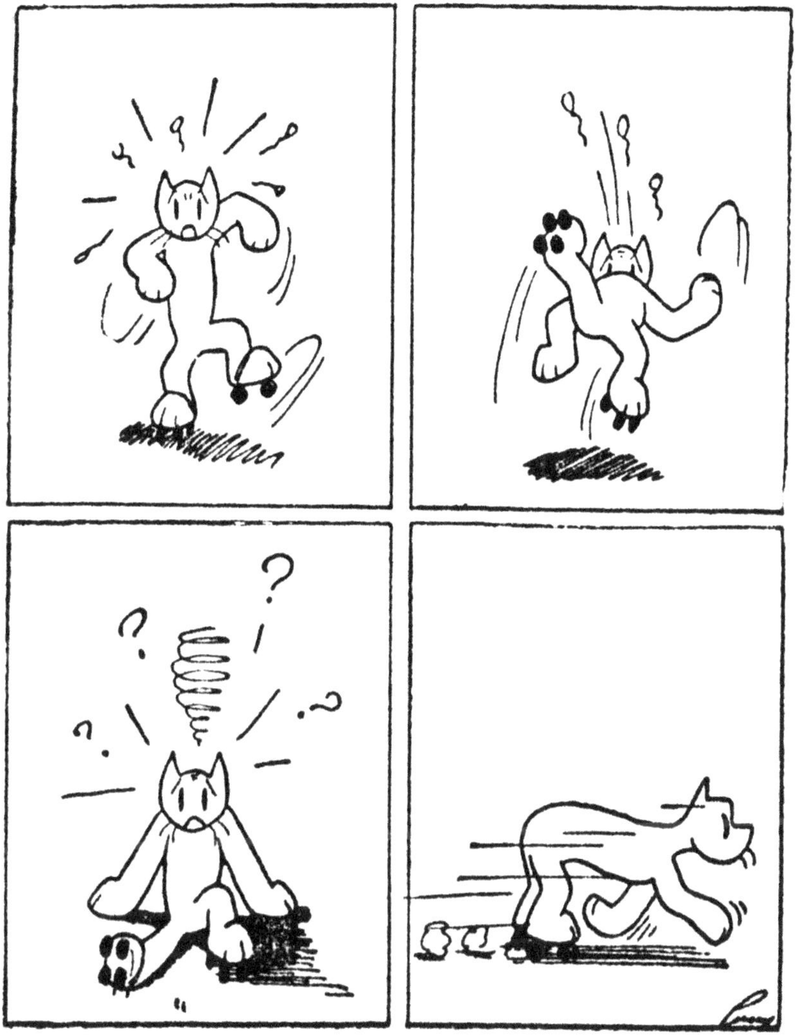

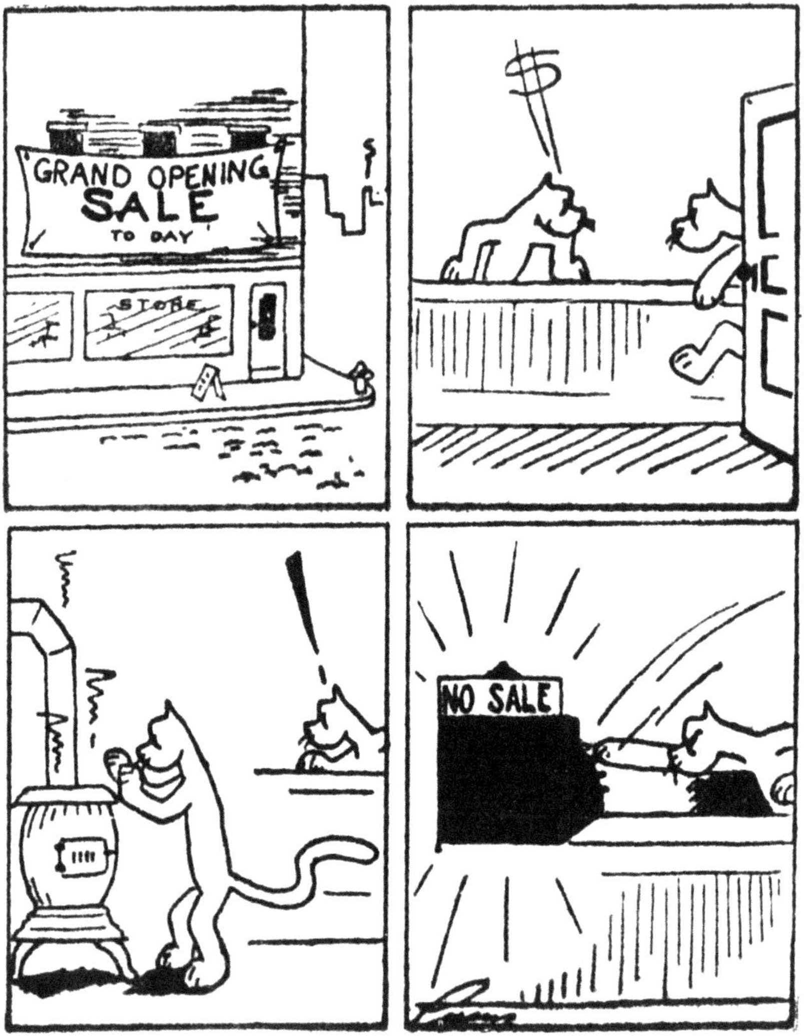
GRAND OPENING
SALE
TO DAY
STORE
$
!
NO SALE

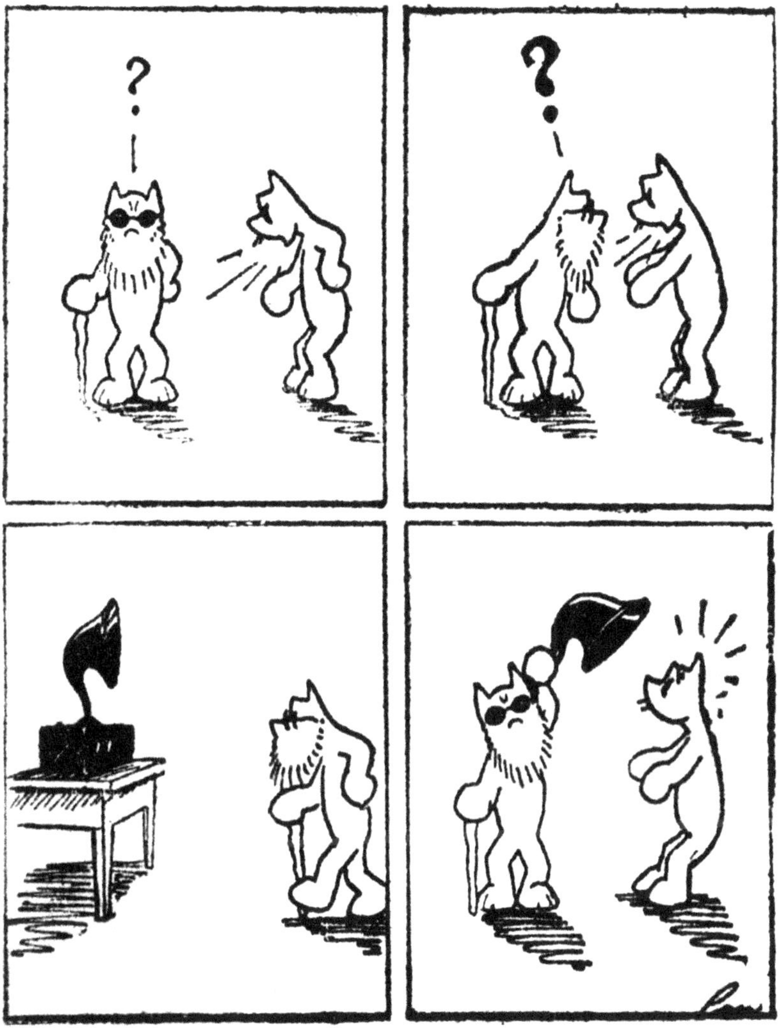

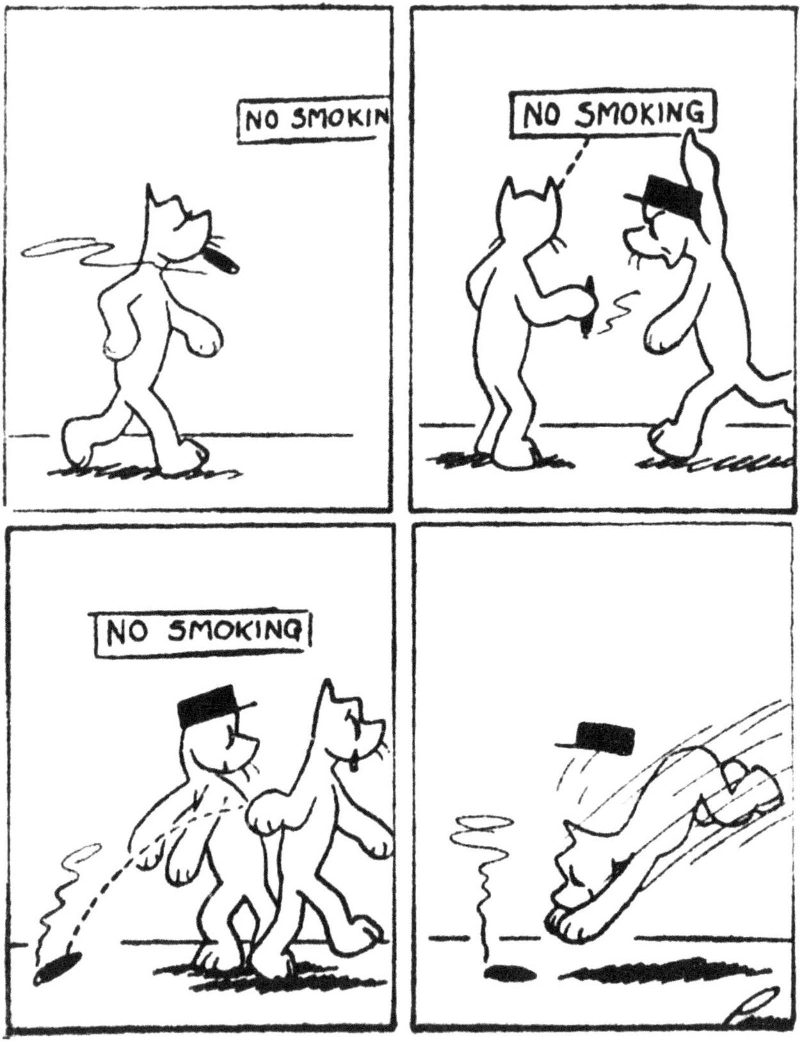
NO SMOKIN
NO SMOKING
NO SMOKING

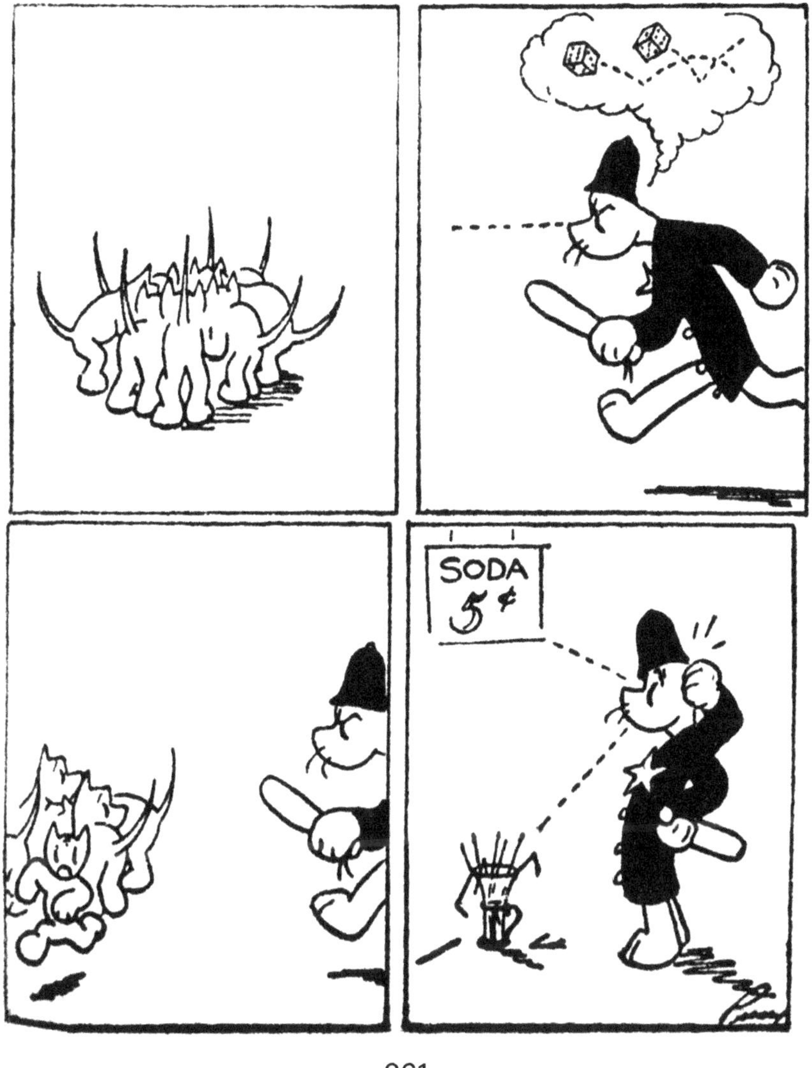
SODA
5¢

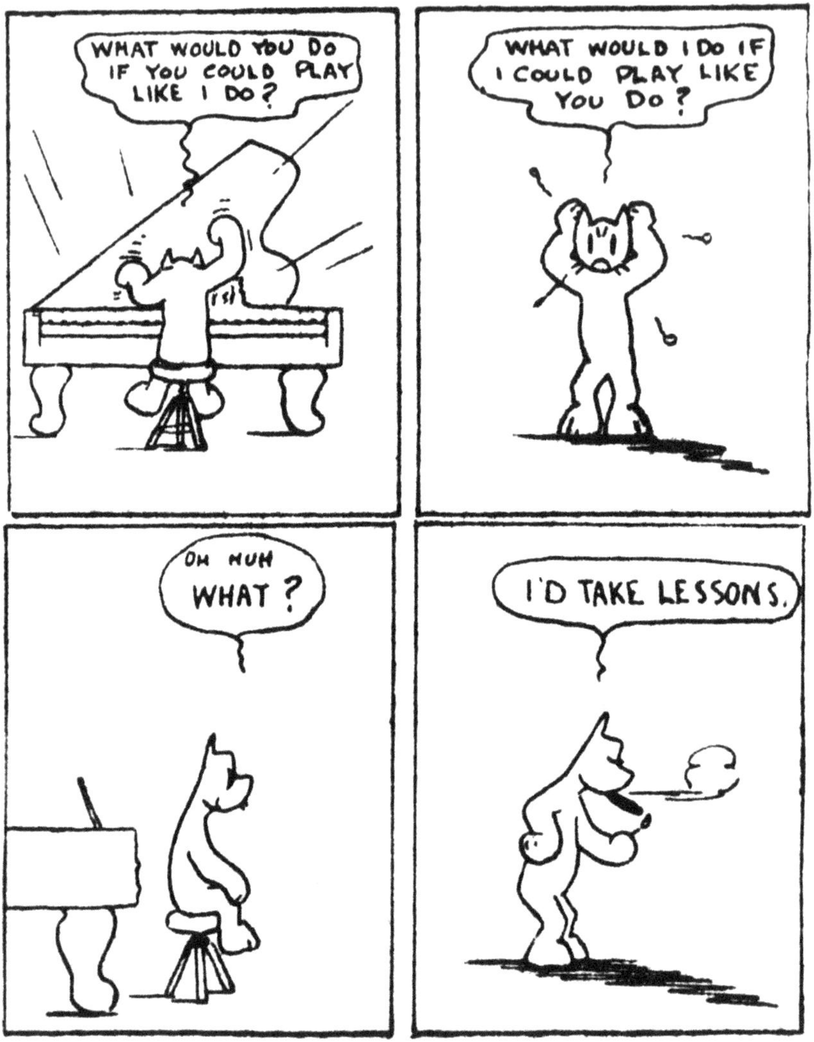
WHAT WOULD YOU DO IF YOU COULD PLAY LIKE I DO?
WHAT WOULD I DO IF I COULD PLAY LIKE YOU DO?
OH HUH WHAT?
I'D TAKE LESSONS.

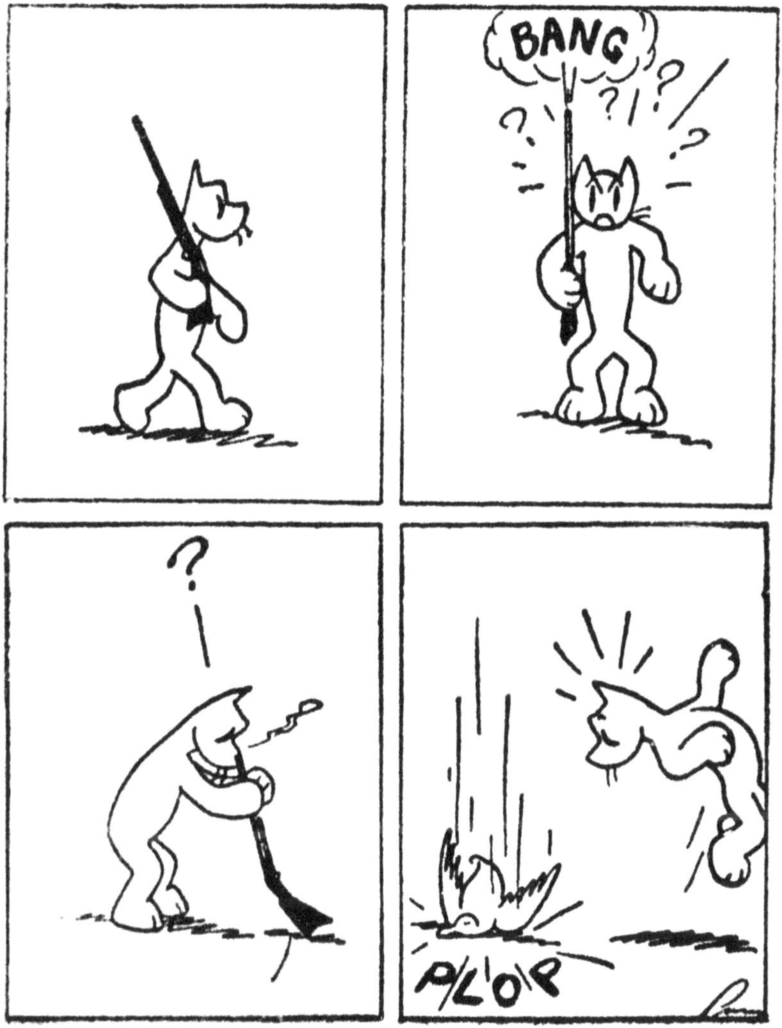
BANG
PLOP

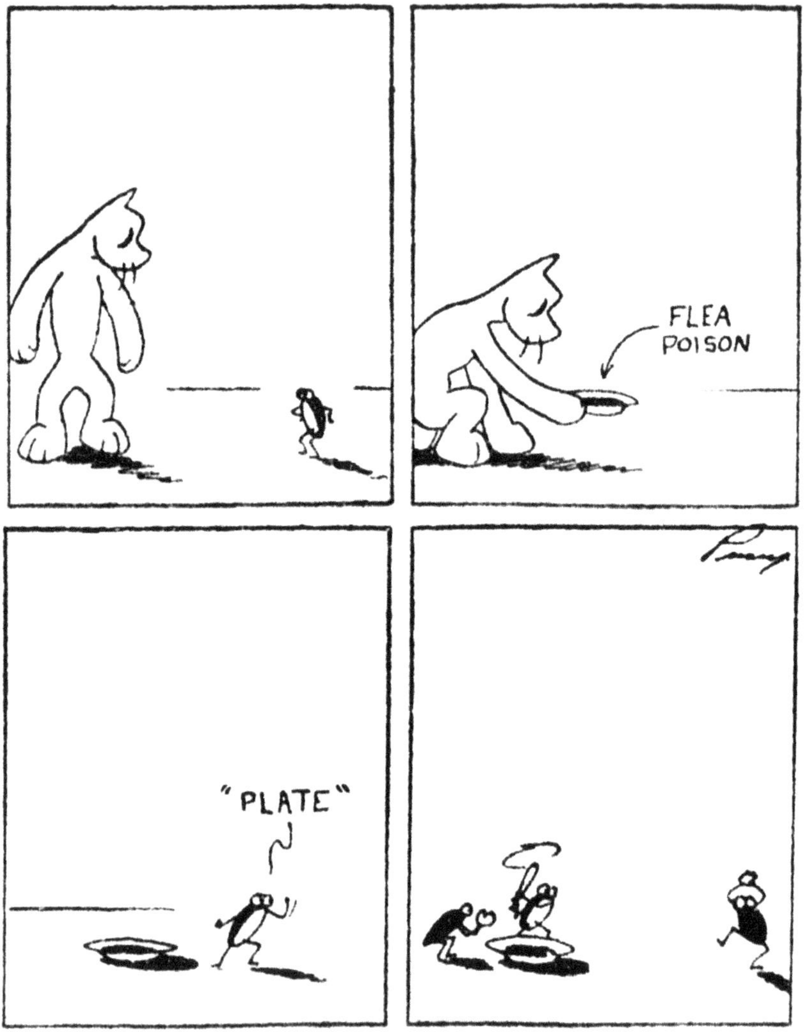
FLEA
POISON
"PLATE"

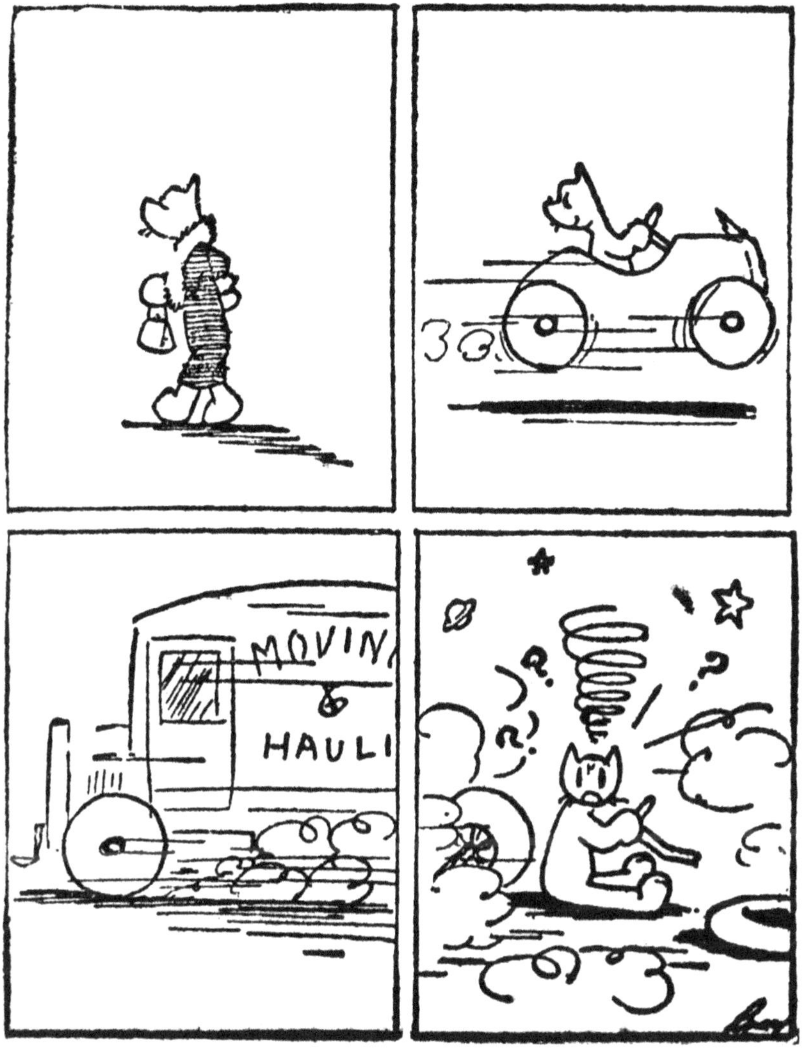
MOVIN
&
HAULI

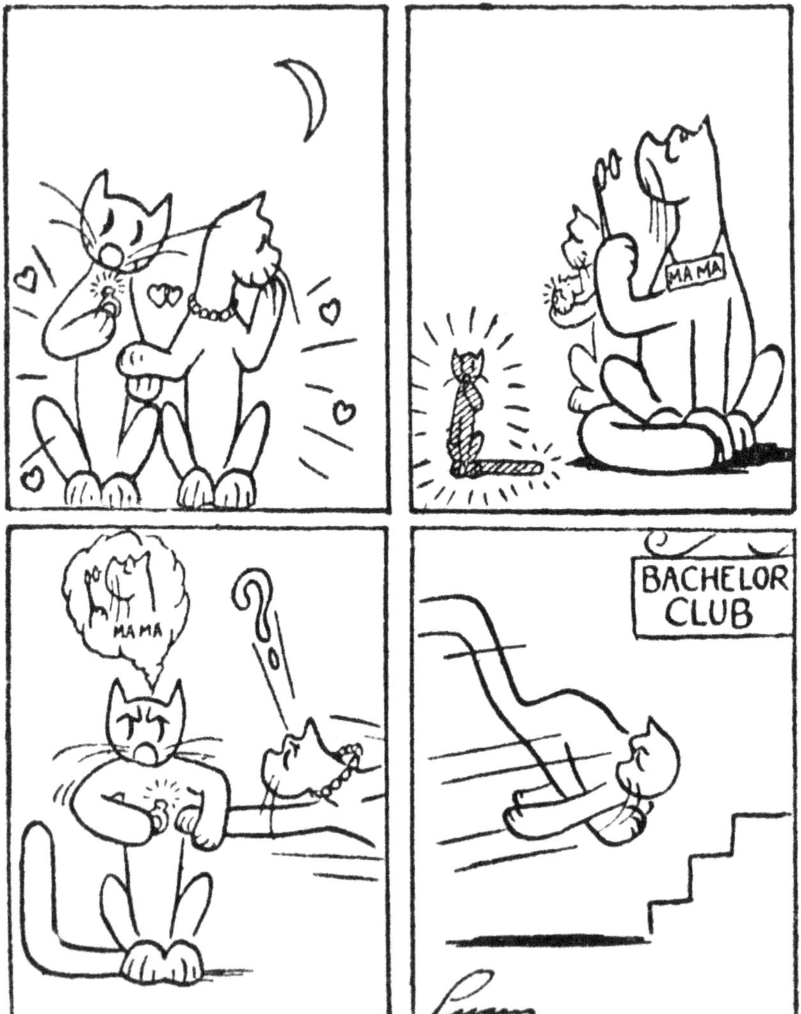
MA MA
MA MA
BACHELOR CLUB

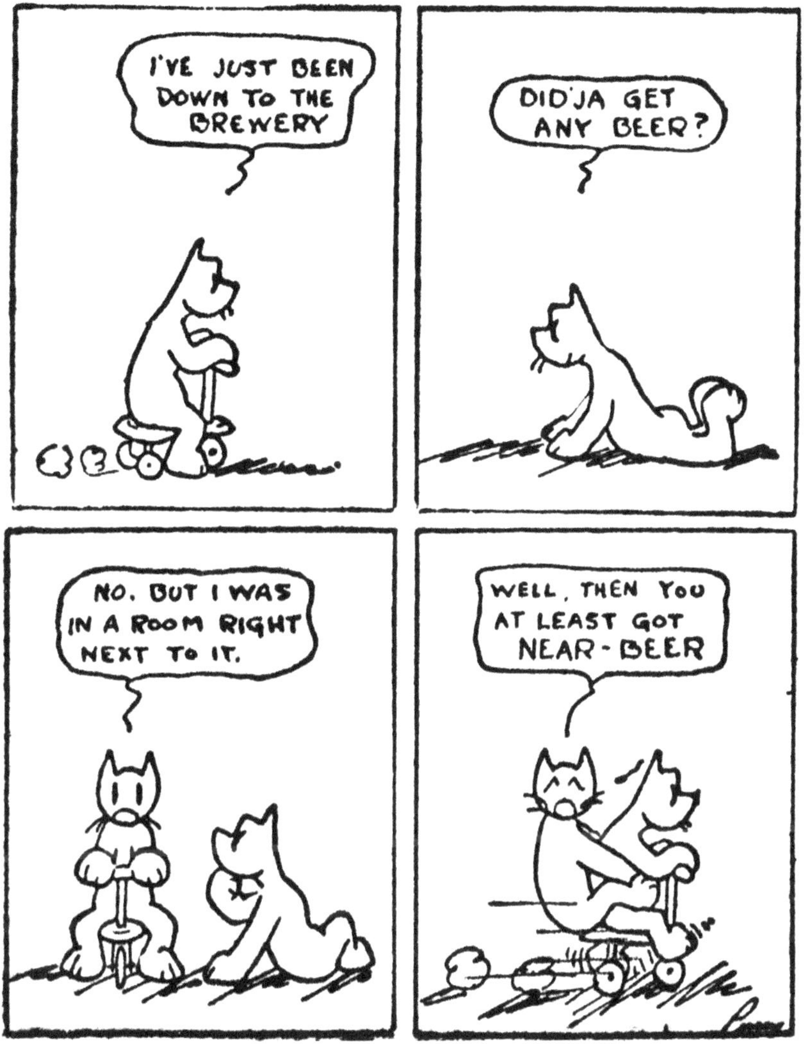
I'VE JUST BEEN DOWN TO THE BREWERY
DID'JA GET ANY BEER?
NO. BUT I WAS IN A ROOM RIGHT NEXT TO IT.
WELL, THEN YOU AT LEAST GOT NEAR-BEER

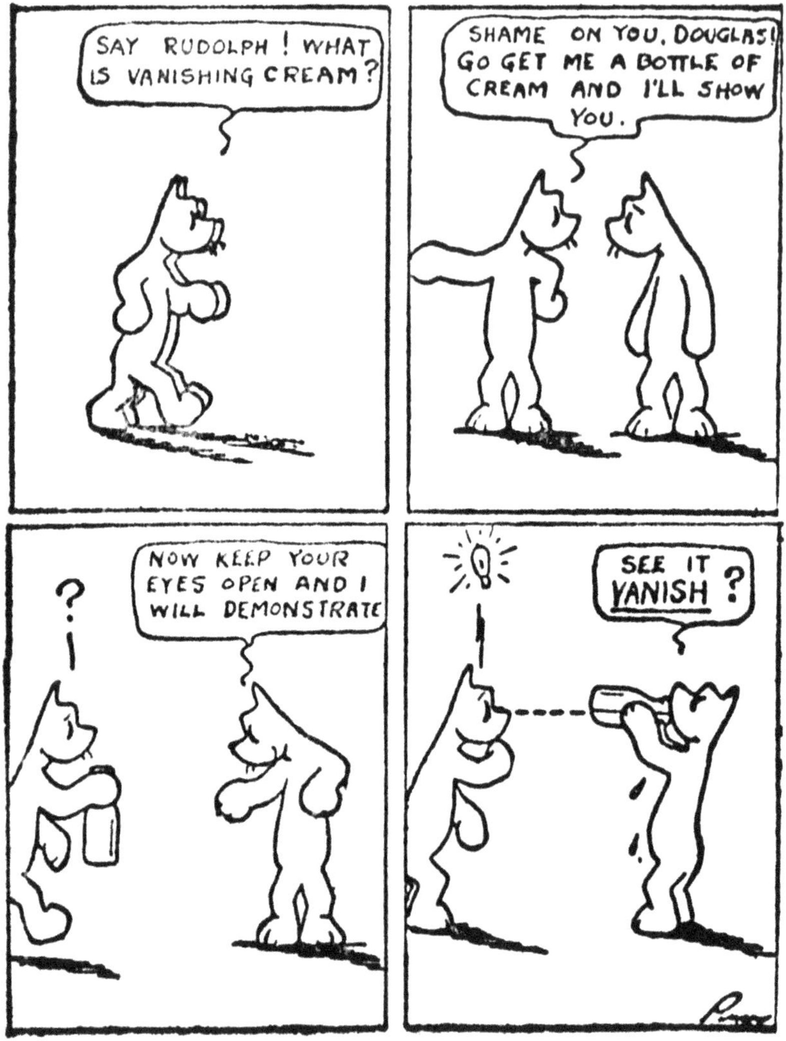
SAY RUDOLPH ! WHAT IS VANISHING CREAM ?
SHAME ON YOU, DOUGLAS! GO GET ME A BOTTLE OF CREAM AND I'LL SHOW YOU.
?
NOW KEEP YOUR EYES OPEN AND I WILL DEMONSTRATE
SEE IT VANISH ?

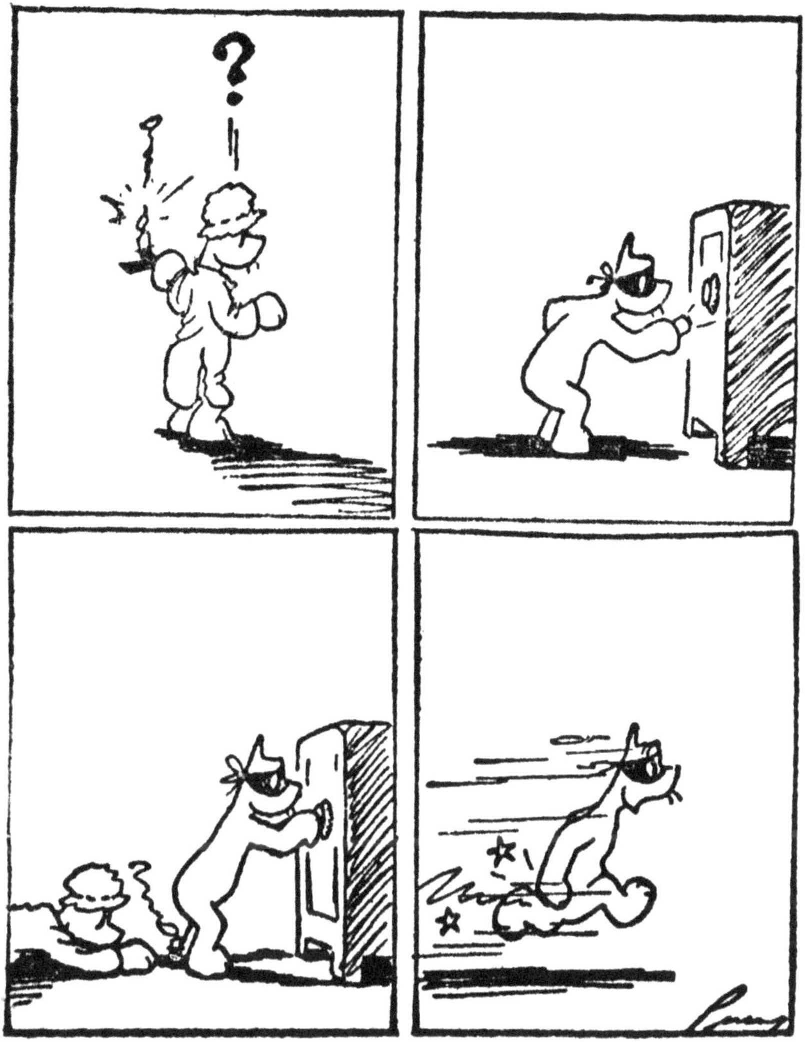

IDEA
B-R-R-R
B-R-R
VACUUM
CLEANER
B-R-R-R
ACUUM
LEANER
B-R-R-R-R-R
B-R-R
B-R-R-R
B-R
ACUUM
LEANER
B-R-R
B-R-R-R
B-R-R

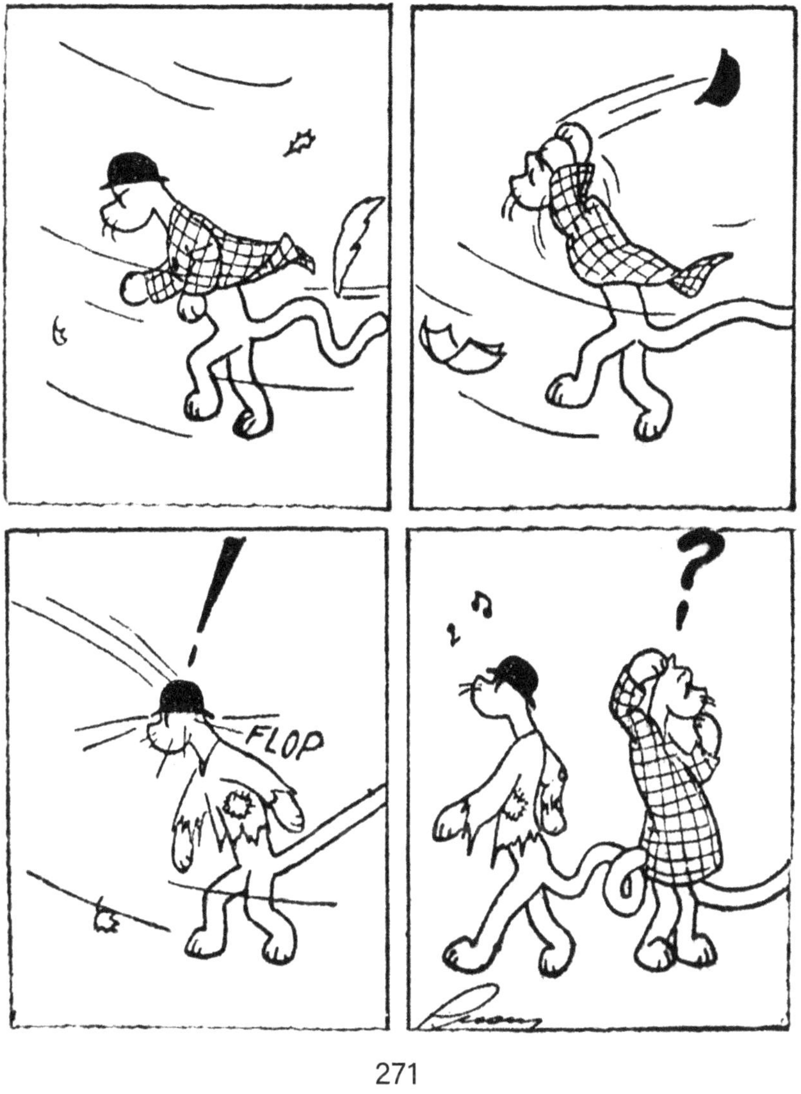
!
FLOP
?

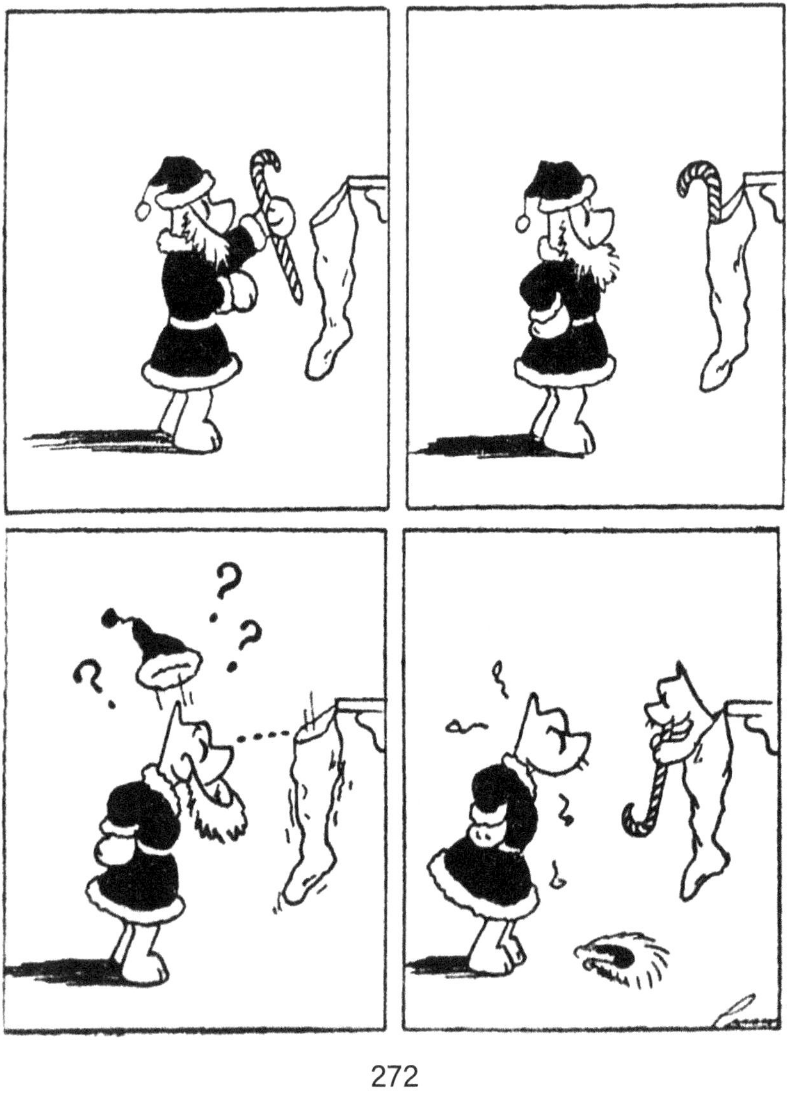

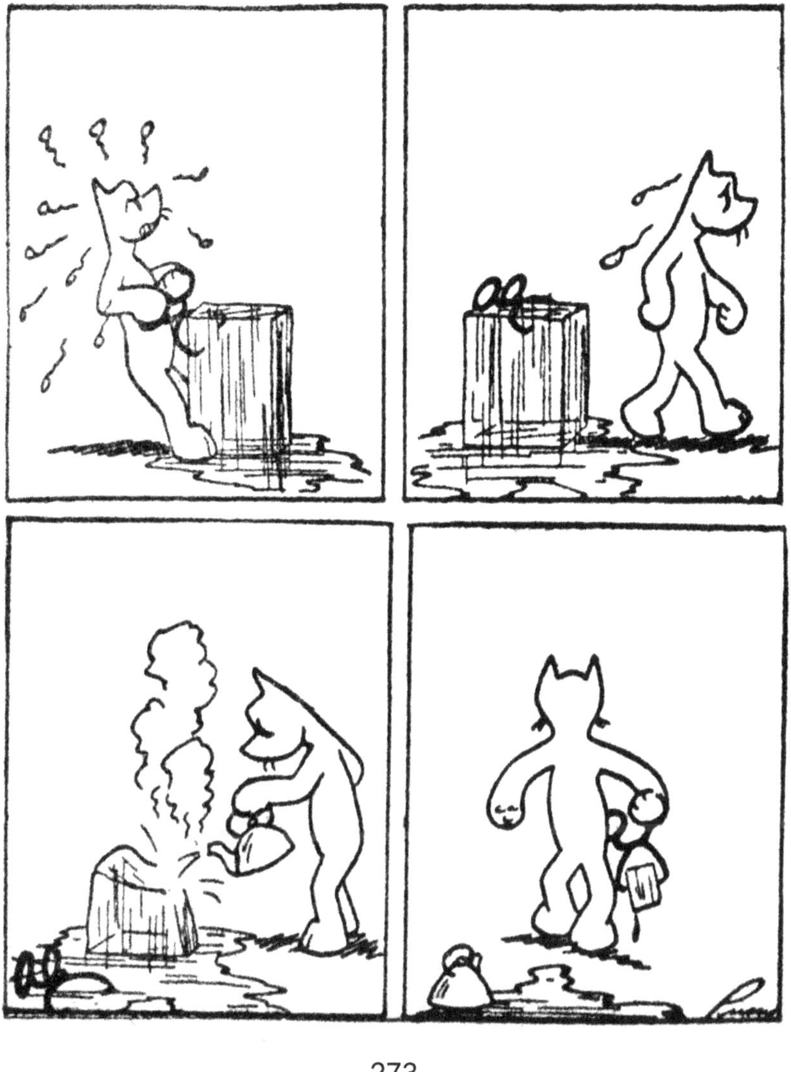

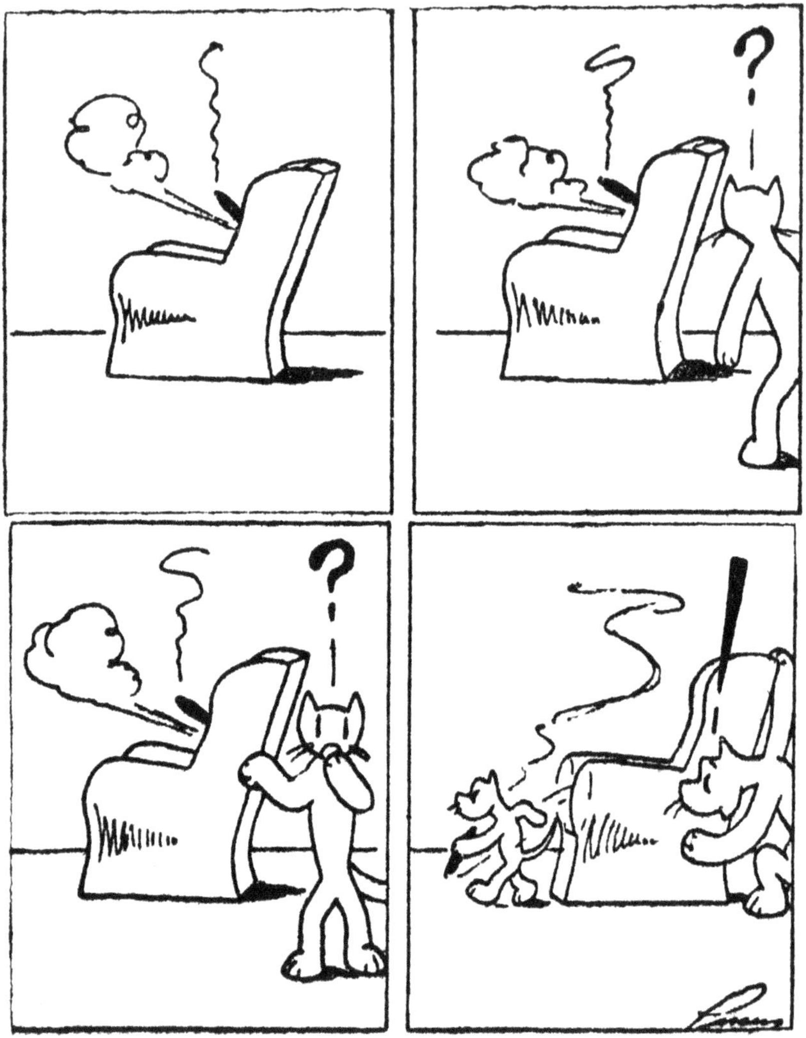

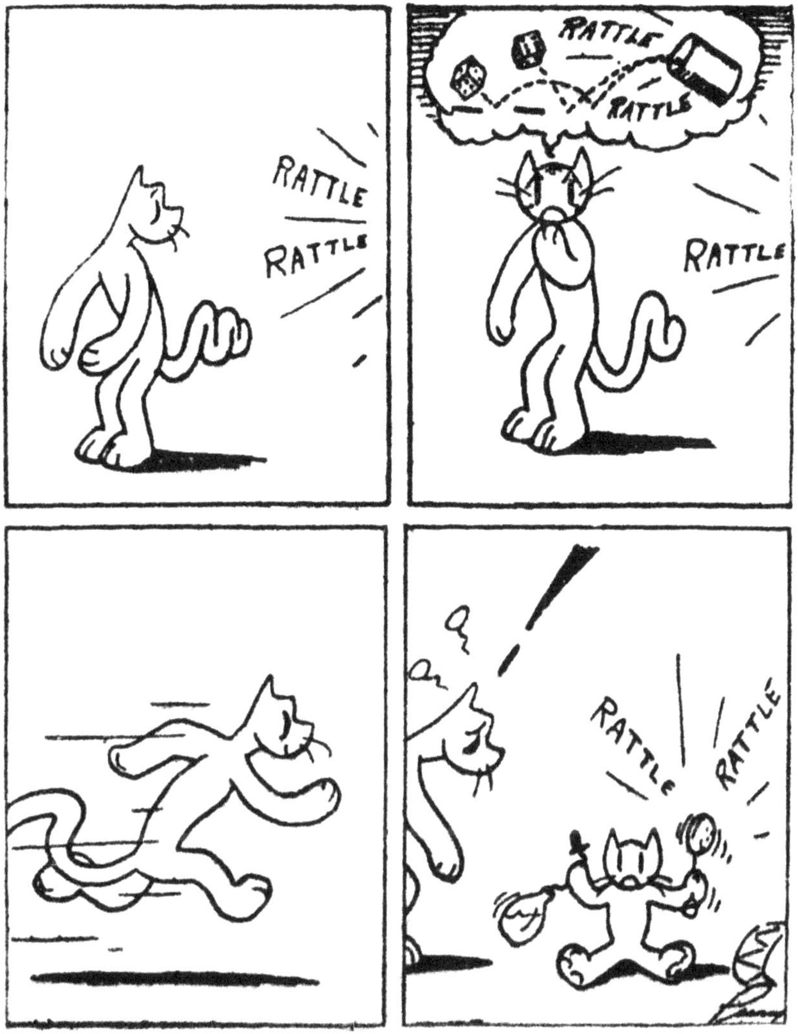
RATTLE
RATTLE
RATTLE
RATTLE
RATTLE
RATTLE
RATTLE
RATTLE

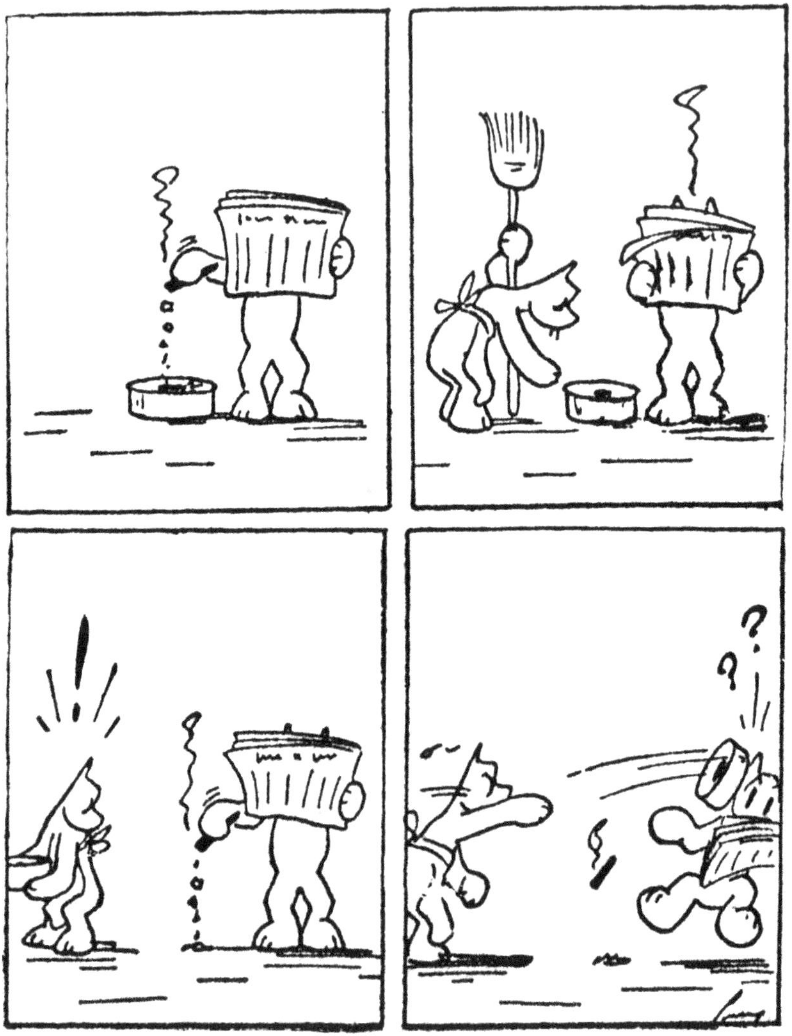

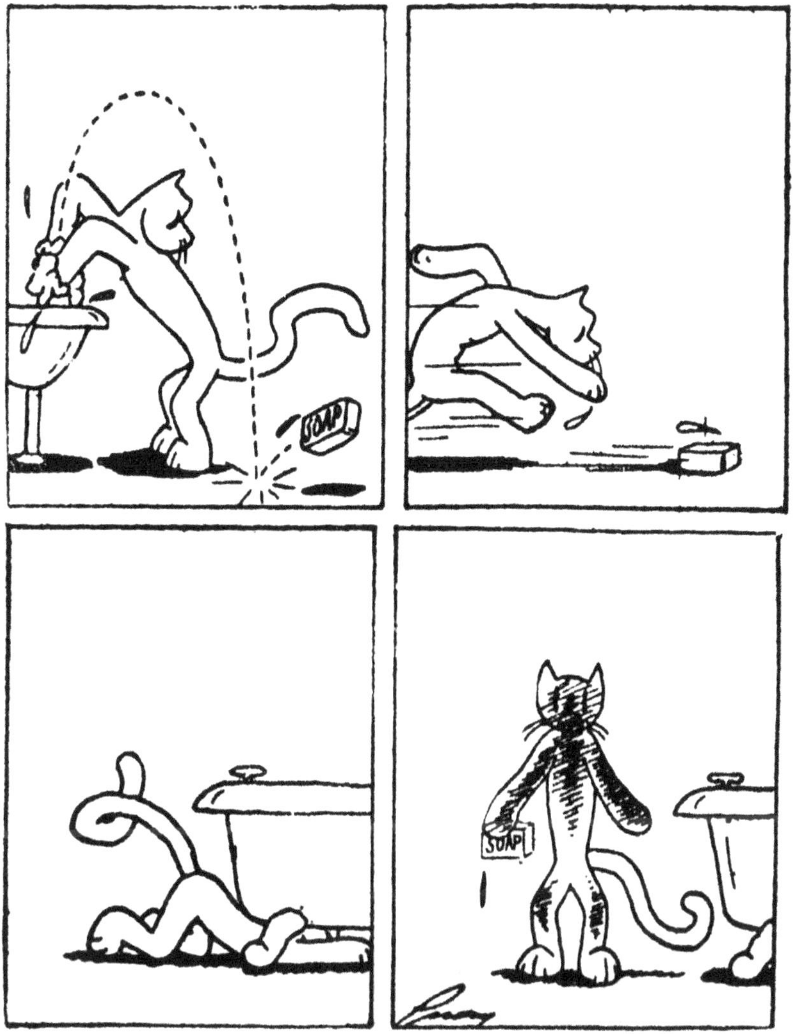
SOAP
SOAP

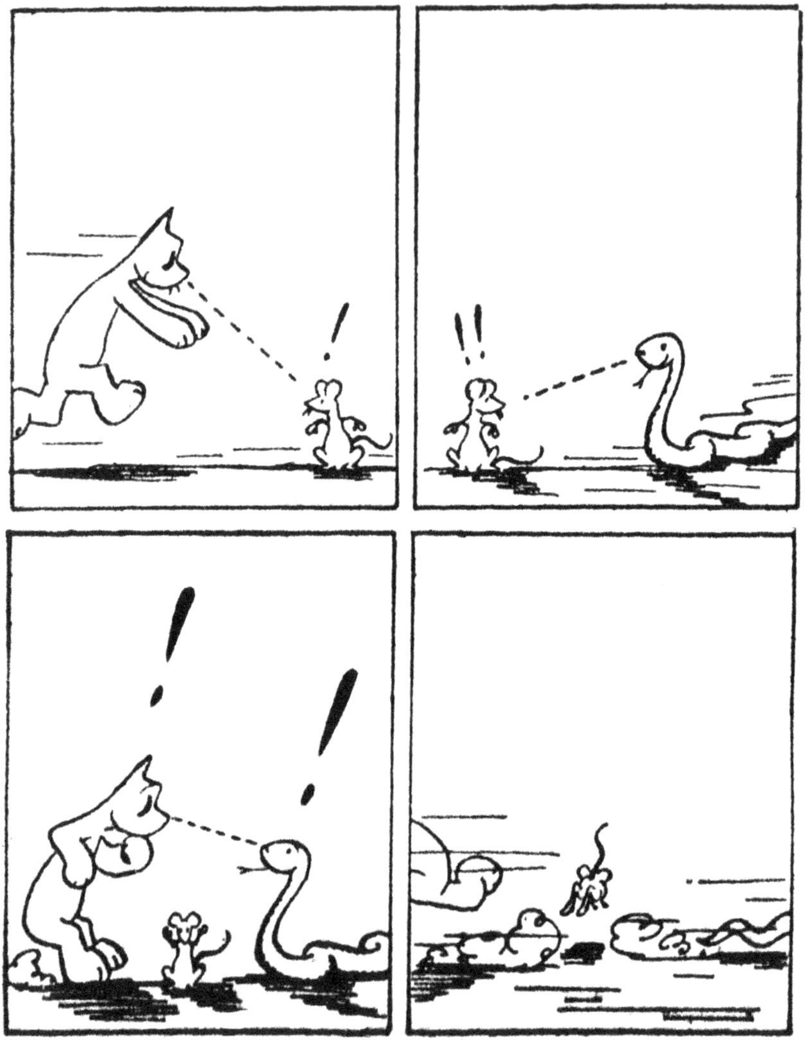
!
!!
!
!

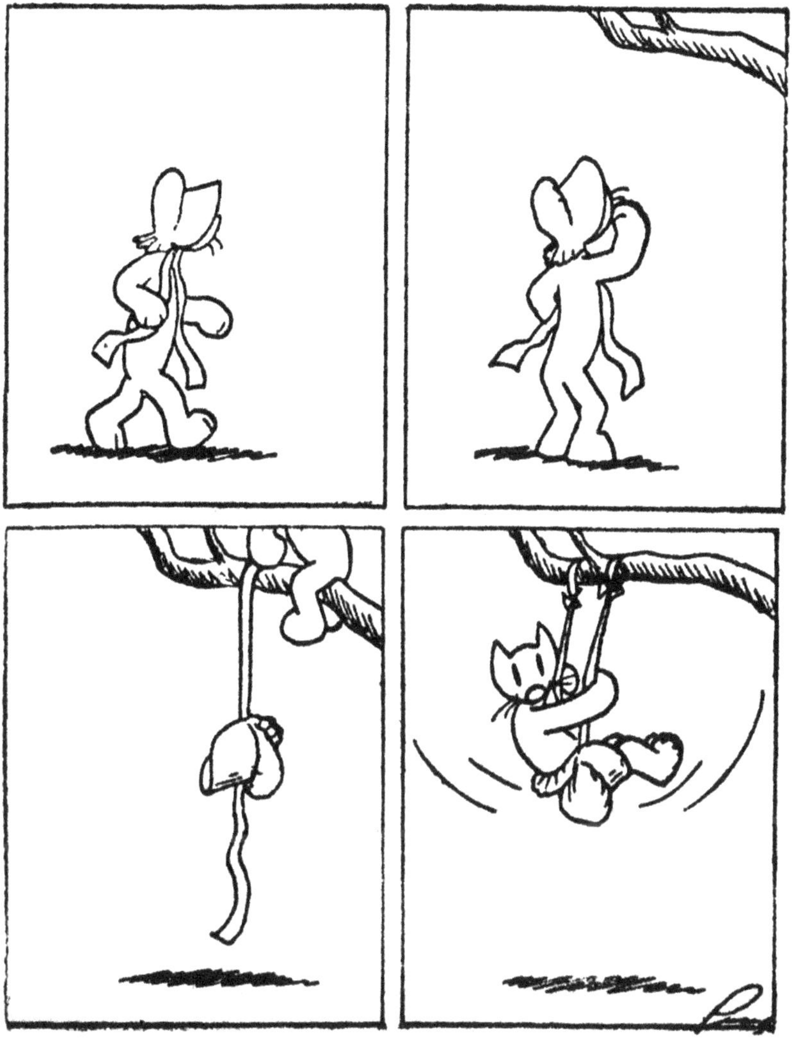

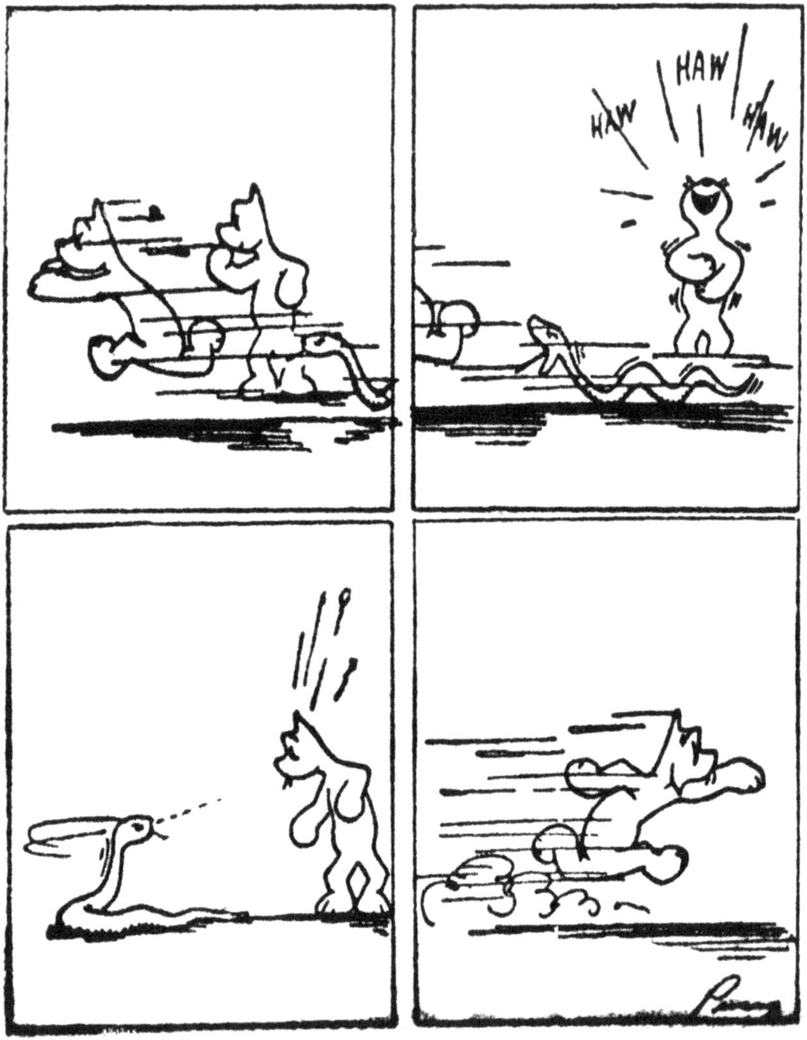
HAW
HAW
HAW

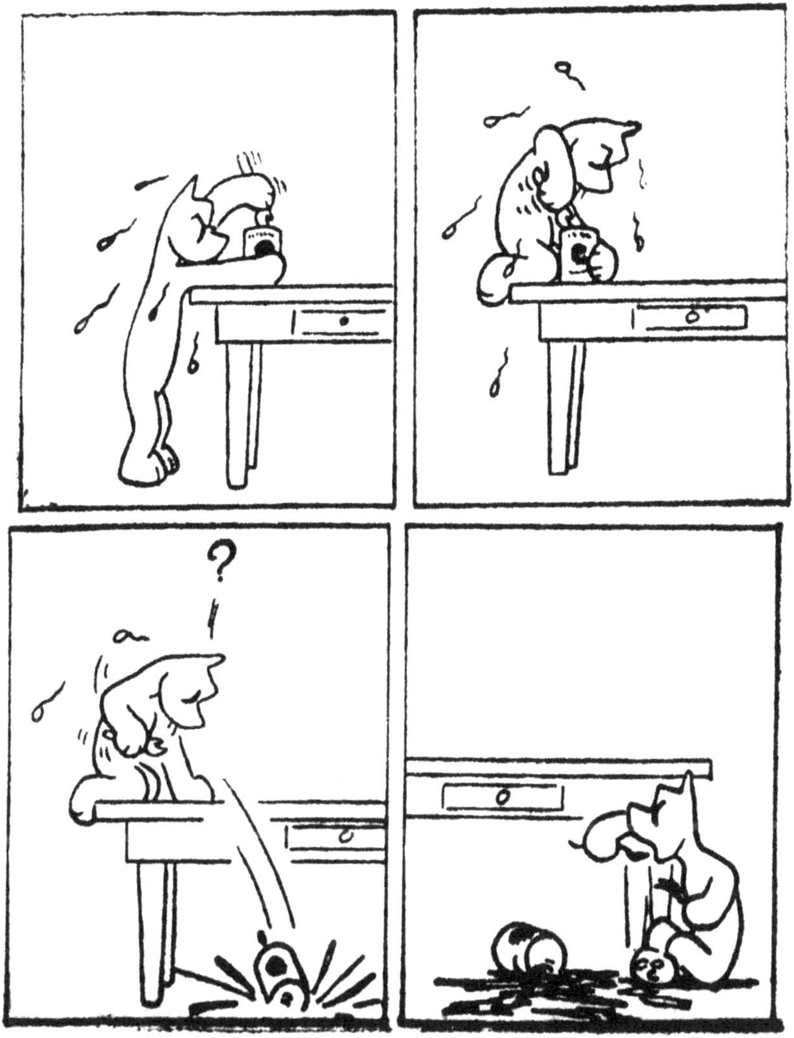

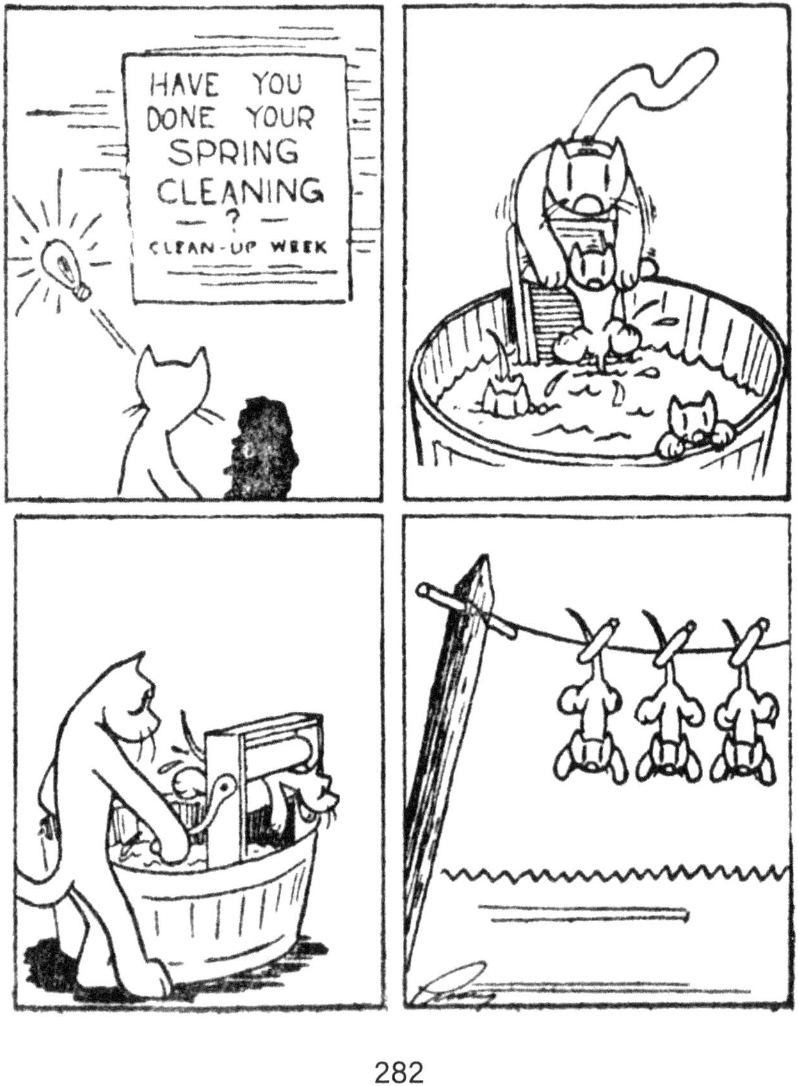
HAVE YOU DONE YOUR SPRING CLEANING ?
CLEAN-UP WEEK

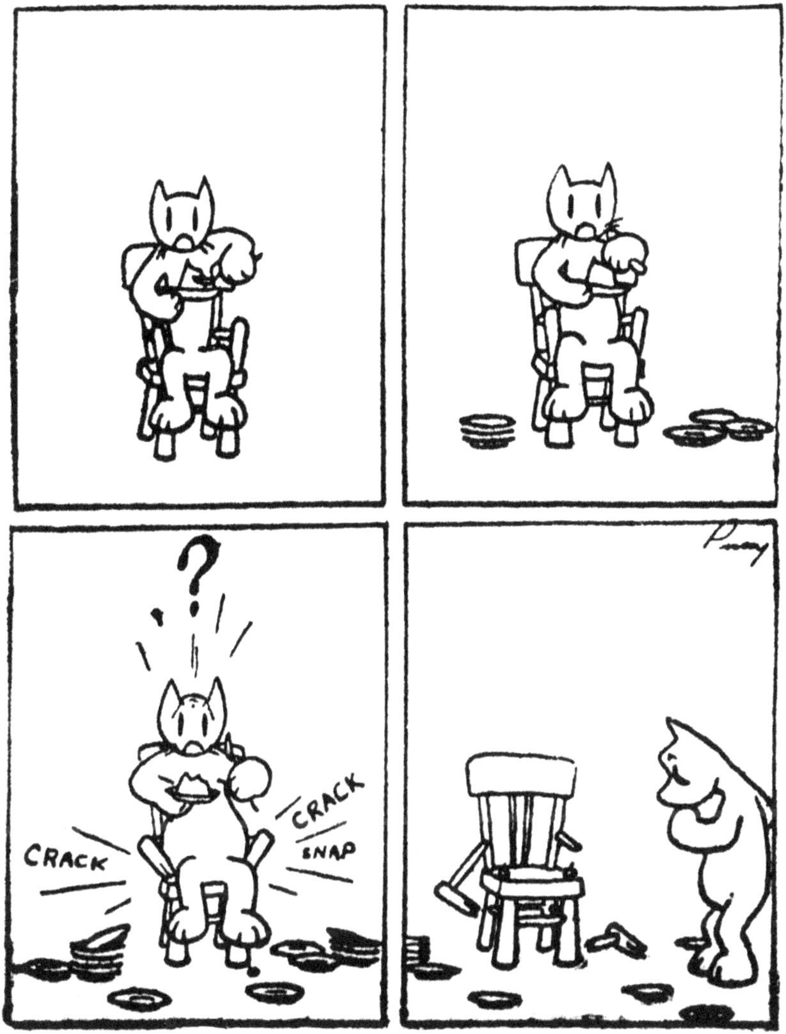
?
CRACK
CRACK
SNAP

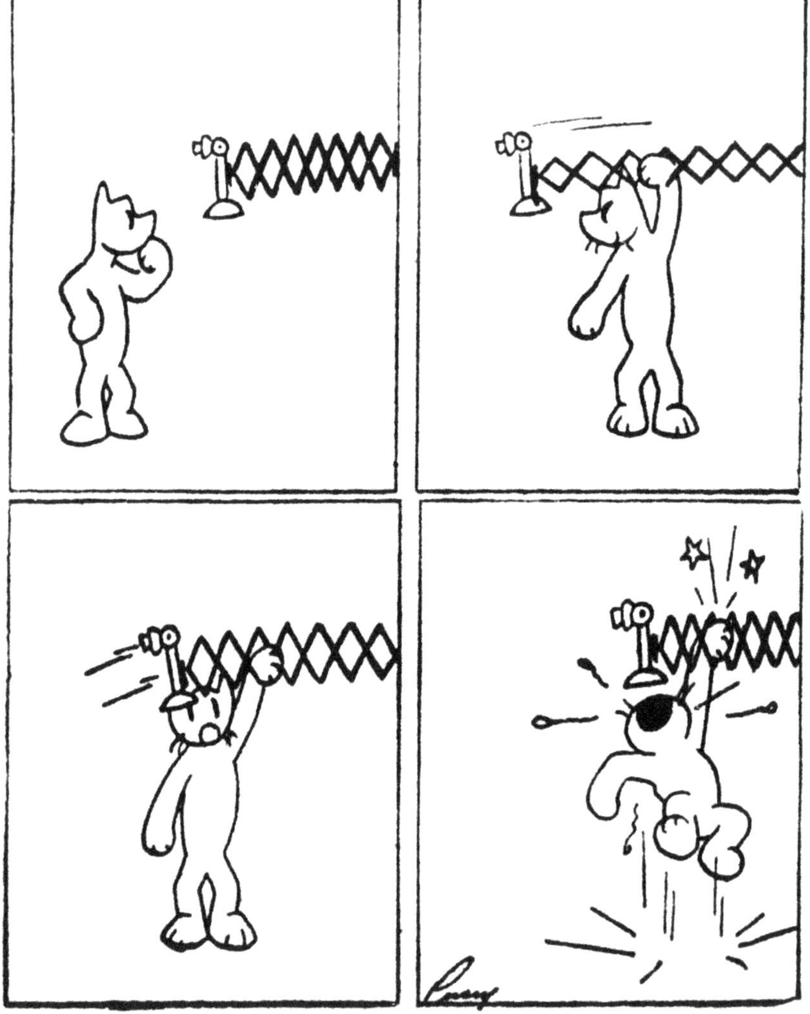

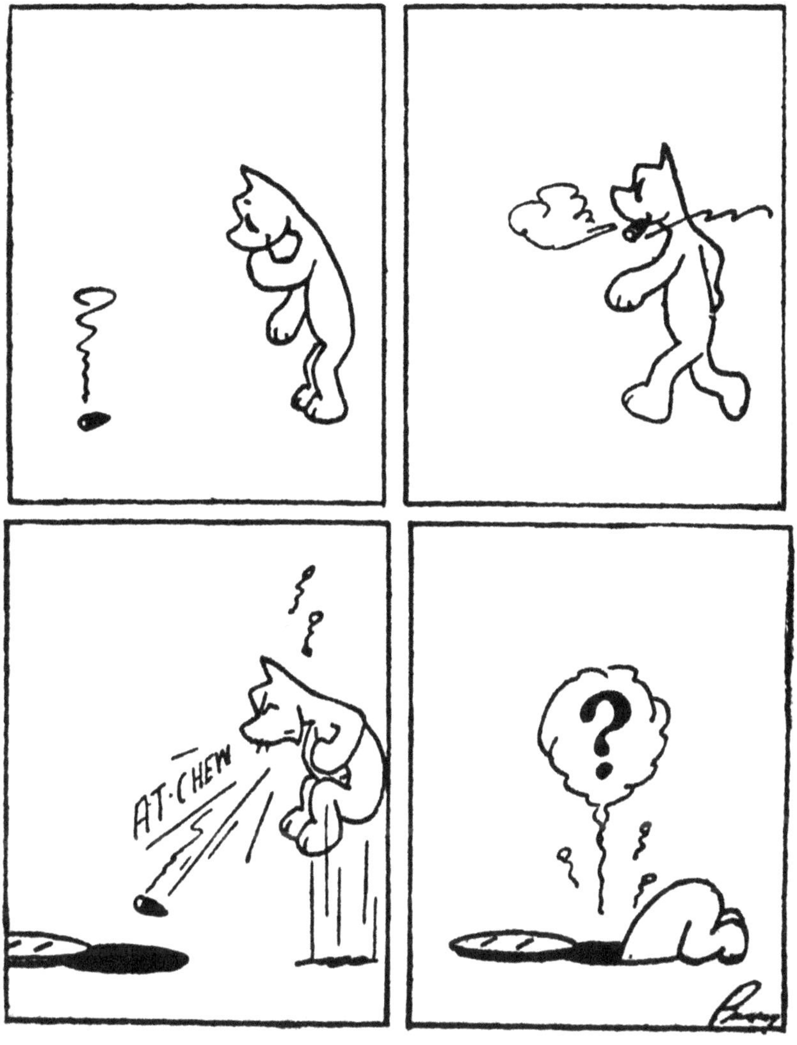
AT-CHEW

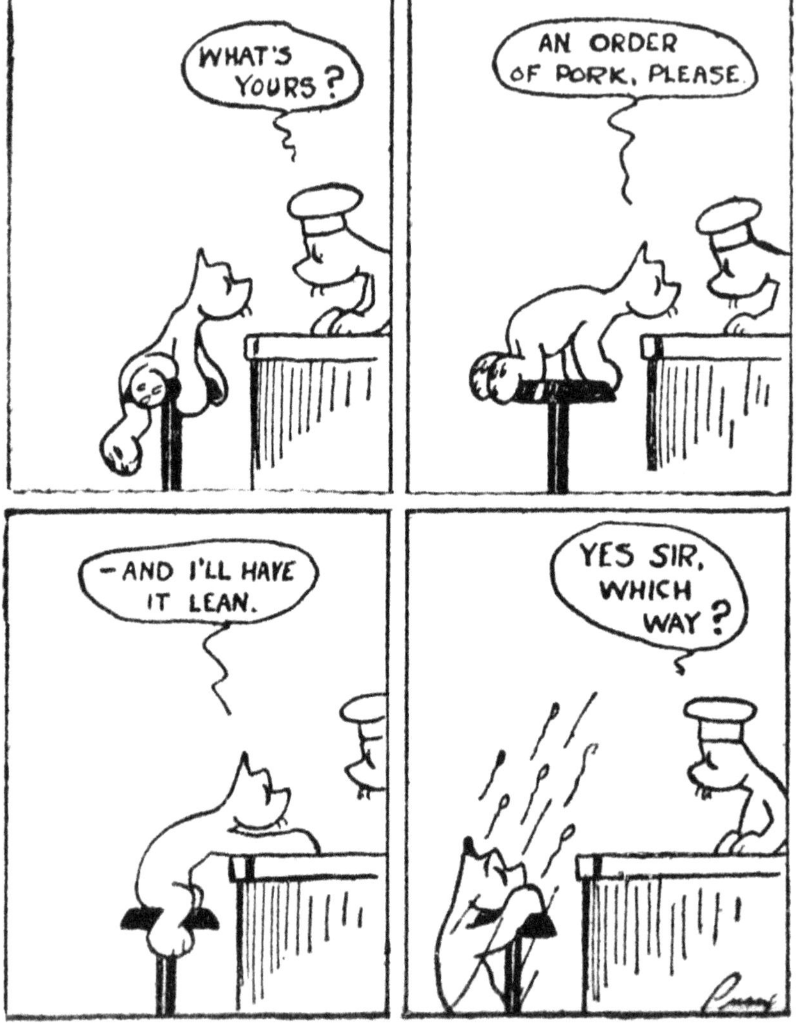
WHAT'S YOURS?
AN ORDER OF PORK, PLEASE.
—AND I'LL HAVE IT LEAN.
YES SIR, WHICH WAY?

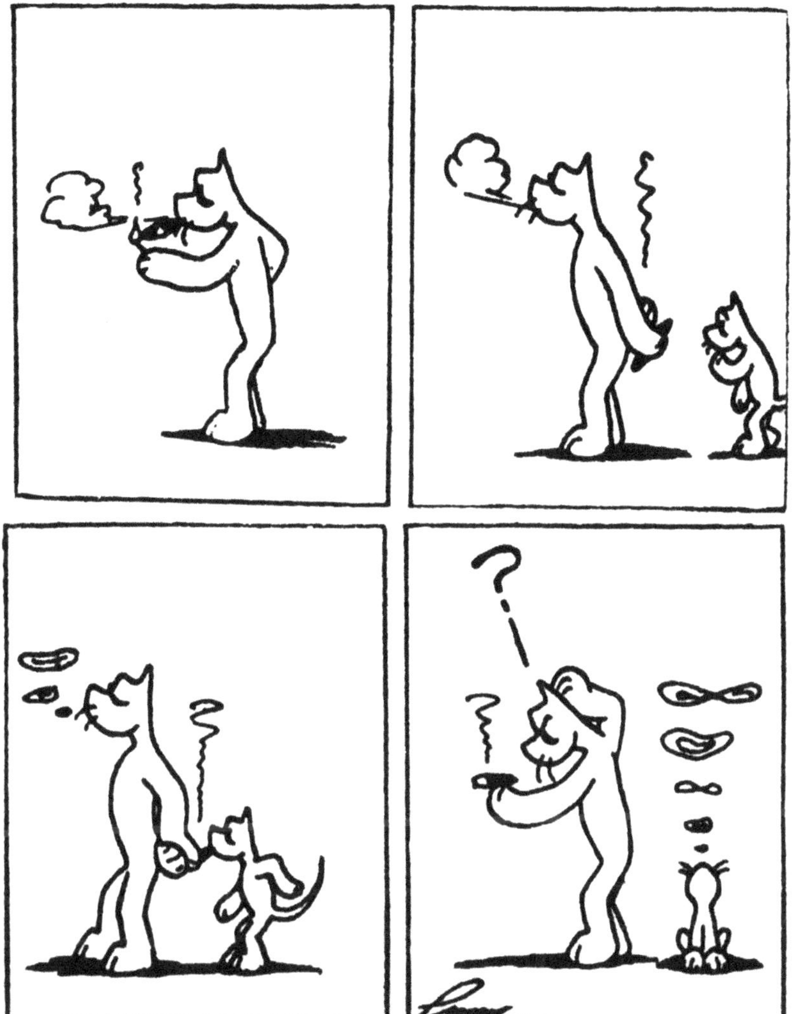
?

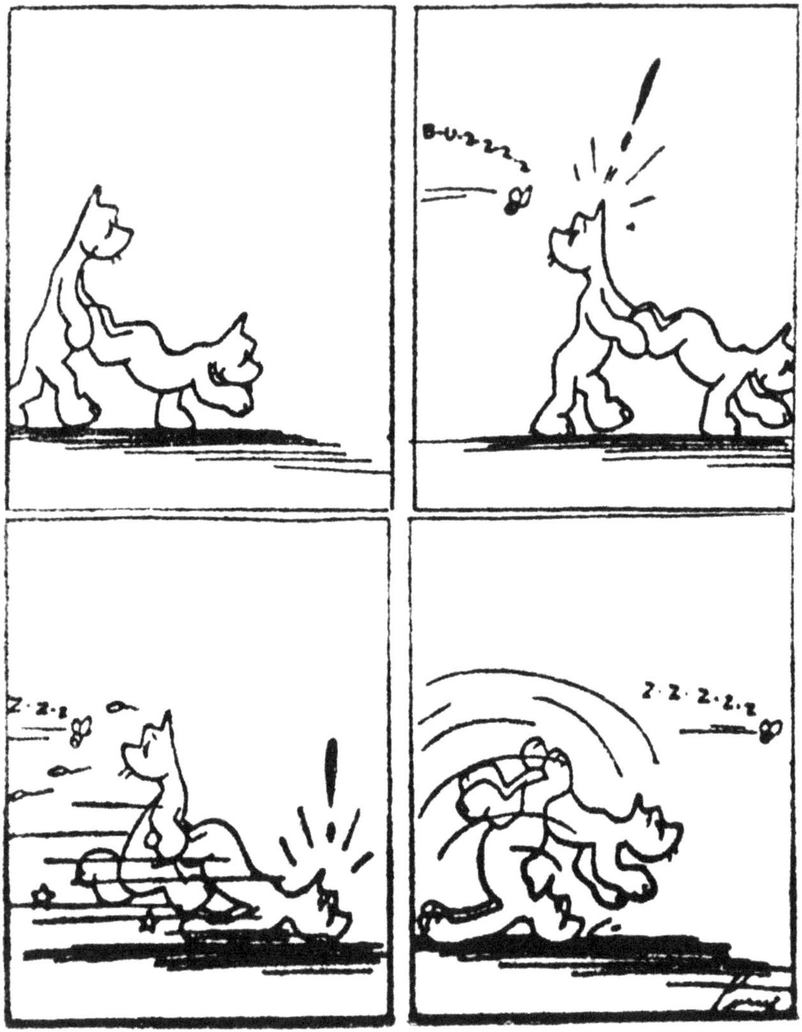
B-U-Z-Z-Z-Z
!
Z-Z-Z
!
Z-Z-Z-Z-Z

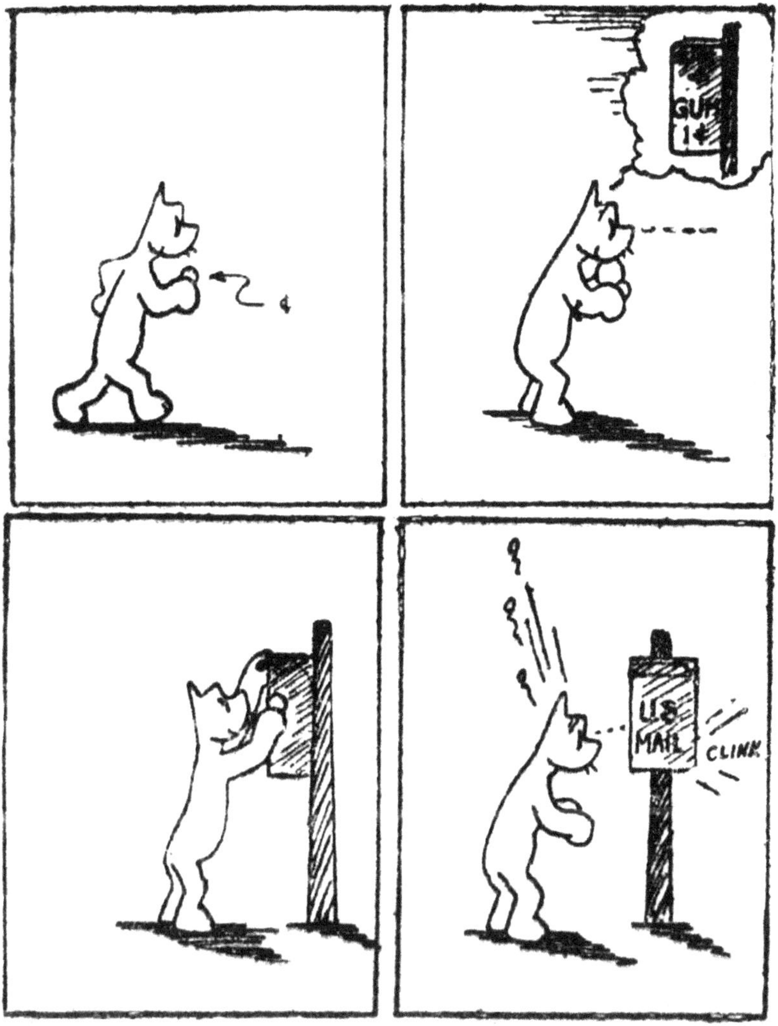
¢
GUM
1¢
U.S.
MAIL
CLINK

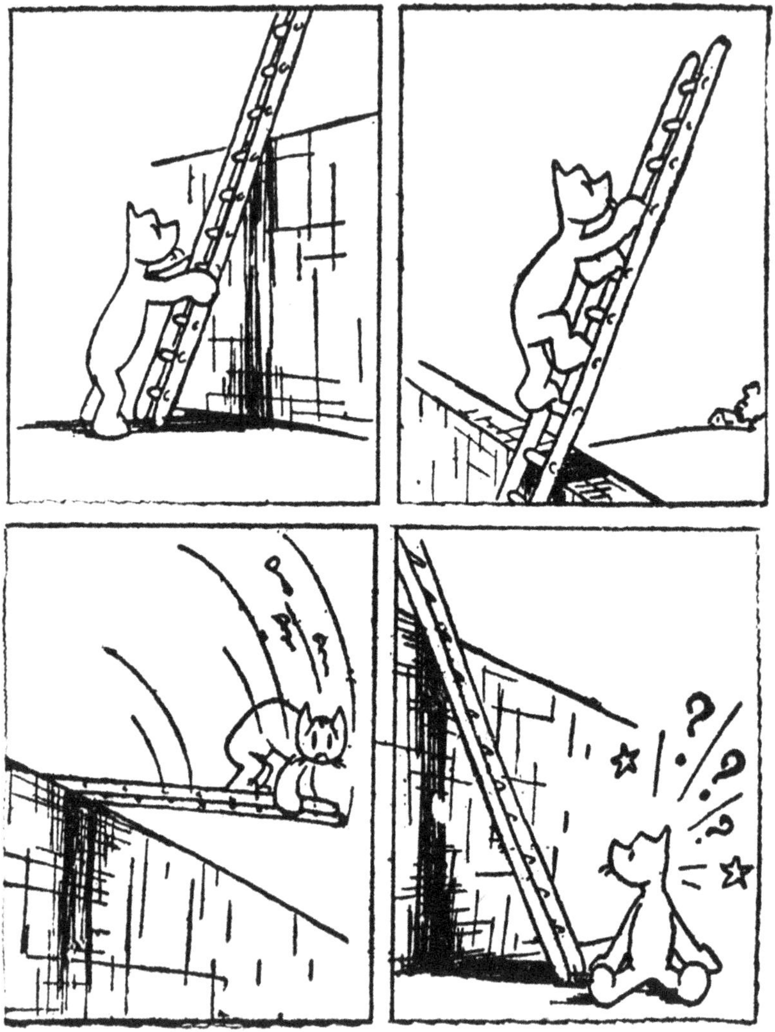

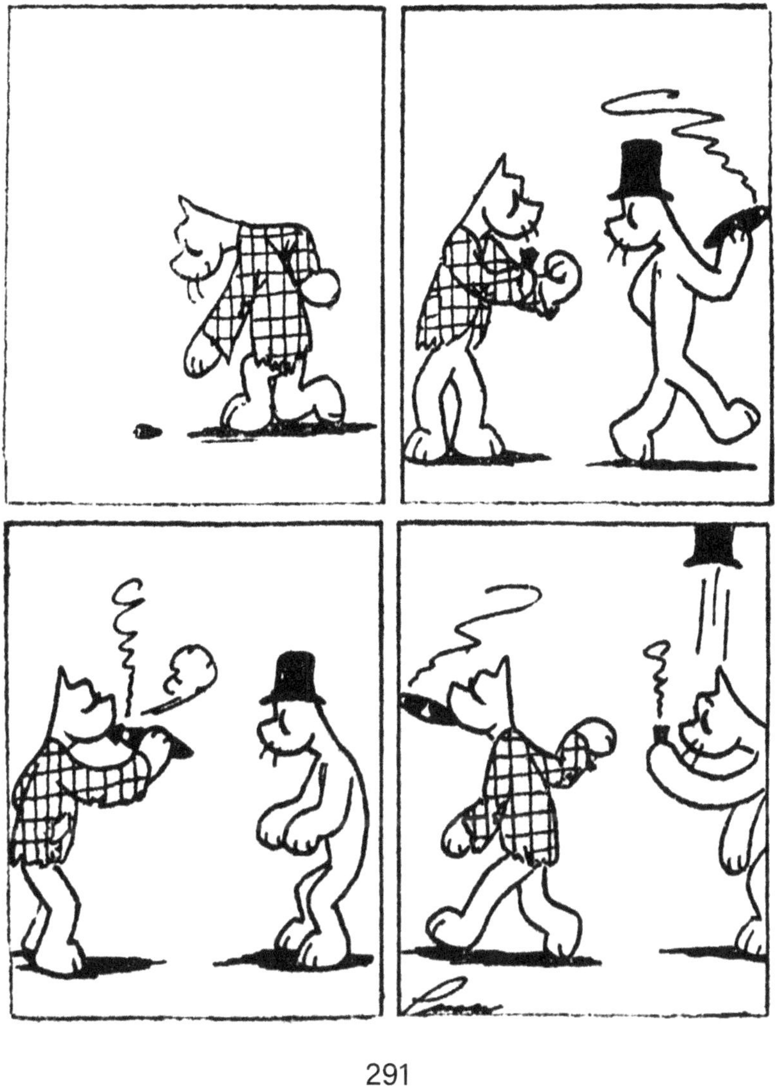

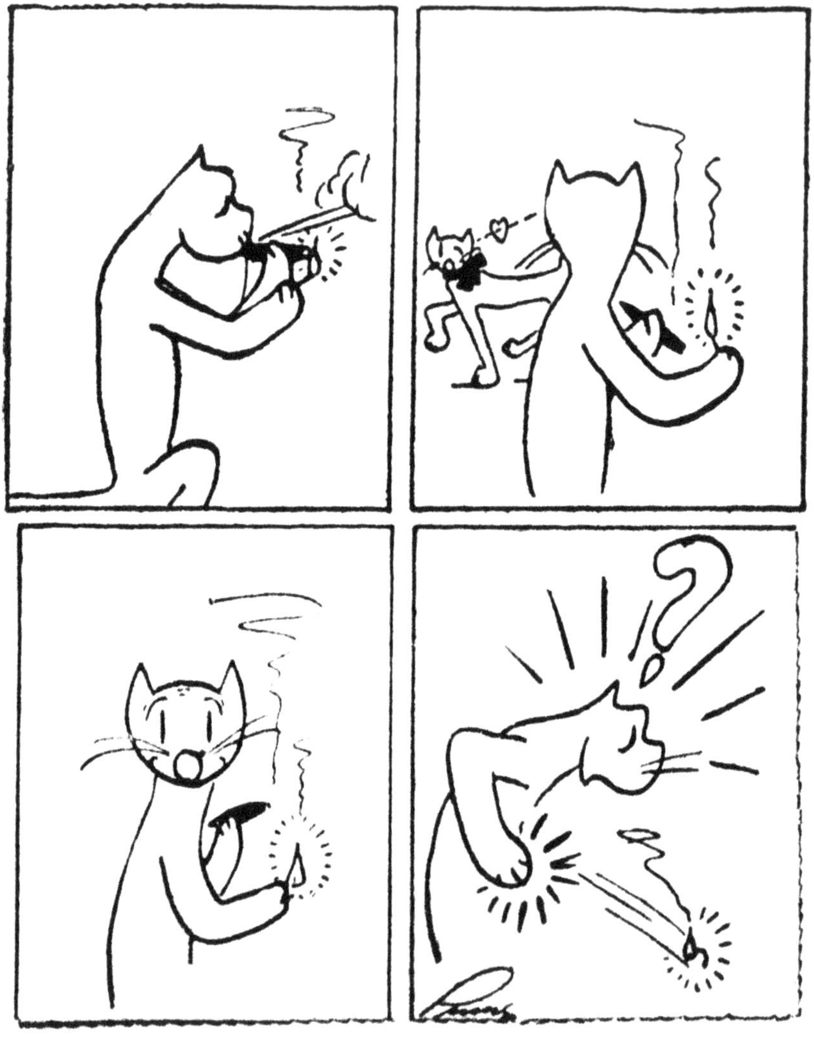

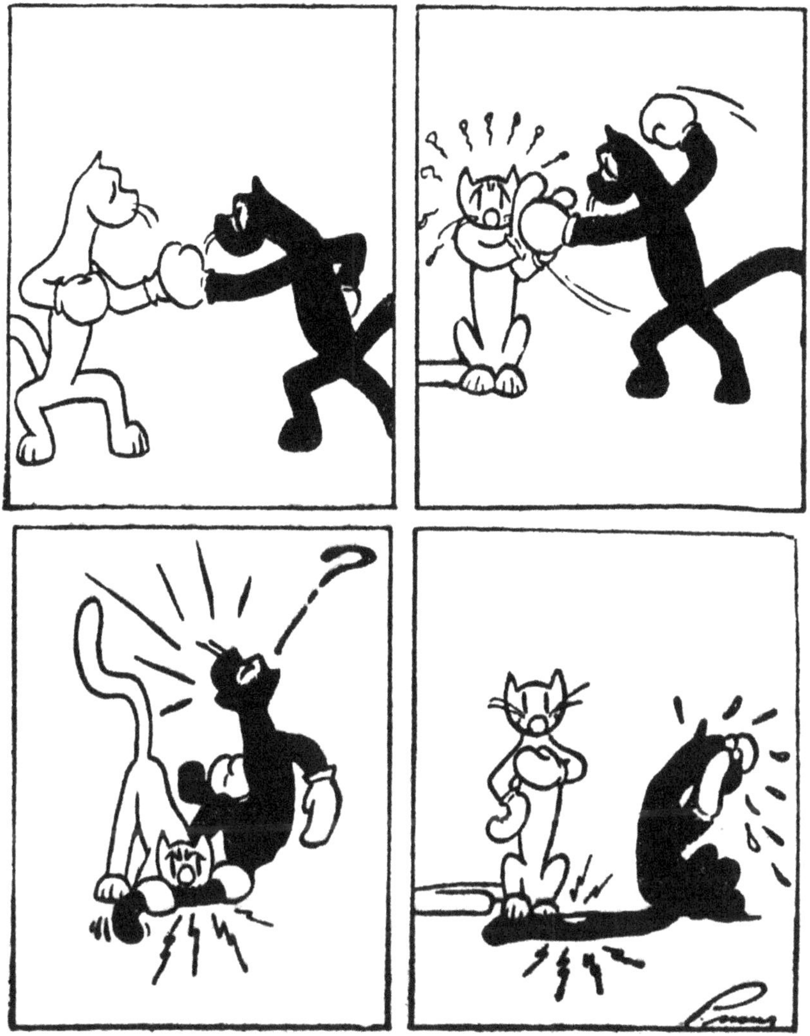

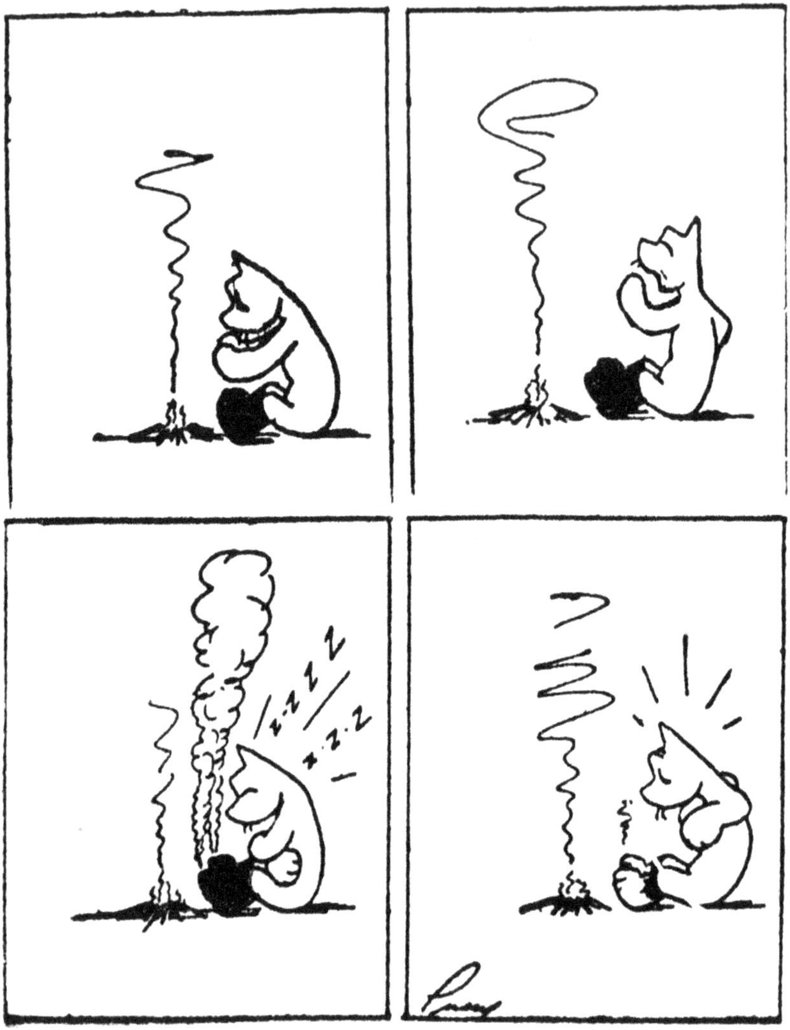
z·z z z
z·z·z

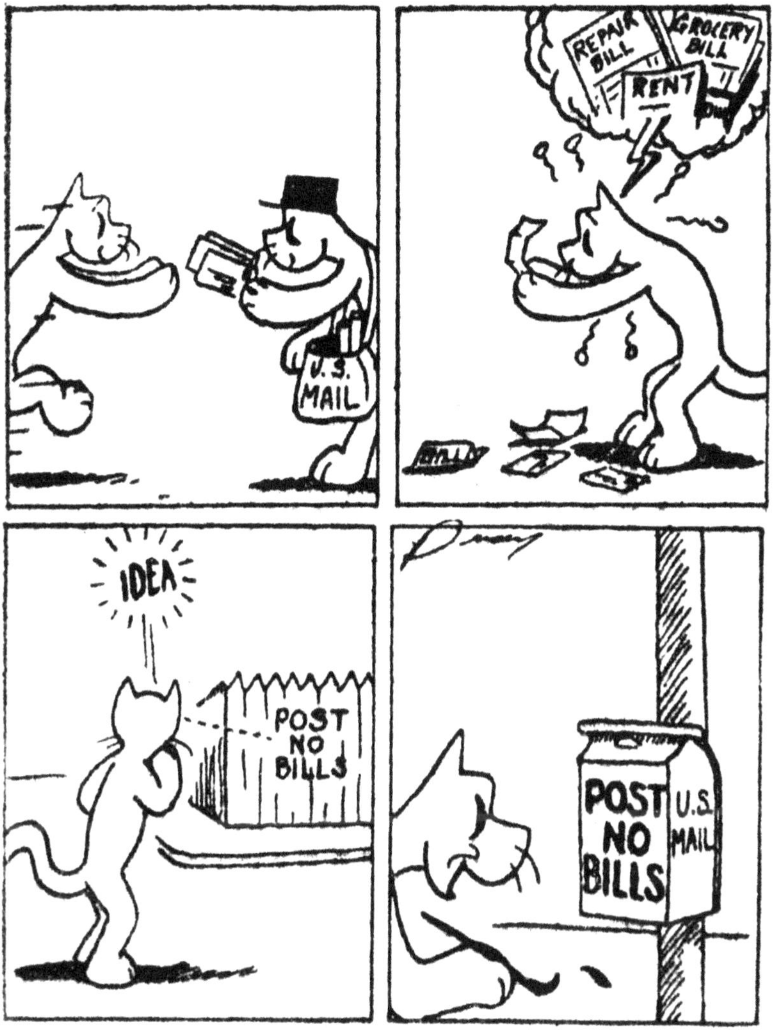
U.S.
MAIL
REPAIR
BILL
GROCERY
BILL
RENT
IDEA
POST
NO
BILLS
POST
NO
BILLS
U.S.
MAIL

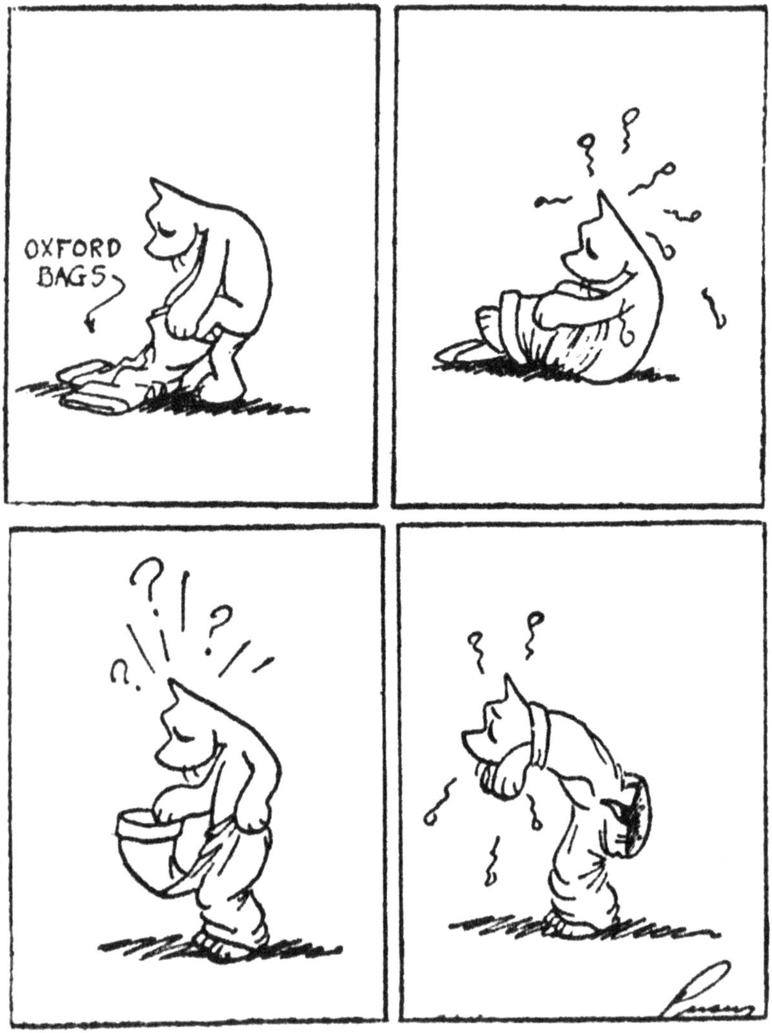
OXFORD
BAGS

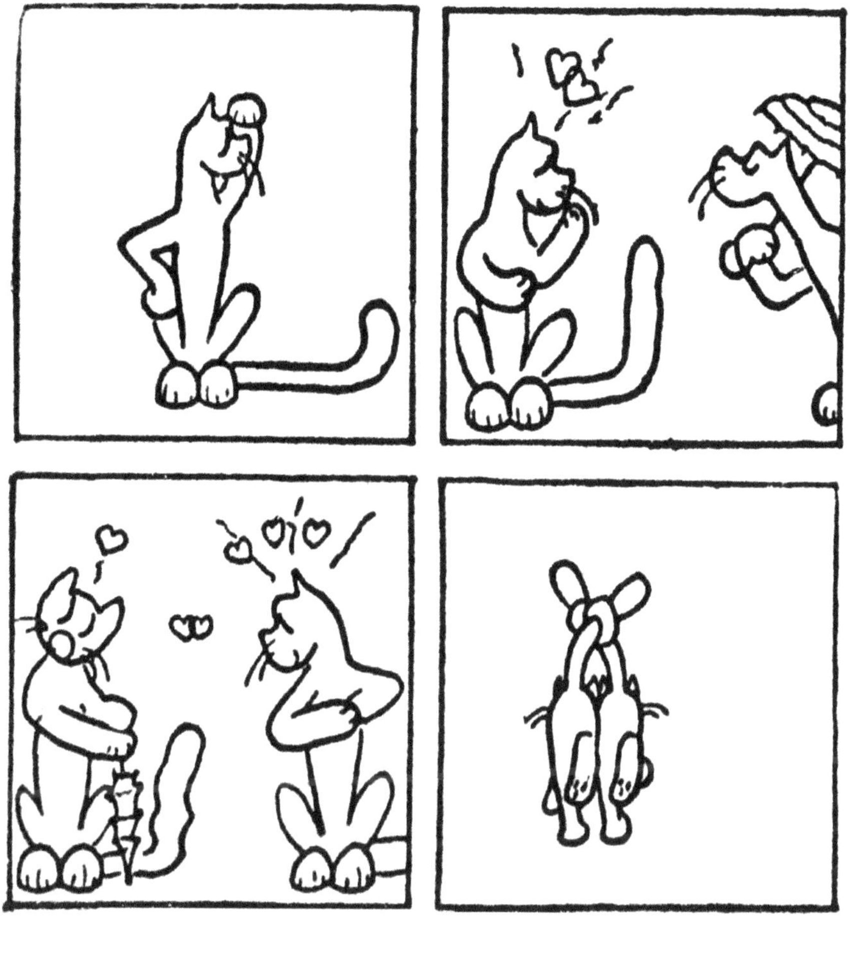

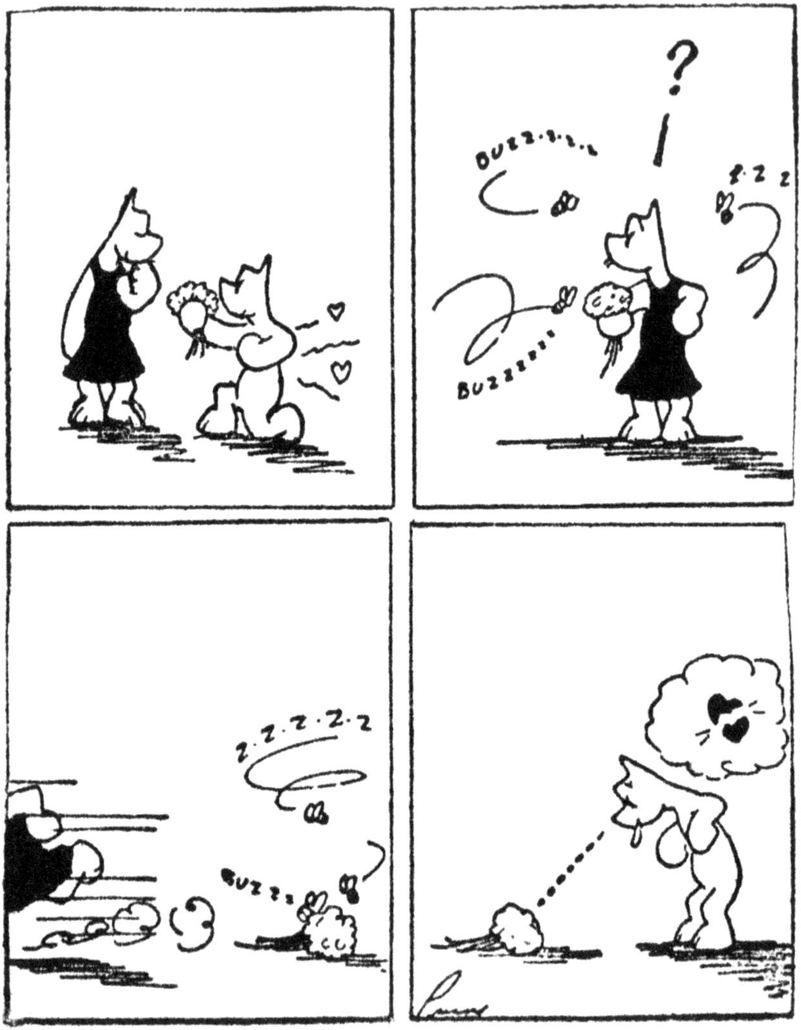
BUZZ.Z.Z.Z
Z.Z Z
BUZZZZZZ
Z.Z.Z.Z.Z
BUZZZ

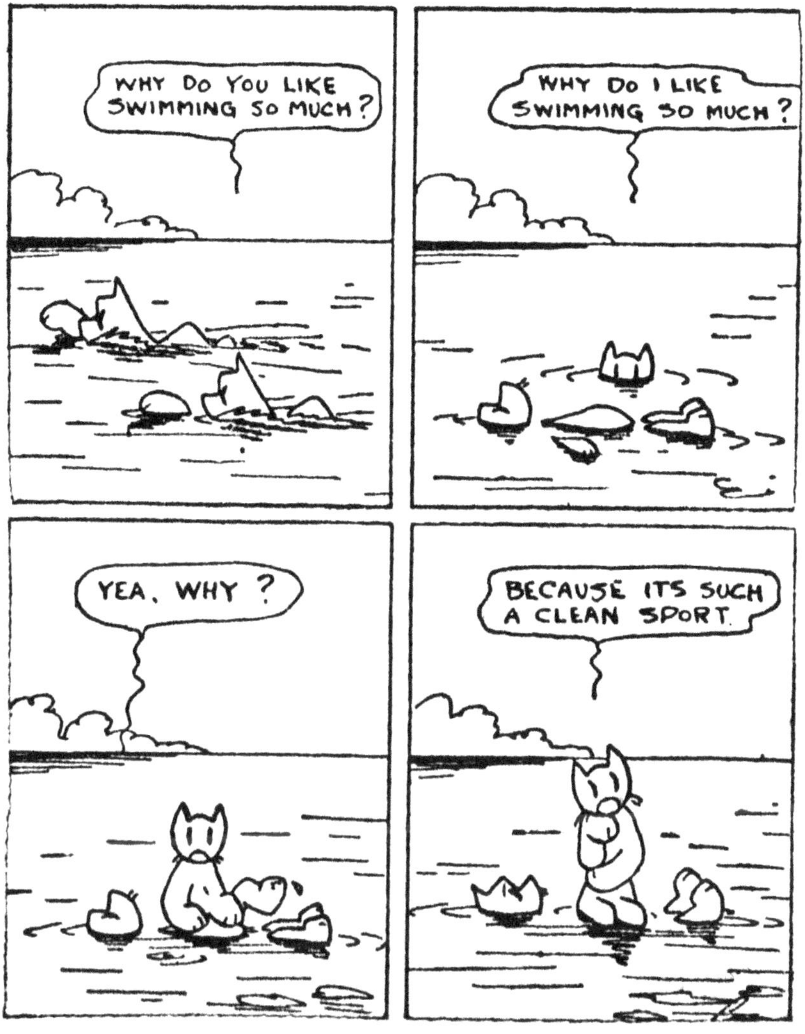
WHY DO YOU LIKE SWIMMING SO MUCH?
WHY DO I LIKE SWIMMING SO MUCH?
YEA, WHY?
BECAUSE ITS SUCH A CLEAN SPORT.

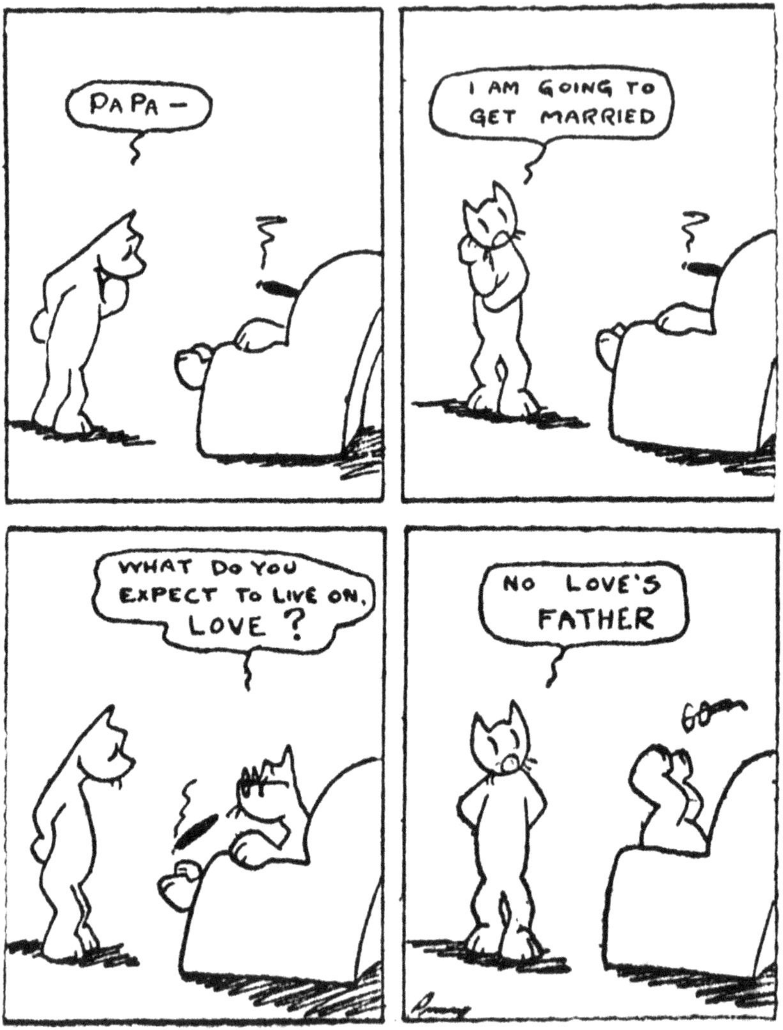
PAPA —
I AM GOING TO GET MARRIED
WHAT DO YOU EXPECT TO LIVE ON, LOVE ?
NO LOVE'S FATHER

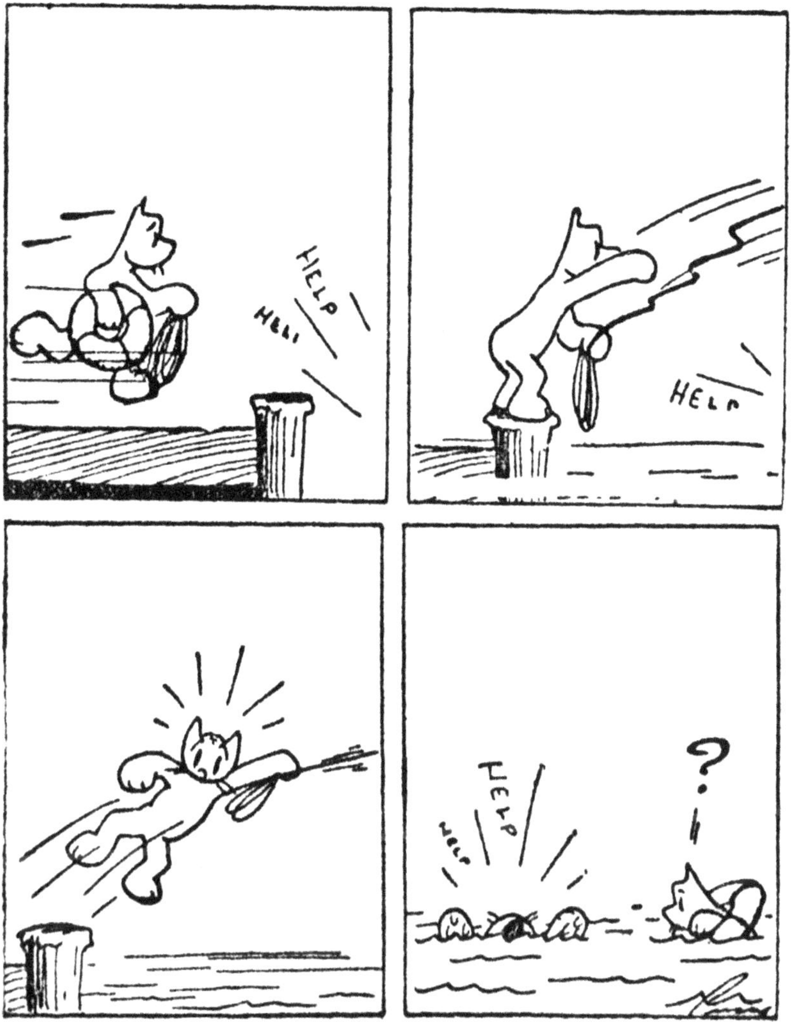
HELP
HELP
?

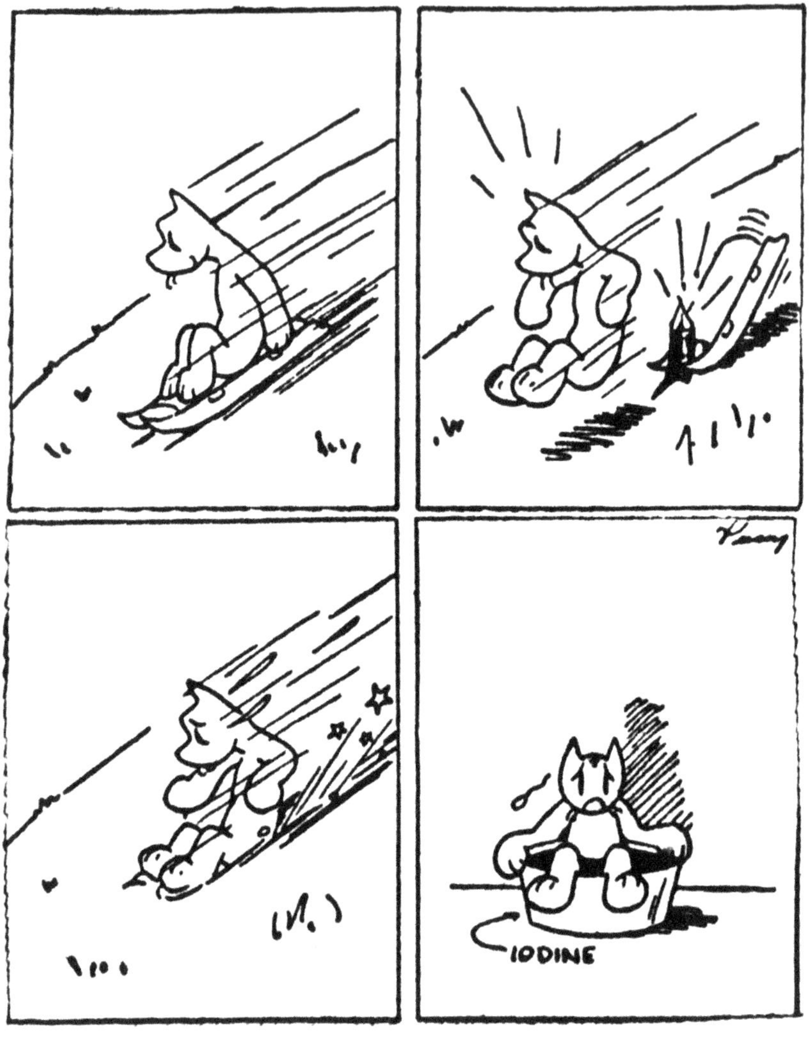
IODINE

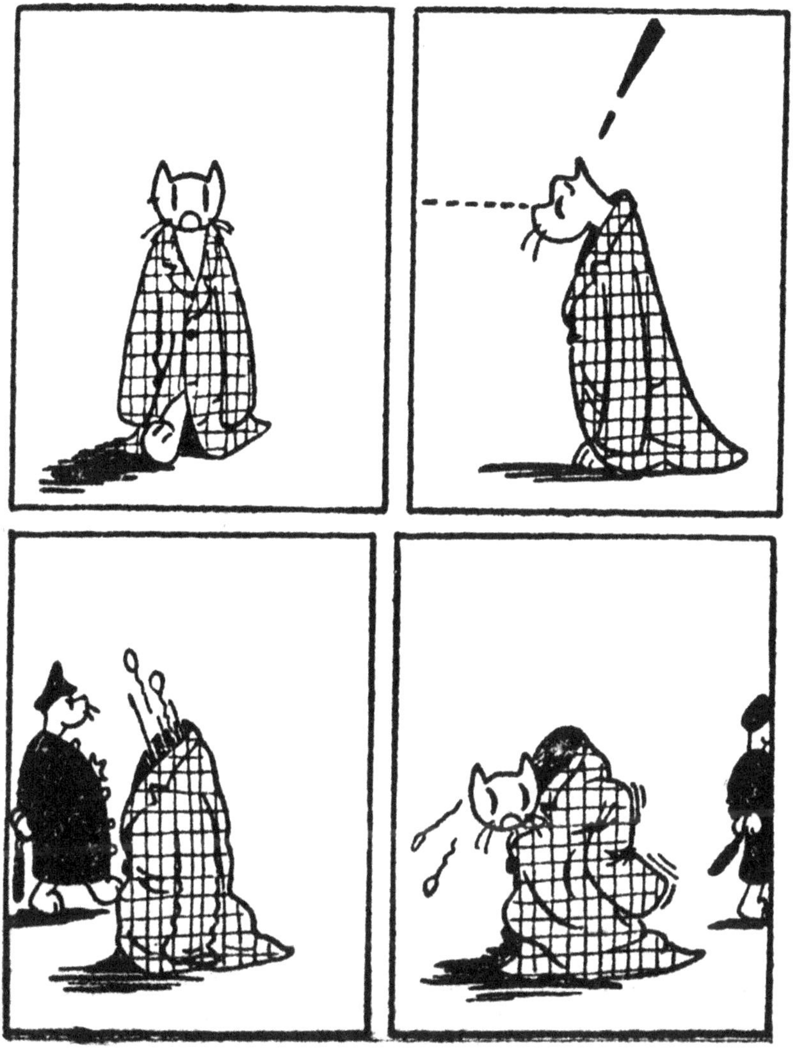

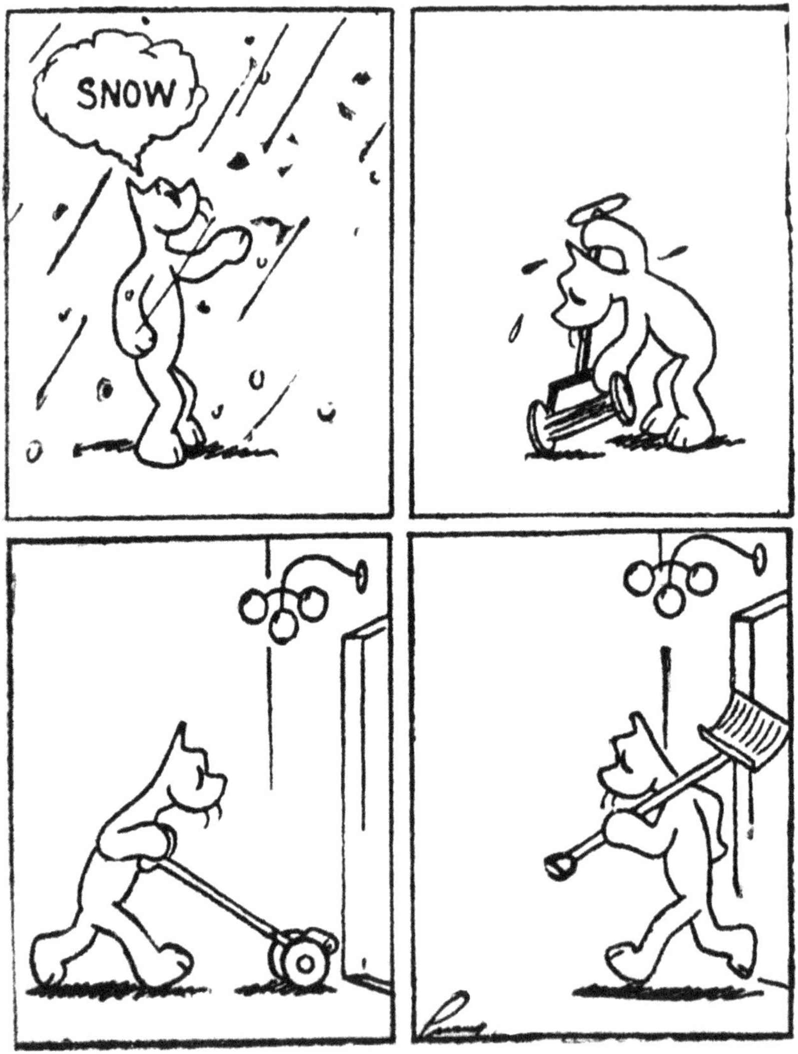
SNOW

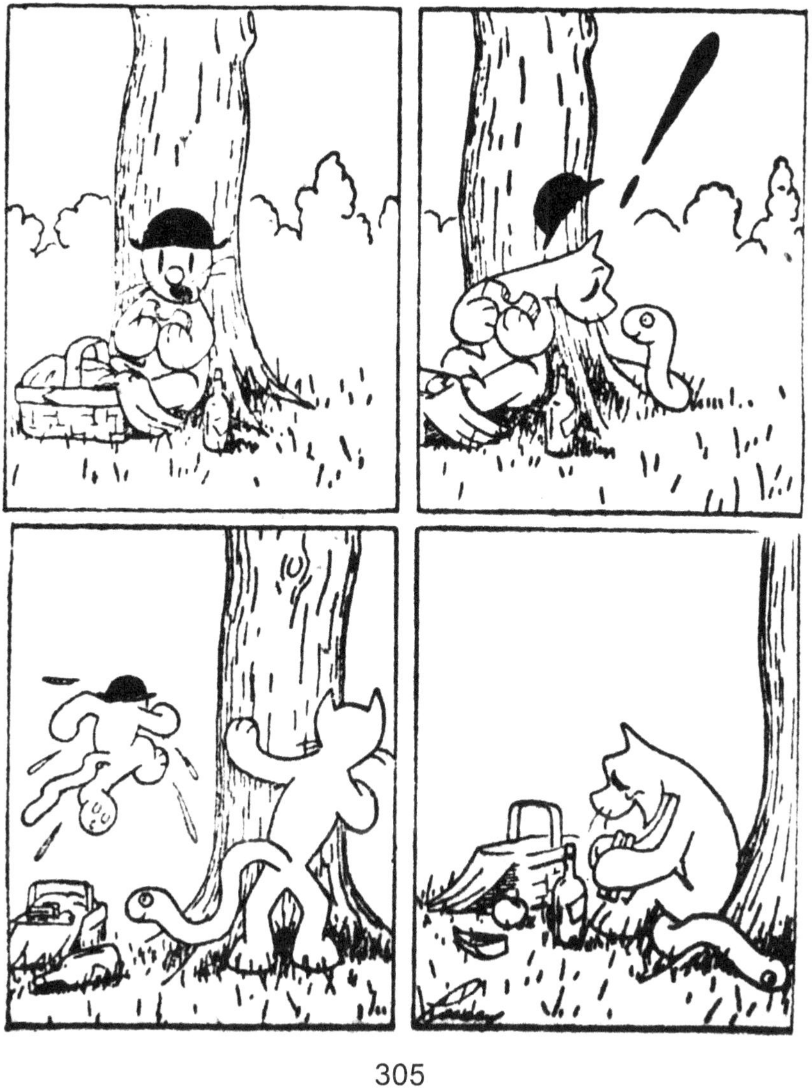

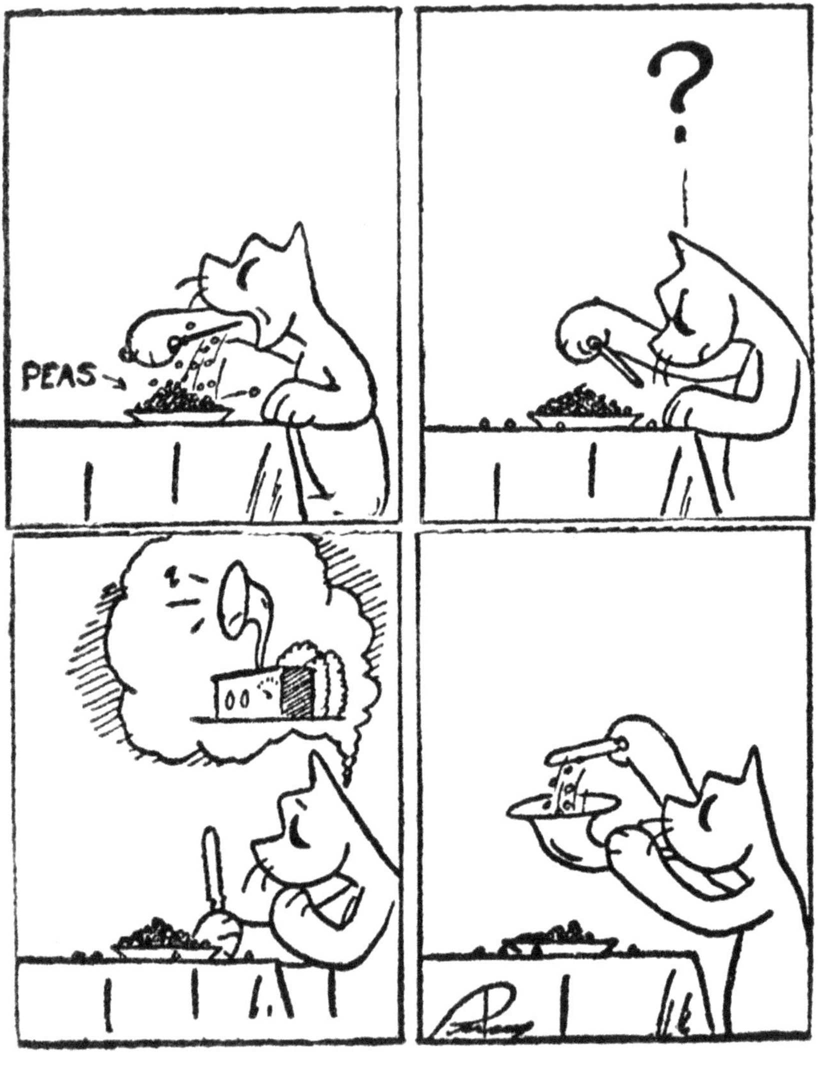
PEAS
?

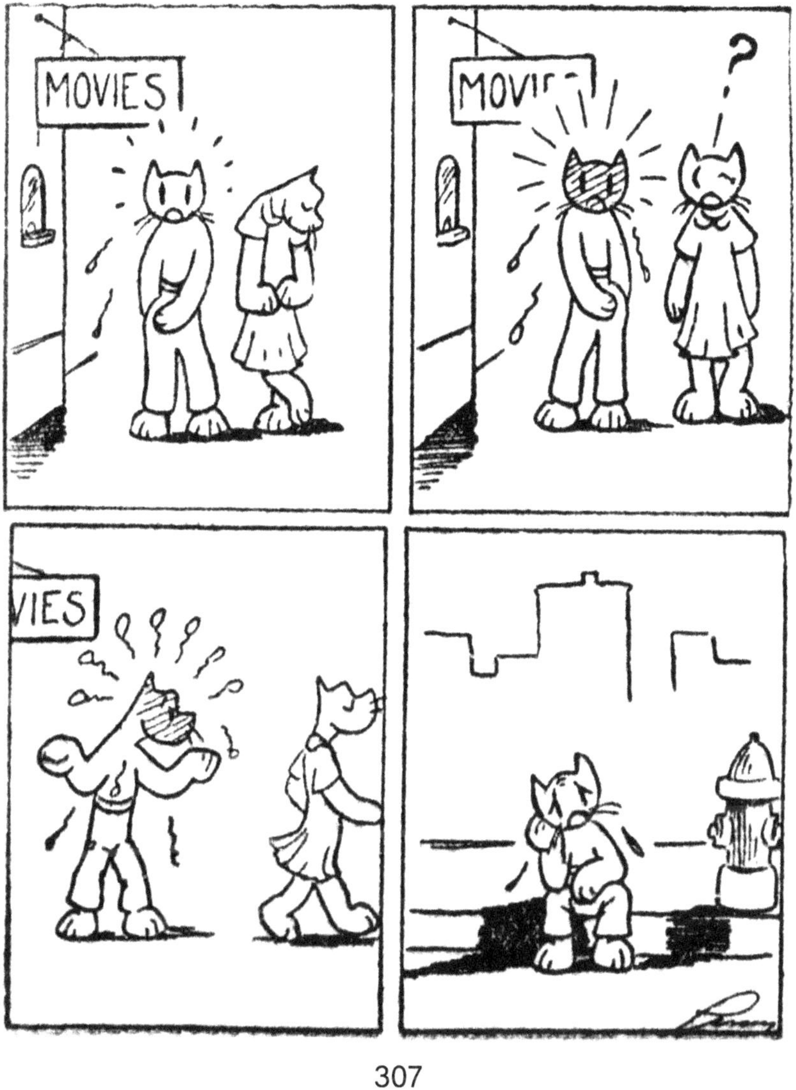
MOVIES
MOVI
?
VIES

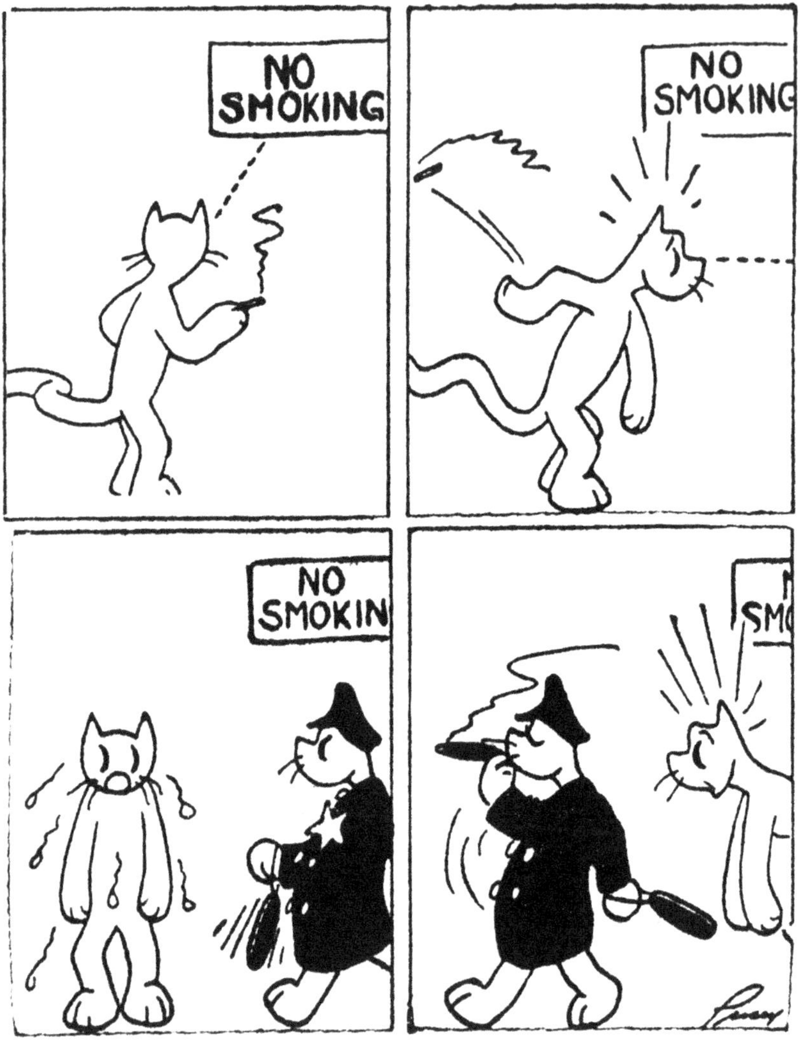
NO SMOKING
NO SMOKING
NO SMOKIN

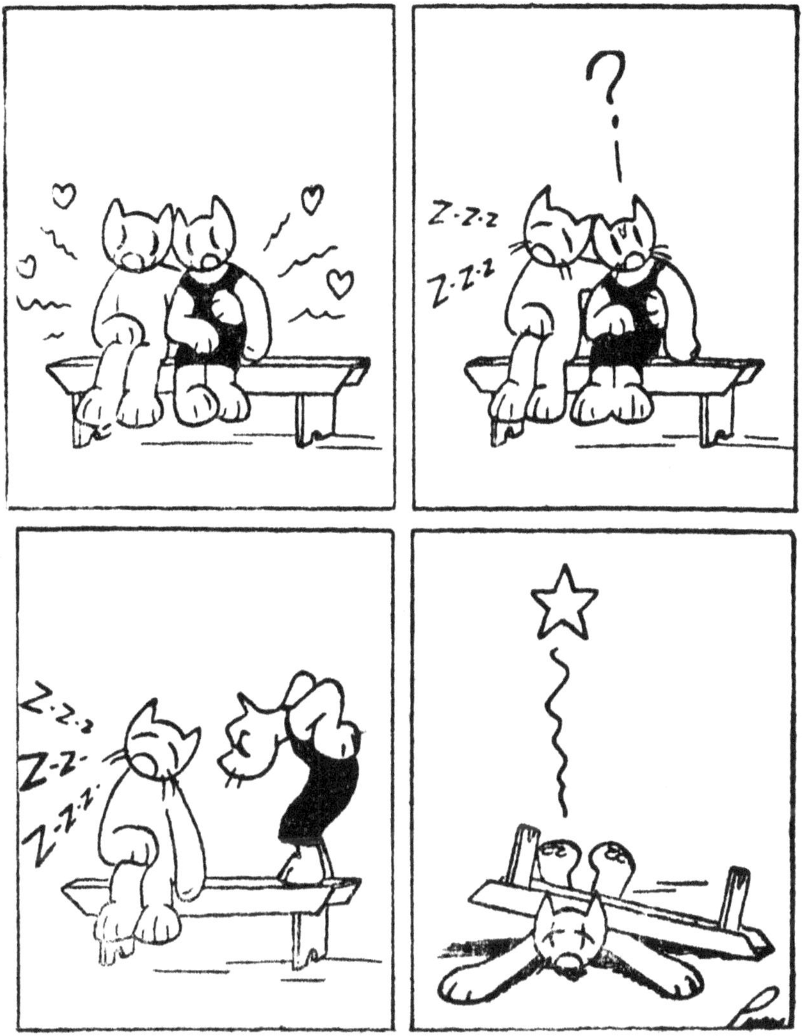
Z-Z-Z
Z-Z-Z
Z-Z-Z
Z-Z-
Z-Z-Z-

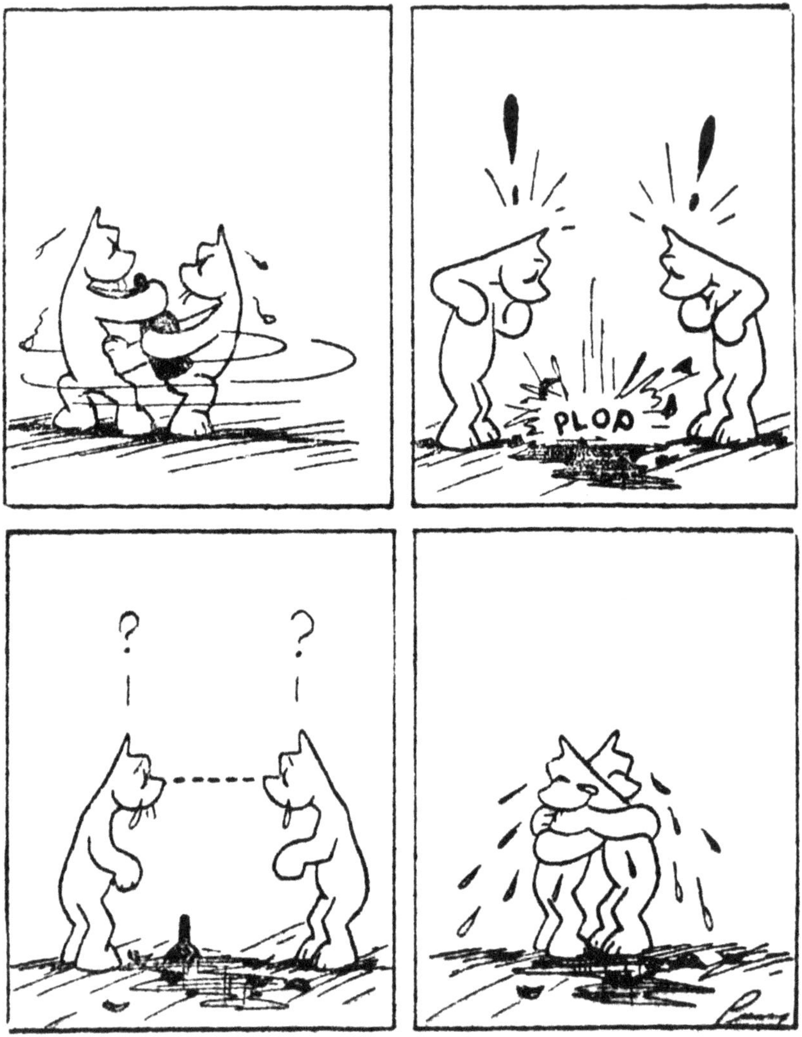
PLOP

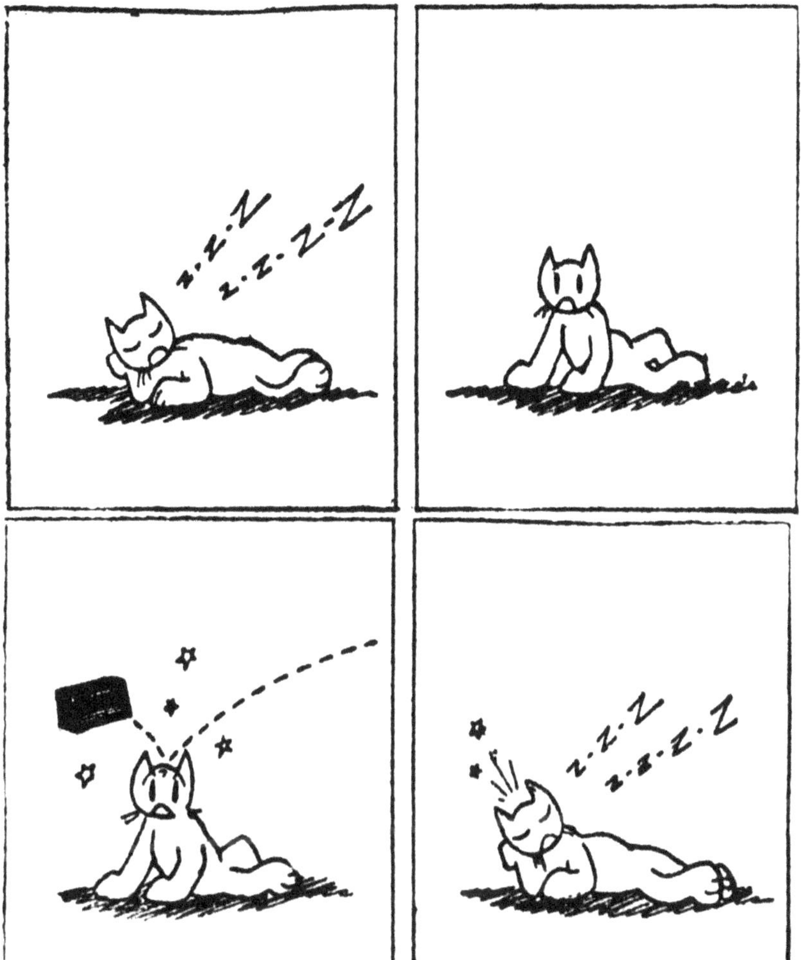
z·z·Z
z·z·Z·Z
z·z·Z
z·z·z·Z

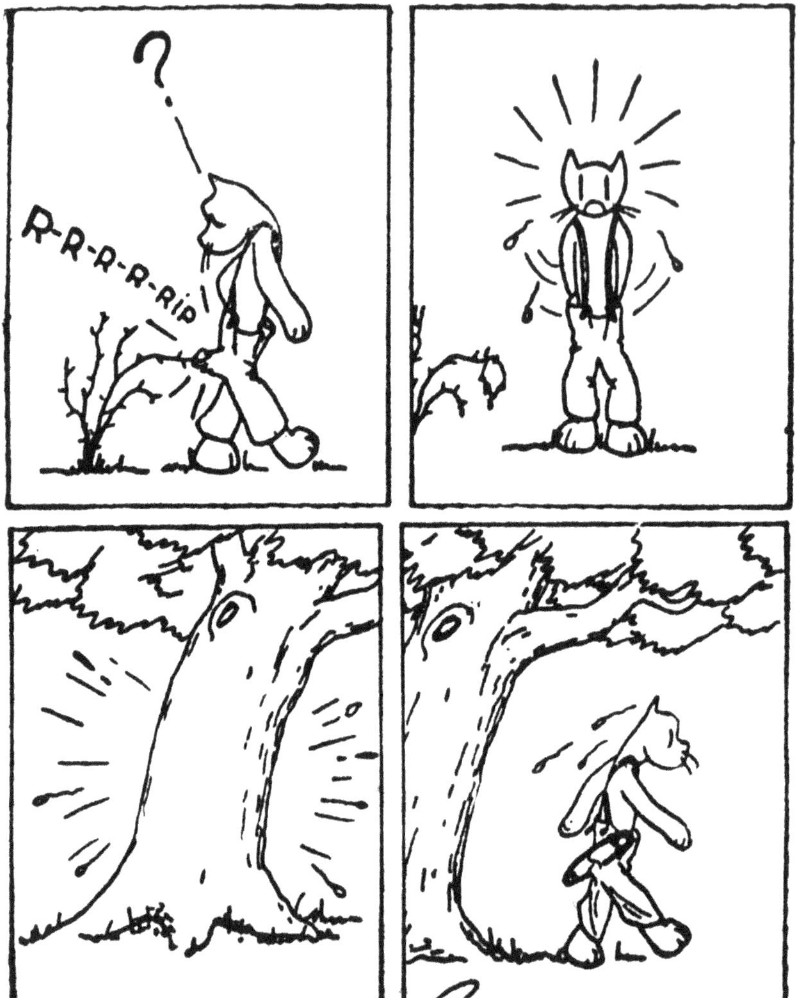
?
R-R-R-R-R-RIP

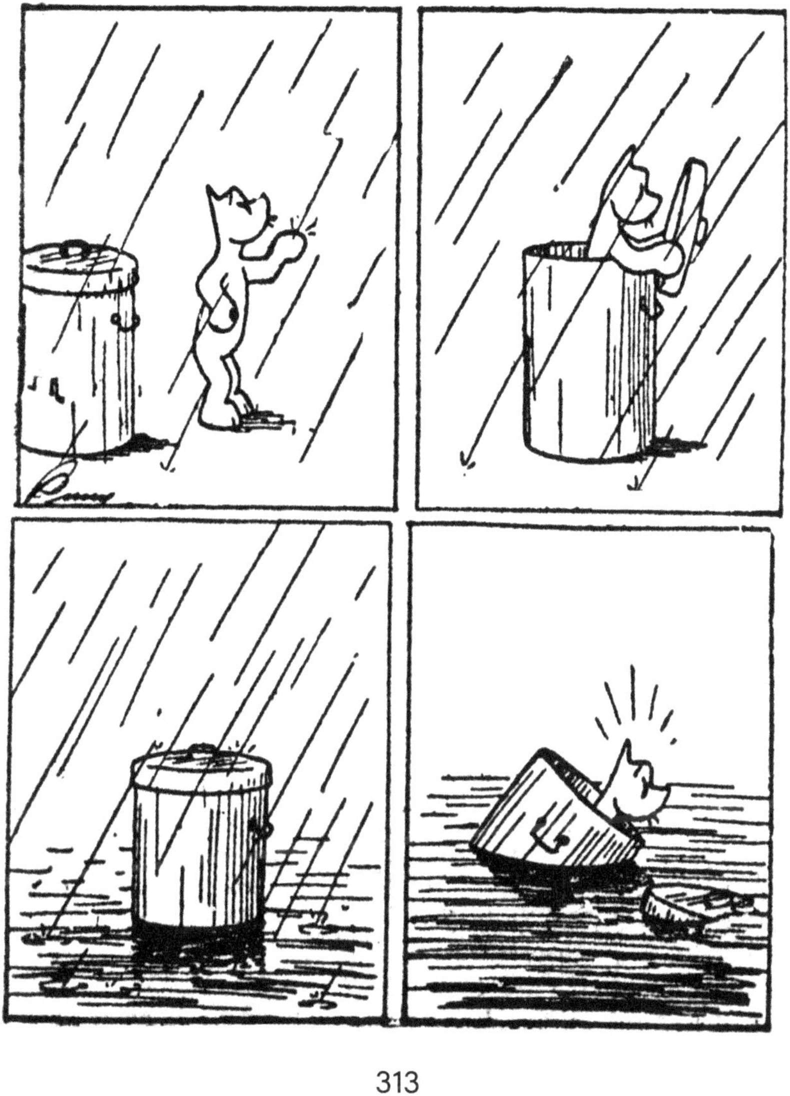

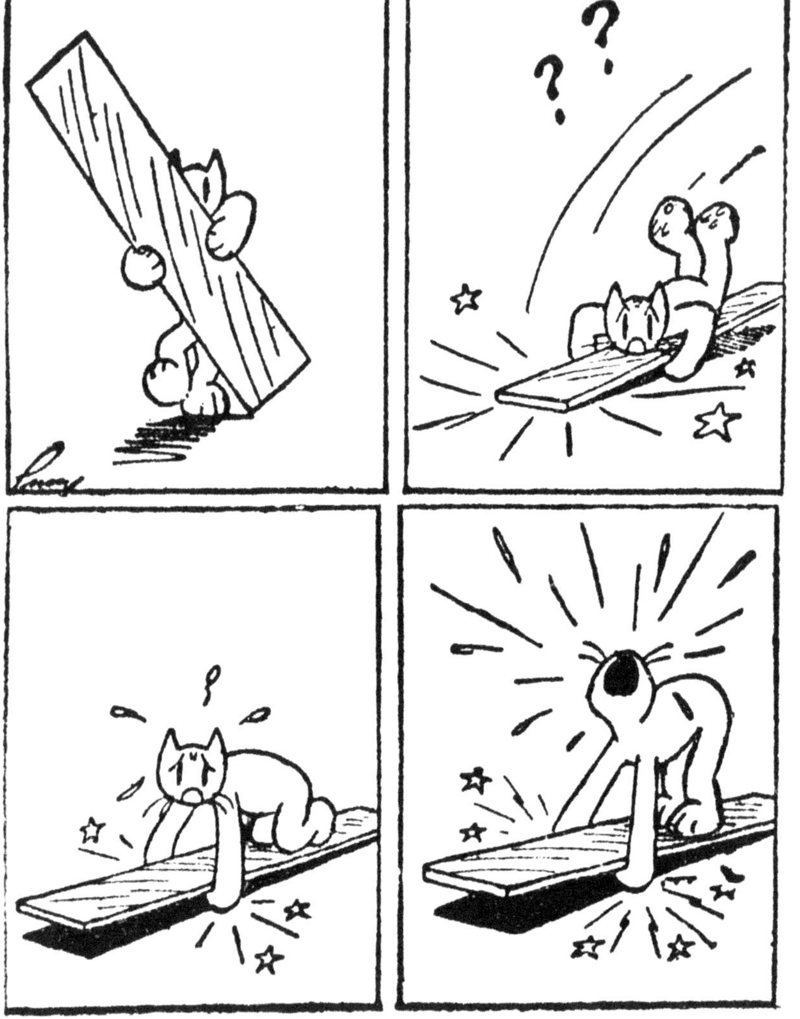

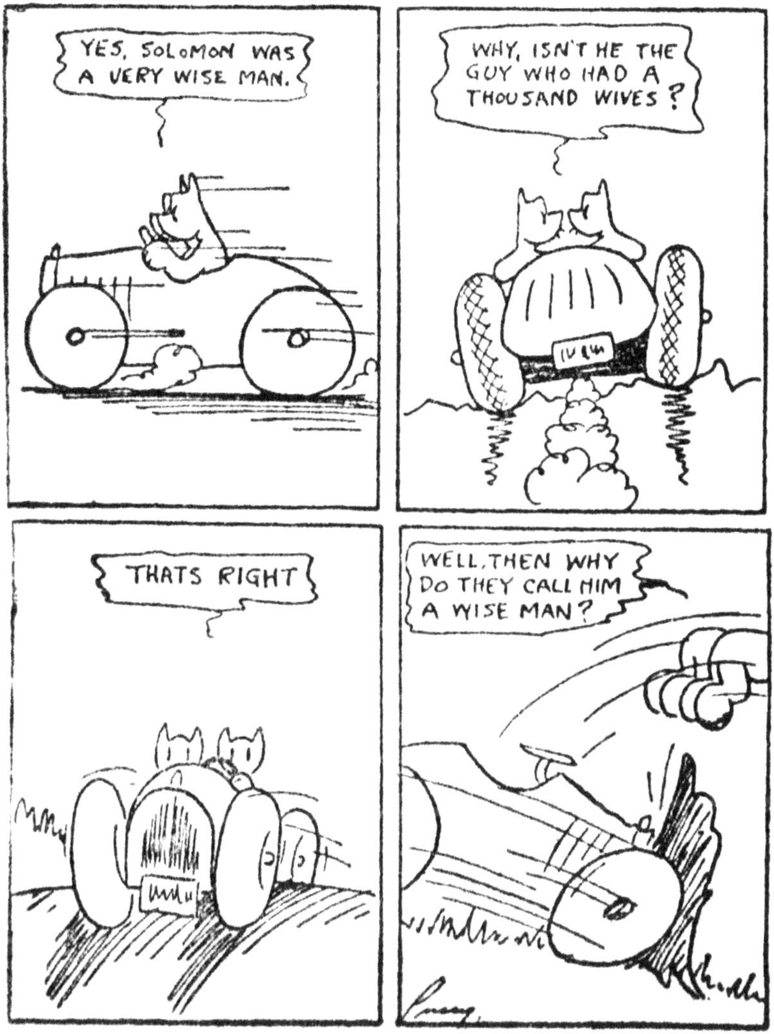
YES, SOLOMON WAS A VERY WISE MAN.
WHY, ISN'T HE THE GUY WHO HAD A THOUSAND WIVES?
THATS RIGHT
WELL, THEN WHY DO THEY CALL HIM A WISE MAN?

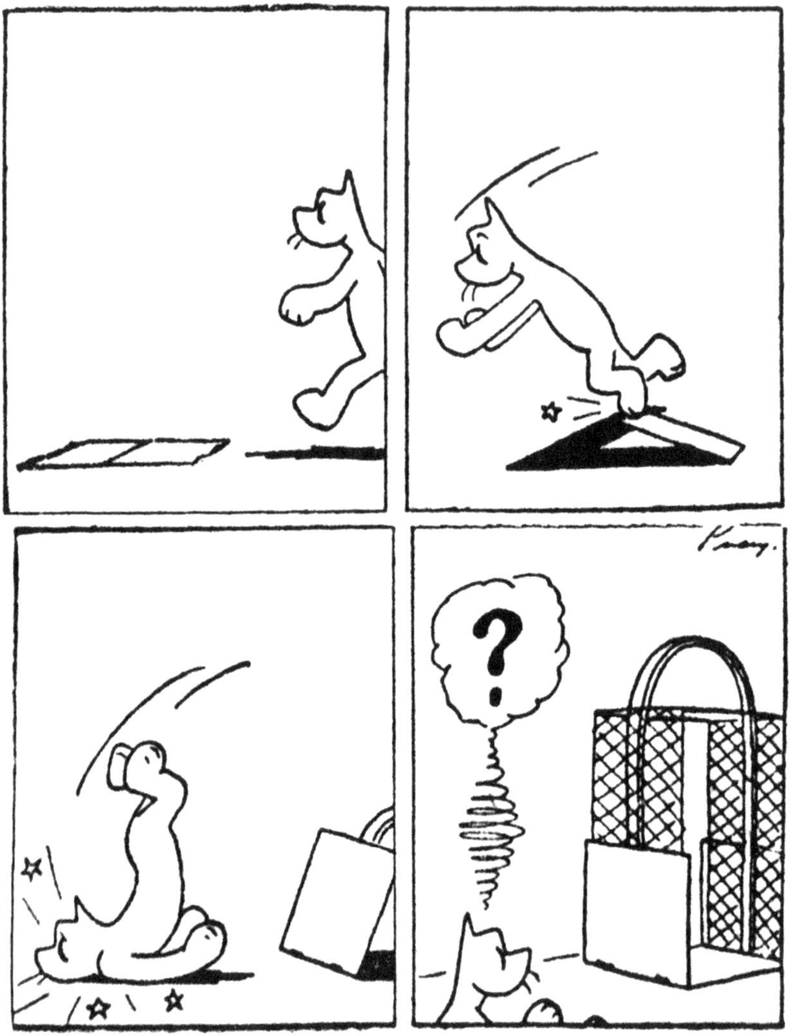
?

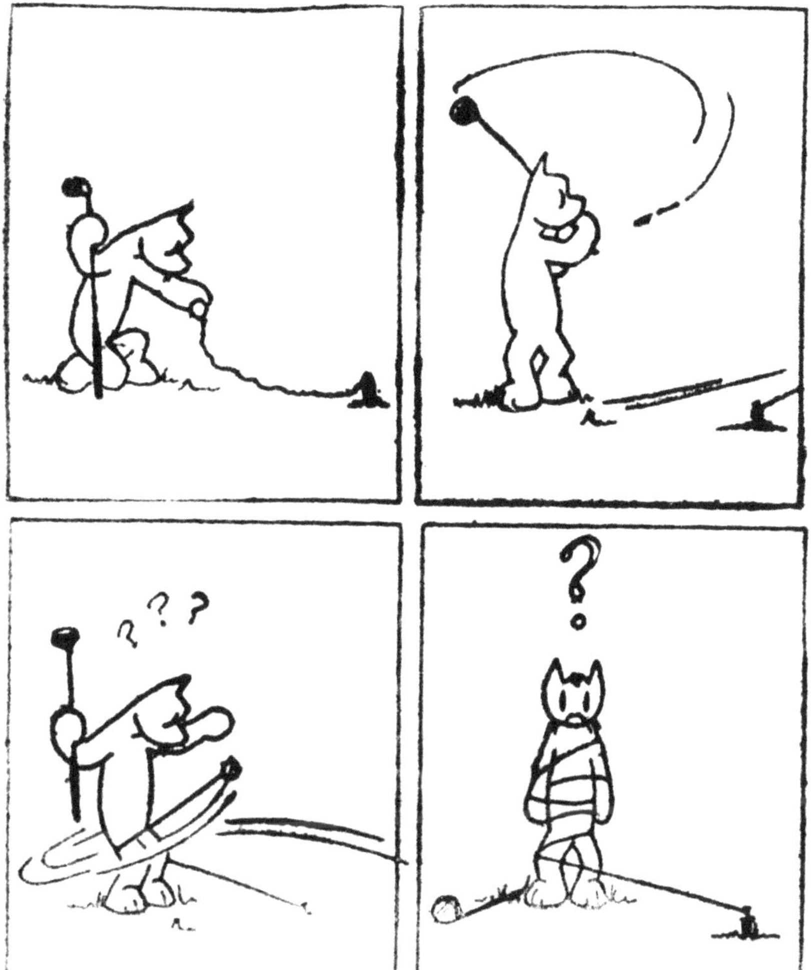

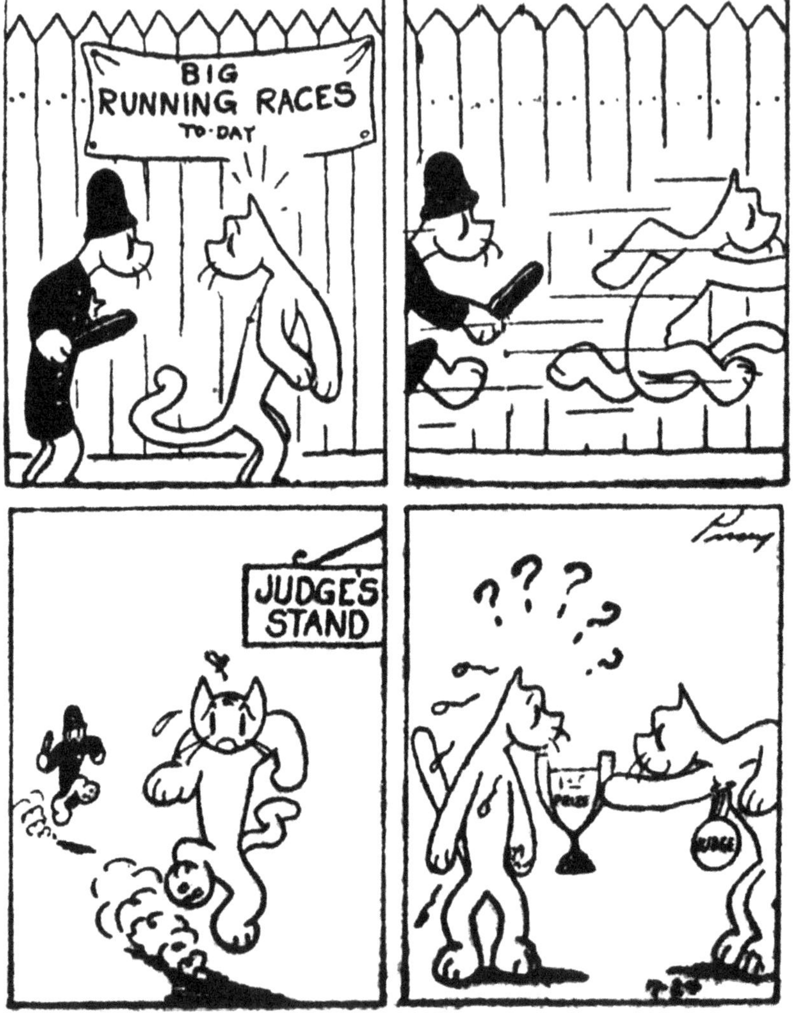
BIG
RUNNING RACES
TO-DAY
JUDGE'S
STAND
JUDGE

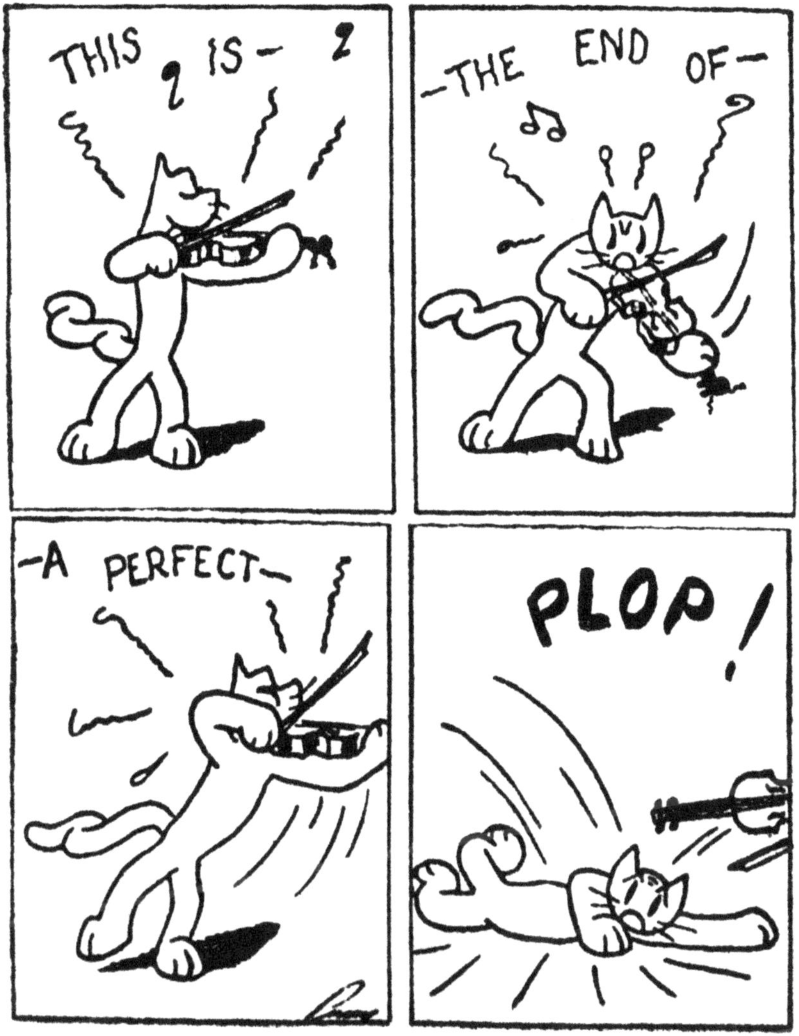
THIS IS —
— THE END OF —
— A PERFECT —
PLOP!

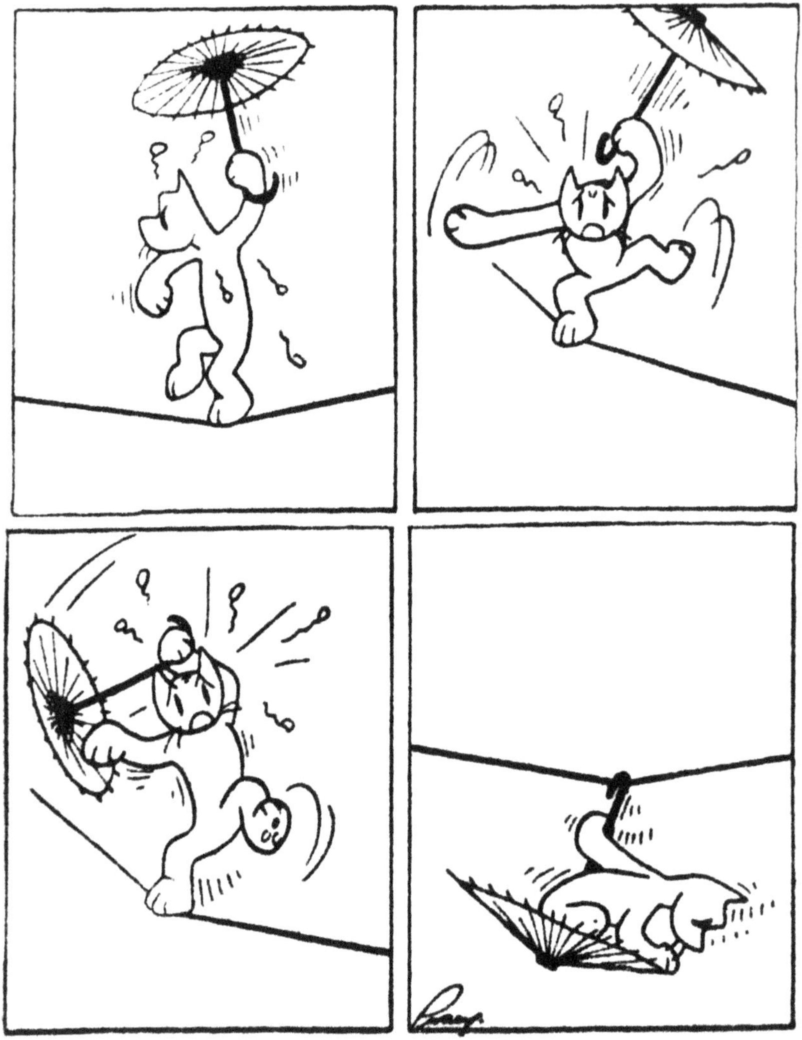

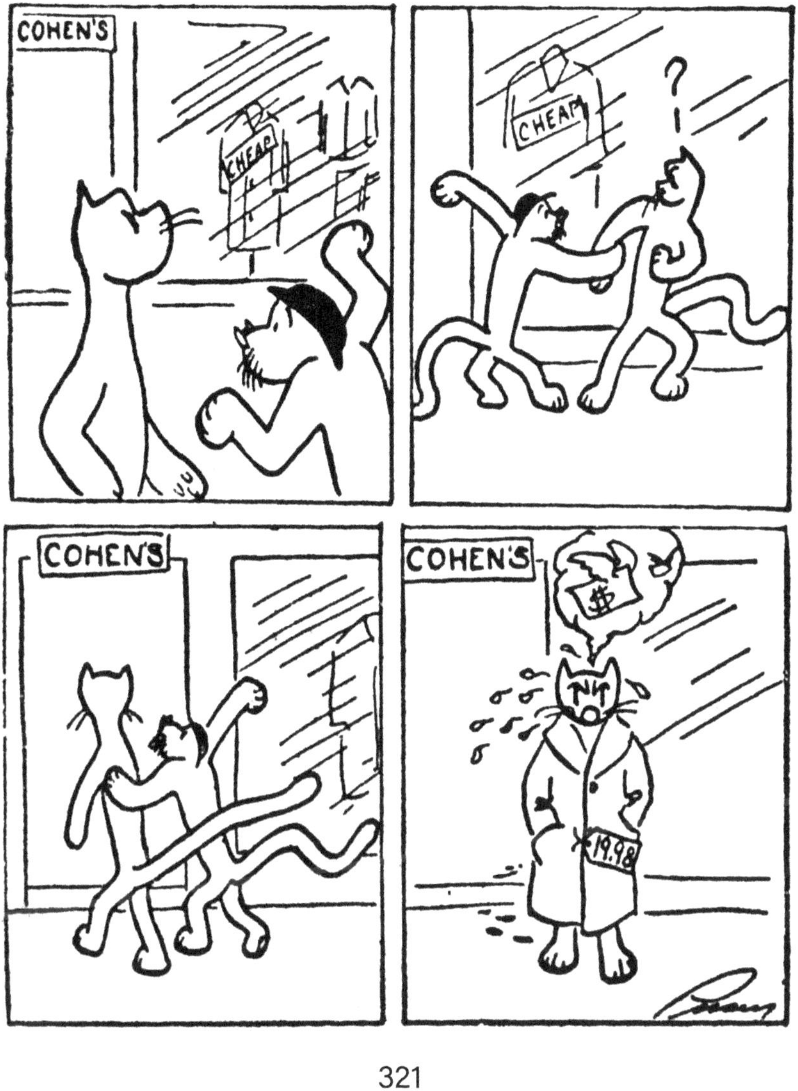
COHEN'S
CHEAP
?
CHEAP
COHEN'S
COHEN'S
19.98

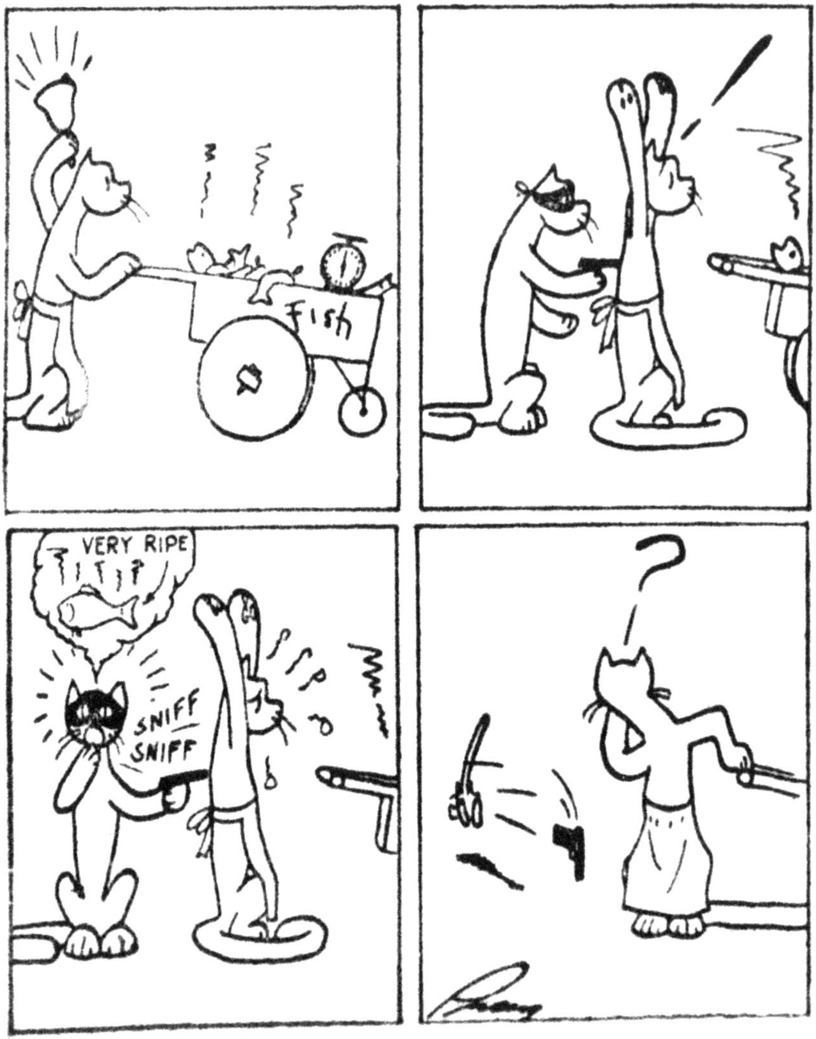
Fish
VERY RIPE
SNIFF
SNIFF

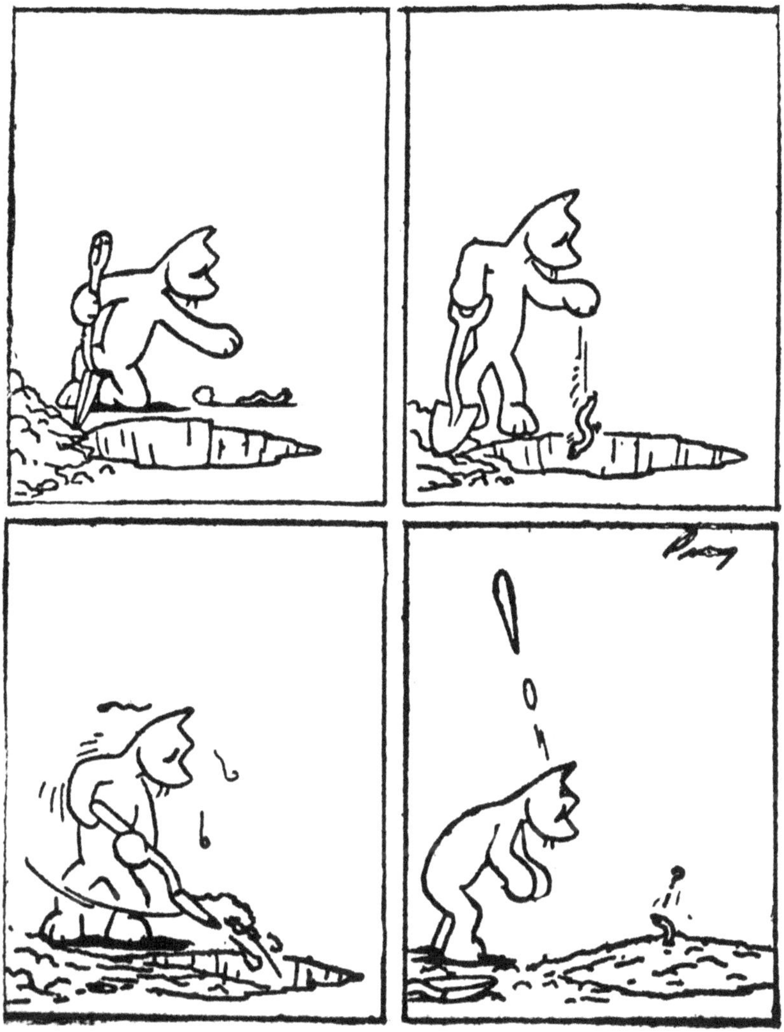

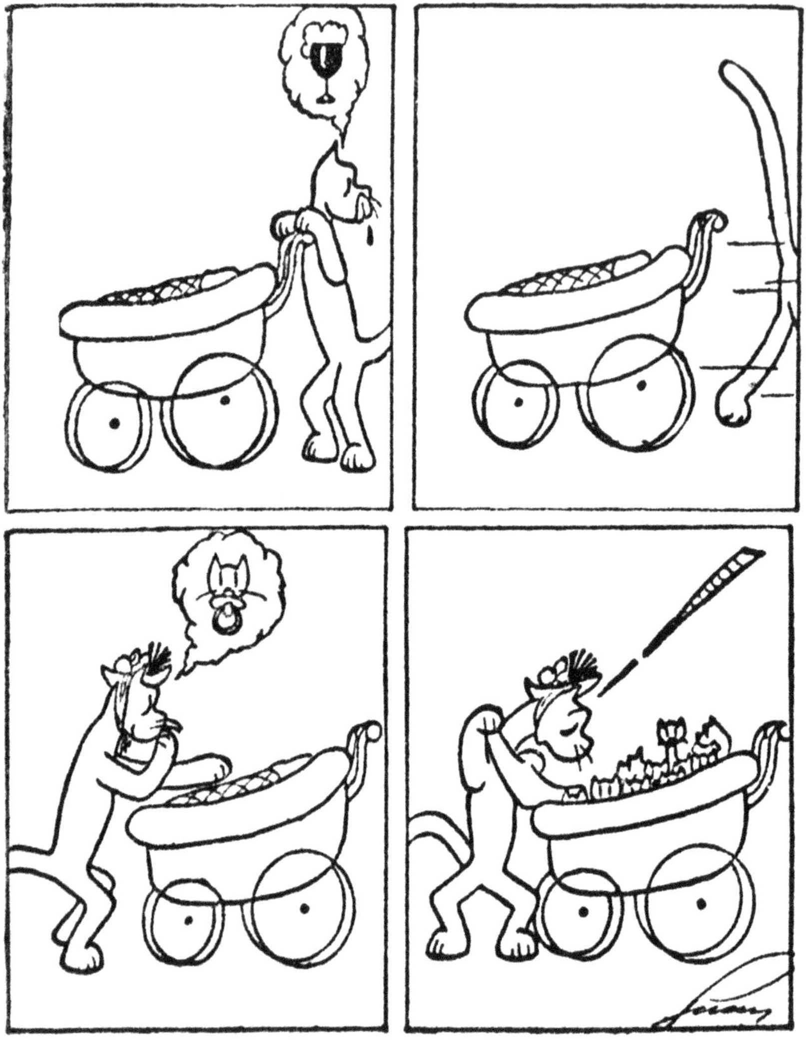

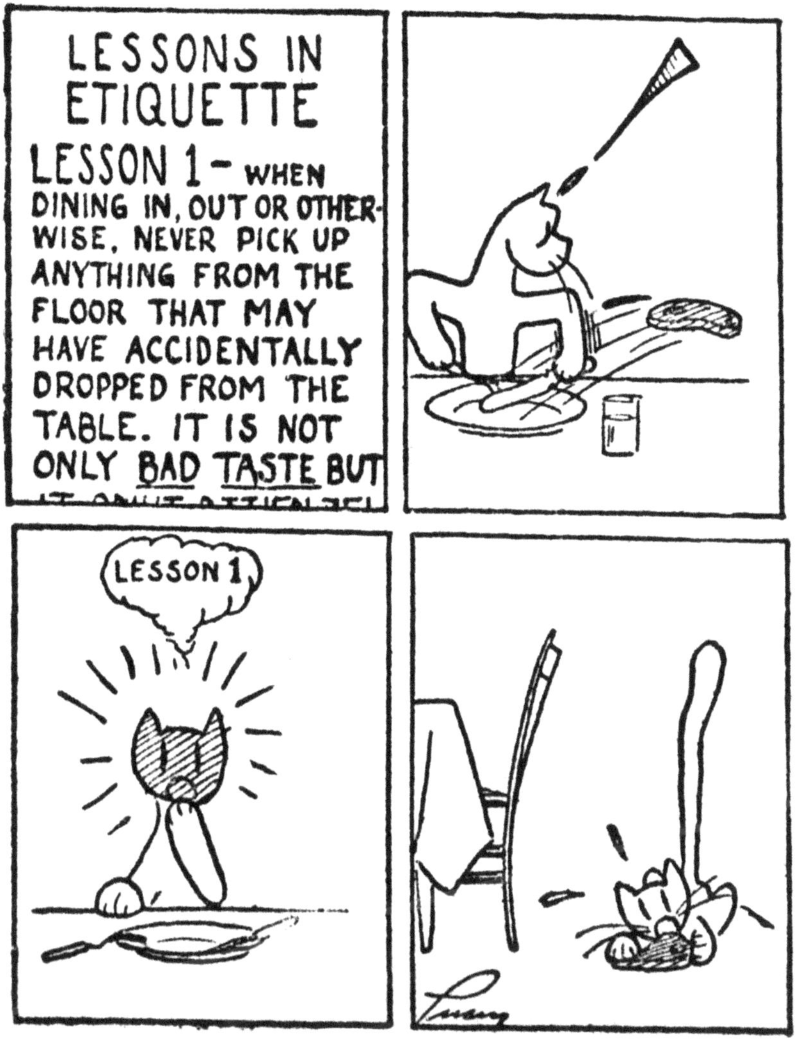
LESSONS IN ETIQUETTE
LESSON 1 – WHEN DINING IN, OUT OR OTHER-WISE, NEVER PICK UP ANYTHING FROM THE FLOOR THAT MAY HAVE ACCIDENTALLY DROPPED FROM THE TABLE. IT IS NOT ONLY BAD TASTE BUT
LESSON 1

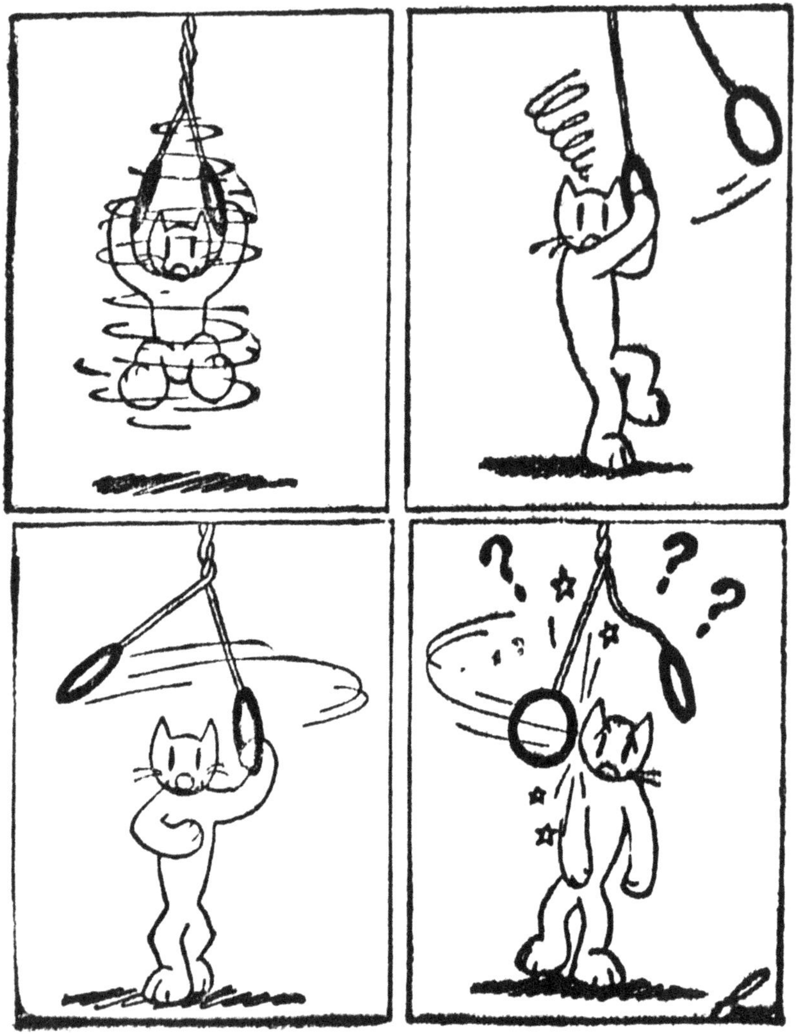

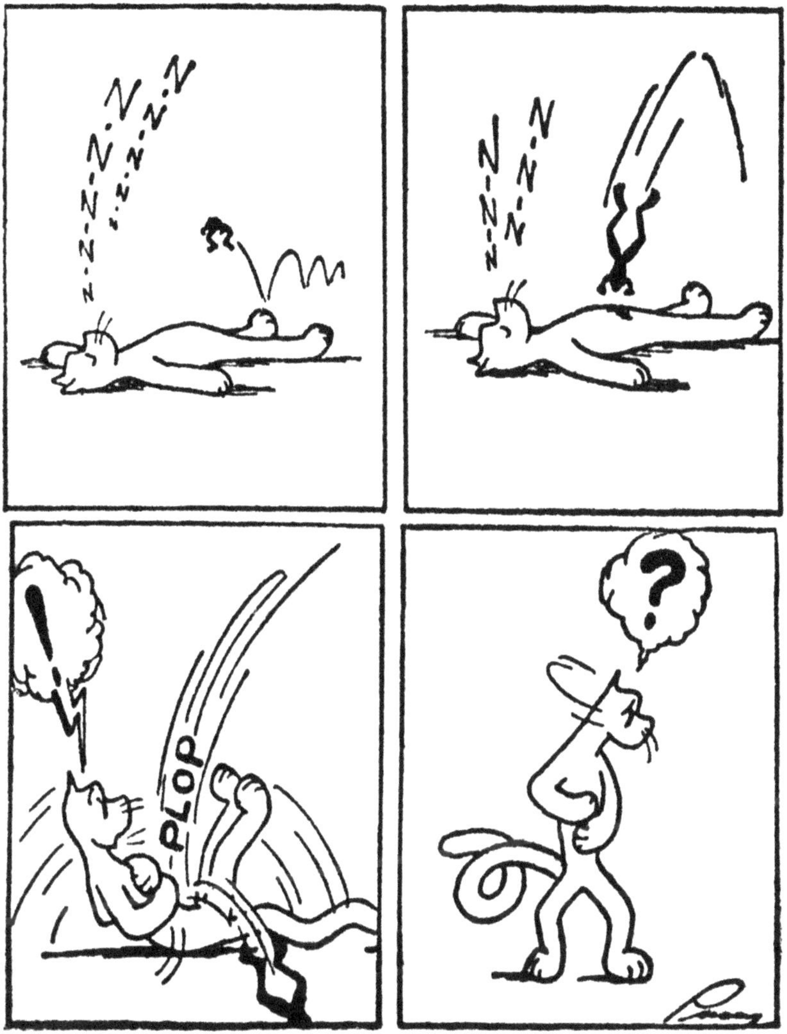
!
PLOP
?

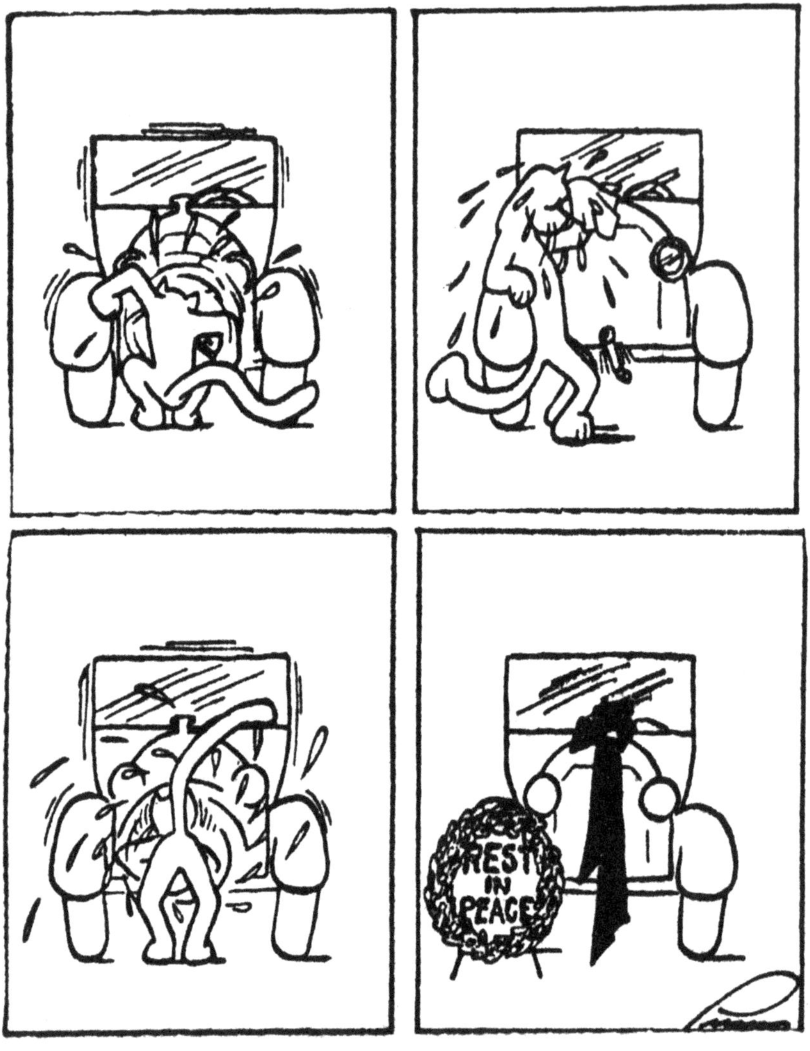
REST
IN
PEACE

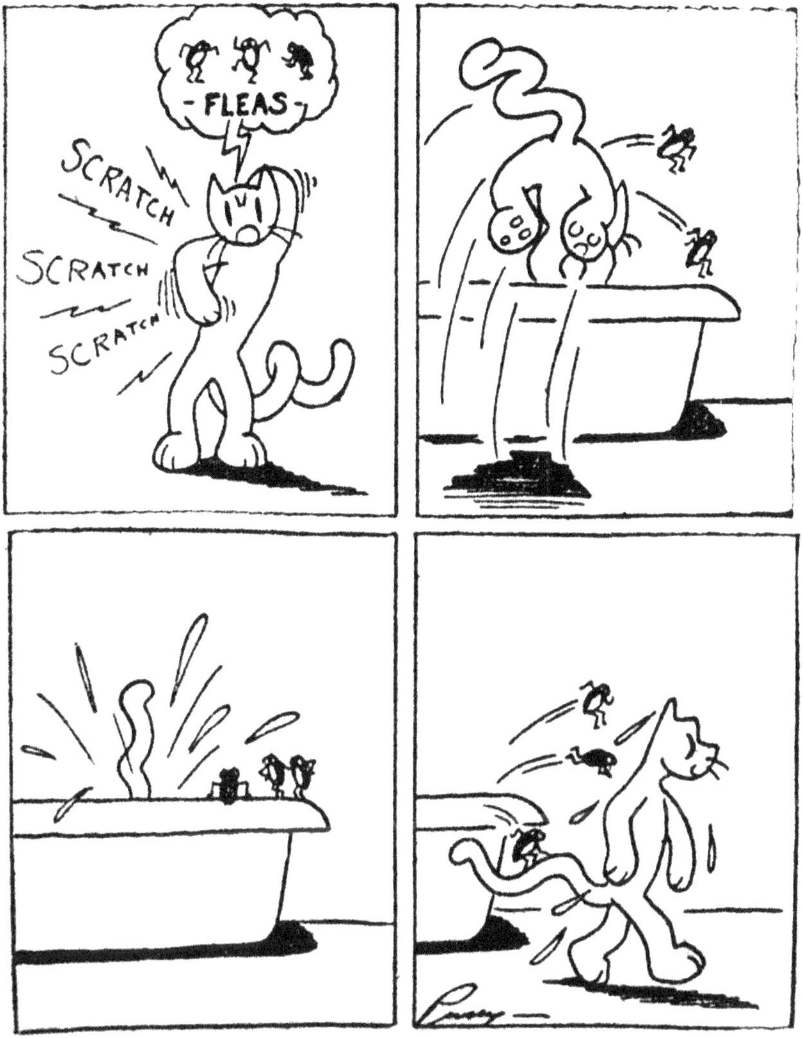
FLEAS
SCRATCH
SCRATCH
SCRATCH

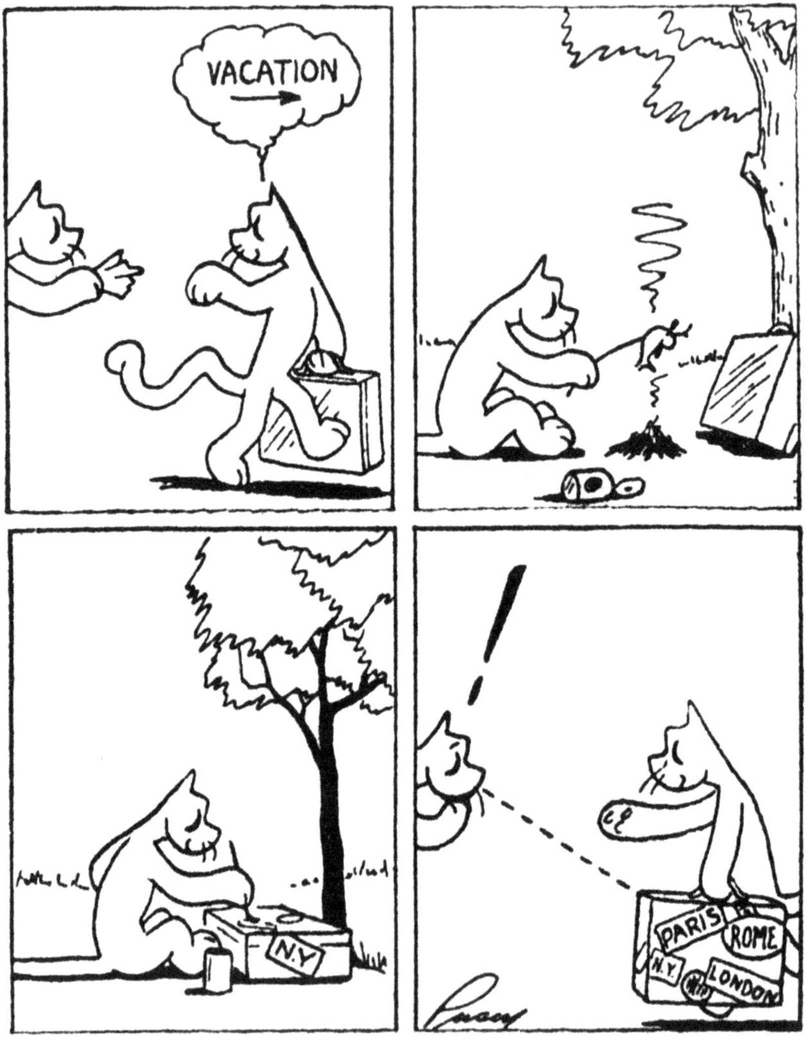
VACATION
N.Y
PARIS
ROME
N.Y.
LONDON

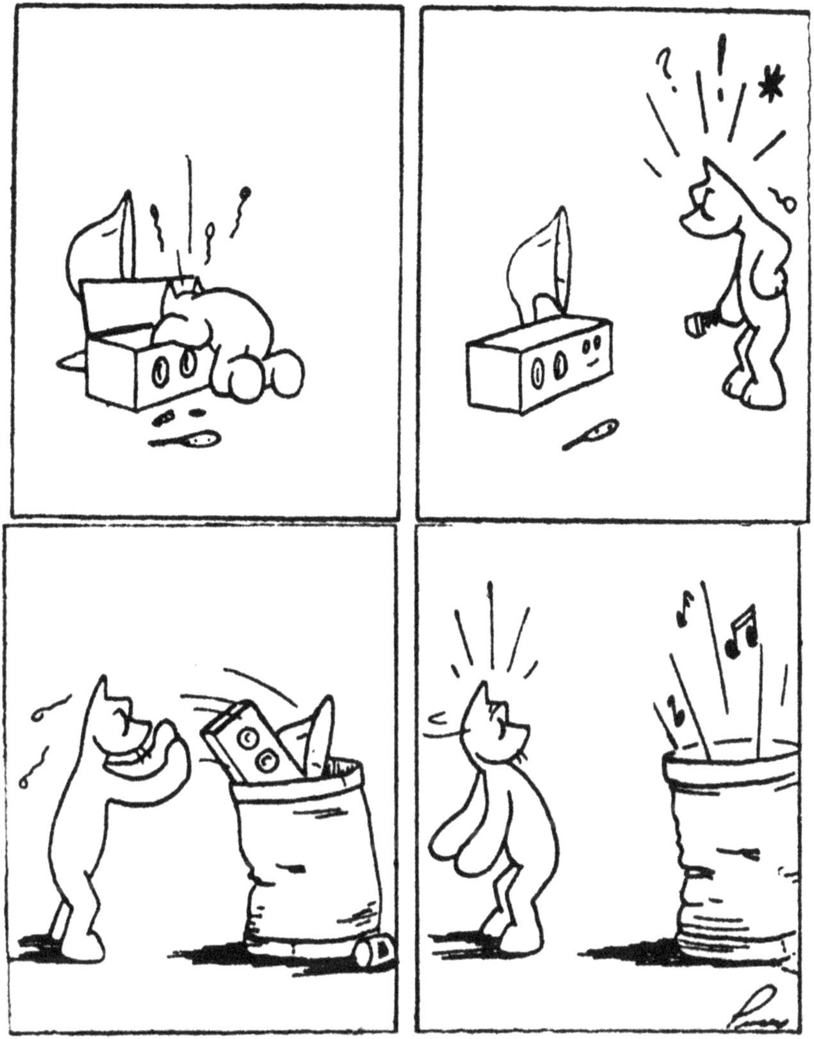

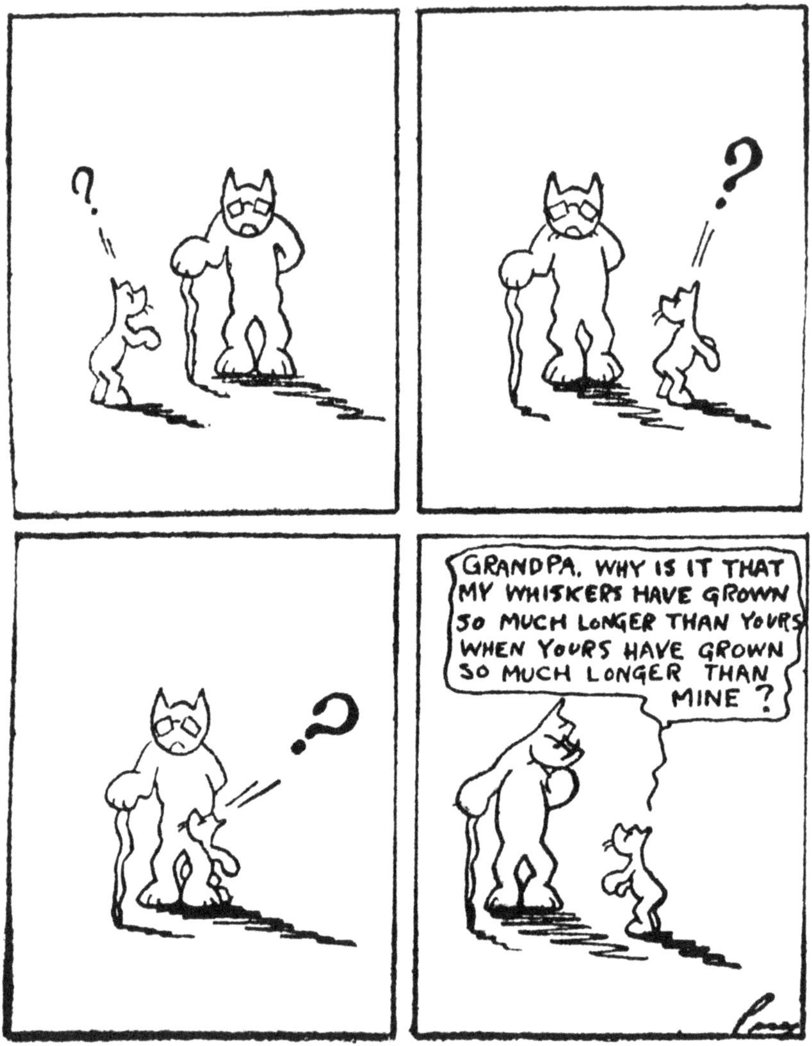
?
?
?
GRANDPA, WHY IS IT THAT MY WHISKERS HAVE GROWN SO MUCH LONGER THAN YOURS WHEN YOURS HAVE GROWN SO MUCH LONGER THAN MINE ?

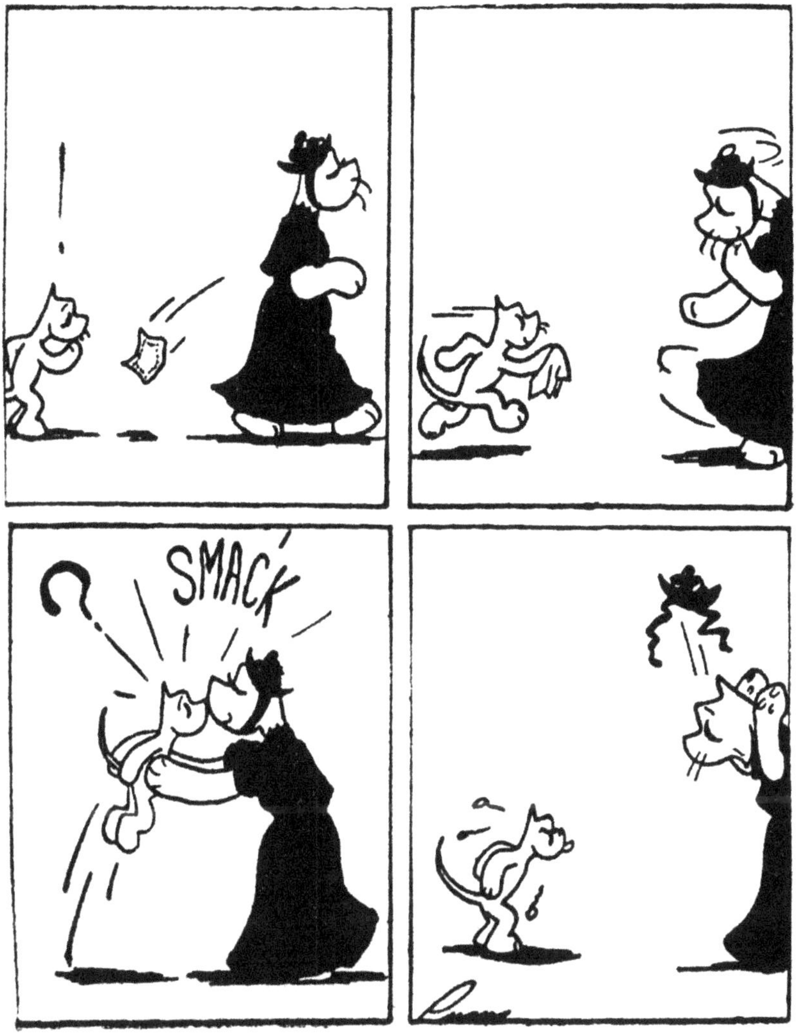
SMACK

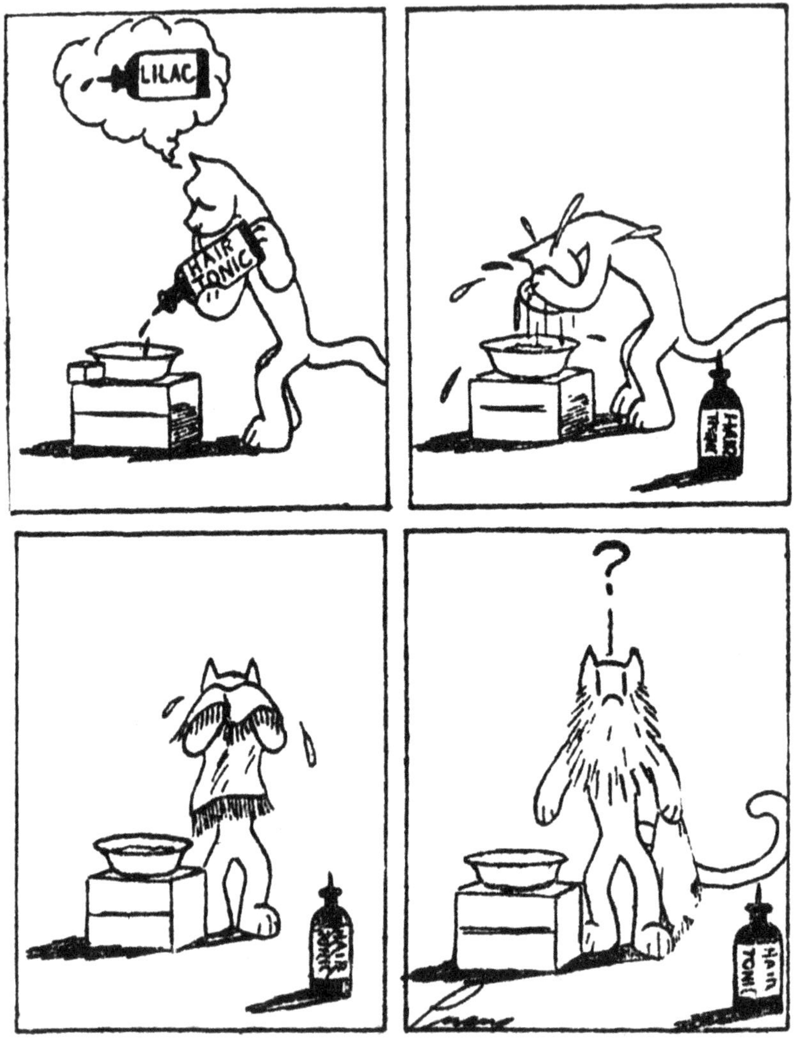
LILAC
HAIR TONIC
HAIR TONIC
?
HAIR TONIC

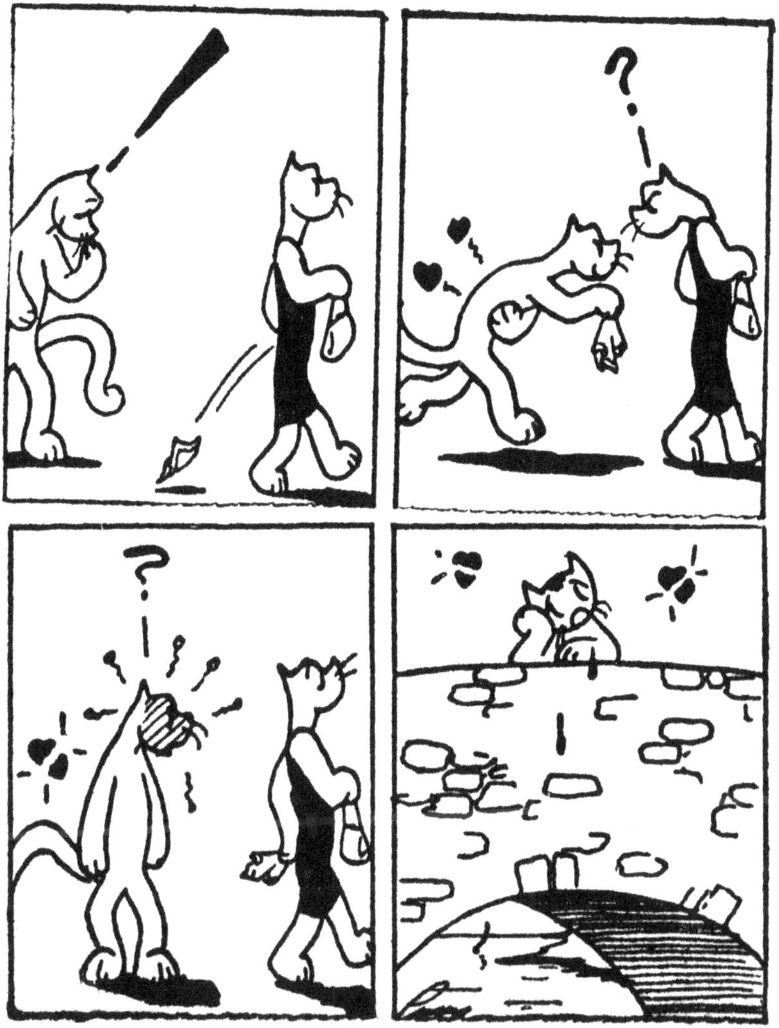

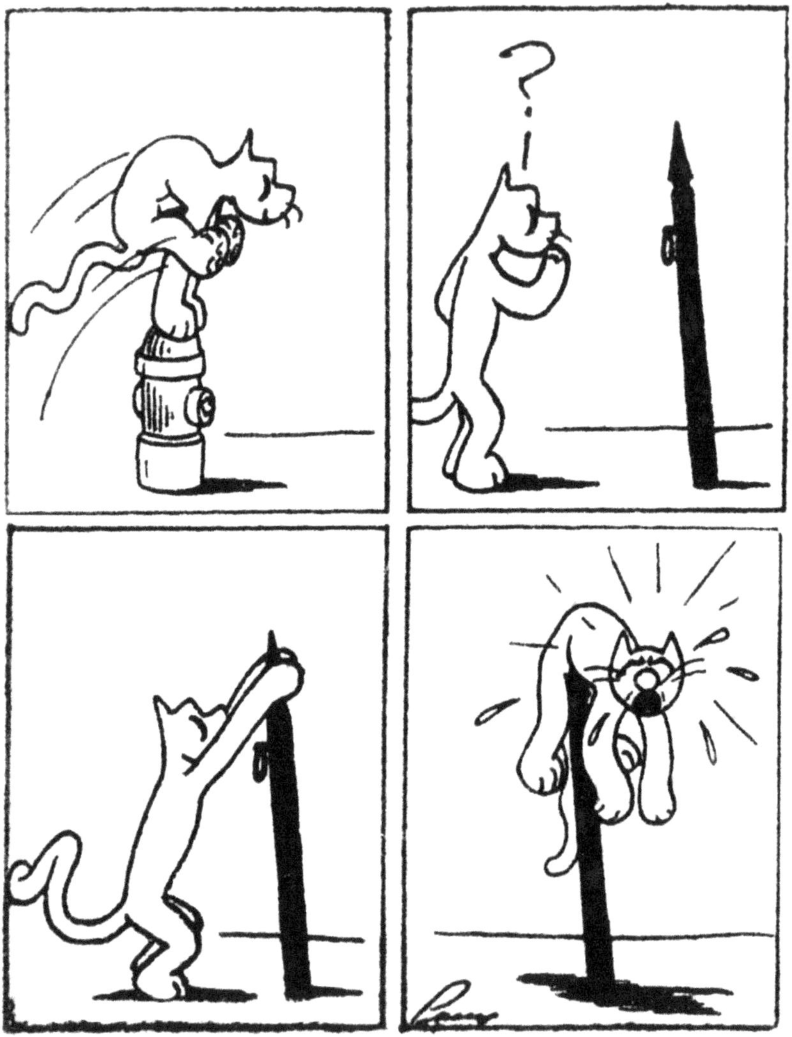

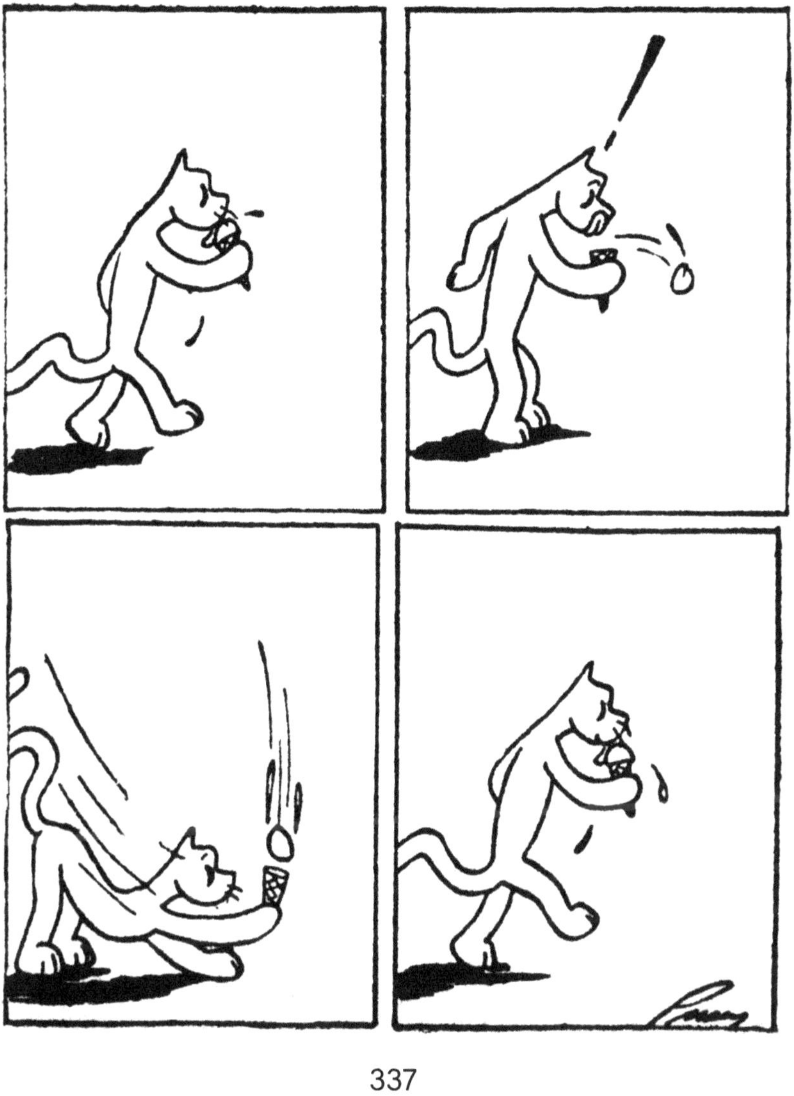

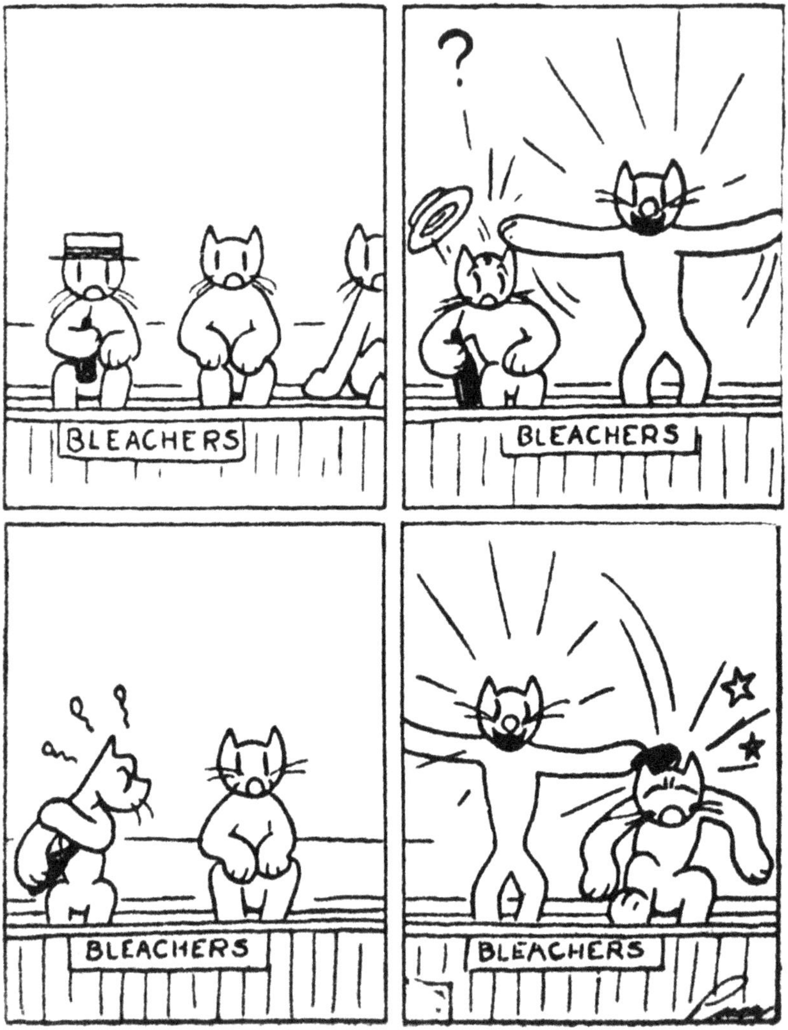
BLEACHERS
?
BLEACHERS
BLEACHERS
BLEACHERS

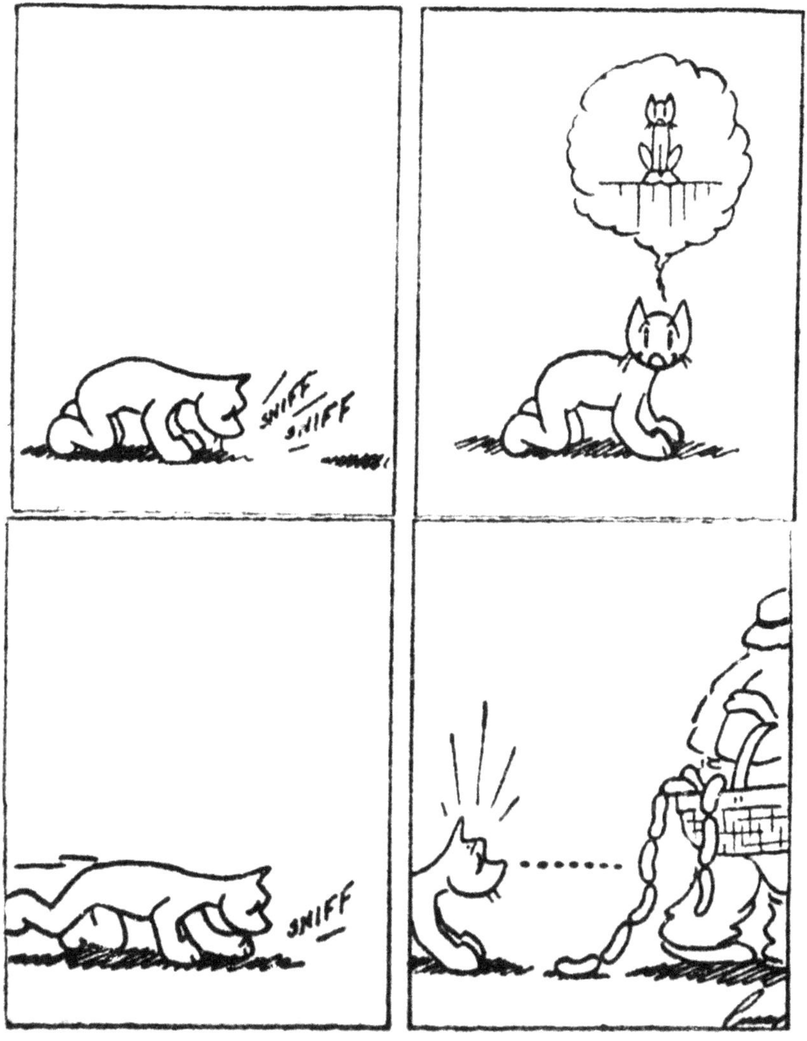
SNIFF
SNIFF
SNIFF

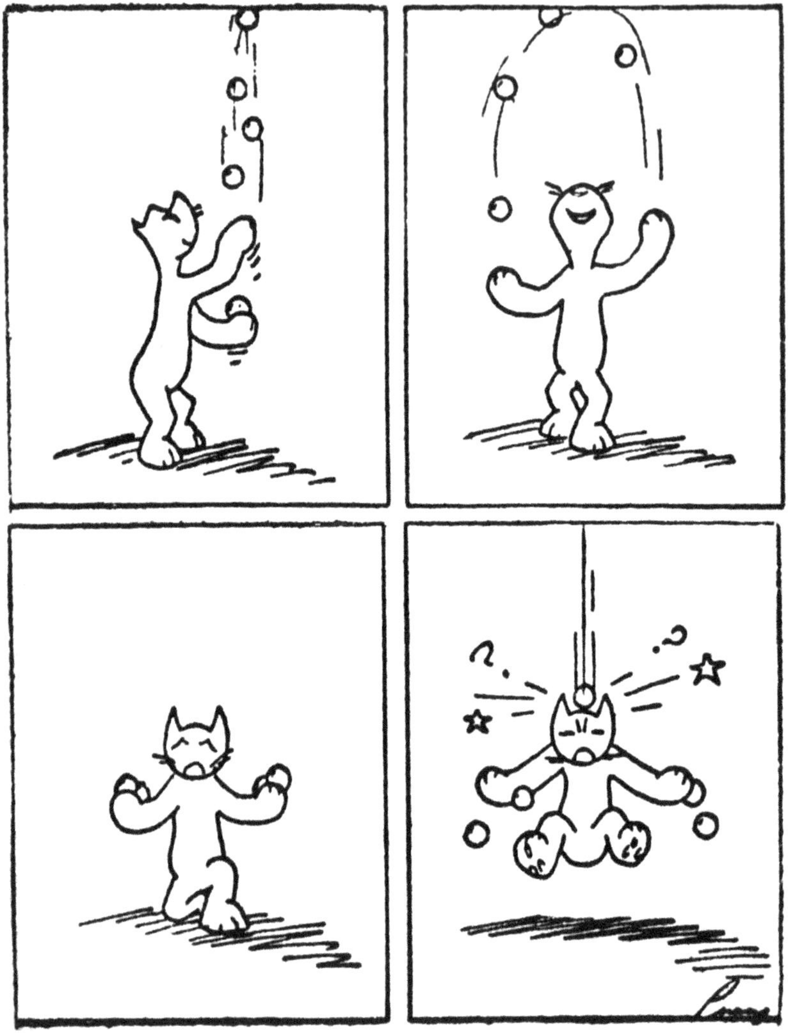

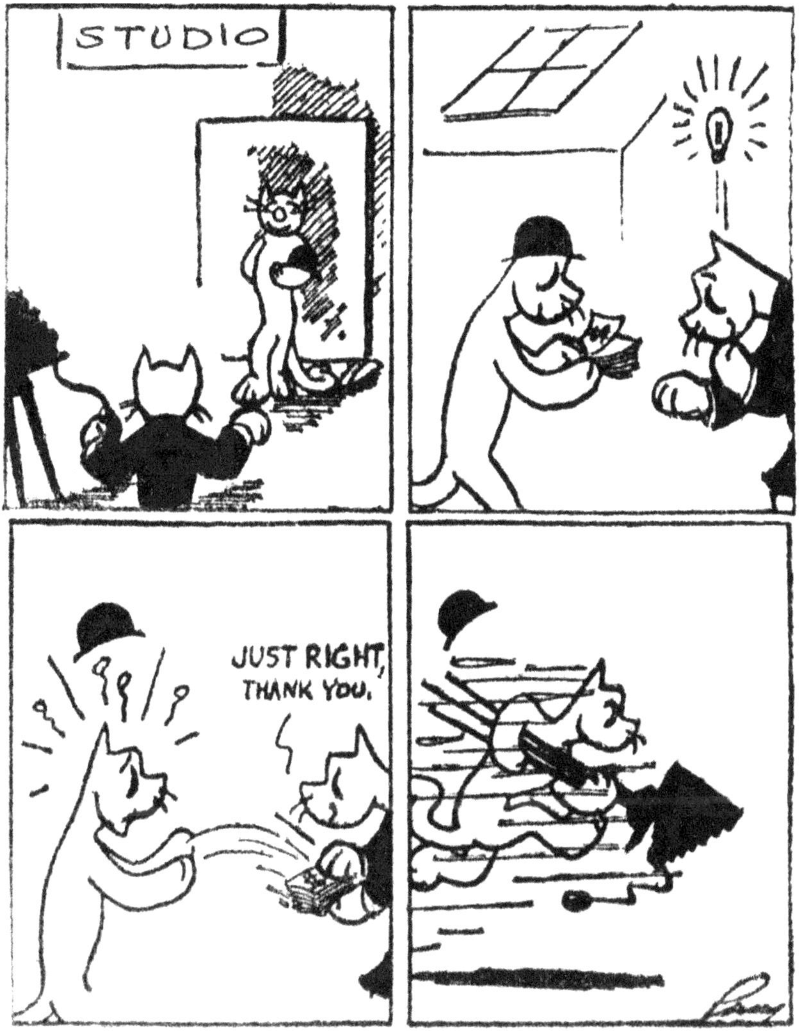
STUDIO
JUST RIGHT, THANK YOU.

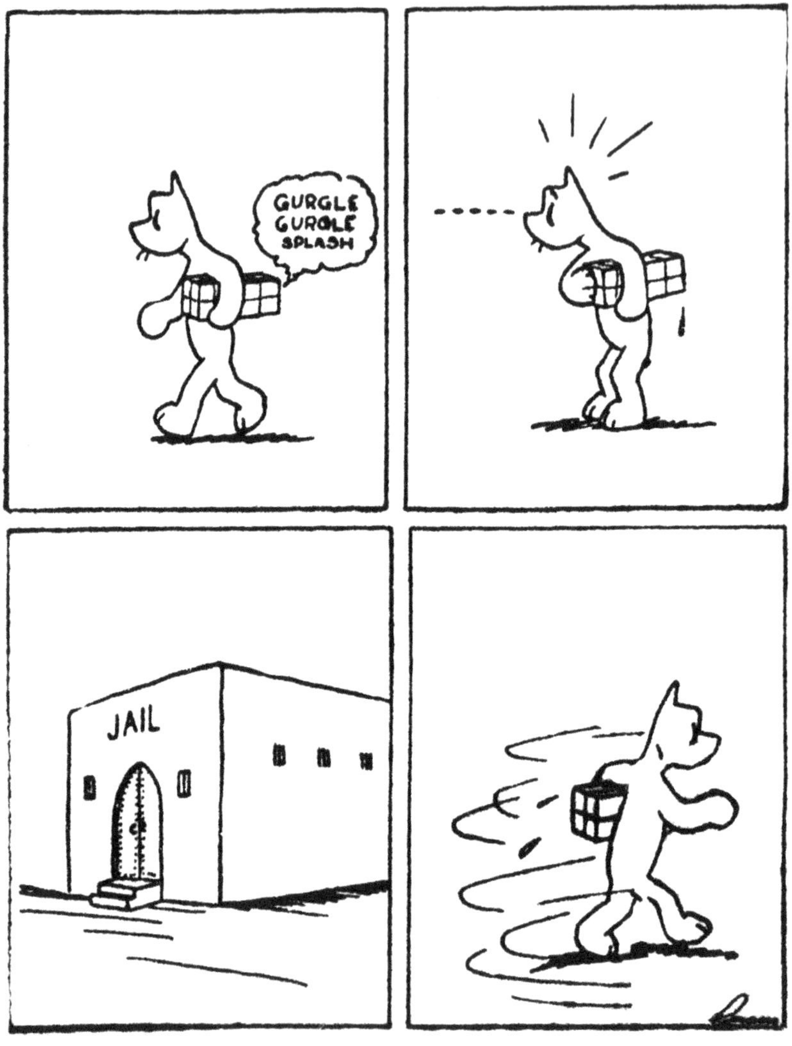
GURGLE
GURGLE
SPLASH
JAIL

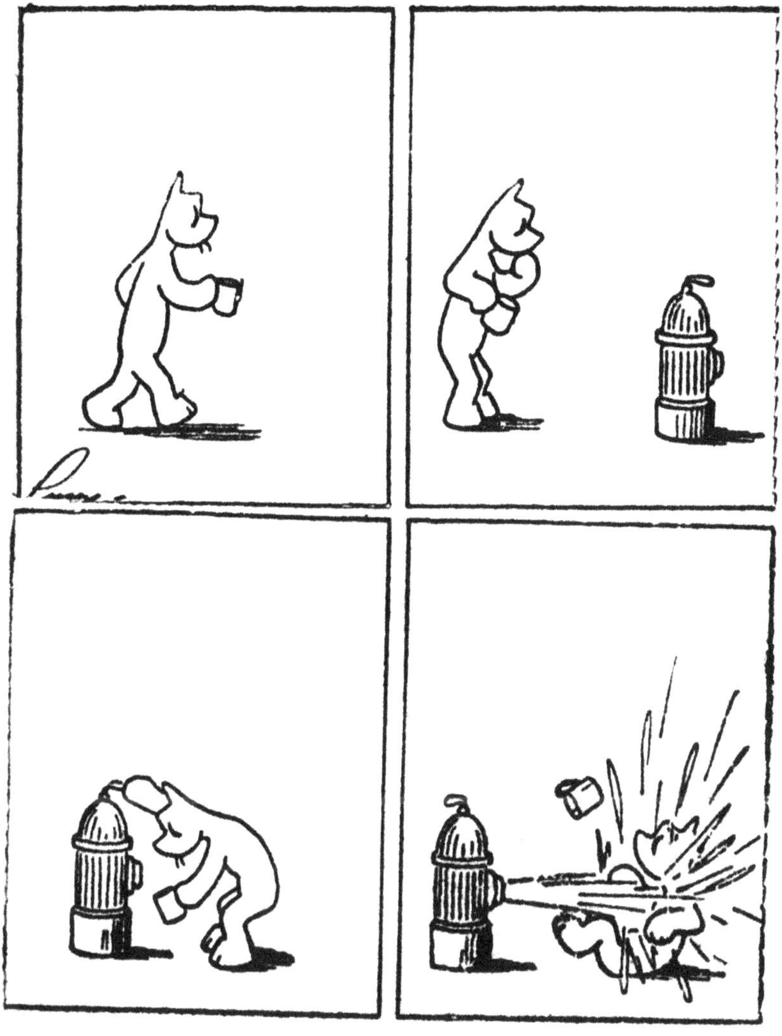

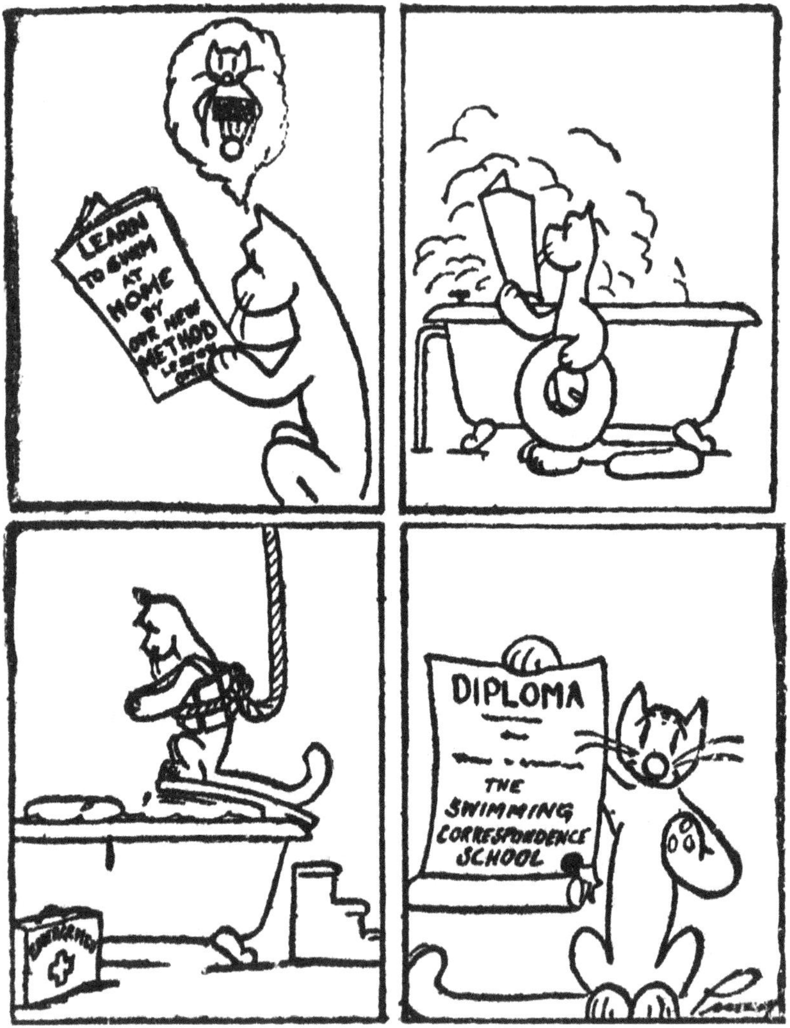
LEARN TO SWIM AT HOME BY OUR NEW METHOD
DIPLOMA
THE SWIMMING CORRESPONDENCE SCHOOL

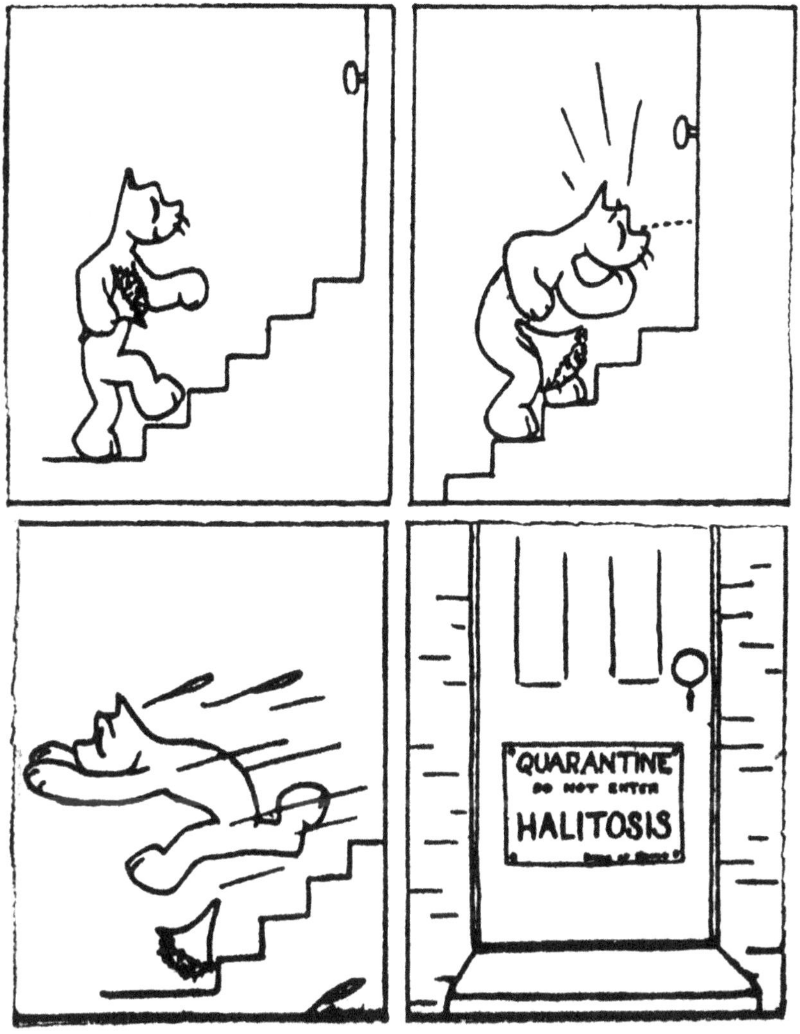
QUARANTINE
DO NOT ENTER
HALITOSIS

SOCK
ICE
WATER

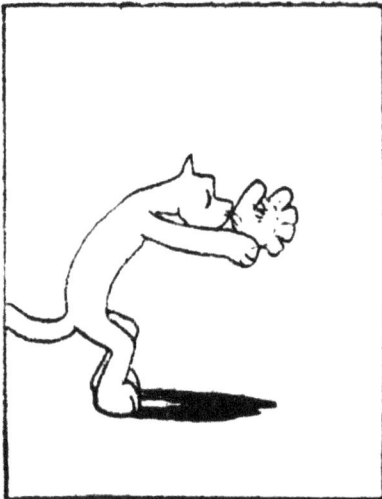

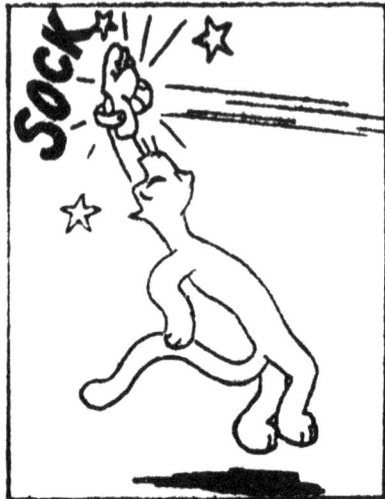

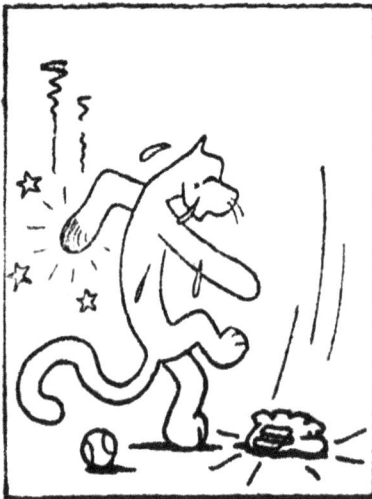

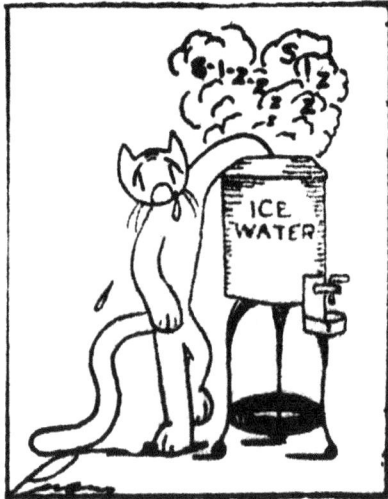

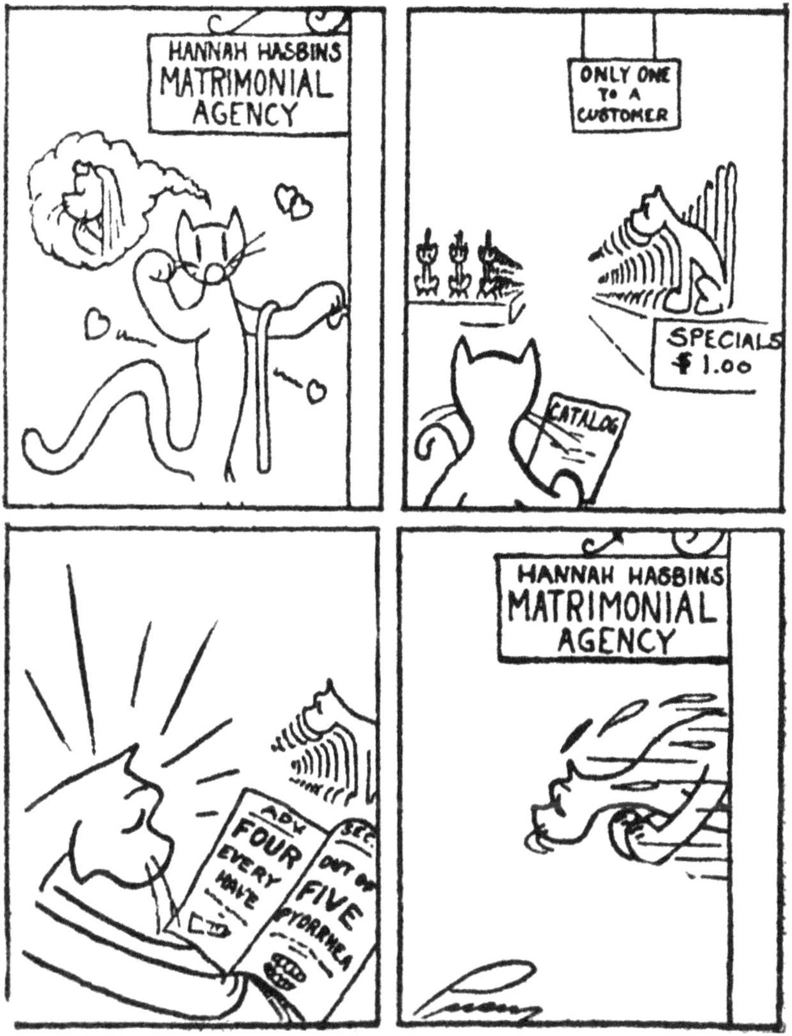
HANNAH HASBINS
MATRIMONIAL
AGENCY
ONLY ONE
TO A
CUSTOMER
SPECIALS
$ 1.00
CATALOG
ADV
FOUR
EVERY
HAVE
SEC.
OUT OF
FIVE
PYORRHEA
HANNAH HASBINS
MATRIMONIAL
AGENCY

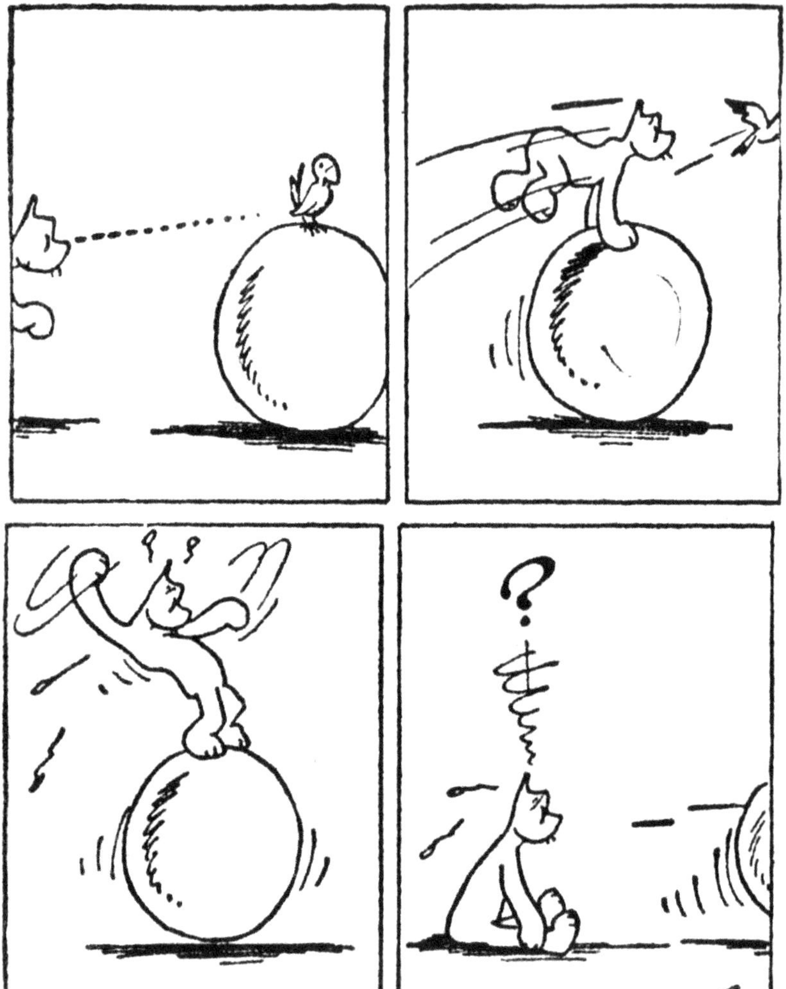
? ?
?

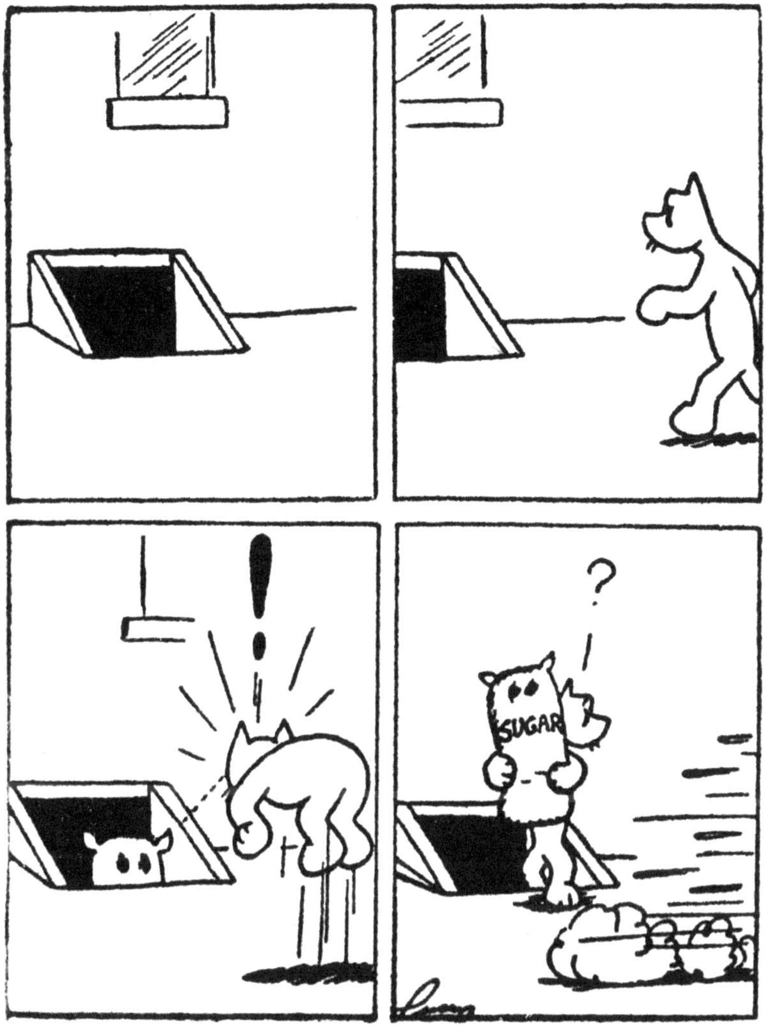
!
?
SUGAR

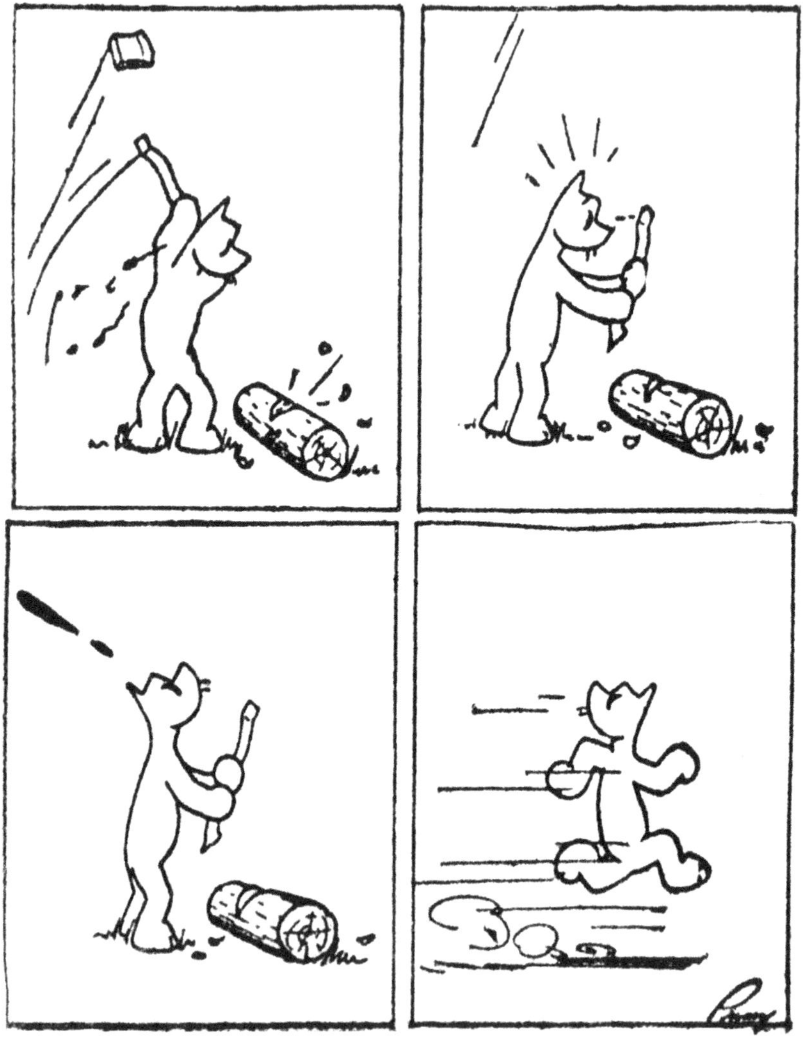

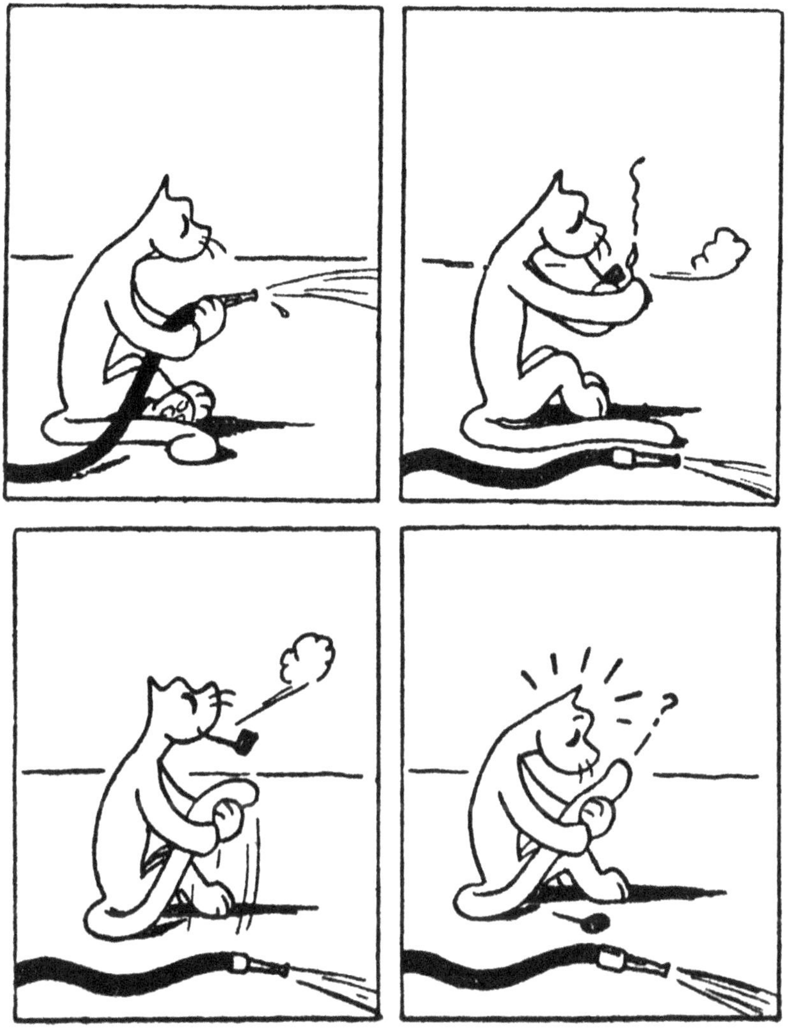

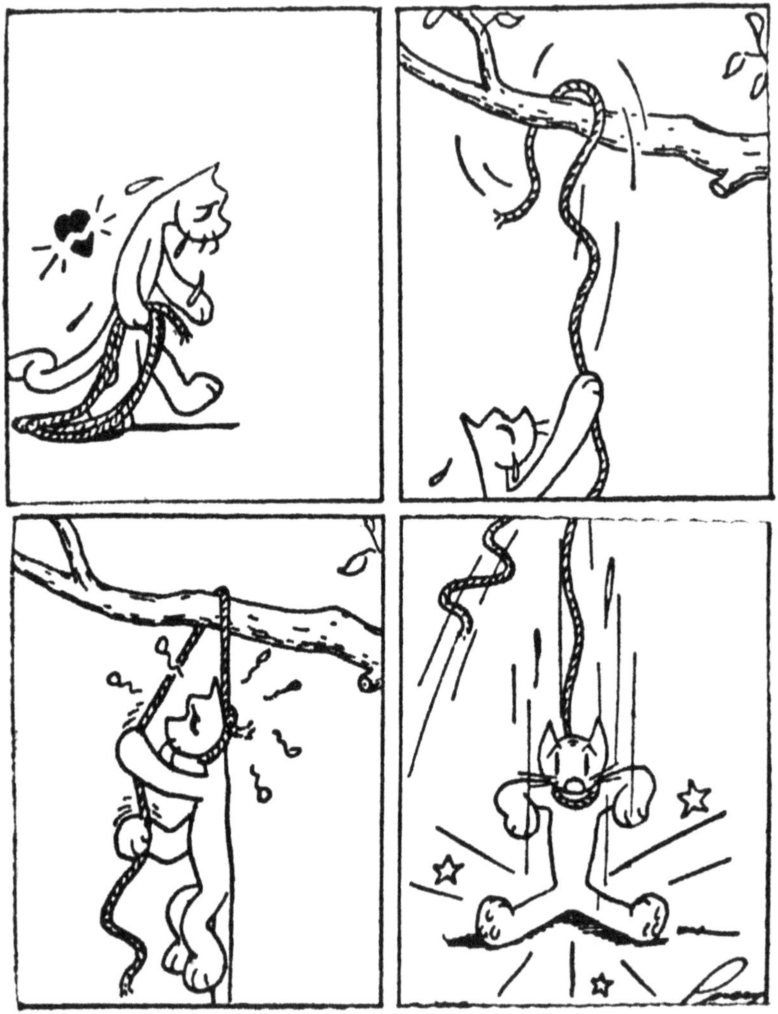

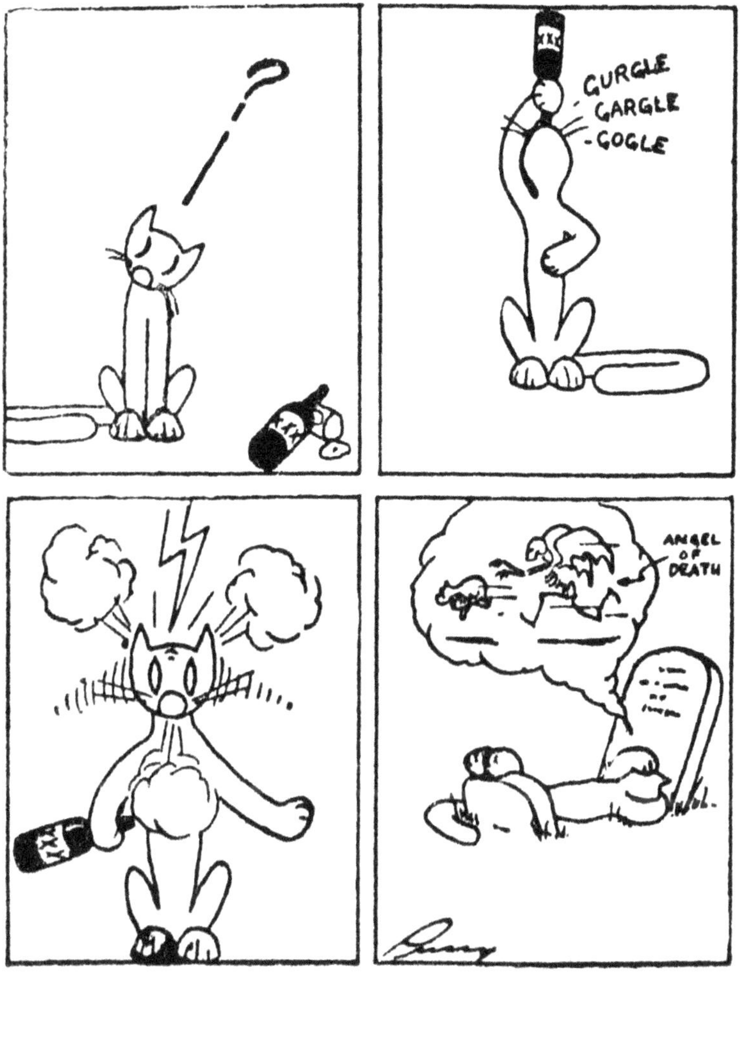
GURGLE
GARGLE
GOGLE
ANGEL OF DEATH

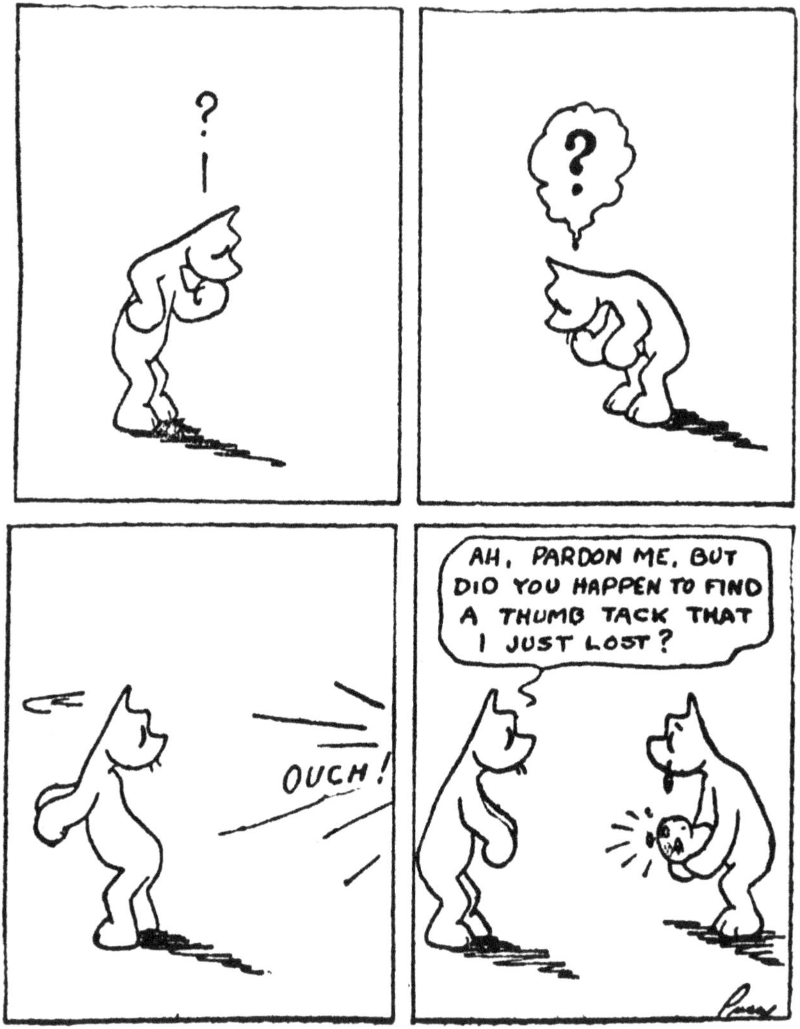
?
?
OUCH!
AH, PARDON ME, BUT DID YOU HAPPEN TO FIND A THUMB TACK THAT I JUST LOST?

That Little Game

BERT LINK

Details at
CoachwhipBooks.com

Available from your favorite online retailers

Foolish
Questions

RUBE GOLDBERG

Details at
CoachwhipBooks.com

Available from your favorite online retailers

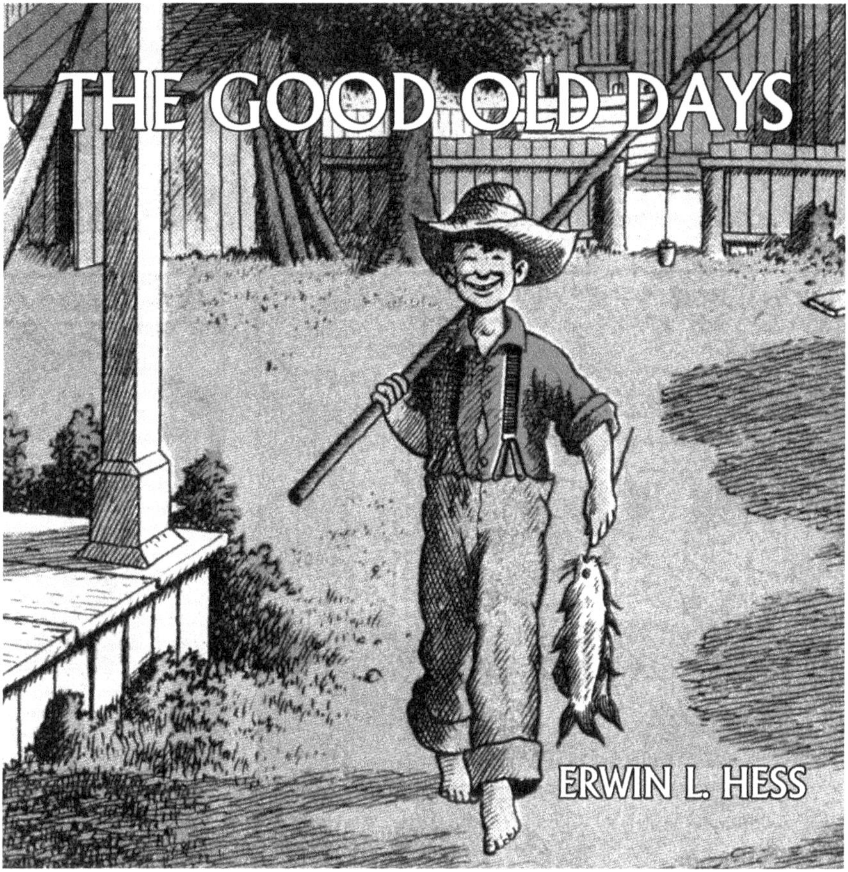
THE GOOD OLD DAYS
ERWIN L. HESS

Details at
CoachwhipBooks.com

Available from your favorite online retailers

Details at
CoachwhipBooks.com

Available from your favorite online retailers

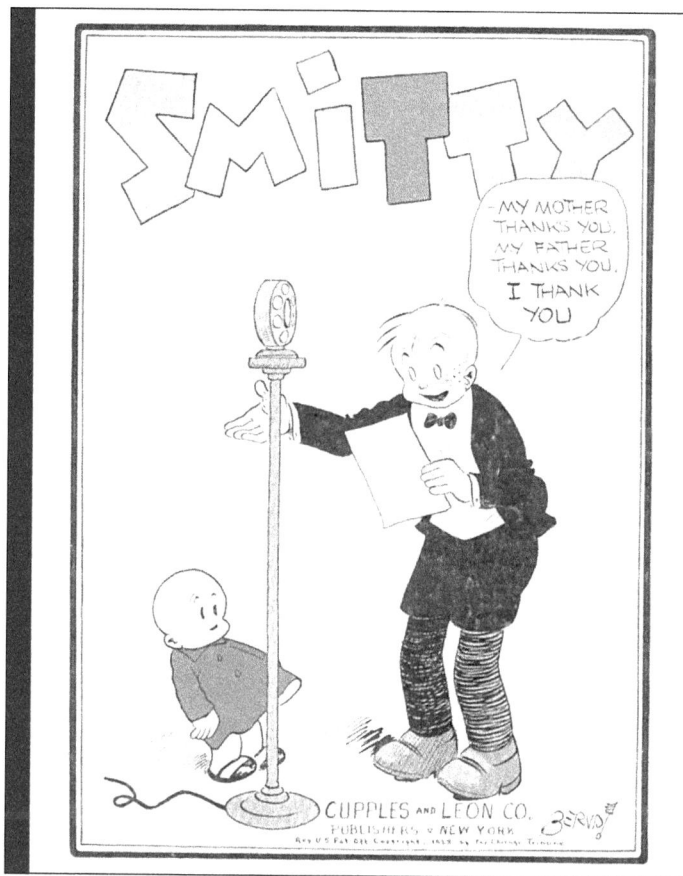

Details at
CoachwhipBooks.com

Available from your favorite online retailers

www.ingramcontent.com/pod-product-compliance
Lightning Source LLC
Chambersburg PA
CBHW060242100426
42742CB00011B/1612